Social Issues in
the English Classroom

Social Issues in the English Classroom

Edited by

C. Mark Hurlbert
Indiana University of Pennsylvania

Samuel Totten
University of Arkansas at Fayetteville

National Council of Teachers of English
1111 Kenyon Road, Urbana, Illinois 61801

Project/Production Editor: Robert A. Heister

Manuscript Editor: William J. Tucker

Interior Design: Tom Kovacs for TGK Design

Cover Design: Barbara Yale-Read

NCTE Stock Number 45043–3050

Library of Congress Cataloging-in-Publication Data

Social issues in the English classroom / edited by Mark Hurlbert
and Samuel Totten.
    p. cm.
   Includes bibliographical references and index.
   ISBN 0-8141-4504-3
   1. English language—Study and teaching—United States. 2. Social
teaching—United States. Literature—Study and teaching.
   I. Hurlbert, C. Mark. II. Totten, Samuel.
LB1576.S65 1992
428′.007—dc20
                                           92-14843
                                              CIP

C. Mark Hurlbert wishes to dedicate his efforts on *Social Issues in the English Classroom* to the memory of Anne C. Johnstone. Anne's personal and professional commitment to teaching excellence and social justice is a model from which all who knew her continue to learn.

Samuel Totten wishes to dedicate his efforts on *Social Issues in the English Classroom* to his brother Michael Price Totten, an intellectual/social activist with a keen mind, generous heart, and a deep and abiding love for the Earth and its inhabitants.

Contents

IV. Teaching Literature for Social Responsibility

V. Politics, Change, and Social Responsibility

Acknowledgments

While putting this collection together, we, the editors, have learned a lot about generosity. We would like to thank those who have helped us see the teaching of social issues in the English classroom in new ways: namely the contributors to this volume. In addition, we would like to thank Arlene Mitchell of NCTE's Committee on Contemporary Issues for providing moral support in the bad times. We also wish to offer a heartfelt thanks to Michael Spooner, Senior Editor for Publications at NCTE, for his tireless moral support, patience, and guidance.

Foreword

C. Mark Hurlbert
Indiana University of Pennsylvania

Samuel Totten
University of Arkansas at Fayetteville

Racism, sexism, classism, terrorism, homophobia, pollution, AIDS, nuclear weapons proliferation—the list of social issues demanding the attention, energies, and resources of all who live in the last decade of the twentieth century goes on and on. Ours is a time when the number and magnitude of the social issues troubling our country and world could easily overwhelm and silence anyone calling for change. Now, more than ever, we need to listen to teachers like the ones who have contributed to *Social Issues in the English Classroom*. These educators face the problems that trouble us all and demonstrate that we need not give in to anyone or anything that would undermine the efforts of those working for social justice. They articulate a dramatic reminder that something can and must be done to alleviate the social, economic, and political oppressions that marginalize and disenfranchise people. Their thinking and teaching tell us to resist those who corrupt our environment, terrorize others, refuse to recognize the rights and dignities of others, as well as those who are slow to commit the resources needed to battle the epidemics afflicting—and killing—us. In the work of these educators, we see that hope is still alive as long as we continue to teach in the belief that social transformation is possible and as long as we realize that our students are still our best hope for a better future.

As a book, *Social Issues in the English Classroom* demonstrates that many teachers, ones with international reputations and ones with district-wide respect, believe that the English classroom should be more than a place where students learn the literacies of work or the research, critical, and rhetorical skills of the next grade level. The English classroom should be more than a place where students compete

1

individually and in isolation to finish assigned and easily consumable, easily categorized, easily gradable readings and writings. The English classroom, the educators in this collection say, is a good place to begin reading and writing and talking and listening together for a more democratic and ethical society and for a safer and healthier world. The English classroom is a good place for students and teachers to explore, through whole language philosophies and pedagogies, in cooperative and socially responsible ways, the issues and conditions affecting this time and the public lives we lead in it.

Social Issues in the English Classroom is divided into five sections. In the introductory section, "Social Consciousness and Social Responsibility," Samuel Totten presents English teachers with reasons for and ways of including social issues in the English curriculum and classroom. His essay, "Educating for the Development of Social Consciousness and Social Responsibility," provides an overview of what educators are doing and saying to prepare students for participation in the American democratic process and suggests the roles that organizations such as NCTE might play in educating for social responsibility.

Section two of *Social Issues in the English Classroom*, "Dialogue and Social Responsibility," includes essays by educators who have created meaningful contexts in which their students might engage each other, as well as others from their hometowns and from around the planet, in dialogue about social issues. The objective is to help students develop greater understanding of themselves, others, their local communities, and the world. In a personal narrative, "Dismantling White/ Male Supremacy," doris davenport recounts the resistances she faces from students as she teaches for social consciousness. In "Dealing with Conflict: A Structured Cooperative Controversy Procedure," Edythe Johnson Holubec, David W. Johnson, and Roger T. Johnson explain a procedure for helping students to consider the many sides of a social issue by encouraging them to discuss, in a cooperative environment, the complexities of a social issue before they make up their minds about where they stand. Alan Shapiro, a member of Educators for Social Responsibility, offers, in "Cultivating Vision: The Believing Game," yet another way in which to structure classroom dialogue about social issues. Drawing upon Peter Elbow's conception of the believing game, as well as exploring its philosophical tradition, Shapiro explains how students can be brought through a process of believing and doubting to a deeper understanding of difficult and complex issues such as state-sponsored terrorism. In "Learning to Be at Home: Oral Histories of a Black Community," Carol Stumbo presents a personal narrative of how her students' field research in the hollows around

Wheelwright, Kentucky, brought them to a greater understanding of the lives of the families of black miners and the prejudices they have faced. This dialogic research culminated in the students' publishing *Mantrip*, a magazine devoted to the oral histories they conducted. Completing section two, William Wright, who directs Bread Loaf's telecommunications project, Breadnet, recounts how his high school students used computers to participate in a worldwide symposium on the environment. "Telecomputing and Social Action" chronicles both the exchanges among these students from Canada, Indonesia, Peru, the Soviet Union, and the United States, and the students' commitment to changing how we all abuse our planet.

Section three, "Teaching Writing for Social Responsibility," begins with a continuation of the topic of concern for our planet. In "Empowering the Voiceless to Preserve the Earth," Daniel Zins explains how he organizes his composition class around the theme of the nuclear threat to our world. But more than merely teaching about this topic, Zins explores how students can gain a sense of the power of their voices to create change in the face of problems that would seem to be out of their hands. Next, Ellen Louise Hart and Sarah-Hope Parmeter describe, in " 'Writing in the Margins': A Lesbian- and Gay-Inclusive Course," the rationale and methodology for a course they teach at the University of California at Santa Cruz. The double goals of this composition course are to teach students to write better and to help them discover how to live more ethical, less violent, and less homophobic lives. In "Public School and University Compañeros," Debbie Bell tells readers about the important work she is doing at Ohlone Elementary School in Watsonville, California. In this narrative, Bell recounts how she and Sarah-Hope Parmeter have been engaged in a cross-age writing project where at-risk elementary students and university "basic writers" write to and tutor each other about their writing and their lives. In "Ethnographic Writing for Critical Consciousness," James Thomas Zebroski and Nancy Mack explain the rationale and the methodology they use to have their students do ethnographic kinds of research on the topic of work. This process not only helps their students to see themselves as readers and writers and researchers, it also helps them to develop a critical consciousness about issues of class and oppression. M. Daphne Kutzer closes this section with "A Ghostly Chorus: AIDS in the English Classroom." In this dramatic narrative, Kutzer shows how she has, at her students' request, taught about AIDS. Beginning with how she has structured a highly successful composition course around the subject of AIDS, Kutzer then considers her literature class and honestly faces the reasons why her literature students resisted her pedagogy.

Section four, "Teaching Literature for Social Responsibility," begins with two articles about teaching high school students. In "Breaking the Silence: Addressing Homophobia with *The Color Purple*," Vincent Lankewish explains how he teaches about the relationship between Celie and Shug in *The Color Purple* in such a way as to help his high school students come to terms with their own homophobic thinking. In "Using *Native Son* to Explore Language and Stereotype," Jimmie Mason describes how she uses the racially loaded language of *Native Son* to help both her African American and European American high school students to understand the social consequences of the words they use to talk to and about each other. In the next essay, "Racism and the Marvelous Real," Cecilia Rodríguez Milanés discusses how she combines the teaching of works by African American realist writers with literature of the marvelous real by Latina/Latino writers to teach her students about fiction and about their own racism. Rodríguez Milanés documents her interactions with her mostly white middle-class university students, analyzing the ways in which she both succeeded and failed to get them to confront the cultural differences that mark their relationships with the material of the course. Closing section four, two graduate teaching assistants, John Tassoni and Gail Tayko, explain their attempt to include their African American students in the creation of material for their courses. As they tell us in " 'I'm not a poor slave': Student-Generated Curricula and Race Relations," it didn't work out as well as they hoped. Their rationale for their actions and their description of their students' responses are a challenge to all educators, first, to work for democratic teaching materials and methods and, second, to critique their own teaching about social issues. This may be the only way for us to create pedagogies that are true to the ideals we espouse.

The last section of *Social Issues in the English Classroom* is entitled "Politics, Change, and Social Responsibility." The educators who contribute to it challenge readers to consider the political and ethical implications of, as well as the effectiveness of, the ways in which English teachers actually teach about social issues. First, C. Mark Hurlbert and Michael Blitz discuss, in "Rumors of Change: *The* Classroom, *Our* Classrooms, and *Big* Business," how corporate interest in education stands in the way of English teachers' efforts toward social transformation. While acknowledging that English educators have written and taught about social issues in meaningful ways, Hurlbert and Blitz call on readers to pay greater attention to how "big business" currently influences the federal government's control of literacy education in America and how conservative educators work to institute curriculum changes that promote no cultural change. Sandra Stotsky then offers readers another warning in "Ethical Guidelines for Writing Assignments." Working from a more conservative perspective than the other writers in this collection, Stotsky claims that the only ethical way to teach about a social issue is to balance social critique with appreciation for the positive characteristics of American society. Students must investigate a social issue from multiple perspectives and in great depth, Stotsky argues, if they are to understand how difficult it is to address any of the many social issues we face. We, the editors, include this controversial essay in hope that it will encourage serious critique of all curricula promoting social responsibility. In "Textual Authority and the Role of Teachers as Public Intellectuals," Henry A. Giroux describes how different theoretical perspectives on literacy cause teachers to create widely different pedagogies which support widely different ideologies. Giroux further argues that English teachers can teach a discourse of morality in their classrooms, but to do so they must create classrooms in which the voices of the differing communities from which students come are valued. Also working from an ideological perspective, Kathleen Weiler closes *Social Issues in the English Classroom* with "Teaching, Feminism, and Social Change." Weiler explores the responsibility that all English teachers have to make a difference where they teach. If teachers draw upon the principles of feminism, Weiler suggests, they are put in touch with a historically significant movement and a wider collective that is already working for social reform.

Taken together, the writers for *Social Issues in the English Classroom* teach at every level from elementary school to graduate school. They are from different parts of the country. They are from different racial and ethnic backgrounds, and they teach students of different racial and ethnic backgrounds. They have differing sexual preferences, and they no doubt teach students with differing sexual preferences. They claim different political affiliations, and they no doubt teach students who claim different political affiliations. And, finally, they teach about a variety of social issues.

But we, the editors, make no claim to complete coverage in *Social Issues in the English Classroom*. We know that we have not included the concerns of all Americans and that we have not addressed all of the multitude of social issues faced by the citizens of our world. One of the saddest things we have relearned while creating this collection is that there are just too many social issues to fit into any book. *Social*

Issues in the English Classroom is, however, a collection of writings by some teachers who, though they may not agree on many basic issues, such as whether America even *is* a participatory democracy, at least are, whether they be conservatives, liberals, or radicals, devoted to working for social justice and ethical teaching practices. It is our hope that *Social Issues in the English Classroom* will show what can be done and why it should be done. It is our hope that it will contribute to the efforts of those English teachers who are already working for social justice in their classrooms. And it is our further hope that it will encourage still others to begin the work of changing, with students, their classrooms, their communities, this society, and our world. As we said at the outset, the number and the magnitude of the social issues troubling us could easily overwhelm and silence anyone calling for change. But precisely because they are teachers of language, literature, composition, and culture, English teachers have the power to design pedagogies that encourage students and teachers alike to turn the silences forced upon them, and to which they sometimes become resigned, into eloquent and collective calls for change.

I Social Consciousness and Social Responsibility

1 Educating for the Development of Social Consciousness and Social Responsibility

Samuel Totten
University of Arkansas at Fayetteville

Introduction

Well over one hundred years ago, Herbert Spencer (1860) raised the question "What Knowledge Is of Most Worth?" In the subsequent years, it is a question that has intrigued and perplexed innumerable educators—especially curriculum theorists—and rightly so. At the same time, however, it is also a question that has been ignored by far too many curriculum specialists and classroom teachers.

In this "age of information," such a question is even more difficult to tackle. This is true not only because there is such a plethora of information readily available today, but because of some of the negative ramifications of that deluge of information. For example, William Shawcross (1984) has perspicaciously pointed out the irony that "the flood of instant information in the world today—at least in the Western industrialized world—sometimes seems not to further, but to retard, education; not to excite, but to dampen, curiosity; not to enlighten, but merely to dismay" (11). In a similar, but more graphic, vein, Milan Kundera (1980) has noted in *The Book of Laughter and Forgetting* that "the bloody massacre in Bangladesh quickly covered the memory of the Russian invasion of Czechoslovakia; the assassination of Allende drowned out the groans of Bangladesh; the war in the Sinai desert made people forget Allende; the Cambodian massacre made people forget Sinai; and so on and so forth, until ultimately everyone lets everything be forgotten" (2). Concern over the same sort of problem moved poet Archibald MacLeish to remark that "we are deluged with facts but we have lost or are losing our human ability to feel them" (Shawcross 1984, 1).

Too often, an "unexamined curriculum" is not worth teaching, let alone learning. In far too many cases, such a curriculum constitutes no more than a perfunctory exercise to get through a pile of infor-

9

mation—a pile that is often largely comprised of "inert facts" (Whitehead 1971, 178–79). It is a curriculum whose relevance is either not readily recognized by the student or simply not relevant. Put another way, such information is taught simply because it is "there" (e.g., in a curriculum guide or in a textbook) or solely because it is going to be a question on a teacher-made quiz or a standardized test. It is a curriculum that is often taught in an unimaginative, unengaging, and ineffective manner. I have termed such a curriculum the "perfunctory curriculum."

The "study" of such a perfunctory curriculum is possibly why so many students are bored and apathetic in school today; they end up "going through the motions," rather than being intrigued and motivated to explore new ideas and concepts. Far too rarely do teachers posit or ponder the following questions prior to teaching something to their students: Is this knowledge really valuable? If so, why? If not, why are we continuing to teach it? How will this new-found knowledge affect the students' lives? Will it possibly make them better persons? More insightful? More critically aware? More wide-awake? More moral? More creative? More confident? More curious? More competent vis-à-vis truly valuable skills? If so, how? If not, why is it being taught? Where, when, and how will students possibly be able to put the knowledge/skills to use in their current lives? And finally, as the Coalition of Essential Schools personnel (1989) continually asks in the course of their pedagogical efforts, "So what? What does it [the information, knowledge, skills] matter? What does it all mean?" (2).

Vito Perrone (1990), Director of Teachers of Education at Harvard University's School of Graduate Education, has raised the following points regarding such concerns:

> By and large . . . we tend, in most of our schools, to be more attentive to technical than moral and intellectual directions, the isolated pieces, the trees and not the forest. . . . There is, it seems, more concern about whether children learn the mechanics of reading and writing than grow to love deeply reading and writing: learn *about* democratic practice than have practice in democracy; hear about knowledge . . . than gain experience in constructing knowledge; engage in competition rather than learn the power of cooperation and collaborative thought; see the world narrowly, as simple and ordered rather than broad, complex, and uncertain; come to accept the vested authority that exists around them in organizational structures and text rather than challenge such authority, bringing a healthy skepticism to the world. . . . To invest so much in the technical aspects of education is to assure an uninspiring education, one that will surely miss most of the moral

imperatives which surround children and young people and are related directly to concerns of social responsibility. (22)

It is the thesis of this essay, then, that the thorough and well-structured study of social issues,[1] educating for the development of social consciousness[2] and social responsibility,[3] *and* the processes for doing so (e.g., reflective inquiry, examining problems from various perspectives, developing an ability to be open to diverse solutions, the development of a moral imagination, and the sensibilities and abilities to act upon it), constitute some of the most significant learning a student can undertake; and for that reason, such pedagogical concerns are of "most worth." Put another way, at its best, education is capable of assisting in the development of a citizenry that is knowledgeable, mindful, caring, and, ultimately, capable of stewardship. This, of course, is a Herculean and complex task, but it is also one that should be the concern and focus of teachers in all curricular areas.

Why Study Social Issues?

There are numerous reasons for which educators advocate the study and teaching of social issues and/or teaching for social consciousness and social responsibility. Among the many rationales that have been developed over the past nine decades, the following are worthy of serious consideration:

1. To raise students' awareness of key issues in their society.

2. To provide students with a means to analyze and evaluate problems in the world, including their lives/communities/states/nation, so that they are not only more aware of the problems, but also able to examine any issue in an efficacious manner and weigh the feasibility and strengths/weaknesses of various solutions/options as well as generate their own unique solutions.

3. To provide the means and abilities for students to examine their lives, to assist them in pondering and thoroughly assessing why they think and believe as they do, and to engender wide-awakeness so they can act on their new-found knowledge and awareness.

4. To assist the students in coming to understand and appreciate their own "connectedness" to "the larger world around them" (Mathews 1985, 680).

5. To enable students to come to appreciate and understand that

individuals, communities, and governments continually confront choices that can have an impact on social concerns.

6. To assist students to gain a "perspective consciousness . . . [or] the realization that one's values, beliefs, and world view are a matter of perspective" (Hahn 1985, 480).

7. To create in students a deep and abiding passion about how they live their lives, about the fate of others, and about the world around them.

8. To "enable students to find their voices, to think about their own thinking, to open themselves to others, to perceive continuities in their experience, to deal with disequilibrium and dissonance and chaos" (Greene 1990, 77).

9. To give students a sense of not being "afraid to confront, to listen, to see the world unveiled" (Freire 1972, 40).

10. To assist students in coming to understand, appreciate, and gain the ability to "envisage things as they could be otherwise" (Greene 1988, 16).

11. To provide students with a means to take an active and responsible role as citizens in what should be a participatory democracy.

12. To engender praxis, i.e., "reflection and action upon the world in order to transform it" (Freire 1970, 36).

13. To produce in students "civil courage": "the importance of citizenship and mature iconoclasm" (Friedlander 1979, 532).

Resistance to Teaching about Social Issues and/or for Social Consciousness and Social Responsibility

Upon close scrutiny of school curricula across the United States, it becomes painfully obvious that preparing students to become competent social critics and/or socially active citizens is not a high priority in our nation's schools. Certainly indicative of this is the fact that the study of social issues in our social studies, English, and science classrooms is still—despite all of the innovative and exciting programs currently in existence—perfunctory at best, and scant at worst. This is also true despite the long history of repeated efforts to develop and incorporate the study of social issues into the curriculum. Such efforts include the following:

In the early part of this century (late 1920s and on into the 1930s) the Progressives and the Reconstructionists (the radical wing of the Progressives) argued for the incorporation of social issues and developed theories and curricula for teaching about social issues and/or educating for the transformation of society;

The Rugg brothers (Harold and Earle), who developed a series of mimeographed sheets and textbooks throughout the 1920s, 1930s, and 1940s in which they integrated major social issues of the times, asserted that their major goal was to "strengthen the capacity of students to rationally and intelligently handle complex social problems through greater understanding of significant generalizations about human social behavior" (Isham and Mehaffy 1985, 571);

George Counts, whose *Dare the Schools Build a New Social Order?* is considered a classic in educational literature, was vitally concerned about the socioeconomic inequities in the U.S. and challenged educators in the 1930s to design educational programs for the express purpose of reconstructing U.S. society in order to make it more just;

The "New Frontier Thinkers" (in addition to the Ruggs and Counts, there were such individuals as Jesse Newlon and Theodore Brameld) initiated and contributed to a journal entitled *The New Frontier* whose sole purpose was to serve as a forum for addressing and debating the role of education about key social issues;

Hilda Taba, in the latter half of the 1930s, as part of her work with the Progressive Education Association's Eight-Year Study, attempted to identify categories of abilities "related to developing greater social sensitivity—including the ability to apply social facts and generalizations in interpreting social changes, to apply social values in the solution of social problems, and to use relevant and accurate information in the analyses of social problems" (Isham and Mehaffy 1985, 572);

The development in the 1940s of the "Building America" series (monthly magazines published and distributed by the Association for Supervision and Curriculum Development) that highlighted various social issues and delineated their importance to U.S. citizens;

The efforts of Byron Massialas and Benjamin Cox in the early 1960s to develop the Social Inquiry Model whose focus was "social problem solving, primarily through academic inquiry and logical reasoning" (Joyce and Weil 1980, 12);

The development of the Jurisprudential Model of teaching in the 1960s by Harvard's Donald Oliver and James P. Shaver, which was designed "primarily to teach the jurisprudential frame of reference as a way of thinking about and resolving social issues" (Joyce and Weil 1980, 12);

The attempt by Newmann and others (Newmann 1975; Newmann 1981; Newmann and Rutter 1977; Newmann and Rutter 1986; and Newmann, Bertocci, and Landsness 1977) to forge a connection between ways of thinking and resolving social issues and citizen participation;

The theory-building efforts of Samuel Shermis and James L. Barth, authors of *Defining Social Problems* (1979);

The work of such organizations as Facing History and Ourselves (from the mid-1970s to the present) and Educators for Social Responsibility (from the early 1980s to the present) to not only design curricula on key social issues but to attempt to develop curricula and teaching strategies that take into serious consideration the developmental concerns of adolescents, the need for reflection, and the development of social consciousness;

The efforts of the National Council for the Social Studies to develop and implement a Public Issues Program (PIP) which "includes four approaches to participatory citizenship—National Issues Forums (NIF), Jefferson Meetings, the Great Decisions Programs, and C-SPAN (McFarland 1989);[4]

The pioneering work of science educators Norris Harms, Rostum Roy, Peter A. Rubba, and Robert E. Yager in the 1980s and 1990s to develop and implement Science/Technology/Society (STS) programs;

And the current work of the critical and feminist pedagogues who examine (and prod others to critically examine) the systemic problems inherent in our educational system and society in order to better understand its "true" (versus its "stated") goals and purposes, to work toward overcoming "silent and often invisible" injustices, and to empower people to become agents of freedom.

Again, despite this rich history, in more cases than not, teaching about social issues and/or for social consciousness and social responsibility constitutes what Elliot Eisner (1979) calls "the null curriculum":

> What schools do not teach may be as important as what they do teach.
> . . . ignorance is not simply a neutral void; it has important

effects on the kind of options one is able to consider, the alternatives from which one can view a situation or problem. The
absence of a set of considerations or processes or the inability to
use certain processes for appraising a context biases the evidence
one is able to take into account. A parochial perspective or
simplistic analysis is the inevitable progeny of ignorance. (83)

There are numerous reasons as to why the current study of social
issues constitutes the null curriculum, including the following: there
is a fear by teachers that principals, community members, school
boards, and others may disapprove of their teaching about social issues
that are controversial; some adults want to "protect" young people
from certain disturbing issues; certain segments of society prefer—
some consciously, some unconsciously—that the young accept the
status quo and not question it; some believe that certain issues are too
complex and/or volatile for the "average person" to truly understand;
there is a general indifference by the public *and* educators to certain
issues; certain teachers are either ignorant about key issues or only
have a minimal understanding of them, and thus they are more
comfortable simply avoiding the issues in class; already tight schedules
may ostensibly preclude addressing social issues and other concomitant
concerns, which are often perceived as adjunct areas and not as an
integral part of the curriculum; teachers may simply lack an interest
in teaching about social issues; and some teachers may have no sense
as to how to even begin teaching about issues outside of their areas
of expertise—particularly if there is a lack of attention to them in the
textbooks that they use.

It seems that members of our society should have learned long ago
that it can be truly dangerous to "leave [social problems] to the
experts." Too many times in the recent past, as well as today, innocent
people have suffered because of this leave-it-to-the-experts attitude:
people of color who have been denied their basic rights simply due
to the color of their skin, the "downwinders" in Utah who were
subjected to radioactivity from the nuclear weapons tests in the 1950s
and 60s, the Native Americans whose land and bodies have been
contaminated by the radioactive tailings left behind from the uranium
mining on their property, those who resided in the poisoned Love
Canal area in upstate New York, tobacco users who have blindly
believed the tobacco industry's blatant lies that the evidence is still
inconclusive as to whether or not tobacco use and secondhand smoke
are dangerous, the poor and the homeless who "litter" our streets and
are treated like trash, the "voiceless" and exploited who are led to
believe "that's just the way it is," all of us who are threatened by

huge piles of nuclear weapons and increasingly sophisticated delivery systems, ad nauseam. By not insisting on and supporting the teaching of its young about key social issues and for social consciousness and social responsibility, the public is inadvertently supporting the leave-it-to-the-experts attitude.

Years ago, Green (1966) commented that "anything can be introduced as a topic of study in the public schools provided it is a matter about which nobody cares a great deal or a matter . . . widely believed to have no practical consequences" (31). As cynical as that statement may appear, many teachers feel just that way. In relation to this concern, educational critic Joel Spring (1989) has argued that

> the political structure of schooling in the United States makes it impossible to protect freedom of expression in American education. In fact, because of the political organization of the system, teachers and administrators feel that their jobs will be threatened if controversial political and economic ideas are taught in the classroom. (268)

Spring goes on to argue that this problem is

> compounded by the conservative actions of publishers and testing corporations. Therefore, we have the ironic situation that the supposed protectors of democracy, the public schools, do little to promote a political culture that would help a democratic society survive. In this sense, public schools, as they are currently structured, might be destructive of American democratic culture. (268)

That some teachers fear their jobs may be in jeopardy if they teach something controversial is disconcerting. This raises the issue as to why public school teachers, unlike their counterparts in colleges and universities, do not have the same academic freedom in their classrooms. The amount of academic freedom a teacher has seems to depend on "where you teach and what the climate happens to be in a particular community. In a very real sense, what this boils down to is local control of the curriculum" (Hirsh and Kemerer 1982). Another question that arises, of course, is whether such an important issue should be left to local control. And this, in turn, raises the question of whether or not the citizens of the United States truly wish to prepare their young to be critically and creatively thinking, active citizens, or something closer to docile, non-questioning followers. This type of "fear" speaks to the need for teachers, administrators, school board members, and local citizenry to engage in a dialogue about what schools are for, the lack of power teachers have (or at least feel they have) in regard to making curricular decisions, and what our students need to know in order to truly be prepared to take an active part in establishing our nation's agenda and assisting in its welfare. It also focuses on the need for school districts to develop and implement procedures for teaching about social issues.[5] Likewise, it speaks loudly to the need for state and national educational organizations to band together in order to encourage, support, and protect teachers who teach about social issues and/or for social consciousness and social responsibility. Significantly, still others—the critical theorists and certain advocates of feminist pedagogy—think, believe, and eloquently argue that the entire system should not simply be reformed but radically changed from its roots up.

As for the point that the study of certain social issues may be too complex for students, I agree with Bruner's (1960) supposition that "any subject can be taught effectively in some intellectually honest form to any child at any stage of development" (33). Simply stated, students are often capable of a lot more than most give them credit for; and if given sound guidance along with an opportunity to conduct research into a topic that is truly meaningful to them, most can do a remarkably fine job. The same is true, of course, in regard to work on civic projects.

At the other end of the spectrum, it is also a fact that many dedicated teachers, staffs, and their administrators have worked and continue to work extremely hard in order to increase their students' knowledge about various social issues, and many are working just as ardently to instill a sense of social consciousness and social responsibility in their students. Such individuals, it seems, would agree with Shaver's (1985) comment that any democratic society is going to continue to "have controversy, because even rational people do not agree on solutions (or often even on the problems for the simple reason that they bring different frames of reference to specific situations, thereby coming to different policy decisions) . . . [Be that as it may,] the hope of the schools is not to educate students to be rational so as to do away with social problems (for it is inherent in a democratic society that dissension and confrontation will persist), but to educate them so that those problems will be addressed in the context of our basic values, with a minimum of human suffering and violence" (197).

Certainly one way to overcome the sense of nervousness about going it alone and/or the inertia of an organization's (e.g., a department, a school, or a district) lack of support for the teaching of social issues and social responsibility is to plug into a nationally or regionally recognized network or program. This, at the very least, provides teachers with a sense of credibility that they might not have on their own. It will also provide the teacher with a support group as well as a source for new ideas on how to teach about social issues in a pedagogically sound and innovative manner. There are numerous programs currently in existence, including the following: CIVITAS, Educators for Social Responsibility, Facing History and Ourselves National Foundation, Inc., The Governor's School on Public Issues of New Jersey, the Institute for Democracy in Education, National Issues Forum in the Classroom, QUEST, and the STS Program and National STS Network.[6]

Possibly the greatest source of inspiration (not to mention some of the most outstanding ideas) a teacher can gain in regard to teaching about social issues, social consciousness, and social responsibility is the work that individual teachers are doing in their own classrooms. Such information/knowledge demonstrates that caring and concerned individuals can make a difference in a single classroom and can forge ahead on their own if they have the desire and tenacity to do so. (See the rest of the essays in this volume, as well as those in the Fall 1986 special issue, "Teaching Social Issues in the English Classroom," of the *Arizona English Bulletin*, Volume 29, No. 1).

Overview of Various Theoretical and/or Pedagogical Approaches, Models, and Programs

Some of the more common or notable approaches, models, and programs used to teach about social issues, social consciousness, and social responsibility will be reviewed here. It should be understood that none of them is as clear-cut as it appears, and each has its own strengths and weaknesses. Unfortunately, space constraints preclude providing a detailed description, let alone a solid critique, of each one. However, key works will be cited for those readers who wish to obtain more information regarding any of them.

As Hahn (1991) has noted, "Empirical evidence gathered over the past twenty-five years, although meager and often coming from nonrepresentative samples, consistently supports the position that positive citizenship outcomes are associated with giving students opportunities to explore controversial issues in an open, supportive classroom atmosphere" (470). Accordingly, some teachers believe that certain social issues are so significant to both the body politic and lives of individuals that students need to be, *at the very least*, cognizant of their existence. Consequently, these teachers provide their students with *general information* (e.g., several of the major concerns inherent in the issue; its key players; its impact on society; and the significance of the issue for the individual, in particular, and humanity, in general) about a "hot" topic. Such studies also generally attempt to teach students how to examine, dissect, and weigh the issues as "objectively" as possible (e.g., providing various sides to an issue, encouraging the discussion and/or debate of various perspectives). Over the course of the past sixty or so years, many teachers (in the areas of English, science, and particularly the social studies), have conducted "awareness raising" mini-units on such "hot" topics as racism, prejudice, censorship, the death penalty, the environment, the nuclear arms race, and nuclear war.

While awareness of and knowledge about social issues are vitally significant, they hardly provide one with the abilities to cope with, let alone solve, such problems. Too often—and in reality, probably more often than not—the study of such issues was and still is comprised of a string of simple (often watered-down) facts, and is bereft of the depth that is needed to truly understand the complexity and numerous ramifications of the issue, let alone ways to address it in an efficacious manner. Every effort, of course, should be made to *avoid* presenting students with a simplistic view of an issue and naively idealistic notions as to how it can be ameliorated.

While such units are often very brief and lack the depth that many teachers desire and aspire towards, they are a valuable first step in a student's awareness about a major issue. For if a person is not aware of a problem there is absolutely no way that he or she can act upon it. The units may also serve to sensitize students to being more open-minded should they encounter the issue in the future. Furthermore, a study such as this may, in fact, be the catalyst for further study by students. Concomitantly, it can provide an opening for classes to discuss why people may remain unaware of certain issues, and the profound ramifications of such ignorance. When all is said and done, the significance of this type of study should *not* be underestimated.

Perrone (1990) relates an interesting story that is relevant to the points above:

> At a recent Peace Studies Symposium at the University of North Dakota, Brian Petkau, a Canadian teacher, presented *A Prairie Puzzle*, a powerful personal statement about the presence of nuclear missiles across the North Dakota landscape and what these weapons represent in terms of danger to human life. Several young North Dakota students who were in the audience expressed considerable anger about "how little they knew." They asked why they hadn't learned more about the missile fields, the kinds of weapons that existed and something about their control mechanisms, the cost of these weapons, and importantly, they stressed,

their potential as targets. In not making the nuclear arms in North
Dakota, or in the country, or in the world, a matter of serious
study in the schools these students attended, what kinds of values
were being expressed? Were the students being prepared for active
citizenship? (25)

It seems as if the concluding interrogatives are questions all educators
should ask themselves in regard to what they do and do not teach
their students and why.

Some teachers go a step beyond the previously discussed approach
in believing that students who live in a democracy not only need to
be informed about certain social issues but also need to understand
and appreciate how individuals or groups can have a say and impact
concerning those issues. Thus, these teachers teach about social issues
not only to inform their students about the issues but to impress upon
them the role of an active citizen in a democracy. Such a study might
involve studying why and how various individuals and groups have
addressed a social issue in their communities, state, and nation, and
the results of their efforts. It also might include an examination of the
type of resistance that these efforts met and why, how the resistance
was countered and overcome (if, in fact, it was), what methods worked
and did not work and why, and the short- and long-term outcomes.
The same caveats mentioned in regard to the first method also apply
here.

Still other educators (mainly researchers in the areas of the social
studies and science) have developed research-based teaching approaches, models, and programs specifically for use in the study of
key social or policy issues. One of the most highly respected models
along this line was the one developed by the Harvard Social Studies
Project in which students were instructed in the use of a "jurisprudential
approach" to analyze controversial public policy issues (Levin, Newmann, and Oliver 1969; Oliver and Shaver 1966/1974). One of the
many strengths of this program is that it, unlike a great many of the
other units/programs, was thoroughly evaluated (using a battery of
methods, including "standardized critical thinking tests, Social Issues
Analysis Tests developed by the project staff, [and] a measure of
interest in current events" Hahn 1991, 474) to test the developers'
hypothesis that "it is possible to teach adolescent students to use an
abstract conceptual model for analyzing and clarifying public controversy" (Oliver and Shaver 1966/1974, 257).[7]

Many, if not most, of the advocates of the aforementioned approaches
neglect to examine the systemic and often oppressive structures (social,
economical, cultural) at work in society that not only constitute the

root causes of many social issues but are also the very factors that work against ameliorating or solving them. An approach or study that examines systemic issues and works toward a transformation "of the relation between human capacities and social forms so as to make possible and enable the realization of differentiated human capacities" (Simon 1988, 1) is commonly referred to as "critical pedagogy." (As Ellsworth (1989) notes, the "different emphases [of critical pedagogy] are reflected in the labels given to them, such as 'critical pedagogy,' 'pedagogy of critique and possibility,' 'pedagogy of student voice,' 'pedagogy of empowerment,' 'radical pedagogy,' 'pedagogy for radical democracy,' and 'pedagogy of possibility' " [298].)

A study addressing such concerns would involve an initial (but also ongoing) "critical" examination of the root or underlying causes of many and vastly different key issues (e.g., authoritarian and oppressive social structures at various levels of life, including government, school, and the family; how and why the current dominant structure in society has been developed and the impediments it imposes to creating a fair and just society; control of knowledge and information in society; the marginalization of certain peoples and the silencing of their voices; poverty and lack of opportunity in society at large; conditions at home, on the job, and in school; the type of knowledge that is taught in schools; "how schools are places that represent forms of knowledge, language practices, and social relations and values that are represent-ative of a particular selection and an exclusion from the wider culture" (Giroux 1985, 379); "how schools serve to introduce and legitimate *particular* forms of social life" (Giroux 1985, 379); and, "the banking system of education" (Freire 1979, 58–74). What is also emphasized is the need to go beyond the given, and the taken for granted, to expose and thoroughly examine dominant concepts and ideologies in order to uncover that which "masks and distorts" (Gilbert 1985) our true understanding of a situation. Such a study, though, would only be the first—albeit a vitally significant—step in working toward a transformation of all aspects of the school, community, and larger society in which we live, bringing about a more just society for all.[8]

What the "radical critique/approach" means in pedagogical terms is delineated in the following passage by Henry Giroux (1985):

> Central to the category of transformative intellectual is the ne-cessity of making the pedagogical more political and the political more pedagogical. Making the pedagogical more political means inserting schooling directly into the political sphere by arguing that schooling represents both a struggle to define meaning and a struggle over power relations. Within this perspective, critical

reflection and action become part of a fundamental social project to help students develop a deep and abiding faith in the struggle to overcome economic, political and social injustices and to further humanize themselves as part of this struggle.

... Making the political more pedagogical means utilizing forms of pedagogy that embody political interests that are emancipatory in nature; that is, using forms of pedagogy that treat students as critical agents; make knowledge problematic; utilize critical and affirming dialogue; and make the case for struggling for a qualitatively better world for all people. In part, this suggests that transformative intellectuals take seriously the need to give students an active voice in their learning experiences. It also means developing a critical vernacular that is attentive to problems experienced at the level of everyday life, particularly as they are related to pedagogical experiences connected to classroom practice. As such, the pedagogical starting point for such intellectuals is not the isolated student but individuals and groups in their various cultural, class, racial, historical and gender settings, along with the particularity of their diverse problems, hopes and dreams.

... At the same time, [teachers] must work to create the conditions that give students the opportunity to become citizens who have the knowledge and courage to struggle in order to make despair unconvincing and hope practical. (379)

The centrality of these systemic concerns, a critical pedagogue would say, is such that if they are not addressed in a "critical" and "transformative" manner then most (if not all) of the well-intentioned efforts to effect equitable and lasting change will be nothing more than perfunctory and, ultimately, cosmetic.

As befitting pedagogues who advocate a critical stance, the critical pedagogists have provided ample and solid critiques of their own and their colleagues' arguments/positions. On the other hand, many conservatives and moderates have argued that the ideas of the critical pedagogists are "too radical"; still others have complained that their thoughts are couched in language that is so dense that it is extremely difficult to understand. Still others have argued that the ideas of the critical pedagogists are not easily incorporated into a public school setting and that they have not provided teachers with enough practical ideas. Some of the most stinging critiques have been written by feminist theorists/pedagogues. A particularly provocative critique by a feminist educator can be found in Elizabeth Ellsworth's (1989) essay, "Why Doesn't This Feel Empowering? Working Through the Repressive Myths of Critical Pedagogy." Ellsworth argues, in part, that "key assumptions, goals, and pedagogical practices fundamental to the literature on critical pedagogy—namely 'empowerment,' 'student voice,' 'dialogue,' and even the term 'critical'—are repressive myths that perpetuate relations of domination" (298). A key reason for this, she asserts, is that such assumptions, goals, and practices are based on rationalist assumptions. Her discussion of each of these assumptions, goals, and practices is detailed and thought-provoking. All educators, but especially critical pedagogists and those who have co-opted such terms as "empowerment," "student voice," "dialogue," and "critical," should take into serious consideration what she has to say.

Speaking of rationalist assumptions, Ellsworth (1989) argues that they

> have led to the following goals: the teaching of analytic and critical skills for judging the truth and merit of propositions, and the interrogation and selective appropriation of potentially trans- formative moments in the dominant culture. As long as educators define pedagogy against oppressive formations in these ways the role of the critical pedagogue will be to guarantee that the foundation for classroom interaction is reason. In other words, the critical pedagogue is one who enforces the rules of reason in the classroom—"a series of rules of thought that any ideal rational person might adopt if his/her purpose was to achieve propositions of universal validity." Under these conditions, and given the coded nature of the political agenda of critical pedagogy, only one "political" gesture appears to be available to critical pedagogues. They can ensure that students are given the chance to arrive logically at the "universally valid proposition" underlying the disclosure of critical pedagogy—namely, that all people have a right to freedom from oppression guaranteed by the democratic social contract, and that in the classroom, this proposition be given equal time vis-à-vis other "sufficiently articulated and rea- sonably distinct moral positions."
>
> Yet educators who have constructed classroom practices de- pendent upon analytic critical judgment can no longer regard the enforcement of rationalism as a self-evident political act against relations of domination. Literary criticism, cultural studies, post- structuralism, feminist studies, comparative studies, and media studies have by now amassed overwhelming evidence of the extent to which the myths of the ideal rational person and the "universality" of propositions have been oppressive to those who are not European, white, male, middle class, Christian, ablebodied, thin, and heterosexual. Writings by many literary and cultural critics, both women of color and White women who are concerned with explaining the intersections and interactions among relations of racism, colonialism, sexism, and so forth, are now employing, either implicitly or explicitly, concepts and analytical methods that could be called feminist poststructuralism. While poststructuralism, like rationalism, is a tool that can be used to dominate, it has also facilitated a devastating critique of the violence of rationalism against its Others. It has demonstrated that as a discursive practice, rationalism's regulated and systematic use of elements of language

constitutes rational competence "as a series of exclusions—of women, people of color, of nature as historical agent, of the true value of art." In contrast, poststructuralist thought is not bound to reason, but "to discourse, literary narratives about the world that are admittedly *partial*." Indeed, one of the crucial features of discourse is the intimate tie between knowledge and interest, the latter being understood as a "standpoint" from which to grasp "reality." (303–304)

As one can readily ascertain, there is ample food for thought in her critique. (Also see Weiler's "Teaching, Feminism, and Social Change" in this volume.)

Feminist pedagogy is another approach that not only has direct bearing on the issues under discussion here, but on the entire framework of schooling. While it shares many of the same concerns as one would find in critical pedagogy, its primary concerns are "gender justice" and a pedagogy in which the "subjective" is integral (e.g., "knowledge must be contextualized and rooted in a particular framework and world view, and should have an emotional component, a feeling component that comes from the knower's sense of purpose, sense of connection to the material and particular context" [Maher 1987, 96]).

Speaking of the reasons for the development and emergence of feminist pedagogy, Maher (1987) reports that

feminist pedagogy has emerged in large part as a response to the traditional content and theory of knowledge purveyed in most college classrooms. Traditionally, the experience, viewpoint, and goals of white, Western, elite males are taken as representing all of human experience. The histories, experiences, and consciousness of other groups, whether women, all people of color, or all working-class people, are either ignored, condemned as inferior, or judged as deviant. Furthermore, in this process of universalizing the experience of one particular group, claims are laid for the primacy of a certain kind of thinking and problem solving, namely, the scientific method. The constructing of hypotheses provable or disprovable by empirical data, the process by which generalizations are formed from selected particulars and then considered "true," the idea that abstract reasoning and critical thinking can lead to an accurate understanding of "objective reality"—this kind of thinking and the knowledge derived from it are seen to constitute the only valid process and content of knowledge itself. (91–92)

In an essay entitled "What Is Feminist Pedagogy?" Shrewsbury (1987) describes "feminist pedagogy" in the following manner:

Feminist pedagogy begins with a vision of what education might be like but frequently is not. This is a vision of the classroom as a liberatory environment in which we, teacher-student and student-teacher, act as subjects, not objects. Feminist pedagogy is engaged teaching/learning—engaged with self in a continuing reflective process; engaged actively with the material being studied; engaged with others in a struggle to get beyond our sexism and racism and classism and homophobia and other destructive hatred and to work together to enhance our knowledge; engaged with the community, with traditional organizations, and with movements for social change.

. . . At its simplest level, feminist pedagogy is concerned with gender justice and overcoming oppressions. It recognizes the genderedness of all social relations and consequently of all societal institutions and structures. Thus, fundamental to a feminist perspective is a commitment to growth, to renewal, to life. The vision itself must continue to evolve. (6–7)

While the theory and practical applications of feminist pedagogy are still evolving, it is an approach that educators ignore at peril to both themselves and their students. Again, if educators hope to educate for social consciousness and social responsibility, it behooves them not only to become conversant with the most salient issues and nuances of feminist pedagogy but also to begin to reexamine their own philosophy and pedagogical efforts in this "new light" and then act accordingly.[9]

Shelley Berman (President of Educators for Social Responsibility) and a few select others, most of whom are associated with Educators for Social Responsibility, have begun what appears to be promising work on the development of an approach that attempts to integrate and fuse many components of the previously mentioned approaches, theories, and conceptual frameworks into a practical teaching strategy. The approach's main focus is teaching for social consciousness and social responsibility. In my mind, social consciousness is akin to what Maxine Greene (1978) calls "wide-awakeness":

The social philosopher Alfred Schutz has talked of wide-awakeness as an achievement, a type of awareness, "a plane of consciousness of highest tension originating in an attitude of full attention to life and its requirements." This attentiveness, this *interest* in things, is the direct opposite of the attitude of bland conventionality and indifference so characteristic of our time.

We are all familiar with the number of individuals who live their lives immersed, as it were, in daily life, in the mechanical round of habitual activities. We are all aware how few people ask themselves what they have done with their own lives, whether or not they have used their freedom or simply acceded to the imposition of patterned behavior and the assignment of roles.

. . . The opposite of morality, it has often been said, is indifference—a lack of care, an absence of concern. Lacking wide-awakeness, I want to argue, individuals are likely to drift, to act

on impulses of expediency. They are unlikely to identify situations
as moral ones or to set themselves to assessing their demands. In
such cases, it seems to me, it is meaningless to talk of obligation;
it may be futile to speak of consequential choice. (42–43)

Berman (1990b), for one, contends that there are five basic steps to
educating for social consciousness and social responsibility:

1. "Helping students develop an understanding of our social and
   ecological interdependence" (8);

2. "Giving students the opportunity to contribute to the lives of
   others and to the improvement of the world around them" (9);

3. "Becoming aware of group needs . . . [that is] developing a 'consciousness of the group' so that an individual begins to sense
   the atmosphere or climate that is present in the group, to observe
   how people's interaction influences the productivity of the group,
   and to understand the impact his or her actions have on the
   group as a whole" (10);

4. "Developing basic participatory understandings and skills" which
   are comprised of: "acquainting students with our political institutions and history" (12–13), and such skills as organizing,
   consensus-building, problem-solving, and long-term thinking (13);
   "stepping out of one's own perspective" (13);

5. And "help[ing] students enter the dialogue about the real world
   issues that concern them" (15). (For a discussion of these and
   other related issues see Berman's (1990b) "The Real Ropes Course:
   The Development of Social Consciousness.")

Berman (1990b) argues that educating along this line

> means emphasizing a different set of questions: What does the
> way I lead my life mean for the lives of others? What is my hope
> for the future? Are my actions consistent with the way I would
> like the world to be? What can we do *together* as a community,
> as a society, and as a world community, that will promote our
> common good and our common wealth? How can I contribute in
> a meaningful way to creating a more just, peaceful, and ecologically
> sound world? Educationally, this means balancing our focus on
> personal self-realization and collective achievement. (8)

Elsewhere, Berman (1987) has argued that this involves "synthesis
thinking":

> Rather than closing in on a narrowly focused critique, it seeks to
> broaden the focus and enlarge the vision. . . . It means helping
> students enter into the positions of others in an attempt to see
> the world through others' eyes, [to] find the root agreements

among positions as well as the root differences, ... [and to] see the open-ended nature of the problems we face—whether they be the global problems of the threat of nuclear war, threats to the environment, social injustice, or a whole range of local or personal problems—and letting students know that they will have a role in creating better solutions. (1)

As intriguing and ostensibly valuable as the effort is to develop this "social consciousness and social responsibility strategy," the model in its present form is not without key problems. It is exciting in that it attempts to incorporate the ideas of many disparate theorists (moral education theory, empathy theory, critical pedagogy, feminist theory, and developmental theory) into what could be a new useful pedagogical approach; however, instead of being thoroughly grounded in such theories and integrated into a solid amalgamation, it seems to be rather disjointedly comprised of bits and pieces of the theories. Put another way, its "theoretical" base is weak. Thus, it is not only in need of a stronger theoretical base, but one in which the theories are fully and harmoniously integrated into a research-based strategy. If, as I assume, the development of the strategy is still in its nascent stage then it can be expected that this problem will be addressed as the model is field-tested, evaluated, and revised.

Having a social consciousness, of course, does not automatically lead to "social responsibility." There are those individuals who are vitally concerned about the type of life they lead and the welfare of others, but neglect to act upon their awareness. Some may well argue that one can hardly be *truly* socially conscious and *not* socially responsible; that is, they are not mutually exclusive. I, however, disagree with that position. In my view, to become "socially conscious" means to work towards a "wide-awakeness" in which one constantly examines one's thoughts and actions as they relate to the betterment of the world, while being "socially responsible" means *acting upon* that "social consciousness"—to engage in work and actions that assist in the betterment of the world.

As for the need to educate for social responsibility, Barber (1989) argues that

if the point were just to get students to mature into voters who watch television news diligently and pull a voting machine lever once every few years, traditional civics courses would suffice. But if students are to become actively engaged in public forms of thinking and participate thoughtfully in the whole spectrum of civic activities, [educational programs] require a strong element of practical civic experience—real participation and empowerment. (355)

The key term here is "real participation." If the activities in which the students end up participating are meaningless to them or ones in which they are simply going through the motions in order to meet a requirement, then the activities are almost, if not completely, useless. Concomitantly, if the students do not gain, at least gradually, a sense of self-efficacy from the activities, then, in all likelihood, the impact of the participation will have been ephemeral at best and discouragingly frustrating at worst. It is also true, of course, that simply carrying out certain socially responsible actions does not mean one has a deep and abiding social consciousness. What social consciousness and social responsibility call for is a critical stance in regard to one's world and life (including how and where one gains knowledge; how one examines one's knowledge base, understandings, and perspectives; how one uses such knowledge; one's motives and actions; and the far-reaching ramifications of one's actions).

There are numerous educational programs today which encourage or assist students in becoming actively engaged in various types of civic projects. The strongest of these not only move the students from being passive learners to being active participants, but provide the students with a solid understanding of the major concerns, controversies, and perspectives surrounding the issue at hand while at the same time striving to develop a sense of "social consciousness" in the students. It is simply not adequate to have the students work on a project in which they do not have a solid foundation of knowledge regarding the issue or are in the dark concerning the larger significance of the project/issue in relation to their own lives as well as to the larger world.[10] Most, if not all, of these programs, however, are bereft of a truly transformative approach as advocated by the critical and/ or feminist theorists.

At this point in time, "evidence from quantitative methodologies is somewhat limited, though a body of research does exist that tends to show that social, personal, and academic development are fostered by community service. Evidence from qualitative, anecdotal studies suggests even more strongly and consistently that community service can be a worthwhile, useful, enjoyable, and powerful learning experience" (Conrad and Hedin 1991, 746).[11] Additional research needs to be done to develop and evaluate the efficacy of such programs and to ascertain how they can be strengthened.

All of the previously mentioned approaches/models/programs are certainly worthwhile in their own right; however, not all of them are equally valuable. That said, no matter which approach teachers and their students select, it should involve the teachers and the students in becoming social critics and not simply accepting the status quo (Stanley 1982, 590).

It is also true that the approaches mentioned in this chapter are not the only ones available; in fact, there are numerous others—some entirely different, and others that use various components of those programs described above but with some innovative twists.[12]

Finally, another promising practice that deserves to be studied, refined, and ultimately implemented is the engagement of students in the use of computer networking with those organizations that focus on social issues, social consciousness, and social responsibility. In this age of information and interdependence, the use of the computer is a magnificent way to encourage students to create, share, and evaluate information as well as to make connections across the continent and globe. Such activities will not only graphically illustrate how social issues affect different parts of the globe, but provide crucial insights into the fact that other people in other places are also working on similar issues. This makes for a lesson on interdependence that the students will not soon forget. (For information on these types of programs, see Sagar's (1990) "Educating for Living in a Nuclear Age," and William Wright's essay, "Telecomputing and Social Action," the latter of which appears in this volume.)

Moral Development/Education and Prosocial Education

Over the past two decades or so, numerous educational theories, approaches, models, and programs have been developed or revised in respect to the issues of moral development, moral education, and prosocial education. While certain researchers and educators who are interested in teaching about social issues, social consciousness, and/ or social responsibility have incorporated such theories and practices into their work, many have not. Instead, many teachers and researchers have had a propensity to latch onto one theory, model, or program while totally neglecting to examine the array of other options available to them. That is unfortunate, because the goals of moral development, moral education, and prosocial education are definitely germane to many of the concerns, aims, and goals of the former group. Ignoring such concerns, it seems, is analogous to English teachers teaching the so-called "traditional" canon to the exclusion of all others. It is a distinct possibility that some of the new theories, models, and programs that have been developed by moral and/or prosocial researchers/ advocates may, in fact, prove to be the most efficacious of all in obtaining the results aimed for by those who advocate the teaching of social issues for social consciousness and social responsibility. The answer, it seems, to such a supposition will be provided once the requisite research has been conducted.

Again, space constraints unfortunately preclude even a cursory examination of the aforementioned theories, models, and programs. At the very least they demand to be highlighted. Thus, succinct descriptions of each area will be presented, as will a brief listing of key citations (e.g., description, key research, and critiques) for those who wish to examine the area in more detail.

Numerous theories, models, and programs of moral education have been developed, including but not limited to the following: *Kohlberg's,* in which moral reasoning and universal ethical principles are the main focus *(for a description,* see Kohlberg 1976; Kohlberg 1978; Kohlberg 1979; Kohlberg 1981; *for research,* see Blasi 1980; Colby, Kohlberg, Gibbs, and Lieberman 1983; Schaefli, Rest, and Thoma 1985; *for critiques and/or response to critiques,* see Enright, Lapsley, and Levy 1983; Gilligan 1982, 1987; Johnson 1983; Kohlberg 1985; Kohlberg, Levine, and Hewer 1985; Leming 1981; Lockwood 1978; Schaefli, Rest, and Thoma 1985; Weiler 1992); *Damon's,* in which issues of positive justice (e.g., issues of economic and social equity) reasoning is the focus *(for a description,* see Damon 1975; *for research,* see Damon 1980; Enright 1981; Enright, Enright, and Lapsley 1981; Enright, et al. 1984; Enright, et al. 1980; Krogh 1985); *Nucci's,* in which social conventional reasoning ("an effort to distinguish the concept of morality from that of social convention," Scott 1991, 361) is the main focus *(for a description,* see Nucci 1982; Nucci 1989; *for research,* see Nucci and Nucci 1982; Smetana 1983; *for critiques or an alternative view,* see Kohlberg, et al. 1985; Shweder, Mahapatra, and Miller 1987); *Gilligan's* model of care, responsiveness, and responsibility *(for a description,* see Gilligan 1977; Gilligan 1982; Gilligan 1987; Gilligan and Wiggins 1987; *for research,* see Gilligan 1977; Gilligan 1982; Johnston 1985; Lyons 1983; Lyons 1987; *for critiques,* see Kohlberg, et al. 1985; Brabeck 1987; Nunner-Winkler 1984; Sichel 1985; Walker, de Vries, and Trevethan 1987); and *Rest's,* in which he proposes "an integrated model that portrays morality as a series of distinct processes, each involving thoughts, feelings, and action" (Scott 1991, 363) *(for a description,* see Rest 1983; Rest 1984; *for critiques,* see Blasi 1980; Blasi 1983).[13] (For additional insights on the feminist perspective, see the special issue ["Feminist Perspectives on Moral Education and Development."] of *The Journal of Moral Education,* 16(3). For a discussion of how to incorporate moral education into the classroom through "moral discourse," see Oser 1986.)

As for prosocial education, it has been defined as "the provision of experiences designed to develop effective helping behaviors without regard for external rewards" (Oliner 1985/1986, 389). Prosocial education is basically comprised of four objectives: "developing prosocial intentions and values, developing basic prosocial skills, promoting intellectual processes involved in prosocial decision making, and participating in effective prosocial behaviors" (Oliner 1985/1986). *For descriptions*, see Mussen and Eisenberg-Berg 1977; Oliner 1983a; Oliner 1983b; Oliner 1985/1986; Scott 1991; and *for research* see, Battistich, et al. in press; Eisenberg 1982; Feshbach 1979; Feshbach 1982a; Feshbach 1982b; Radke-Yarrow, Zahn-Waxler, and Chapman 1983; Solomon, et al. 1985; Staub 1979.

The Study of Social Issues in the English Classroom

It should be readily apparent that in a republic such as ours, instruction about social issues and/or for social consciousness and social responsibility should *not* be the sole concern of one curricular area as it often is (e.g., the social studies class). Aside from the simple but profound fact that such issues truly cut across the curriculum, it is also true that such concerns are simply too important to leave to one curricular area. Certainly the curriculum that is primarily concerned with enabling students to become competent in the areas of reading, writing, speaking, and listening (i.e., English)—all of which are needed for an intelligent citizenry—is also a sound candidate for addressing such concerns. The ability to be a competent reader suggests that one is capable of doing more than simply decoding words or detecting the surface meaning of groups of words, sentences, or paragraphs. Similarly, to write or to speak in a competent manner means more than simply stringing words together in a coherent fashion, as important as that is. And to listen means more than simply to hear; rather it refers to engaged and critical listening. One also needs to be able to analyze ideas critically, to question assumptions, to detect biases, to put forth arguments that are well researched and well thought out, and much more.

The study of language is an outstanding place to begin an examination of social issues in our society. Students can learn a great deal by studying the use and misuse (some might say "abuse") of language (e.g., "doublespeak," "nukespeak," propaganda, political rhetoric), and the reasons for such use. As an example of such language, the

euphemistic and "acronymic" vocabulary of nuclear planners immediately comes to mind. As the eminent psychiatrist and author Robert
Jay Lifton has noted:

> . . . we domesticate these weapons in our language and attitudes.
> Rather than feel their malignant actuality, we render them benign.
> In calling them "nukes," for instance, we render them small and
> cute, something on the order of a household pet. . . . Quite simply,
> these words provide a way of talking about them. In them we
> find nothing about billions of human beings incinerated or melted,
> nothing about millions of corpses. Rather, the weapons come to
> seem ordinary and manageable or even mildly pleasant (a "nuclear
> exchange" sounds something like mutual gift-giving). (Lifton and
> Falk 1982, 106–107)

Commendably, the National Council of Teachers of English has repeatedly noted the danger of using language in such a manner, and
even awarded its tenth annual Doublespeak Award to President Reagan
for using "nukespeak" to describe the MX missile as the "peacekeeper."

The significance of such euphemistic language does not, of course,
end with blurred perceptions: "It also covertly tends to quell citizen
involvement and decision making about key issues by insinuating that
the 'real thinking' should be left to the experts" (Lifton 1981, 107).
The general public can counter that attitude by becoming informed
about the use of such language and its purposes. The English classroom
is an ideal place to prepare our young citizens to deal with such
language.

Stories (both nonfiction and fiction) are at the heart of the English
curriculum and they should also be at the core of any study of social
issues, social consciousness, and social responsibility. As for the power
of literature (and the possibilities of its use in the study of social issues,
especially the concept of social consciousness), Greene (1982) has
argued that "one of the functions of the arts and humanities—beyond
the enlargement of vision they make possible, beyond the pleasures
they provide—is to provoke self-reflectiveness, to help us recover our
lost spontaneity—to be present in the first person to the world. Another
is to nurture wide-awakeness, the capacity to attend, to search, to
transcend" (9).

Literature is, of course, replete with characters who are blind to the
world around them or to their own attitudes, feelings, beliefs, moti-
vations, or actions, and we (the readers) often gain invaluable insights
from studying and pondering the thoughts and actions of such characters. Those characters that immediately come to mind include numerous personages in Twain's *Adventures of Huckleberry Finn;* Mr.

Head in O'Connor's "The Artificial Nigger"; Homer A. Barbee, the blind preacher in Ellison's *Invisible Man;* and the prosecutor in Kafka's *The Trial.* Conversely, literature is also blessed with innumerable situations where the characters eventually come to an understanding of themselves as well as of certain situations or events, and dare to make difficult moral decisions in the face of great adversity based on those revelations. Those that immediately come to mind are Antigone, King Lear, Huck Finn, Silas Marner, Anna Karenina, Ivan Ilych, Nora in *The Doll's House,* Frederick Henry in *A Farewell to Arms,* Gene Forrester in *A Separate Peace,* Celie in *The Color Purple,* the narrator in *The Moviegoer,* and the unnamed protagonist in *Invisible Man* (who seems to be on the way to an awakening and transformation as the novel comes to a close).

On the importance of fictional stories as they relate to the lives of young people, Greene (1988) notes that

> there have been many reports on classroom discussion of issues ostensibly of moment to the students: cheating, betraying confidences, nonviolent resistance, sexual relations, discrimination. Not only has there been little evidence that the participants take such issues personally; there has been little sign of any transfer to situations in the "real world," even when there were opportunities (say, in a peace demonstration) to act on what were affirmed as guiding principles. . . . It seems clear, as Oliver and Bane have said, that young people "need the opportunity to project themselves in rich hypothetical worlds created by their own imagination or those of dramatic artists. More important, they need the opportunity to test out new forms of social order—and only then to reason about their moral implications." (Oliver and Bane 1971, 270) (Greene 1982, 119)

Totten (1986), Berman (1990b), and others have also suggested that a powerful method for teaching about social issues available to English (and other) teachers is that of focusing on the literature of social change, a phrase which can be read several ways (e.g., literature calling for social change, literature about social change taking place, and literature that can be examined in regard to changes that have taken place in society). A wealth of outstanding works (nonfiction and fiction) immediately come to mind when contemplating this approach, including the following: Baldwin's *The Fire Next Time,* Camus's *The Plague,* Fugard's *Statement After an Arrest Under the Immorality Act* and *The Island,* Gaines's *The Autobiography of Miss Jane Pittman,* Gordimer's *July's People,* Lee's *To Kill a Mockingbird,* Huxley's *Brave New World,* Kafka's *The Trial,* King's "Letter from Birmingham Jail," Koestler's *Darkness at Noon,* Olsen's "O Yes," Orwell's *Animal Farm* and *1984,*

Rand's *Anthem*, Sinclair's *The Jungle*, Solzhenitsyn's *One Day in the Life Of Ivan Denisovich, Cancer Ward*, and *First Circle*, Steinbeck's *The Grapes of Wrath*, Stowe's *Uncle Tom's Cabin*, Thoreau's "On Civil Disobedience," Twain's *The Adventures of Huckleberry Finn*, and Wright's *Native Son*. (English teachers will also find a discussion and description of a host of wonderfully engaging methods for conducting such a study in both this volume as well as in a special issue of the *Arizona English Bulletin* ["Teaching Social Issues in the English Classroom," Fall 1986, Volume 29, No. 10]. The latter volume is available from NCTE.)

It is in the realm of language and stories that English teachers can make a tremendously significant contribution to the type of education being discussed in this essay. For a wonderfully engaging examination of the power of both fictional and personal stories and their use in the classroom, teachers should read *The Call of Stories: Teaching and the Moral Imagination* by Robert Coles, the eminent psychiatrist and Harvard professor. Coles tells one story after another about English teachers at the university and secondary school level who engage their students in remarkable discoveries about themselves, their families, their friends, and their society through the study of a short story, a novel, or a play. At one point in his book, Coles (1989) says, "Again and again, instructed by novelists, students remind themselves of life's contingencies; and in doing so, they take matters of choice and commitment more seriously than they might otherwise have done" (90).

Of course, such insights and revelations are not always automatic; students need guidance and prodding and encouragement to reach such insights. Each chapter of *The Call of Stories* is packed with testimony (from Coles, his friends, his patients, and students, as well as from high school teachers and their students) regarding the magical allure of stories and their power to provoke us to examine our lives and question our basic assumptions and actions: "Their stories, yours, mine—it's what we all carry with us on this trip we take, and we owe it to each other to respect our stories and learn from them" (William Carlos Williams to Coles) (30); "I don't know how I ever could have got my students to take a look at themselves, an honest look, without that story" (an Atlanta English teacher speaking about Tillie Olsen's "O Yes") (55); "The way the teacher taught it [the story], you stopped and asked yourself a hell of a lot of questions. You begin to realize that we're all in trouble, one way or the other" (a white, sixteen-year-old male high school student in a suburban Boston school after reading Tillie Olsen's "Hey Sailor, What Ship?") (53); and "I can't believe

Hardy didn't want the Oxford and Cambridge teachers and students who read *Jude* to take the novel to heart—to be made nervous by reading certain parts of it . . . , to be made *ashamed,* not only of what used to happen, but what is still happening. One way to read a novel like that is to see it as a challenge to your conscience, not just your intellect. Aren't we here to grow a little in that direction—to become self-critical as well as critical?" (a junior at Harvard University) (81).

On a similar front, Lyn Mikel Brown and Mark B. Tappan are engaged in fascinating work in which they are working for the "recovery and re-application of the role that storytelling and narra- tive—particularly oral narrative—can play in moral education" (1989, 183). In their thought-provoking essay entitled "Stories Told and Lessons Learned: Toward a Narrative Approach to Moral Development and Moral Education," they argue that "individuals develop morally by 'authoring' their own moral stories and by learning the moral lessons in the stories they tell about their own experiences" (183–184). English teachers should find the ideas in this essay (where Brown and Tappan present their theoretical base as well as practical applications) particularly germane to the English classroom.

Time and again, researchers and classroom teachers have commented on the need to introduce the students to the stories of those individuals (both the famous and the non-famous) who have been socially conscious and acted in a socially responsible manner. From them, students will not only glean various ways individuals have acted but these stories are capable of providing opportunities for deep reflection. In this regard, Berman (1990) asserts that

> It is . . . important for teachers to tell young people about the success stories of others, students who have reclaimed forests, cleaned up rivers, improved their school environment, helped the homeless. They need to hear about the Mother Teresas and the Martin Luther Kings, of course, but also about the people who live down the street who are doing what they can to improve the neighborhood and about the many organizations that make a difference in our communities. We must put students in touch with these people and organizations so that they can see how deeply people care about their world and how worthwhile it is to participate in creating change. (78)

There is a need, of course, to not only note the resounding successes of such individuals but also their trials and tribulations, their fears and frustrations, their disappointments, the limitations of their efforts, their tenacious and resilient spirit in the face of adversity, and their dedication to work on the behalf of others for the betterment of society. This can be done in numerous ways, including the following:

reading biographies, autobiographies, news stories, oral histories, etc.; having guest speakers come to class to interact with the students; and having the students conduct oral histories/interviews.[14]

On a different, but still related, note, Keen and Keen (1990) make the observation that "the sharing of stories in the encounter with the other has tremendous power to lead us into the experience of compassion and trust. The imagination has the capacity then to apprehend a larger and more adequate whole that begins to enrich and transform our own stories. Our own stories thus become inclusive of the other— of diversity, of pluralism" (67). That type of component is exactly what is needed if the study of social issues is going to reach beyond factual knowledge and become personalized, and ultimately lead to a wider awareness, a deepening social consciousness and, possibly, a greater sense of social responsibility. It cannot be emphasized too strongly that the students' own stories, as well as the stories of their families, friends, and fellow community members, should be the core of such a study. (Also see Witherell and Noddings's *Stories Lives Tell: Narrative and Dialogue in Education.*)

Finally, one of the most powerful ways for English teachers to integrate the issues of social consciousness and social responsibility into the extant curriculum is to co-design interdisciplinary units with teachers in other curricular areas (e.g., social studies, government, general science, biology, physics, chemistry, health, art, etc.). For example, during a year-long program on the environment at Mosier Elementary School in South Hadley, Massachusetts, the teachers incorporated "novels with relevant themes" into their curriculum. Midyear, one teacher (a former Greenpeace worker) helped her students make "daily informational announcements over the public address system about energy use and waste, the effects of the Amazon forests on our climate"; and they had a spring festival which included "performances of students' original plays, a chorus program featuring songs about Mother Earth, and displays throughout the school" (Page 1990, 94).

By developing interdisciplinary units, teachers can address the issue from their particular strengths and expertise; but even more importantly, the study will provide students with insights into the interdependence of ideas and a much richer understanding of the complexity of the issue(s). It is worth noting that a number of recent reports "by the American Association for the Advancement of Science (1989), the National Council of Teachers of Mathematics (Commission 1989), and the National Council of Teachers of English (Lloyd-Jones and Lunsford 1989) each advocates greater correlation among school subjects than is the present case, and emphasizes the shared responsibility of all subjects for the superordinate aim of education for democratic citizenship" (Wraga and Hlebowitsh 1990, 195).[15]

What has not been addressed herein is the beauty, power, and significance of using writing as a means of assisting students to explore their own lives and the world around them. There are myriad ways, some of which are suggested by contributors to this volume. (See particularly Part III, "Teaching Writing for Social Responsibility.")

Some Key Concerns to Take into Consideration when Addressing Social Issues in the Classroom

Many educators have argued that the processes used in a carefully structured study of social issues (where systemic concerns are examined, and in which there is an emphasis on social consciousness and social responsibility) can help to prepare students to live and participate fully in a democratic society: "not merely to increase the rate or amount of social participation, but to develop student competence to influence public affairs in accordance with democratic and ethical principles" (Newmann 1989, 357); *and* nurture the belief that each and every individual's thoughts and actions do matter and that they can—either individually or in concert with others—make a difference (Facing History and Ourselves 1990, 3).

But, as is often the case, things are not as simple as they appear. Shermis and Barth (1985) have argued that

> present practices in teaching about social issues have created an illusion by seducing teachers and the public into believing that young people are truly grappling with these serious problems. Because students have little stake in a pseudo problem—a proposition handed to them without either their concern or complicity—there is precious little understanding of the reality of social problems. (193)

Aside from the fact that Shermis and Barth's criticism of "current practices" is somewhat dated (for, in fact, a good number of innovative programs/strategies have been developed over the past eight years or so—though they certainly are not used as widely as they could or should be), their concern about the study of "pseudo problems" is vitally significant. Not only should the study of problems be pertinent to the students' lives, but teachers also need to help "students to define [social] problems in terms they comprehend and to develop 'ownership' of the problems" (Shaver 1985, 196). If this is not done, then it is probable that the study will be for naught.

A different, but related, concern is the need for teachers to avoid conducting a study that results in a simplistic understanding of complex issues and processes (e.g., where the complexity of the problem is underplayed, key components are left out, and where simplistic solutions are suggested and accepted). To do so could, ultimately and ironically, lead to a sense of frustration and disenfranchisement when students expect to see changes and *don't*. As Perrone (1990) states, students should not see "ambiguity and uncertainty as something to remedy, but as the soil for deep learning. . . . The simple and the certain is not the road to social responsibility" (28). Students are capable of understanding and examining complex issues if they are provided with the tools to do so.

In regard to examining the amelioration of social problems, educators also need to conduct studies in which various and realistic (not to mention creative) solutions are examined and discussed, if not put into action (e.g., at least at the school site or community level). Again, as Perrone (1990) suggests, "There is a need for new understandings that the world, however defined, is not static, that change is possible, and that change demands a personal and collective investment. An education of consequence ought to encourage such understandings" (28).

Over the past sixty years or so, one issue that has surfaced time and again in the on-going debate surrounding the teaching of social issues is that of indoctrination. If asked, most educators would probably argue that indoctrination has no place in schools. At the same time, however, some educational critics have convincingly argued that "indoctrination" has a long tradition in our nation's schools. Kozol (1981), for example, asserts that the pledge to the flag is the "most obvious form of pure indoctrination in the public school" (75). In fact, if one examines the public schools in a bit more depth, one will discover that indoctrination is rife throughout both the hidden curriculum (e.g., inculcation of patriotism, loyalty, the work ethic, punctuality) and the explicit curriculum (e.g., inculcating that representative democracy is the best form of government) that is taught.

That said, many teachers who teach about social issues, social consciousness, and social responsibility find themselves wrestling with the issue of indoctrination as they prepare to teach about certain subjects or develop methods for doing so. Some suggest that teachers should avoid indoctrination at all costs and primarily concentrate on teaching students the process of problem solving, while others suggest that while it is certainly legitimate to reinforce the core values of a democratic society, a key concern should be to teach students "the skills required to make policy decisions" (Stanley 1985, 385). Still others assert that the nation is so inequitable in its distribution of wealth, opportunity, and justice that nothing short of an imposition of certain values is needed.

Most, it seems, would readily agree that when teaching about a particular issue (e.g., capital punishment, the nuclear arms race, the environment), there is no place for the imposition of a specific agenda or insistence on a right and wrong answer. Instead of leading to a situation where students are encouraged to use their abilities to thoroughly analyze an issue and come to a conclusion, the insistence on one right answer or position encourages mindlessness. The engendering of such mindlessness constitutes nothing less than mis-education.

A question that comes to mind, though, is: "Are those teachers who are teaching for social responsibility guilty of indoctrination? Are these educators guilty of what Boyd Bode (a close associate of John Dewey and a highly influential teacher educator in the 1930s and 1940s) criticized Jack Childs (another highly influential teacher educator during the same period) of: "favoring good indoctrination and being opposed to bad indoctrination" (Shermis and Barth 1985, 192). Some, of course, would say "yes," others "no." Purpel, for one, "calls upon schools explicitly to abandon the myth of neutrality and involve students in continuous moral discourse that rekindles personal commitment to compassion and the common good" (Newmann 1989, 358). To some that may appear to be sage advice; to others it may smack, once again, of indoctrination.

The issue of indoctrination, then, is not as simple a problem as it initially appears to be. One of the soundest suggestions that can be made is that every teacher who teaches about social issues and/or for social consciousness and social responsibility become conversant with the salient points of view (and they are many and varied) concerning the issue of indoctrination and imposition. At the very least, the individuals then should assess their goals, motives, objectives, materials and methods prior to developing any unit of study and entering the classroom. It is also imperative for teachers to constantly assess their interaction with the students, the students' interactions with one another, and the overall climate of the classroom in order to determine and assure that there is an open, positive, and supportive climate for the consideration of varied opinions and insights. It seems that if a teacher is going to be as pedagogically sound, fair, and effective as he or she can be, then such an assessment is imperative.[16]

Another major problem frequently observed in those classrooms where social issues are taught is that some teachers have a propensity for simply or primarily dwelling on the negative aspects and consequences of a problem to the exclusion of what can be done to ameliorate the problem. This may result in a situation where "students see only the overwhelming or depressing nature of our problems and the political conflict and stalemate that prevent us from solving these problems. Then they feel despair rather than empowerment" (Berman 1990, 79). What teachers need to do is not only help students focus on the systemic issues of the problem and how they are manifested in society and in peoples' individual lives, but also assist them to discover, examine, and possibly create ways the problems can be solved. Inherent in such a study should be an examination of how real people—people like their parents, fellow community members, social activists, politicians, and young people like themselves—have tackled and solved, or attempted to solve, real problems at either the local, regional, state, national, or international levels.

Another key problem is that there is *still* a lack of ample and conclusive research into what constitutes effective methods for teaching about social issues and for social consciousness and social responsibility. The absence of such research creates a situation where teachers end up working in the dark and hoping, rather than knowing, that something is effective. (A suggested research agenda is outlined in the next section of this essay.)

Finally, as is commonly known, very few teachers at the upper elementary through high school and college levels use educational research to assist them in developing their goals, objectives, lesson plans, materials, or their teaching strategies. This is also true, of course, of many of those who teach about social issues, and/or for social consciousness and social responsibility. It is also true of many curriculum and program developers who design curricula and programs in these areas of concern.[17] This situation must change if we are to become more effective in these particular pedagogical endeavors.

Research Questions In Need of Study

As previously mentioned, in order to strengthen teaching about social issues and for social consciousness and social responsibility, additional research needs to be done. What follows are a number of suggestions regarding a possible research agenda (ideas other than those of the author are noted):

1. Do students who study about social issues in school have a greater interest in such issues outside of school?

2. Is exposure to social issues associated with positive changes in attitudes (e.g., increased levels of political interest, political confidence, social integration, efficacy, and trust [Hahn 1991, 472])?

3. Is exposure to social issues in the classroom positively associated with toleration of dissent?

4. Do "different subgroups of students (e.g., age, gender, race, and class) think about controversial issues" in different ways (Hahn 1991, 478)?

5. What needs to be done to overcome the resistance to incorporating the study of social issues, social consciousness, and social responsibility into the public schools' curricula?

6. What are the most effective means for incorporating the study of social issues into the English curriculum?

7. What teaching strategies are the most effective for teaching students at different developmental levels about complex social issues?

8. Does the study of social issues (or for social consciousness or social responsibility) have an impact on students' long-term attitudes and beliefs vis-à-vis social consciousness, civic-mindedness, participation, social responsibility? If so, to what extent and why? If not, why not?

9. What "kinds of attitudes, knowledge, skills, and behaviors distinguish active from inactive citizens" (Ferguson 1991, 396)?

10. Do critical pedagogical practices "actually alter specific power relations outside or inside schools" (Ellsworth 1989, 301)? If so, how and to what extent? If not, why not?

11. How does moral decision-making take place (Scott 1991, 364)?

12. "Does exposure to controversial issues contribute to moral reasoning" (Hahn 1991, 478)?

13. Does the moral development of children impact on their sense of social consciousness and/or social responsibility? If so, how?

14. Does empathy development in children and young adolescents have a direct influence on the development of social consciousness and/or social responsibility?

15. What are the most efficacious ways to assist in the development of a child's empathic and prosocial behavior?

16. What are "the most effective methods for teaching civic participation" (Ferguson 1991, 391)?

17. What impact does participation in civic projects have on a student's long-term sense of social responsibility?

18. What are the most efficacious projects and studies that can be incorporated into the English classroom in order to "help nurture a person's potential to be an active citizen in the democratic process" (Facing History and Ourselves 1990, 2)?

19. How pervasive is teachers' fear of introducing controversial issues into their courses?

20. "How do mass media presentations interact with social studies of controversy to influence student learning" (Hahn 1991, 478)?

Hahn (1991) has also suggested that "longitudinal studies are needed in which classroom observations are combined with student interviews to determine whether controversial-issues discussions in an open environment foster positive civic attitudes in students" (476).

Recommendations

Certain actions can be taken immediately to begin to assist teachers in teaching about social issues and for social consciousness and social responsibility. Among my suggestions are the following:

1. The National Council of Teachers of English (NCTE), in conjunction with other educational organizations (e.g., the American Federation of Teachers (AFT), the Association of Supervision and Curriculum Development (ASCD), the National Association for Science/Technology/Society (NASTS), the National Association of Secondary School Principals (NASSP), the National Council for the Social Studies (NCSS), the National Council of Teachers of Mathematics (NCTM), the National Science Teachers Association (NSTA), National Education Association (NEA),) should sponsor research into what constitutes the most effective curricula and pedagogical methods for teaching about social issues to elementary- and secondary-level students.

2. NCTE should establish a committee to design sound and research-based curricula which incorporate social issues into the extant English curricula.

3. NCTE should establish a regular column and/or section in the *English Journal* (much the way the Association of Supervision and Curriculum Development does in its journal *Educational Leadership*) that addresses key social issues and methods for incorporating them into the English curriculum.

4. NCTE, along with AFT, ASCD, NASSP, NASTS, NCSS, NCTM, and NSTA, should urge the National Assessment of Educational Progress (NAEP) to conduct a major study which examines U.S. students' depth and breadth of knowledge of today's key social issues.

5. NCTE, NCSS, NASTS, NCTM, and NSTA could cosponsor the development of interdisciplinary units on key social issues and then encourage their various members to team up at their respective schools to teach the units.

6. NCTE, NCSS, NASTS, NCTM, and NSTA could cosponsor the development of and then offer inservice programs for those teachers who are interested in developing and teaching interdisciplinary units on key social issues.

7. Along with other national teacher and educator associations, NCTE could cosponsor the development of a series of national and/or international interactive video conferences that addresses the teaching of social issues in an interdisciplinary manner.

8. In concert with others, NCTE could lobby state departments of education to implement a required semester- or year-long course at the senior year for all high school students across the nation on the subject of social issues (National Issues Forum in the Classroom 1989; Parker 1990, 21).

9. In concert with other educational organizations, NCTE could sponsor the development of a research-based, year-long "national curriculum" in which four to six key social issues are addressed in depth.

10. In concert with other national teacher and educator associations, NCTE could cosponsor the development and implementation of a year-round on-line computer network system whose express purpose is to provide students and teachers with opportunities to network with others (e.g., other teachers and students; community, regional, national, and international activists; subject area experts; politicians, etc.) who are addressing social issues in their own unique ways.

11. NCTE could sponsor and publish an annotated bibliography that includes the most creative and effective teaching units, curricula, and resources on the teaching of social issues for use in the English classroom.

12. NCTE and other educational organizations could cosponsor the development of an annotated bibliography that includes the most

creative and effective interdisciplinary teaching units, curricula, and resources on the teaching of social issues *across* the curriculum.

Conclusion

Teachers, administrators, school board members, and parents need to realize that students are not going to become socially responsible citizens through osmosis. The schools of our nation have a vitally significant role to play in this most important of endeavors, and they need to quit simply giving "lip service" to that role and become actively and courageously involved in order to make it a reality. As Ernest Boyer (1990), the President of the Carnegie Foundation for the Advancement of Teaching, has said:

> Educators are often confused—even abused—if they try to examine touchy social problems and to help students debate what constitutes the common good. Yet to ignore controversial issues is to offer students an incomplete education, and incapacity to think carefully about life's most important concerns. I am convinced that even in matters where society is sharply divided, schools have an especially important role to play, one that goes beyond silence or the extension of the status quo.
>
> If we hope to make progress toward resolving deep conflicts in the culture, we must encourage open and sensitive classroom discussion about choices, even in such controversial areas as sex, drugs, cultural differences, and religious beliefs. . . . And in the guidance of such inquiry, teachers must be trusted.
>
> If we postpone such involvement for students while they're young, there is a good probability that it will be deferred for a lifetime. Clearly citizenship is not something to be deferred. It should be demonstrated in every institution in which the student is involved, especially at school. (6)

Notes

1. "Social issues" simply refers to those complex problems/issues faced by society. There may or may not be a consensus as to the cause and/or solution of the problems, and many, in fact, may be controversial.

2. Whereas "consciousness" generally refers to "the state of being conscious; awareness of one's own feelings, what is happening around one; the totality of one's thoughts, feelings, and impressions" (Guralnik 1970, 302), "social consciousness" refers to making an effort to constantly and thoroughly critically examine and evaluate one's beliefs, positions, and actions, taking an active interest in the world around one, being conversant with key issues, making an effort to become as informed as one possibly can vis-à-vis the

causes of the problem, viewing the problem and solutions from different perspectives, and living a life that is imbued with a sense of care and justice.

3. In this context "social responsibility" does *not* mean "adherence to social rules and role expectations" (Wentzel 1991); rather it means "acting on one's best knowledge and assessment of a situation/problem and working (either individually or in concert with others) to bring about a fairer and more just society for all, and doing so in a manner that is just."

4. "NIF forums are a modern incarnation of a respected institution, the town meeting. [The express purpose of the forums is to help] Americans get back into the practice of direct democracy. . . . Three national issues are chosen each year. . . . The 1989–90 issues were the Environment at Risk, The Drug Crisis, and The Day-Care Dilemma. . . . National Issues Forums in the Classroom not only educates participants about national issues, but asks them to make policy choices" (McFarland 1989, 365). In the Great Decisions program, "high school and college students and faculty study eight U.S. foreign policy topics in *Great Decisions* along with the accompanying videotapes and *Activity Book*" (McFarland 1989, 365). And in the Public Issues Series (which was originally developed by the Harvard Social Studies Project of the 1960s and 1970s), "the major purpose is . . . to help students analyze and discuss persisting human dilemmas related to public issues . . . throughout history and across cultures" (McFarland 1989, 365).

5. For some specific ideas along this line, see the Association for Supervision and Curriculum Development staff 1987, 1, 3; Dronka 1987, 1, 6; and Sanchez 1984/1985.

6. CIVITAS, c/o the Council for the Advancement of Citizenship, 1724 Massachusetts Ave., N.W., Washington, D.C. 20036; Educators for Social Responsibility, 23 Garden St., Cambridge, MA 02138; Facing History and Ourselves National Foundation, Inc., 25 Kennard Rd., Brookline, MA 02146; The Governor's School on Public Issues of New Jersey, c/o Professors Cheryl H. Keen and James P. Keen, Monmouth College, West Long Branch, NJ 07764; Institute for Democracy in Education, 119 McCracken Hall, Ohio University, Athens, OH 45701-2979; National Issues Forum in the Classroom, c/o Dayton, Ohio; and QUEST, c/o 537 Jones Rd., P.O. Box 566, Granville, OH 43023; STS Program and National STS Network, The Pennsylvania State University, 117 Willard Building, University Park, PA 16802.

7. For a more in-depth discussion of this program as well as others, see Hahn 1991; Parker 1991; and Giese, Parisi, and Bybee 1991.

8. There is a vast and growing literature about these issues. See, for example, Anyon 1980; Apple 1982; Apple 1983; Apple 1984; Carnoy and Shearer 1980; Ellsworth 1989; Fine 1987; Freire 1973; Giroux 1981; Giroux 1983; Giroux 1985; Giroux 1986; Giroux 1988; Giroux and McLaren; Shor 1980; Shor and Freire 1988; Simon 1987; Simon 1988; and Weiler 1988.

9. For a more in-depth view into the various theories/forms and critiques of feminist pedagogy, see: Belenky, et al. 1986; Bunch and Pollack 1983; Culley and Portuges 1985; Gilligan 1982; Maher 1985; Maher 1987; Maher and Schniedewind 1987; Noddings 1984; Noddings 1987; Shrewsbury 1987a; Shrewsbury 1987b; and Weiler 1988.

10. For a discussion of participatory projects, see *Educational Leadership*'s special issue on "Social Responsibility" (November 1990, Volume 48, No. 3);

Social Education's special issue on "Participatory Citizenship" (October 1989, Volume 53, No. 6); and, the *Phi Delta Kappan's* special issue "Youth Service" (June 1991, Volume 72, No. 10).

11. For a breakdown of specific findings and a discussion and listing of various empirical and qualitative studies, see Conrad and Hedin's "School-Based Community Service: What We Know from Research and Theory," *Phi Delta Kappan,* June 1991, 743–49.

12. See, for example: Clark 1989; Facing History and Ourselves 1990; Lodish 1990; Mathews 1985; Nebgen and McPherson 1990; Newmann 1989; Newmann and Rutter 1986; Purpel 1989; Rutter and Newmann 1989; and Wood 1990.

13. The author gratefully acknowledges the work of Kathryn P. Scott (1991) in his preparation of this section.

14. An excellent source for stories about actual people who have effected change is Facing History and Ourselves' *Choosing to Participate: A Critical Examination of Citizenship in American History.* Another resource is Educators for Social Responsibility's *Making History.*

15. For some interesting ideas on how to address social issues through an interdisciplinary study, see Gloria Siegel Moss's (1991) "An English and Social Studies Interdisciplinary Program" in *Social Education.* For a solid overview of design and implementation issues see Heidi Hayes Jacobs's (1989) *Interdisciplinary Curriculum: Design and Implementation.*

16. For interesting and informative discussions on the issue of indoctrination and the teaching of social issues, see Moore 1972; Shermis and Barth 1985; Snook 1972; Stanley 1981; Stanley 1985; and Wilson 1972.

17. It should also be noted that many organizations—such as Educators for Social Responsibility, Educating for Living in a Nuclear Age, and Facing History and Ourselves—have and continue to use such research in the development of their programs. Such organizations have also contributed to the research.

References

Anyon, J. Winter 1980. "Social Class and the Hidden Curriculum of Work." *Journal of Education,* 162:67–92.

Apple, M.W. 1982. *Education and Power.* Boston: Routledge & Kegan Paul.

Apple, M.W. Fall 1984. "The Political Economy of Textbook Publishing." *Educational Theory,* 34:307–19.

Apple, M.W. Spring 1983. "Work, Gender, and Teaching." *Teachers College Record,* 31:611–28.

Association for Supervision and Curriculum Development. June 1987. *ASCD Update,* 29(4).

Barber, B.R. 1989. "Public Talk and Civic Action: Education for Participation in a Strong Democracy." *Social Education,* 53(6):355–61, 370.

Barth, J.L., and S.S. Shermis. Fall 1980. "Nineteenth-Century Origins of the Social Studies Movement: Understanding the Continuity Between Older and Contemporary Civic and U.S. History Textbooks." *Theory and Research in Social Education,* 8(3):29–49.

Battistich, V., M. Watson, D. Solomon, E. Schaps, and J. Solomon. In press. "The Child Development Project: A Comprehensive Program for the Development of Prosocial Character." In W.M. Kurtines and J.L. Gerwirtz (Eds.). *Moral Behavior and Development: Advances in Theory, Research, and Application* (Vol. 1). Hillsdale, New Jersey: Erlbaum.

Belenky, M.F., B.M. Clinchy, N. Goldberger, and J.M. Tarule. 1986. *Women's Ways of Knowing: The Development of Self, Body and Mind.* New York: Basic Books.

Berman, S. Summer 1987. "Beyond Critical Thinking: Teaching for Synthesis—Methodological Belief and Dialogue in the Classroom." *Educators for Social Responsibility Forum,* 6(1): 1, 10.

Berman, S. 1990a. "Educating for Social Responsibility." *Educational Leadership,* 48(3): 75–80.

Berman, S. 1990b. "The Real Ropes Course: The Development of Social Consciousness." *ESR Journal,* 1: 1–18.

Blasi, A. 1980. "Bridging Moral Cognition and Moral Action: A Critical Review of the Literature." *Psychological Bulletin,* 88(1): 1–45.

Blasi, A. 1983. "Moral Cognition and Moral Action: A Theoretical Perspective." *Developmental Review,* 3(2): 178–210.

Boyer, E.L. November 1990. "Civic Education for Responsible Citizens." *Educational Leadership,* 48(3): 4–7.

Brabeck, M. (Ed.) 1987. "Feminist Perspectives on Moral Education and Development." Special issue of *Journal of Moral Education,* 16(3).

Bivner, J. 1960. *The Process of Education.* New York: Vintage Books.

Bunch, C., and S. Pollack. 1983. *Learning Our Way: Essays in Feminist Education.* Trumansburg, NY: Crossing Press.

Carnoy, M., and D. Shearer. 1980. *Economic Democracy.* New York: M.E. Sharpe.

Clark, T. October 1989. "Youth Community Service." *Social Education,* 53(6): 367.

The Coalition of Essential Schools. June 1989. "Asking the Essential Questions: Curriculum Development." *Horace,* 5(5): 1–6.

Colby, A., L. Kohlberg, L. Gibbs, and M. Lieberman. 1983. *A Longitudinal Study of Moral Judgment.* Chicago: University of Chicago Press.

Coles, R. 1989. *The Call of Stories: Teaching and the Moral Imagination.* Boston: Houghton Mifflin.

Conrad, D., and D. Hedin. June 1991. "School-Based Community Service: What We Know from Research and Theory." *Phi Delta Kappan,* 72(10): 743–49.

Culley, M., and C. Portuges. (Eds.) 1985. *Gendered Subjects: The Dynamics of Feminist Teaching.* Boston: Routledge & Kegan Paul.

Damon, W. 1975. "Early Conceptions of Positive Justice as Related to the Development of Logical Operations." *Child Development,* 46(2): 301–12.

Dronka, P. March 1987. "Forums for Curriculum Critics Settle Some Disputes:

Clash Persists on Students' Thinking about Controversy." *ASCD Update,* 1, 6.

Educators for Social Responsibility. 1990. *Making History.* Cambridge, MA: Author.

Eisenberg, N. 1986. *Altruistic Emotion, Cognition, and Behavior.* Hillsdale, NJ: Erlbaum.

Eisenberg, N. (Ed.) 1982. *The Development of Prosocial Behavior.* New York: Academic Press.

Eisner, E. 1979. *The Educational Imagination: On the Design and Evaluation of School Programs.* New York: Macmillan Publishing Co.

Ellsworth, E. August 1989. "Why Doesn't This Feel Empowering? Working through the Repressive Myths of Critical Pedagogy." *Harvard Educational Review,* 59(3): 297–324.

Enright, R. 1981. "A Classroom Discipline Model for Promoting Social Cognitive Development in Early Childhood." *Journal of Moral Education,* 11(1): 47–60.

Enright, R., A. Bjerstedt, W. Enright, V. Levy, D. Lapsley, R. Buss, M. Harwell, and M. Zindler. 1984. "Distributive Justice Development: Cross-Cultural, Contextual, and Longitudinal Evaluations." *Child Development,* 55(5): 1737–45.

Enright, R., W. Enright, and D. Lapsley. 1981. "Distributive Justice Development and Social Class: A Replication." *Developmental Psychology,* 17(6): 826–32.

Enright, R., D. Lapsley, and V. Levy. 1983. "Moral Education Strategies." In M. Pressley and J. Levin (Eds.). *Cognitive Strategy Research: Educational Applications.* 443–83. New York: Springer-Verlag.

Enright, R., W. Enright, L. Mankeim, and B. E. Harris. 1980. "Distributive Justice Development and Social Class." *Developmental Psychology,* 17: 826–32.

Facing History and Ourselves. 1990. *Choosing to Participate: A Critical Examination of Citizenship in American History.* Brookline, MA: Facing History and Ourselves.

Ferguson, P. 1990. "Impacts on Social and Political Participation." In J.P. Shaver (Ed.) *Handbook of Research on Social Studies Teaching and Learning.* New York: Macmillan.

Fesbach, N.D. 1979. "Empathy Training: A Field Study in Affective Education." In S. Feshbach and A. Fraczek (Eds.) *Aggression and Behavior Change.* 234–49. New York: Praeger.

Fesbach, N.D. 1982a. "Empathy Training and the Regulation of Aggression: Potentialities and Limitations." *Academic Psychology Bulletin,* 4(3): 399–413.

Fesbach, N.D. 1982b. "Sex Differences in Empathy and Social Behavior in Children." In N. Eisenberg (Ed.). *The Development of Prosocial Behavior.* 315–38. New York: Academic Press.

Fine, M. 1987. "Silencing in the Public Schools." *Language Arts,* 64(2): 157–74.

Flood, J., J.M. Jensen, D. Lapp, and J.R. Squire. (Eds.) 1991. *Handbook of*

Research on Teaching the English Language Arts. New York: Macmillan Publishing Company.

Freire, P. 1973. *Education for Critical Consciousness*. New York: Seabury Press.

Freire, P. 1970. *Pedagogy of the Oppressed*. New York: Herder and Herder.

Friedlander, H. 1979. "Toward a Methodology of Teaching About the Holocaust." *Teachers College Record*, 89(3): 519–42.

Giese, J.R., L. Parisi, and R.W. Bybee. 1991. "The Science-Technology-Society (STS) Theme and Social Studies." In James P. Shaver (Ed.). *Handbook of Research on Social Studies Teaching and Learning*. 559–66. New York: Macmillan Publishing Company.

Gilbert, R.J. May 1985. "Social Knowledge, Action and the Curriculum." *Social Education*, 49(5): 380–83.

Gilligan, C. 1982. *In a Different Voice: Psychological Theory and Women's Development*. Cambridge, MA: Harvard University.

Gilligan, C. 1977. "In a Different Voice: Women's Conception of the Self and of Morality." *Harvard Educational Review*, 47(4): 481–517.

Gilligan, C. 1987. "Moral Orientation and Moral Development." In E.F. Kittay and D.T. Meyers (Eds.). *Women and Moral Theory*, 19–36. Towata, NJ: Rowman and Littlefield.

Gilligan, C., and G. Wiggins. 1987. "The Origins of Morality in Early Childhood Relationships." In J. Kagan and S. Lamb (Eds.). *The Emergence of Morality in Young Children*. Chicago: University of Chicago Press.

Giroux, H. 1981. *Ideology, Culture, and the Process of Schooling*. Philadelphia, PA: Temple University Press.

Giroux, H. 1986. "Radical Pedagogy and the Politics of Student Voice." *Interchange*, 17: 48–69.

Giroux, H. 1988. *Schooling and the Struggle for Public Life: Critical Pedagogy in the Modern Age*. Minneapolis: University of Minnesota Press.

Giroux, H. May 1985. "Teachers as Transformative Intellectuals." *Social Education*, 49(5): 376–79.

Giroux, H. 1983. *Theory and Resistance in Education*. South Hadley, MA: Bergin and Garvey.

Giroux, H., and P. McLaren. 1986. "Teacher Education and the Politics of Engagement: The Case for Democratic Schooling." *Harvard Educational Review*, 56(3): 213–38.

Green, T. 1966. *Education and Pluralism*. Syracuse, NY: Syracuse University Press.

Greene, M. 1988. *The Dialectic of Freedom*. New York: Teachers College Press.

Greene, M. 1990. "Interpretation and Re-Vision: Toward Another Story." In J. Sears and J. Marshall (Eds.). *Teaching and Thinking about Curriculum: Critical Inquiries*. New York: Teachers College Press.

Greene, M. 1978. *Landscapes of Learning*. New York: Teachers College Press.

Greene, M. 1982. "Wide-Awakeness in Dark Times." Speech delivered at Teachers College, Columbia University, 1982.

Guralnik, D.B. 1970. *Webster's New World Dictionary of the American Language*. Englewood Cliffs, NJ: Prentice Hall, Inc.

Hahn, C.L. 1991. "Controversial Issues in Social Studies." In J.P. Shaver (Ed.). *Handbook of Research on Social Studies Teaching and Learning.* 470–80. New York: Macmillan Publishing Company.

Hahn, C.L. September 1985. "Human Rights: An Essential Part of the Social Studies Curriculum." *Social Education,* 49(6): 480–84.

Hedin, D., and D. Conrad. 1981. "Executive Summary of the Final Report of the Experiential Education Evaluation Project." Center for Youth Development and Research, University of Minnesota.

Hirsh, S.A., and F.R. Kemerer. February 1982. "Academic Freedom in the Classroom." *Educational Leadership,* 39(5): 375–77.

Hoffman, M.L. 1982. "Development of Prosocial Motivation: Empathy and Guilt." In N. Eisenberg (Ed.). *The Development of Prosocial Behavior.* 281–311. New York: Academic Press.

Hullfish, G. (Ed.) 1953. *Educational Freedom in an Age of Anxiety.* New York: Harper & Row Publishers.

Isham, M.M., and G.L. Mehaffy. October 1985. "Issues in Social Studies Education: Experimentation in the Social Studies." *Social Education,* 49(7): 571–74.

Jacobs, H.H. (Ed.) 1989. *Interdisciplinary Curriculum: Design and Implementation.* Alexandria, VA: Association for Supervision and Curriculum Development.

Johnson, H.C. 1983. "Moral Education." In H.E. Mitzel (Ed.). *Encyclopedia of Educational Research,* 1235–56. Vol. 3 (5th ed.). New York: Free Press.

Johnston, K. 1985. "Two Moral Orientations—Two Problem-Solving Strategies: Adolescents' Solutions to Dilemmas in Fables." Unpublished doctoral dissertation, Harvard University.

Joyce, B., and M. Weil. 1980. *Models of Teaching.* Englewood Cliffs, NJ: Prentice Hall, Inc.

Keen, C.H., and J.P. Keen. November 1990. "The Governor's School on Public Issues and the Future." *Educational Leadership,* 48(3): 66–68.

Kohlberg, L. 1981. "The Just Community Approach to Moral Education in Theory and Practice." In M. Berkowitz and F. Oser (Eds.). *Moral Education: Theory and Application.* 27–87. Hillsdale, NJ: Erlbaum.

Kohlberg, L. 1979. *The Meaning and Measurement of Moral Development.* Worcester, MA: Clark University.

Kohlberg, L. 1974. "Moral Stages and Moralization: The Cognitive-Developmental Approach." In T. Lickona (Ed.). *Moral Development and Behavior: Theory, Research, and Social Issues.* 29–53. San Francisco: Jossey-Bass.

Kohlberg, L. 1978. "Revisions in the Theory and Practice of Moral Development." In W. Damon (Ed.). *New Directions for Child Development,* 83–88. San Francisco: Jossey-Bass.

Kohlberg, L., C. Levine, and A. Hewer. 1985. *Moral Stages: A Current Formulation and a Response to Critics.* New York: Karger.

Kozol, J. 1981. *On Being a Teacher.* New York: The Continuum Publishing Corporation.

Krogh, S.L. 1985. "Encouraging Positive Justice Reasoning and Perspective Taking Skills." *Journal of Moral Development,* 14: 102–10.

Kundera, M. 1981. *The Book of Laughter and Forgetting.* New York: Penguin Books.

Leming, J.S. 1981. "Curricular Effectiveness in Moral/Values Education. A Review of Research." *Journal of Moral Education,* 10(3): 147–64.

Levin, M., F.M. Newmann, and D.W. Oliver. 1969. "A Law and Social Science Curriculum Based on the Analysis of Public Issues" (Final Report Project No. HS-058, Grant No. OE310142). Washington, DC: U.S. Department of Health, Education, and Welfare, Office of Education.

Lifton, R.J. Fall 1982. "Beyond Nuclear Numbing." *Teachers College Record,* 84(1): 15–29.

Lifton, R.J., and R. Falk. 1982. *Indefensible Weapons: The Political and Psychological Case Against Nuclearism.* New York: Basic Books.

Liston, D.P., and K.M. Zeichner. 1987. "Critical Pedagogy and Teacher Education." *Journal of Education,* 169: 117–37.

Lodish, R. 1990. "A Lesson for a Lifetime." *Educational Leadership,* 48(3): 92–93.

Lockwood, A.L. 1978. "The Effects of Values Clarification and Moral Development Curricula on School-Age Subjects: A Critical Review of Recent Research." *Review of Educational Research,* 48(3): 325–64.

Lyons, N.P. 1983. "Two Perspectives: On Self, Relationships, and Morality." *Harvard Educational Review,* 53(2): 125–45.

Lyons, N.P. 1987. "Ways of Knowing, Learning, and Making Moral Choices." *Journal of Moral Education,* 16(3): 226–39.

Maher, F. 1985. "Classroom Pedagogy and the New Scholarship on Women." In M. Culley and C. Portuges (Eds.). *Gendered Subjects: The Dynamics of Feminist Teaching,* 29–48. London: Routledge & Kegan Paul.

Maher, F. 1987. "Toward a Richer Theory of Feminist Pedagogy: A Comparison of 'Liberation' and 'Gender' Models for Teaching and Learning." *Journal of Education,* 169(3): 91–99.

Maher, F. and Schneidewind. 1987. Special Issue ("Feminist Pedagogy") of *Women's Studies Quarterly,* 15(3 and 4).

Mathews, D. November/December 1985. "Civic Intelligence." *Social Education,* 49(8): 678–81.

McFarland, M. October 1989. "The NCSS Public Issues Program." *Social Education,* 53(6): 365–66.

Moore, W. 1972. "Indoctrination and Democratic Method." In I.A. Snook (Ed.). *Concepts of Indoctrination: Philosophical Essays.* Boston: Routledge & Kegan Paul.

Moss, G.S. January 1991. "An English and Social Studies Interdisciplinary Program." *Social Education,* 55(1): 45–51.

Murry, R.N. October 1988. "Paul Hanna: 1902–1988." *Social Education,* 52(7): 413.

Mussen, P., and N. Eisenberg-Berg. 1977. *Roots of Caring, Sharing, and Helping: The Development of Prosocial Behavior in Children.* San Francisco: W. H. Freeman.

National Issues Forum in the Classroom. 1989. *Participation in Government.* Dayton, OH: Author.

Nebgen, M.K., and K. McPherson. November 1990. "Enriching Learning Through Service: A Tale of Three Districts." *Educational Leadership*, 48(3): 90–92.

Newmann, F.M. 1975. *Education for Citizen Action: Challenge for Secondary Curriculum*. Berkeley: McCutchan.

Newmann, F.M. 1981. "Political Participation: An Analytic Review and Proposal." In D. Heater and J.A. Gillespie (Eds.). *Political Education in Flux*. Beverly Hills, CA: Sage Publications.

Newmann, F.M., and R.A. Rutter. 1977. *The Effects of High School Community Service Programs on Students' Social Development*. Madison, WI: Wisconsin Center for Education Research, University of Wisconsin.

Newmann, F.M., and R.A. Rutter. 1986. "A Profile of High School Community Service Programs." *Educational Leadership*, 43(4): 64–71.

Newmann, F.M. October 1989. "Reflective Civic Participation." *Social Education*, 53(6): 357–60, 366.

Newmann, F.M., T.A. Bertocci, and R.M. Landsness. 1977. *Skills in Citizen Action: An English-Social Studies Program for Secondary Schools*. Niles, IL: National Textbook Co.

Noddings, N. 1984. *Caring*. Berkeley: University of California Press.

Noddings, N. 1987. "Do We Really Want to Produce Good People?" *Journal of Moral Education*, 16(3): 177–88.

Nucci, L. 1982. "Conceptual Development in the Moral and Conventional Domains: Implications for Values Education." *Review of Educational Research*, 52(1): 93–122.

Nucci, L. 1989. "Knowledge of the Learner: The Development of Children's Concepts of Self, Morality, and Societal Convention." In M. Reynolds (Ed.). *Knowledge Base for the Beginning Teacher*, 117–27. Oxford: Pergamon Press.

Nucci, L. (Ed.) 1989. *Moral Development and Character Education: A Dialogue*. Berkeley: McCutchan.

Nucci, L., and M. Nucci. 1982. "Children's Responses to Moral and Social Conventional Transgressions in Free-Play Settings." *Child Development*, 53(5): 1337–42.

Nunner-Winkler, G. 1984. "Two Moralities? A Critical Discussion of an Ethic of Care and Responsibility Versus an Ethic of Rights and Justice." In W. Kurtines and J. Gewirtz (Eds.). *Morality, Moral Behavior, and Moral Development*, 348–61. New York: Wiley.

Oliner, P.M. 1985/1986. "Legitimating and Implementing Prosocial Education." *Humboldt Journal of Social Relations*, 13(1 and 2): 389–408.

Oliner, P.M. April 1983a. "Putting Compassion and Caring into Social Studies Classrooms." *Social Education*, 47(4): 273–76.

Oliner, P.M. Summer 1983b. "Putting 'Community' into Citizenship Education: The Need for Prosociality." *Theory and Research in Social Education*, 11(2): 65–81.

Oliver, D.W., and M.J. Bane. 1971. "Moral Education: Is Reasoning Enough?" In C.M. Beck, B.S. Crittenden, and E.V. Sullivan (Eds.). *Moral Education: Interdisciplinary Approaches*. New York: Newman Press.

Oliver, D.W., and J.P. Shaver. 1974. *Teaching Public Issues in the High School.* Logan, UT: Utah State University Press. (Original work published 1966.)

Oser, F.K. 1986. "Moral Education and Values Education: The Discourse Perspective." In M. Wittrock (Ed.). *Handbook of Research on Teaching* (3rd Ed.), 917–41. New York: Macmillan.

Page, A. November 1990. "Raising Students' Social Consciousness in South Hadley, Massachusetts." *Educational Leadership,* 48(3): 93–94.

Parker, W. November 1990. "Assessing Citizenship." *Educational Leadership,* 48(3): 17–22.

Parker, W.C. 1991. "Achieving Thinking and Decision-Making Objectives in Social Studies." In J.P. Shaver (Ed.). *Handbook of Research on Social Studies Teaching and Learning,* 3345–56. New York: Macmillan.

Parks, S. 1987. *The Critical Years.* San Francisco: Harper & Row.

Perrone, V. 1990. "What Should Schools Teach and Students Learn?" *ESR Journal,* 1: 21–29.

Purpel, D.E. 1989. *The Moral and Spiritual Crisis in Education: A Curriculum for Justice and Compassion in Education.* Granby, MA: Bergin and Garvey.

Radke-Yarrow, M., C. Zahn-Waxler, and M. Chapman. 1983. "Children's Prosocial Dispositions and Behavior." In P. Mussen (Ed.) *Handbook of Child Psychology* (Vol. 3), 469–545. New York: Wiley.

Rest, J. 1984. "The Major Components of Morality." In W.M. Kurtines and J.L. Gewirtz (Eds.). *Morality, Moral Behavior, and Moral Development,* 24–40. New York: Wiley.

Rest, J. 1983. "Morality." In P. Mussen (Ed.). *Handbook of Child Psychology* (Vol. 3), 470–545. New York: Wiley.

Rutter, R.A., and F.M. Newmann. October 1989. "The Potential of Community Service to Enhance Civic Responsibility." *Social Education,* 53(6): 371–74.

Sagar, R. November 1990. "Educating for Living in a Nuclear Age." *Educational Leadership,* 48(3): 81–83.

Sanchez, L.E. December 1984/January 1985. "Controversial Issues: Practical Considerations." *Educational Leadership,* 42(4): 64.

Schaefli, A., J. Rest, and S. Thoma. 1985. "Does Moral Education Improve Moral Judgment? A Meta-Analysis of Intervention Studies Using the Defining Issues Test." *Review of Educational Research,* 55(3): 319–52.

Scott, K.P. 1991. "Achieving Social Studies Affective Aims: Values, Empathy, and Moral Development." In J.P. Shaver (Ed.). *Handbook of Research on Social Studies Teaching and Learning,* 357–69. New York: Macmillan.

Shaver, J.P. March 1985. "Commitment to Values and the Study of Social Problems in Citizenship Education." *Social Education,* 49(3): 194–97.

Shawcross, W. 1984. *The Quality of Mercy: Cambodia, Holocaust and Modern Conscience.* New York: Simon and Schuster.

Shermis, S.S., and J.L. Barth. Spring 1979. "Defining Social Problems." *Theory and Research in Social Education,* 7(1): 1–19.

Shermis, S.S., and J.L. Barth. March 1985. "Indoctrination and the Study of Social Problems: An Examination of the 1930s Debate." *The Social Frontier, Social Education,* 49(3): 190–93.

Shor, I. 1980. *Critical Teaching and Everyday Life.* Boston: South End Press.

Shor, I., and P. Freire. 1987. "What Is the 'Dialogical Method' of Teaching?" *Journal of Education*, 169(3): 11–31.

Shrewsbury, C.M. 1987a. "Feminist Pedagogy: A Bibliography." *Women's Studies Quarterly*, 15(3 and 4): 116–24.

Shrewsbury, C.M. Fall/Winter 1987b. "What Is Feminist Pedagogy?" *Women's Studies Quarterly*, 15(3 and 4): 6–14.

Shweder, R., M. Mahapatra, and J. Miller. 1987. "Culture and Moral Development." In J. Kagan and S. Lamb (Eds.). *The Emergence of Morality in Young Children*, 1–82. Chicago: University of Chicago Press.

Sichel, B. 1985. "Women's Moral Development in Search of Philosophical Assumptions." *Journal of Moral Education*, 14(3): 149–61.

Simon, R. April 1987. "Empowerment as a Pedagogy of Possibility." *Language Arts*, 64(4): 370–81.

Simon, R. February 1988. "For a Pedagogy of Possibility." *Critical Pedagogy Networker*, 1(1): 1–4.

Smetana, J. 1983. "Social Cognition Development: Domain Distinctions and Coordinations." *Developmental Review*, 3(2): 131–47.

Snook, I.A. (Ed.) 1972. *Concepts of Indoctrination: Philosophical Essays*. Boston: Routledge & Kegan Paul.

Solomon, D., M. Watson, V. Battistich, E. Schaps, P. Turck, J. Solomon, C. Cooper, and W. Ritchey. 1985. "A Program to Promote Interpersonal Consideration and Cooperation in Children." In R. Slavin, S. Sharan, S. Kagan, R. Lazarowitz, C. Webb, and R. Schmuck (Eds.). *Learning to Cooperate, Cooperating to Learn*, 371–403. New York: Plenum.

Spencer, H. 1860. "What Knowledge is of Most Worth?" In Spencer (1860) *Education: Intellectual, Moral and Physical*, 5–93. New York: A.L. Burt Company, Publishers.

Spring, J. Winter 1989. "Response to Review of *Conflict of Interests*." *Teachers College Record*, 91(2): 268–70.

Stanley, W.B. May 1985. "Social Reconstruction for Today's Social Education." *Social Education*, 49(5): 384–89.

Stanley, W.B. May 1982. "What Social Education Content Is Most Important?" *Educational Leadership*, 39(8): 588–92.

Staub, E. 1979. *Positive Social Behavior and Morality: Socialization and Development*, Vol. 2. New York: Academic Press.

Tappan, M.B., and L.M. Brown. 1989. "Stories Told and Lessons Learned: Toward a Narrative Approach to Moral Development and Moral Education." *Harvard Educational Review*, 159(2): 182–205.

Totten, S. Fall 1986. "Teaching Social Issues in the English Classroom." Special Issue of the *Arizona English Bulletin*, 29(1).

Turiel, E. 1983. *The Development of Social Knowledge: Morality and Convention*. Cambridge: Cambridge University Press.

Walker, L.J., B. de Vries, and S.D. Trevethan. 1987. "Moral Stages and Moral Orientations in Real-Life and Hypothetical Dilemmas." *Child Development*, 58(3): 842–58.

Weiler, K. 1988. *Women Teaching for Change: Gender, Class & Power*. New York: Bergin and Garvey Publishers.

Weiler, K. 1992. "Teaching, Feminism, and Social Change." In Hurlbert C. M. and S. Totten (Eds.). *Social Issues in the English Classroom.* Urbana, IL: NCTE.

Wentzel, K.R. Spring 1991. "Social Competence at School: Relation Between Social Responsibility and Academic Achievement." *Review of Educational Research,* 61(1): 1–224.

Whitehead, A.N. 1971. "The Aims of Education." In John Paul Strain (Ed.). *Modern Philosophies of Education,* 178–89. New York: Random House.

Wilson, J. 1972. "Indoctrination and Rationality." In I.A. Snook (Ed.). *Concepts of Indoctrination: Philosophical Essays.* Boston: Routledge & Kegan Paul.

Witherell, C., and N. Noddings. 1991. *Stories Lives Tell: Narrative and Dialogue in Education.* New York: Teachers College Press.

Wood, G.H. 1990. "Teachers as Curriculum Workers." In J.T. Sears and J.D. Marshall (Eds.). *Teaching and Thinking About Curriculum: Critical Inquiries,* 97–109. New York: Teachers College Press.

Wraga, W.G., and P.S. Hlebowitsh. April/May 1990. "Science, Technology, and the Social Studies." *Social Education,* 54(4): 194–95.

II Dialogue and Social Responsibility

2 Dismantling White/Male Supremacy

doris davenport

"Why do you keep saying we're white?" a female Women's Studies student asked me a few days ago. "Because you are," I told her. "You ain't 'universal'; you also have 'adjectival definers.' " In a peer-editing session in my composition class, one of the young black males explained to another male, "*Women* don't understand that kind of language." One of the "women" he referred to was me, his teacher. I don't know what I said, since I was shouting at him and two other males were also screaming at me. Nothing like that had ever occurred before; I was really uncomfortable and disgusted with the students, but equally disturbed by my own "unprofessional" behavior, so I sought out the white male chairperson. He merely said, "At least you got them thinking." But earlier, at a departmental meeting, I gave him a written announcement to make: using the term "you guys" is sexist. He announced it, but with a very peculiar, confused look on his face.

No matter who or what we are, or what our focus is, we are surrounded by the inseparable grid (mental iron bars) of racism, sexism, classism, and heterosexism. That network constitutes the "social issue" to me, and these *are* the "master's tools," as Audre Lorde noted.[1] And I, a black-feminist-lesbian-working class-Southern poet, sometimes feel like I am engaged in a 24–7 job of "educating."

As I wrote in another essay, who and what we teachers are, *all* that we are, become major and crucial factors in our teaching. Therefore, we should ask ourselves how we address (or ignore) the issues of class, race, gender, sexual preference, and ethnicity in our teaching and scholarship. What do we bring to the classroom in terms of these issues? The questions (both in this essay as well as the earlier one) center around three major, *intimately* interlocking areas which influence each other in a circular and reciprocal manner in the classroom:

> (1) Our [the teachers'] assumptions and/or pedagogy are po-
> tentially volatile when there are ideological or identity "differ-

ences" between the students and us. Obviously, our assumptions determine text selection.

(2) The materials and texts used can also be explosive if they show any major deviation from what is considered the "status quo." The most upsetting and disturbing materials tend to be by black wimmin and/or lesbian-feminists of any race/class.

(3) The affect on the students, or the classroom dialectics, based in the students' assumptions and value systems, is *the* most crucial aspect. (These dialectics, in turn, influence the choice of texts.) (davenport 1991, 2–4)

It seems inevitable that every "socially conscious" educator must deal with these issues constantly. To do that, we need to examine and articulate our own assumptions. How do we contribute to or dismantle that interlocking network? These and related issues are ongoing concerns for me. Although there is some "theory" involved, I deal mainly with concrete experiences such as those mentioned in the first paragraph. One of my specialty areas is contemporary multi-ethnic wimmin's[2] literature (especially black wimmin's literature). But whatever the course, I inevitably teach from a holistic feminist (not "gender only") perspective. Additionally, I emphasize positive cultural identities (as opposed to reactionary, "oppressed," victimized ones) and transcendent/visionary materials and experiences. My approach and its underlying assumptions frequently lead to confrontations with students, and sometimes, with colleagues. *That is rarely my intention, but it inevitably happens.*

What I *do* do deliberately is make the students question themselves: In what way do they contribute to the system of white-male-heterosexual supremacy? On how many levels are they being co-opted? What happened to their freedom of choice (compulsory heterosexuality)? And, other than an apparent socially sanctioned "right" to oppress or profit from the oppression and exploitation of colored folk and/or wimmin, just what does it mean to be white or to be male? Even when I don't ask these questions, the literature I teach does. Many of the texts force students to question basic assumptions about their identities, or what they consider "reality." For example, even when I use a text mainly because of its style (Morrison's *Song of Solomon,* for instance), it can be problematic for certain students because the idea of an autonomous African American culture is totally alien and therefore "threatening" to them.

So, a directly related concern I have is with how we use (or misuse) certain texts, particularly those by visibly ethnic ("minority") authors. Why do we select the works we do? What do we hope to "teach" with a specific work? What have we learned ourselves, about ourselves?

And, how honest are we willing to be about some of our fundamental assumptions? Most importantly, I am concerned with *intended* positive outcomes, for all concerned in the process.

"Process" is the key word here; "hope" is another. For all my students and for me, I hope for some specific outcomes from our classes. First, and in general, I hope for some basic rethinking and reassessment of what they consider "givens" in their lives. Subsequently, I hope for specific, albeit minor, changes in their cognitive patterns (to recognize manifestations of the interlocking grid of sexism-racism-classism-heterosexism, for example) and behavioral patterns (speech and actions). For me, and other socially conscious educators, I am hoping to better develop my "theory" and to sharpen the skills of my trade, so to speak. I hope to learn how to be a better teacher. ("Better" means improved communication techniques and skills; greater awareness and understanding of others' [my students'] realities; more patience and less sarcasm, among other things.)

I frequently hope—when I explain to someone who is "-ist" in several ways—that that one will say "Oh, wow! How fascinating! Thanks for pointing that out to me, and I'll get to work on it immediately." In other words, I am sometimes a naive, unrealistic, deluded fool. (Fortunately, I keep a good sense of [sick] humor, and laugh at myself often.) And, I was particularly and painfully reminded of this fact daily in my Fall 1990 Women's Studies class, "Introduction to *Feminist* Studies."

In this class I attempted to deal with all the "social issues," since they really are inseparable. This class tested the strength of every "ism" and every facet of the pedagogical and practical concerns that I have as an educator. It also worked every one of my nerves, repeatedly.

The first day of class, I walked in and as usual, said, "Good Morning, folks." Their response was a shocked, questioning silence. I knew what they were responding to, and told them. That yes, their professor was a black womon with dreds, and with a Ph.D.[3] Most of them giggled embarrassedly; they acknowledged that they all expected a white womon professor in this class. Then, I told them what I saw: twenty-four young students—two black wimmin and twenty-two "invisible ethnics" (whitefolk); among them, two males, one male with a ponytail. But, as I told them, I also found their appearance rather bizarre. Heavily made up white faces, and many of the wimmin had "processed" hairdo's (bouffant or "relaxed"). They giggled again. But the major conflict-of-assumptions had to do with the way the course was listed and designed. It was a "writing intensive" course, and could meet one of the general education (GE) requirements for education.

Most of them were in there for that reason, the subject matter was secondary. I, of course, saw the content as primary, and although I had structured in a substantial written and oral (class participation) component, the content was the major focus for me. In other words, our assumptions were in conflict, from day one (or, days 1–21).

Several students said they were "interested" in the topic; one of the males said he wanted to "know what women thought about things." The other male (white, fortyish) mentioned that he felt intimidated—and mentioned castration—surrounded by all these wimmin. Many of the wimmin were intimidated just by the *presence* of those two males, however, and acted out accordingly, for the entire semester. Still, I went ahead with my plan. Overall, the syllabus was designed to move, in three stages, from wimmin's definition by "others" through wimmin (re)defining themselves, to end with wimmin's alternative realities.

Early on (meaning, each meeting day for the first three weeks), I explained that we could not simply focus on "sexism," but rather the interlocking grid of "sexism-racism-classism-heterosexism." It was several weeks before most of them accepted this focus, and a few of them never did. One major aspect of the class, which I repeatedly emphasized, was that our *lives* would also be the "texts." That meant we would attempt an engagement and interaction with the text*books* and with our daily lives. Accordingly, one of the first writing assignments was to identify and/or discuss one aspect of sexism in their lives—from family, friends, lovers; school, job, or casual public encounters. Initially, most of them (especially the two males) denied that sexism existed in their lives. For most of the first three weeks, we engaged in a basic "power play." The textbook and I would suggest or explain certain realities; the students would deny them. By the end of the second week, I wanted to deny *them*—I wanted to cancel that class, period.

Their responses and/or "reaction formations" were very much influenced by their race/gender/ (perceived or self-defined) class. Some of the reactions were quite predictable, and easily anticipated and dealt with. The two blackwimmin were intensely involved, but said very little, *verbally,* for a long while—yet they and I communicated (nonverbally, in a manner unique to blackwimmin) constantly. And what they communicated was a reluctance to deal with sexism as affecting their lives. The two whitemales denied being perpetrators of sexism; they refused to understand how the *system* of sexism was beneficial to them in spite of their individual disclaimers. Many of the whitewimmin did the same with the subject of racism—denying its reality, or attempting to "testify" about their "one good black friend." (Apparently, they did not even conceive of racism against other people of color in America.) Repeatedly, they refused to see that they profit from the *system* of white supremacy which runs America. Only two of the wimmin (one black, one white) mentioned a working-class background, but they left it there—in the *background*. (Interestingly enough, no one denied being heterosexual!) Meanwhile, I went on with the plan.

Again and again, I reminded them that those isms were as pervasive in America as air (pollution) and that all of us had to have been affected. In an attempt to get them to open up, I used examples and anecdotes from my own life when pertinent. I shared my theory that I was mainly hired at the University of North Carolina at Charlotte (UNCC) due to an "affirmative action" need, not because of any special expertise that I had. I alternately corrected, cajoled, teased, and—as several of them told me—enraged, frustrated, and disturbed them. The final and major point that I made was that if they didn't do the reading (and at some point, most of them refused to), and if they refused to get beyond "denial" and/or guilt, they could not possibly contribute meaningfully to class discussions, could do no writing, and would fail the course. I also suggested that many of them might want to drop the course. Surprisingly, only one of them did.

At some point in the (endless, and endlessly grueling) term, I told them that I was always writing essays on pedagogy, and that they, eventually, would wind up in *this* essay. And long before midterm, I congratulated them all on essentially and effectively *subverting* the class! (At midterm, in response to one of the questions about how best to use the remainder of the semester, too many of them wrote about what else *I* could do; they remained consistently too passive, refusing to take responsibility for themselves.) When I wasn't being totally frustrated and aggravated, I actually found them amusing! Most of them stayed, I believe, because even if they did so reluctantly, they were actually learning something—as several of them wrote later on— they were learning something "real" and applicable in daily life, not just some abstract notions about the world, not just some "academic" exercises. Out of, or in spite of, their strong ambivalence, however, they did give written and verbal evidence that the class was actually "working."

We did "life stories," especially on Mondays. One Monday, a whitewoman volunteered: she had told her fiancé that he should no longer expect her to cook for them daily, and related items. (For instance, he would sit near the refrigerator, yet ask her to get him a drink.) According to her, he responded sensibly and sensitively. We all gave her a round of applause. "Ms. Universal," as I jokingly nicknamed one whitewoman, Ms. DeWitt, constantly had stories; one of them dealt with how she sometimes played the "weak, helpless, mindless female" in order to get a male to do manual labor for her. Two of the most silent young whitewimmin told, proudly, how they changed the oil in one of their cars. One of the whitemales told about being harassed by a group of whitemales for just looking different (his ponytail). And the written responses became (maybe four weeks into the class) more honest and specific as well.

One of the blackwimmin wrote about how she had just "accepted" the sexist beliefs of her church; she was beginning to wonder why she did. A whitewoman wrote about questioning why she and her mother had to do maid services for the male family members. Another whitewoman wrote a hilarious paper about thinking she was a boy, since she grew up with five brothers. Once they stopped reacting to (or overreacting to and overpersonalizing) the texts and the ideas, most of the wimmin wrote about some specific engagement with racism or sexism. Indeed, I told one of the blackwimmin that she had written enough about her encounters with racism—what about the other isms? The older whitemale continued to resist, however, except for saying that he didn't want to give up some of his domestic privileges with his wife (like watching football and being waited on, on Sundays). The other whitemale wrote a few "creative" pieces, but could never bring himself to be as honest as he needed to be. (But more about him later.)

I kept reminding them that even though that oppressive grid existed, they all had the opportunity to disengage from it, or attempt to make some changes—first, in themselves, and then, possibly, in those with whom they interacted. I particularly emphasized this point for the few students who planned to teach in elementary and secondary school. Meanwhile, this class was never an "objective" exercise for me either. Since I don't really have a different persona for the classroom and another for "real life," I "lost it" a few times. On the other hand, when we did have a particularly good, stimulating class discussion, I immediately let them know—individually and collectively. As the final exam approached, I had a "rad" idea. I told them about *this* essay, and invited them to write something for me to include—their responses to the class in their own words. Again, I encouraged them to be *honest*, and to think of a much larger audience than just each other.

Only about seven folk chose this option; these were representative of the few who found the course to be a positive, useful experience.

From those seven, I selected essays which seemed at once most inclusive (in addressing the course's contents) and uniquely individual. The following are a few excerpts, with my "analysis." I have made only minor punctuation and/or grammatical corrections; words inserted (for clarity) by me are enclosed in brackets.

One additional option I gave them was a "group" or collective essay. Ms. Beth Davis, Ms. Margaret Thornton, and Ms. Dana Bennett wrote a six-page essay entitled "For the Anthology: Issues of Racism and Sexism." Divided into two sections, then subdivided with their individual responses, it attempts to respond honestly to those two issues. The essay begins:

> Racism is a very difficult topic for us to deal with because subconsciously we are not aware of the verbal abuse and/or physical abuse that white people cause people of color. Racial issues in this class first went into our minds without changing our thoughts. As the course continued, it became difficult for us to ignore and suppress these racial feelings that so strongly influence our lives.

Subsequently, Ms. Thornton wrote about her dating a young man who was "part Korean and part [white] American" in high school. According to her assessment, because of this class, she now realizes that she broke off with him because of her racism. Ms. Bennett, who almost never spoke in class, wrote,

> When I first came to class and heard racist acts and comments being mentioned, I tried so hard not to listen. I kept saying to myself that I'm not racist so why should I listen. As time passed, I began to realize something very important. Being racist doesn't have to be anything that I actually say, but it can be shown through my actions and thoughts. For example, my unwillingness to discuss the issue and deal with it in class was a way of being racist, a way I hadn't considered.

She continues, saying that she is now at least willing to *consider* that she might be racist, sometimes. Ms. Davis, who was always alert and fairly consistent in class discussions, wrote about a classroom exchange:

> When I came to this class I was very racist, yet as the semester progressed I became more aware of how it felt to be discriminated [against] by white women and men . . . I remember specifically in class when I had said the wrong thing about racism. The question I asked was "Do light-skinned black people and dark-skinned black people have differences in their culture?" I had asked for the black people in our class to speak for their [entire] culture. At first I had been furious at the way Dr. Davenport and the class took what I said, but I soon came to realize that I had been oppressing [expressing?] my racism. I was not dealing with my

true feelings in class and more importantly outside of the class. In the end, racism has made me more aware of people of color and how I relate to them on a one to one basis.

Their collective statement about sexism says it was a "much easier issue" than racism for them to handle, since it "surrounds our everyday environment." Their individual responses present how they are now dealing with sexism in their lives. Ms. Thornton, a track star, says she now gets angry at (as opposed to just ignoring) the catcalls and other verbiage she gets from males when she runs. Ms. Bennett is more aware of the unfair distribution of labor in her family. Ms. Davis chided a female friend of hers about her submissiveness to her boyfriend. She told her friend that she "needed to learn to be self-sufficient without him because he was not treating her with respect." Ms. Davis concludes her comment with an explanation of the exemplary, respectful behavior of *her* boyfriend. (No comment.)

Enhanced "awareness" was an increasingly repeated theme/event throughout the semester. Of course, some folk became, or allowed themselves to become, more aware than others did. Of those, I am quoting the next few students' essays almost in their entirety—because of the range and depth of their responses.

Ms. Tamra Perry wrote, in an essay entitled "Women Studies and Me,"

> Women's Studies 3101 has brought on a new dimension to my life. This dimension is one basically of awareness. This awareness is one fundamental thing this class has taught me. Along with this came a clearer sense of myself.
>
> If I were to use one word to describe this class it would have to be "intriguing." By this I mean thought provoking. Never did a class go by without my thinking, "Is that really true? or How does this really affect me?" At least that is what this class did for me. This class was excellent in making me rethink or should I say THINK about my understanding of basic common everyday things.
>
> Class discussions in particular brought on what I consider eye opening experiences. I personally did not know that some people were totally oblivious to some concepts, not excluding myself. Also I did not realize that some people over-generalize extensively. What I mean by this is that people think their comments apply to everyone when they have not obviously considered the supposedly "everyone" they are referring to. Here I am speaking mainly of the white students in class.
>
> Maybe the fact that I am a black female explains why I do not universally try to speak for others if I am not asked to do so. To me this means that my culture has taught me not to make such comments. My question is, "Are cultures that are not the majority

taught that they can not universally speak for others because they can not or should not? Could it possibly be that White Americans are the [numerical] majority therefore they think they have the privilege to do so?" If they honestly think that they can speak on my behalf then they are sadly mistaken.

Women's Studies 3101 not only raised my level of awareness, but also gave me a sense of being. Do not misinterpret what I am trying to say, please, because I have never been ashamed of who I am. This class just reiterated why I should not be ashamed of myself, being a black woman. Regardless of what many others may or may not say, I know I am a beautiful woman and will always be. No white, black, purple, man or woman will ever be able to tell me differently. No one can take that away from me as long as I know who Kendra March is.

Dr. Davenport, I would personally just like to thank you for a class of this nature. Your class has given me the opportunities to learn more about myself while learning about my race and *women*. In my four years here at UNCC, I can truly say that this class has been one of the few that has taught me something that I can use every day in some form or fashion.

As I wrote on her essay, this is a fairly generalized response, yet one with myriad interpretations. Inadvertently, Ms. Perry was positively affected by having an affirmative "role model" in the class. And, as she wrote in an earlier essay, she is normally quite talkative and active in her other classes, as well as in extracurricular activities (the Black Student Union, for instance, and being elected homecoming queen for the basketball team). In Women's Studies, however, she found that she preferred to listen more.

Ms. Jolinda Mills, also a track star, a senior, a very astute, perceptive person, *and* a good writer, wrote a short essay entitled "Anthology Piece: My Experience With Three Social 'Isms.'"

Dr. Davenport's Wimmin's Studies class focused on many important social issues such as sexism, heterosexism, and racism. With her guidance, most people in our class became aware of the existence of these "isms" in the world outside. I began to spot these isms popping up in class, and before long was searching inside myself to see if maybe some of them could have hidden themselves there without my knowing it. This process of self realization reminds me of picking the muscle tissue of a dissected frog; observing which way the fibers run and how deeply they intertwine. Until you start picking, you can't take a look at all the different threads in your personality, and sometimes that seems good because you like to think that none of your threads are bad.

It was tough learning that racism is not as simple as calling someone a "nigger" or "spic": it can be very subtle. I had never realized that not having to be conscious of my whiteness is a

luxury, since my culture is built on a white frame of reference. . . . My instructor warned us that facing our own racism
would not be a pleasant experience, and she was right.

I came face to face with my racism in microbiology lab. I was
working with three other women. One of them was black, one
looked Indian, and the other was also white. I messed something
up and the black woman, Debbie, cracked up. I got pissed off
inside that she was laughing at me, as if because I am white she
should not have made fun of my stupidity. I played it off at the
time, but later my mind kept running over it again. I knew why
it was bothering me so much. I had realized that racism was a
part of me and that pissed me off. I was piqued at Debbie and
Dr. Davenport for two days. Since then I've gotten to know Debbie
and I like her. My own racism did not get in the way of my
making a new friend this time, and I hope that I never forget the
burning inside that made me feel so uncomfortable with myself.

I remember buying a T-shirt from a fraternity as freshman. The
front said "STOP AIDS," and the back portrayed an explicit scene
of two stick figures, decidedly male, performing a sexual act inside
of a circle with a slash across it. Underneath was written, "None
for me, thanks!" Later, I thought about what the words meant
and cut the back out and quit wearing it. My reasoning was that
heterosexuals could get it [AIDS] too; that babies got AIDS from
inside their mothers' wombs, and that people couldn't help it, so
the shirt was indirectly insulting them [male homosexuals]. What
if someone who'd contracted the disease from a transfusion were
to see it? I never considered, until now, that the shirt had nothing
to do with AIDS. It was an attack on homosexuals, and I am
positive that I passed more than one gay person with it on. I
wonder how my shirt made those people feel? Did they hate me?
Were they unhappy? Or was I written off as a close-minded,
homophobic who helped to financially support an all-white-male
homophobic establishment? The answers would not be pleasant,
I'm sure.

I came into this class with a better awareness of sexism than
of the other social isms we discussed. The class sharpened that
awareness. There have been many instances in which I wanted
to speak out against the sexism aimed towards me or other women
around me. In too few, it seems, I have. A close male friend told
me that I am brainwashed by this class, and that I am the worst
"one" on the cross-country team. I assume he meant the worst
brainwashed, radical bitch one. At a concert I attended last night
a male decided he was entitled to grab me just wherever he felt
like grabbing. When I faced him, the wimp pointed to his friend
standing beside him. I was so enraged I didn't know what to do
first. All I managed was "Fuck off," and the most convincing look
of disgust and loathing that he had probably ever seen. It doesn't
seem like enough. Next time it happens I will not wish I had
done or said more, and he will definitely, without a doubt, know
sure enough, that he's got hold of "the wrong bitch."

> The social issues that we discussed throughout the semester are all a part of everyday life. I would not have contemplated the importance of sexism, heterosexism, and racism in my life or society with any depth on my own. I hope to remember my experiences and those of others in the class, and to use them to deal positively with the isms now and in the future.

And then, there was Mr. Carl Simms, the young whitemale with the ponytail. A most exasperating "case study." Mr. Simms is a theater major, a senior, and a very articulate, intelligent person. He was truly consistent in *major* contributions to class discussions; he could even prompt responses when I failed. Yet, something "shut down" in him when it came to written assignments. His midterm exam was essentially a tirade, explaining how I was the reason for his not doing well in the class. Since I "hated white males," he felt unfairly besieged. Those three pages of tirade were some of the most repetitive (I've heard many of them before) and unwarranted, some of the most *projectionary* and hostile reactions, that I'd ever received from one person at one time. After I handed the paper back—with an "R" for "redo"—we talked. He apologized for his attitude; I chastised him for his irresponsible behavior (he should have told me about his frustrations early on); we agreed that he could and would do better. Yet, as demonstrated by the following paper (entitled "White Boy's Lament,") he was never able to be fully honest on paper:

> This class has been a siege for me. It has challenged me on numerous levels that have not been questioned or tested. These variables have been quite comfortable in the social, political, economic climate in the U.S. specifically the state of North Carolina. My reality is that I am a young, white, male heterosexual. All of these traits are ones that are accepted as normal or correct. These are my given circumstances physically. I went into this class accepting unconsciously the normalcy of myself. I did not consider the different characteristics of myself; I did not think about them because as a white male I was not forced to. I went into this class thinking I could redeem my sex and gender. I could be an example of a liberal, open-minded, progressive white boy. I could be proof that not all men were scum (as I projected feminists considered them). I went in with a pat agenda. I was comfortable.
>
> What this class proceeded to lay siege [to] was not what I expected. Rather than speak through my suppositions about what this class should be about and what place I held in it. The class did not deal with my misconceptions but challenged them at the base of the matter, the conditioning I have experienced via parents, media and so forth, to accept my normalcy [his reality as the normative one, all others as "deviant"]. The class gave me a lesson in the subjugation of people of color and especially women of color by members of my sex and race. Universality was no

longer to be envied when lumped together with this group [white males?]. I wanted to show I was different. I wanted my differences recognized.

At the time I most wanted to express myself and work through these questions I found myself at my most inarticulate. My writing was reactionary, shallow and ignorant. I was over-emotional and blamed the professor for the upheaval I was feeling. I lost confidence in my writing and I became very frustrated with the whole class. My intention to acquit myself well in this class was scrubbed in favor of merely getting through.

The issues this women's studies class dealt with: sexism, racism, heterosexism, . . . are critical problems and were presented that way in this class; no points were pulled. A short lifetime of conditioning is still not able to sweep these issues under the rug, as easy as that would be.

On the other hand, there was Ms. Pamela B. Wright, the young woman who wrote brilliantly about her life as a boy early in the semester. Ms. Wright went quickly from self-righteous denial of her racism, complicitous sexism, and other "excuses," into a total engagement with all aspects of the class. She also good-humoredly accepted a few lessons from us Southerners about Northerners (she's from Ohio). Now that I think of it, she is probably an ideal student, in her open-mindedness, her quickness, and her overall inquiring attitude.

Near the end of the term, I brought a photocopied essay to class, Peggy McIntosh's "White Privilege: Unpacking the Invisible Knapsack."[4] After I read a few paragraphs from the article, Ms. Wright asked to borrow it. Her final essay, "The Privileges of Being Heterosexual," is modeled on McIntosh's article. It begins:

When I read "White Privilege: Unpacking the Invisible Knapsack," I didn't like how it made me feel. It's very eye opening to read something that makes you realize that everything you were taught to believe is false. I never thought about being white because I am white. This realization, along with the article, readings in class and comments in class made me start thinking. If I take being white for granted, do I also take being heterosexual for granted? Of course, this society has trained me to.

In the article, Peggy McIntosh focuses on White Privileges; I want to focus on Heterosexual Privileges, as I see them.

Thereafter, she lists fifteen specific "privileges," such as "I don't have to worry about feeling 'normal' when I talk about my sex life. I don't have to face the disapproval of my family and friends because of my sexuality. I don't ever have to 'think' about others sexuality, I just assume they are like me. I can legally get married . . . I can feel accepted in the eyes of God, according to the Bible. I can blame AIDS on others." She continues,

Of course, these fifteen things are only the beginning. There are many benefits of being heterosexual that are so much a part of my life that I don't even notice them. They allow me to be protected from mass hostility, fear, unnecessary distress and unprovoked violence. People consider what I am as "normal."

I've become much more aware of my sexuality, and this awareness raises some questions. Since, in my opinion, being heterosexual is an extension of the patriarchal system, then that means I am choosing to take part in an unfair and repressive system. Once I was programmed to be heterosexual, I was also programmed to be controlled and dominated by others. Therefore, I act out on my own inferiorities by using the system to dominate others. I also have been taught to believe that without a man, and eventually a marriage and family, I'm not really a whole person. Believing in this system only helps to perpetuate the system which only benefits the minority of people.

Now that I'm aware of what my heterosexuality means, I don't really know what that means in my life. I think it means starting inside myself first. I have to work on evaluating what being heterosexual means to me and how I am going to work on preventing myself from benefitting from my choice. I can't allow myself to use my position to dominate others while being dominated myself. I know that the most important thing is that we are all humans and we have to learn to accept each other and ourselves one step at a time.

This essay has several commendable features, but the major one—given my intentions and hopes—is Ms. Wright's attitude of open inquiry. More than any other student I've had anywhere, she opened up to the process and to the materials. She frequently came to class with a slight smile on her face—seemed to actually *enjoy* herself. Another admirable aspect about her paper is that she felt comfortable enough to question her own societally constructed, compulsory heterosexuality. (For the most part, the others seemed to cling to that, if nothing else, as "normal.") In spite of me and Anne Allen Shockley,[5] most of the class saw lesbians/gays as "deviant"—though they were very polite and quiet about it.

These few "testimonies" are indicative of the "successes" of the class. These few people "got it" in spite of quite a few mishandlings on my part. It *was* a stressful semester for me, and I know I recycled that stress in the classroom. (There were days when I simply did not care about the class's outcome, although I continued to care about the students involved.) Otherwise, even on my "best" days, I had a difficult time getting them to avoid "ranking" oppressions. As is evident from the above essays, they did that anyway. It seems that they personalized the issues, and responded most in terms of the specific ism which affected them most, or which they were most "guilty" of. (On several days, it felt like we were an "encounter group" for racism.) One young whitewomon, one of the three eternally silent ones, whose boyfriend accompanied her to class each day, gave a totally different response from the above essays in her final paper. In essence, she resented and resisted the course all semester. She wrote that many of the topics discussed—such as sex, relationships, racism—were, to her, not appropriate for "public" discussion. I'm sure there were some 5–7 others who, more or less, shared her opinion. She also acknowledged her racism; she only saw black folk as "darker than" she, and with "dark, greasy skin." Also, anytime they were in her classes, she just assumed they had scholarships, since they were *all* poor.

In spite of my constant requests for honesty, several students also wrote what they thought I wanted to hear: glib, generalized essays about how much they'd learned, parroting statements, terminology, and ideas which they could not possibly have adopted (nor believed) in so short a time.

The one overall success or accomplishment of the class was, I believe, that I effectively and efficiently destroyed the notion of "universalism" (meaning, white-male-supremacy as the only norm). Thanks to Ms. DeWitt, and her constant "universal," generalized statements, all the students became aware of the particularity of all people, hence, the danger and half-truths of generalities. Yet, speaking *in general*, I believe that I attempted to do too much in the class, from the assigned readings to the expected responses. That is, if "adults" (feminist/lesbian activists, faculty, administrators, etc.) have a difficult time with these topics, it should not be a surprise that many students would have a *very* hard time. One recent issue of *Radical Teacher (Balancing the Curriculum)* is almost entirely about the efforts of faculty to do just that, especially with crosscultural perspectives and/or wimmin's perspectives. Several articles discuss workshops or training sessions for faculty. One of them ("Different Voices: A Model Institute for Integrating Women of Color into Undergraduate American Literature and History Courses" by Johnella E. Butler and Betty Schmitz) mentions the resistance/denial from the teachers involved. If *they (or, we)* resist, how much more must the students?

Evaluation, especially self-evaluation, is a tricky and tenuous thing in academia. As I know from my own life as a student, some of the materials/courses don't really have an effect until much later—often, years later. Yet, I will attempt to give another assessment of this course, via those three major interlocking areas which I mentioned initially, as well as other pertinent areas. This assessment is written with all of us—socially conscious educators—in mind, and I welcome feedback and responses.

Since there was so much conflict between *my* assumptions and those of the students, I will take more time, in the future, to explain and explore these "hidden agendas." The following list of items deals mainly with that concern.

1. Course setup: Begin with information about wimmin's alternative lifestyles, from plumbers and carpenters, to feminist-lesbian publishers, musicians, and artists. We never really got to that material satisfactorily, and that is one colossal failure of the class. Additionally, I would provide an extensive secondary bibliography, require research papers and oral reports.

2. Text selection and order: Begin with the writings of visibly ethnic wimmin of the United States, rather than a "generalized" anthology of mainly whitewimmin. (This should be much more effective at demonstrating the inadequacy of any blanket statements about "universalism" among wimmin.)

3. Others: Emphasize class(ism) *much* more. In fact, I would experiment with introducing the students to the "isms" with a "layered" approach, like someone blending in the ingredients for a cake (a very rich, fattening, high cholesterol, and totally unhealthy cake). Once they totally understood class issues, I would layer in [fold in] sexism, etc.—while simultaneously emphasizing the importance of each "ingredient" in the overall system of oppressions.

   Initially (on day one) I would provide a list of standard responses of denial—projections, excuses, and related kinds of statements—perhaps as a "checklist" or "test yourself on the 'isms.'" There would be periodic checks throughout the semester to see whether students were understanding the *basic* materials of the course.

A few closing observations: In response to *numerous* observations from *assorted* colleagues, I don't see my teaching (nor my lifestyle) as "confrontational." It seems that anything that even looks like it is unorthodox is too hastily labeled "confrontational" or "problematical" by the orthodox-minded. I see myself as merely pointing out a few obvious (and obviously denied/suppressed) facts. In writing this essay, I relived the experiences of that class. If anyone was "confronted," even battered, I was. Simultaneously, I relived most of my "academic career," such as it is. That is, I *know* that my pedagogy (including my style and appearance) is a factor in my status of underpublished "gypsy" scholar. For the most part, a large number of faculty in English departments will not have their boat—a tiny, overladen, leaky, rotten, stinky, corpse-laden, pestilential boat—rocked. But, I don't rock boats. If anything, I stand next to a mountain on dry land, on a clear (unpolluted, unbombed) beach, sending out safety signals. And I am not alone.

A few more people from my Women's Studies class just joined me/ us. I sincerely thank them all for their written contributions to this essay. And I am truly grateful to everyone who is engaged in not just dismantling, but in trying to create a world free of all isms and of other kinds of war.

Notes

1. Lorde's essay, "The Master's Tools Will Never Dismantle the Master's House" is found in her collection of essays, *Sister Outsider: Essays and Speeches* (Trumansburg, NY: The Crossing Press, 1984, 110–113). Lorde gave the speech at a conference "as a Black lesbian feminist . . . within the only panel . . . where the input of Black feminists and lesbians is represented" (110). She notes the limitations of the conference planners as she observes that, in America, "racism, sexism, and homophobia are inseparable" (110).

2. Wimmin, or womon in the singular, is a feminist spelling of the words women and woman. The intention is to emphasize the autonomous existence of wimmin; the spelling—like wimmin's existential being—has no "man" in it. The spelling "wimmin" is now in the *Oxford English Dictionary* (OED).

3. At the risk of seeming hopelessly outdated, old-fashioned, or even, truly invested in "classism," I insist that my students address me as "Dr." They, in turn, are "Ms." or "Mr." to me. I have found this necessary for two reasons, especially in some parts of America. One, most of these students have rarely encountered a black female Ph.D. If they say it enough, it might sink in. Second, I don't encourage undue familiarity. I address my students as adults, expecting they will behave as such.

4. My chairperson put a copy of this article in my mailbox; someone had handed him a copy—but without the necessary documentation (place, date, source of publication). If anyone knows of this article and the pertinent materials, I would appreciate hearing from you.

5. Shockley is a black lesbian writer; we were using her novel *Say Jesus and Come to Me* as a primary text. The novel is both a lesbian love story and a utopian political manifesto.

References

Butler, J.E., and B. Schmitz. 1990. "Different Voices: A Model Institute for Integrating Women of Color Into Undergraduate American Literature and

History Courses." *Radical Teacher (Special Issue: "Balancing the Curriculum: Sister Outsider: Essays & Speeches")* 37, 4–9.

davenport, d. 1989–1990. "Pedagogy &/of Ethnic Literature: The Agony and the Ecstasy" *MELUS,* 16 (Summer):2, 51–62.

Lorde, A. 1984. "The Master's Tools Will Never Dismantle the Master's House." In *Sister Outsider: Essays & Speeches.* Trumansburg, New York: The Crossing Press Feminist Series, 110–13.

McIntosh, P. "White Privilege: Unpacking the Invisible Knapsack."

3 Dealing with Conflict: A Structured Cooperative Controversy Procedure

Edythe Johnson Holubec
University of Minnesota

David W. Johnson
University of Minnesota

Roger T. Johnson
University of Minnesota

> Have you learned lessons only of those
> who admired you, and were tender with you,
> and stood aside for you?
> Have you not learned great lessons from those
> who braced themselves against you,
> and disputed the passage with you?
> —Walt Whitman, 1860

Often, in English classrooms, controversy is handled badly. Either disagreements are negative experiences where sides are drawn and feelings are hurt, or controversy is skirted or glossed over for the sake of classroom harmony. Worse yet, student disinterest toward the social issues contained in literature may make futile any attempt to stimulate thoughtfulness about those issues. However, the clash of ideas, when skillfully handled, can not only deepen student involvement with the English content but can expand student understanding of the perspectives of others and the complexity of the ideas of the present and past.

One such idea is that of civil disobedience. We live in an age where those who have nonviolently challenged legal injustices have been instrumental in changing them. Dissenters such as Henry David Thoreau, Susan B. Anthony, Rosa Parks, Daniel and Phillip Berrigan, Cesar Chàvez, Joan Baez, and Martin Luther King, Jr. have helped make important improvements in our legal and social system. Yet we also find prominent public figures, from Wall Street to the White House, who apparently feel justified in breaking laws for personal or political gain. Because of this, it is of the utmost importance that our students examine that fine line between blind obedience and disobedience where responsible citizens may need to walk.

Should people obey a law of their country if they feel that it is wrong? If so, or if not, what are the implications and responsibilities? Where is that narrow wire on which responsible citizenship may teeter in order to bring attention to legal or social injustices and thereby change them? This issue is found in numerous places in American literature; we have chosen to examine Huck wrestling with the issue of breaking the law in order to help Jim, the runaway slave, during a class reading of *Huckleberry Finn.*

Yet, how do you get students to examine civil disobedience deeply and seriously? One method for getting students involved with controversial ideas is with debate. However, debate, while it may stimulate involvement with ideas, emphasizes taking sides and winning disagreements with superior arguments rather than exploring the complexities. Also, civil disobedience, like many social issues, has at least several sides—the truth may be found only in walking a tightrope between them. A careful consideration of the implications of both, is necessary to find a socially responsible position.

An instructional technique that is tailor-made for examining Huck's dilemma in the English classroom is our method of structured controversy. Over the past twelve years, we have developed and tested a theory about how controversy promotes positive outcomes (D. Johnson 1979, 1980; Johnson and Johnson 1979, 1985). With this method we have students learn to use disagreement as a vehicle for exploring all the possible sides of an issue. Briefly, we assign students to groups of four. Two of these groups prepare a position supporting one side of the issue and the other two prepare a position supporting another side. Each pair argues its position in a structured way; then the partners change sides and argue the other pair's side. Finally, we teach them to drop sides, and all four students write a position paper delineating the truths the controversy uncovered for them.

This essay looks at the rationale for the controversy model, outlines the context of the cooperative classroom, and describes the structured-controversy model, focusing on the social issue of civil disobedience.

Controversy Rationale

Controversy is a type of academic conflict that exists when one person's ideas, information, conclusions, theories, or opinions are incompatible with those of another and the two seek to reach an agreement (Johnson and Johnson 1979). Controversy can be a positive experience which increases learning and improves student relationships, or it can be a negative experience which closes off logical thought and damages relationships—it depends on how it is handled.

Conflicts among ideas, opinions, and alternative courses of action are frequent and inevitable within any learning situation. No two students ever see any situation in exactly the same way. The question is not whether there are differences in perceptions among students, but how different those perceptions are. Yet there exists a practice in school situations of avoiding or suppressing conflicts (Collins 1970, DeCecco and Richards 1974) and of inhibiting discussion which might lead to disagreement or argument. This lack of emphasis on constructive conflict in schools is one possible reason that adults in our society lack the skills and procedures needed for effective conflict management (Blake and Mouton 1961, Deutsch 1973, Johnson 1979). Knowing that there are potential differences in opinions on the social issue of civil disobedience, it makes sense to explore many aspects of the issue before trying to decide which may be the most thoughtful one. This divergence-before-convergence procedure is central to well-rounded thinking and to examining the issue of civil disobedience (or any other controversial social issue) in the structured-controversy model presented here.

Although every controversy is unique and has its own characteristics, there is a broad model which seems to fit the research around cooperative controversy (Johnson and Johnson 1979). When a controversial issue is first approached, there is a "choosing of sides" behavior where the learner takes a position, however tenuous, on the issue. That is described in the model as "Through a Glass Darkly" (see figure 1). Left undisturbed, this position would continue to strengthen as information is added, often selectively. However, opinions and ideas are seldom left undisturbed, and should not be. They are challenged with other positions and perspectives. In the cooperative-controversy model this tends to happen face to face in what we call the "Disputed Passage." This conflict of ideas in a cooperative setting—where students are looking for a most appropriate consensus position—causes uncertainty. This is a time when a competitive orientation could cause a dogmatic entrenchment of ideas if the cooperative structure is not strong enough and/or if the collaborative skills are not present. However, if cooperation is strong, the uncertainty resulting from the "Disputed Passage" leads to a search for more information. This step

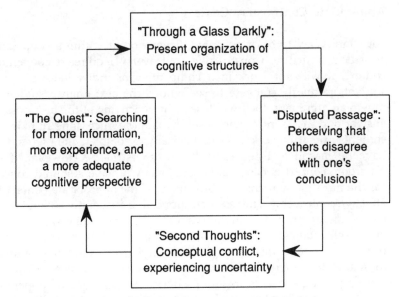

Fig. 1. The process by which controversy promotes learning.

is referred to as "The Quest." The gaining of new information and perspectives then leads back to a position which could be described as "Through a Glass a Little Less Darkly," and the cycle is ready to be repeated. Students may change their positions on answers several times as the controversy process works in their group.

In examining Huck's dilemma, students first may argue whether he was wrong to break the law or right to aid Jim, depending on their position. As they engage in the controversy, however, they may come to see that following laws they cannot believe in is not "right," but breaking these laws at will is also not "right." As they work through the issue, they may come to see that there are consequences for breaking laws which they must confront if they are going to put their personal conscience above the legal system. They need to see the difference between breaking a law for their own convenience versus breaking a law in order to right a wrong and being willing to accept the consequences. Drawing public attention to their actions may be part of their strategy to promote public awareness and support for changing the law. This increasing awareness, then, can lead to a better understanding of civil disobedience, but also to continued examination of the issue.

Appropriate Controversy Context

For controversy to be appropriate, it must occur within a cooperative classroom structure. Constructive controversy requires a cooperative context; it will not work in a competitive or individualistic one. If students primarily compete to see who is the best English student or to win an argument, they will lose sight of arriving at the best possible answer and move into "win/lose" dynamics which stifle thinking. If students primarily work individualistically to complete their work, they have no reason to listen carefully to others' ideas. However, if the classroom context is cooperative, students will have a shared concern for the most rational answer; this provides the appropriate context for effective controversy. The research supporting cooperative relationships in the classroom rather than competitive or individualistic ones has been well established (Johnson and Johnson 1989). In terms of controversy, the cooperative context is essential for motivating students to share ideas in order to find the best possible answer. However, simply putting students in groups does not guarantee a cooperative structure (see figure 2). Five elements need to be present for classroom groups to be cooperative (Johnson and Johnson 1987; Johnson, Johnson, and Holubec 1990).

The first element is positive interdependence. Positive interdependence refers to a "sink-or-swim-together" situation and must be structured carefully. Students must feel that they care about the learning of the others in their group and that others care about their learning. Ways to structure this include having groups produce one product, share materials, and work toward a group-improvement goal.

The second element is individual accountability. There should be no "hitchhiking" in a cooperative group because each student is accountable for taking personal responsibility to learn the material and help the group. Ways to structure this include random oral quizzing, assigning jobs, and individual testing.

The third element is face-to-face interaction. Students need to assist, support, encourage, and promote each other's efforts to learn. Teachers must structure time for students to talk about their learning and provide each other with perspectives, feedback, reteaching, and affirmation.

The fourth element is teaching interpersonal and small-group skills. An interpersonally skillful student is one who says, "I can work with anyone." Teachers will need to teach the appropriate communication, leadership, trust, and conflict-management skills so students can work successfully with others.

The fifth element is group processing. This means giving students

Cooperative Learning Groups	Traditional Learning Groups
Positive interdependence	No interdependence
Individual accountability	No individual accountability
Heterogeneous membership	Homogeneous membership
Shared leadership	One appointed leader
Responsibility for each other	Responsibility only for self
Task and maintenance emphasized	Only task emphasized
Social skills taught directly	Social skills assumed/ignored
Teacher observes and intervenes	Teacher ignores groups
Group processing occurs	No group processing

Fig. 2. What is the difference?

the time and procedures to analyze how well their groups are functioning and how well they are using the necessary cooperative skills. Groups should celebrate their interpersonal successes and plan for future improvement.

Structuring Cooperative Controversy

The goal of the structured controversy exercise is to teach students a method for carefully examining various and conflicting sides of a social issue such as civil disobedience. This gives them a structure for controversy, appropriate practice, and a place to learn and practice the needed controversy skills. While variation is possible, there are essentially eight steps in this strategy.

Step 1: Form heterogeneous groups of four. Four are needed so that partners, rather than individuals, research and argue points of view. The groups should be put together heterogeneously so that every group contains males and females, different ethnic groups if available, and able and struggling students. These heterogeneous groups provide the different perspectives, skills, and needs which make the groups more powerful for learning than homogeneous groupings. If students have not worked together before, have them do some cooperative tasks together before the controversy to help strengthen their feelings of positive interdependence. Such tasks might include guided practice, helping each other learn material, and summarizing and elaborating on readings to each other.

Step 2: Introduce students to the controversy by explaining that the objective of this exercise is for them to examine the issue of Huckleberry Finn's breaking the law in order to help Jim escape slavery so they can write a group report on the role of civil disobedience in a democracy. This precuing of the final cooperative effort puts the rest of the model in perspective and helps to form the mutuality the students need for appropriate controversy. Summarize the overall controversy procedure so that students will know what to expect, and teach the appropriate controversy skills (see "Rules" in Appendix). Then help the students relate this subject to things they have already read, such as *The Diary of Anne Frank* or *To Kill A Mockingbird.*

Step 3: Assign students to pairs and perspectives. Pair students heterogeneously within the foursomes so that each pair is fairly equally matched within the groups. Assign positions and give out supporting materials to read (see "Civil Disobedience Positions" in Appendix). One pair will advocate that it is not right to break laws; the other pair will support the idea that personal conscience dictates breaking a law if a person thinks it is wrong. Have partners move apart from their companion pair and work together to become familiar with their position. Give time for partners to research their positions and gather supporting ideas. The responsibility of each pair is to get to know the arguments supporting their assigned position and then prepare to give a brief overview of their position to the other pair. It is sometimes good to allow partners from different groups with the same perspective to come together near the end of this preparation time to share ideas and give advice. This will take at least fifty minutes. Give students time to research their issue in the library and have available resources such as *The Declaration of Independence* by Thomas Jefferson, "Civil Disobedience" by Henry David Thoreau, "Speech at Cooper Union, New York" by Abraham Lincoln, appropriate sections from *Uncle Tom's Cabin* by Harriet Beecher Stowe, "Letter from Birmingham Jail" by Martin Luther King, Jr., and *The Trial of the Catonsville Nine* by Daniel Berrigan. Easier reading material about the underground railroad, women's suffrage, and the civil rights movement should also be available.

Step 4: Each pair has five minutes to present its conflicting positions to the other pair. Allow no arguing during this time; the sole purpose is to clarify the two positions. The listening pair's job is to take notes and ask clarifying (but not argumentative) questions. Remind students about the reversal coming up: they must listen carefully and take notes so they can argue the opposite side without seeing the other pair's material.

Step 5: Open discussion. Each pair argues the strengths of their assigned position and probes the weaknesses of the other position. Students should ask the other side to give supporting data and to show why its position is a rational one. Because students do not prepare very effectively the first time they go through this model, provide for a "time-out" period, to be called by either you or students when the discussion slows down, during which the pairs can caucus and prepare new arguments before continuing discussion. Encourage students to ask others in the class for help on new arguments or good rebuttals and to read more extensively or do more research between sessions. The discussion should last at least fifty minutes. Do not be discouraged by a slow-down in the conversation after the initial burst. This is the heart of the controversy: the face-to-face cooperative argument where students tend not to get appropriate practice. Expect that students may not be very skillful at digging deeper into the issue until they have had practice. You can help by encouraging new arguments, taking sides when a pair is in trouble, playing devil's advocate, having a group stop to observe a group that is good at it, sending students to the library to do more research, and generally stirring up discussion.

Step 6: Reverse sides. Pairs exchange points of view and argue the other pair's position. We like to have students actually exchange seats for this. Partners can use their own notes, but, in order to emphasize the importance of careful listening, we do not let them exchange notes. Reversals can come at any time but should not be too frequent, perhaps near the end of a class for five minutes and at the end of the discussion step. This is an important part of the procedure as it encourages good listening and tends to unlock students from any one position before they write the group report.

Step 7: Write the report. Now students drop the assigned roles and work as a foursome to write a report representing a consensus position—a position they can all agree upon. Encourage a consensus decision where everyone feels good, rather than a compromise where no one really feels satisfied. This resulting position is usually a third perspective which is more rational than the two assigned. If a group cannot reach consensus in the time allowed, have them write a majority and a minority opinion, but all group members must be able to explain the thinking behind both positions. It is not reaching a consensus that is vital in this part of the procedure but the process of attempting to reach a consensus.

The report should contain a brief description of each civil disobedience position, the group's consensus position on civil disobedience, and a supporting explanation. This report should be assigned as a single report from the group with signatures of each group member indicating that they agree with the report and can explain it.

There should be no "hitchhiking" in the groups, and all group members should be involved in the thinking and writing. If you are not sure about the participation of a group member, intervene by asking that person to explain the group's thinking. If one member has trouble, remind the group that everyone needs to be able to explain the thinking behind the group's report and help the group develop a plan for keeping everyone included.

Step 8: Debrief the exercise by asking students to list the ways they effectively interacted during the controversy, decide whether they met the goals of defining the controversy as an interesting problem to be solved rather than as a win-lose situation, and make a plan for being even better next time.

At this point, teachers should help students understand that the issue is not closed. Students may see through the glass a little less darkly, but should be on the alert for readings or events which will help illuminate this issue even more. Because students have been intellectually and emotionally engaged in examining this issue, they are much more likely to continue in the search for better ideas and answers.

When students automatically start looking at social issues from all angles, see their conclusions as tentative based on what they know and have experienced so far, and continue to search for facts and reasoning to enhance their thinking (rather than their positions) on issues, they have internalized the procedure into a habit of thinking.

This, then, is the ultimate purpose of the controversy procedure: to establish as habits in students the higher-level thinking skills involved in managing disagreements among ideas in order to enhance understanding while they maintain relationships. Students should be able to disagree with each other on ideas while they walk arm-in-arm.

Conclusion

We have outlined a structured procedure for having students examine several sides of the issue of civil disobedience in order to have them learn about it. A cooperative classroom is a necessary prerequisite for students exploring ideas and issues together. In groups of four, one pair argues against breaking laws, the other pair argues for breaking unjust laws; they switch sides and argue for the opposite position; then sides are dropped and the foursome writes a group consensus paper. Our objectives are not only to engage students in an examination of the complexities of the very important social issue of civil disobedience, but also to teach them the lifelong skills they need to uncover ideas and perspectives on all important social issues.

Many, if not all, social issues (or any material, for that matter) in the English curriculum can be adapted to this structured-controversy procedure. For example, teachers can engage their students in such issues as whether individuals have a right to refuse to fight when their country is at war (*All Quiet on the Western Front, Johnny Got His Gun, A Farewell to Arms, The Naked and the Dead, Catch 22*), whether individuals or our social system is responsible for people in the United States living in poverty (*Maggie: A Girl of the Streets, The Grapes of Wrath, Native Son, The Other America*), or whether censorship is an abomination or a necessary check and balance of society (*Farenheit 451, 1984, Anthem*). As we help our students engage in skillful disagreements about important social issues like civil disobedience, we can help them understand that by cooperatively venturing into the disputed passage they can learn great lessons.

References

Blake, R.R., and J.S. Mouton. 1961. "Comprehension of Own and Outgroup Positions Under Intergroup Competition." *Journal of Conflict Resolution*, 5, 304–10.

Collins, B. 1970. *Social Psychology.* Reading, MA: Addison-Wesley.

DeCecco, J., and A. Richards. 1974. *Growing Pains: Uses of School Conflict.* New York: Aberdeen Press.

86 Dialogue and Social Responsibility

Deutsch, M. 1973. *The Resolution of Conflict*. New Haven, CT: Yale University Press.

Goldwin, R.A. (Ed.). 1968. *On Civil Disobedience, American Essays Old and New*. Chicago: Rand McNally.

Johnson, D.W. Winter 1971. "Students Against the School Establishment: Crisis Intervention in School Conflicts and Organizational Change." *Journal of School Psychology*, 9, 84–92.

Johnson, D.W. 1979. *Educational Psychology*. Englewood Cliffs, NJ: Prentice-Hall.

Johnson, D.W. 1980. "Group Processes: Influences of Student-Student Inter-action on School Outcomes." In *The Social Psychology of School Learning*, edited by J. McMillan. New York: Academic Press.

Johnson, D.W., and F. Johnson. 1987. *Joining Together: Group Theory and Group Skills*. 3rd ed. Englewood Cliffs, NJ: Prentice-Hall.

Johnson, D.W., and R. Johnson. Summer 1985. "Classroom Conflict: Contro-versy vs. Debate in Learning Groups." *American Educational Research Journal*, 22, 237–56.

Johnson, D.W., and R. Johnson. Winter 1979. "Conflict in the Classroom: Controversy and Learning." *Review of Educational Research*, 49, 51–61.

Johnson, D.W., and R. Johnson. 1989. *Cooperation and Competition: Theory and Research*. Edina, MN: Interaction Books.

Johnson, D.W., and R. Johnson. 1987. *Learning Together and Alone: Cooperation, Competition, and Individualization*. 2nd ed. Englewood Cliffs, NJ: Prentice-Hall.

Johnson, D.W., R. Johnson, and E. Johnson-Holubec. 1990. *Circles of Learning*. 3rd ed. Edina, MN: Interaction Books.

Johnson, D.W., R. Johnson, and K. Smith. 1986. "Academic Conflict Among Students: Controversy and Learning." In R. Feldman (Ed.): *The Social Psychology of Education*. Cambridge University Press. Weber, D.R. (Ed.). 1978. *Civil Disobedience in America, A Documentary History*. Ithaca, NY: Cornell University Press.

Whitman, W. 1860. *Leaves of Grass*. New York: Viking Press.

Appendix: Student Handouts

Structured Controversy Schedule

1. *Meet with your partner* and plan how to argue effectively for your position. Make sure you and your partner have mastered as much of the position as possible.

2. *Each pair presents its position.* Be forceful and persuasive in presenting your position. Take notes and clarify anything you do not understand when the opposing pair presents its position.

3. *Open discussion.* Argue forcefully and persuasively for your position, presenting as many facts as you can to support your

point of view. Critically listen to the opposing pair's position, asking them for the facts that support their point of view. Remember, this is a complex issue and you need to know the opposing views in order to write a good report. Work together as a total group to get all the facts out. Make sure you understand the facts and ideas that support the opposing points of view.

4. *Role reversal.* Reverse the perspectives in the group by each pair arguing the opposing pair's position. In arguing for the opposing position, be as forceful and persuasive as you can. See if you can think of any new facts or ideas that the opposing pair did not think of. Elaborate on their position.

5. *Come to a group decision* that all four of you can agree with. Summarize the best arguments for both points of view. Detail the facts you know and what you believe about the issue. When you have consensus in your group, organize your arguments and write your position paper. Prepare to explain your thinking to the class as a whole.

Controversy Skill Rules

1. I am critical of ideas, not people.
2. I focus on making the best decision possible, not on "winning."
3. I encourage everyone to participate and master all the relevant information.
4. I listen to everyone's ideas, even if I do not agree.
5. I restate (paraphrase) what someone has said if it is not clear.
6. I first bring out all the ideas and facts supporting the opposing sides and then try to put them together in a way that makes sense.
7. I try to understand the opposing sides of the issue.
8. I change my mind when the evidence clearly indicates that I should do so.

Civil Disobedience Report Assignment

The objective of this exercise is for your group to examine the issue of an individual breaking a law as a matter of individual conscience so that your group can write a well-thought-out report on the role of civil disobedience in maintaining a democracy. Should a person obey a law of their country if he/she feels that it is wrong? If so, or if not, what are the implications and responsibilities? Where is that narrow wire on which responsible citizenship may need to teeter in order to bring attention to legal or social injustices and thereby change them? This issue is found in numerous places in American literature: one such place is in *Huckleberry Finn* by Mark Twain, where Huck has to wrestle with the issue of breaking the law in order to help Jim, the runaway slave. Other sources include *The Declaration of Independence;* "Civil Disobedience," by Henry David Thoreau; and "Letter from a Birmingham Jail," by Martin Luther King.

To gather ideas, you will participate in a structured controversy with one pair advocating that it is wrong to break laws at will and the other pair supporting the right to break a law when a person thinks it is wrong. After the controversy, you are to drop positions and gather together the ideas and facts you all can agree on. Your group's paper should contain a brief description of each opposing position argued, your group's consensus position, and, most importantly, a supporting explanation. Be sure to include everyone's ideas: when you sign your group's paper it means that you agree with and can explain the report and you are certain that your group members agree with and can explain the report.

Civil Disobedience Positions

It Is Not Right to Break a Law

Even though Huck's intentions were good, it was not right for him to break the law to aid Jim. Laws are the very foundation of civilization. Without laws, humans are unable to live together. Breaking laws shakes the very foundation on which civilization stands. What would happen if everyone went around breaking the laws? We would have economic and political collapse. Without laws, we would become savages again, not able to live, work, and produce goods and services together. Look at the problems we have in our society today. They are largely due to people who feel free to impinge on the rights of others. Our prisons are full of such law-breakers. Is their lawlessness good for our country? Breaking laws, for however noble a reason, sets a dangerous example for those who are not so noble.

In a democracy, laws are made by our elected representatives who serve the will of the majority. If someone breaks a law, they are going against the majority. True, there have been some bad laws, but if people disagree with a law, there are ways within our democratic system to change it without disobeying it. It is important for the future of our form of government that we stay within the legal system even when we feel a law is wrong.

Conscience Sometimes Dictates Breaking a Law

Huck was right to follow his instinct and help Jim escape from slavery. The trouble with our country is that we have too many people who blindly follow laws that are made by those who have their own self-interest at heart. Too many times, laws are made to support the rich and powerful over the rights of the young, the poor, and the elderly. In fact, many laws have been changed by those who have refused to follow them; it is a way of keeping the majority responsive to the rights of the minority. When laws are obviously wrong, it is the duty of responsible citizens to follow their consciences, which sometimes means breaking a law.

There is a higher law than that of a nation, and that is the moral law to which all humankind should adhere. If a country's law clashes with moral law, then citizens should do what is right, not follow a law and do moral wrong. Look at Nazi Germany. That is an example of how blind obedience to laws allowed citizens to commit one of the worst atrocities of all human history: the cold-blooded killings of many people. If people don't stand up for what is right, the moral fiber of society collapses and such atrocities are permitted. And, sometimes, that means that a responsible person must deliberately break a law.

4 Cultivating Vision: The Believing Game

Alan Shapiro
Educators for Social Responsibility

"If people don't obey the law you can't have a decent society. Creon's right even if you don't like him."

"Listen to what he says: 'There is no greater wrong than disobedience. This ruins cities. . . .' (Grene and Lattimore 1954, 182). Look at New York City. A perfect example. Muggings in Central Park. Addicts everywhere. Kids taking guns to school. Breaking the law ruins a city."

"But Antigone isn't doing things like that. All she wants to do is bury her brother. What kind of law is worth anything that won't let you do that?"

The scene is an English classroom. The subject is *Antigone*. The argument centers on the conflict between Creon's conviction that the ruler of the state "must have/obedient hearing to his least command" (Grene and Lattimore 1954, 182) and Antigone's passionate insistence that no laws of mortals can "over-run/the gods' unwritten and unfailing laws" (174). The student discussion is lively and combative. Creon's supporters point to the violence in our streets, Antigone's to Martin Luther King, Jr. The debate exhausts the period, and when the bell rings students continue to argue as they leave the room.

Satisfied though the teacher may be by the excitement a 2,400-year-old play has generated, he or she may not have noted the ironic replication among the students of the obduracy displayed by Creon and Antigone. The debate has produced sharp disagreement, some cogent arguments, and a good deal of heat. What it has not produced are a recognition of complexity; a sense of the strength and worth of a position not one's own; a movement, a change, however slight, in one's thinking; a desire to go on thinking. We teachers are often better

Criticism of a draft of this paper by Steve Weimar of Educators for Social Responsibility and discussions with him about methodological belief have contributed significantly to the author's thinking. The author, however, is solely responsible for the final version of "Cultivating Vision: The Believing Game."

at stimulating exciting arguments than at complicating and deepening understandings.

In recent years, many have argued that more attention be given in our schools to critical thinking. Such skills as asking good, probing questions, recognizing underlying assumptions, examining evidence for accuracy and logic, and looking for bias and prejudice are part of the Western intellectual tradition of critical thinking. They stem from inquiry methods Peter Elbow (1986) calls "methodological doubt," that is, "the systematic, disciplined, and conscious attempt to criticize everything no matter how compelling it might seem—to find flaws or contradictions we might otherwise miss" (257).

Developed by such thinkers as Descartes, this tradition has produced independent individuals who have developed habits of mind and skills of inquiry that enable them to learn how to learn and to think for themselves and who have challenged conventional truths. It is easier, though, to apply these habits and skills to conclusions based on observations than to opinions on public policies or questions of moral behavior. Yet it is precisely such issues as racism, homelessness, abortion, the environment, the arms race, and foreign policy that high school students need to learn how to think about.

These issues breed controversy. When conventional critical thinking is applied to them, the result is usually a confrontation, a zero-sum game in which the object is to demonstrate that virtue and enlightenment are on one side, ignorance and prejudice on the other. But solutions to the problems that matter most to us demand mutual understanding and collective effort. What we need is a mode of thinking that significantly improves our capacity while we work together to generate good ideas about major issues, to think rigorously without polarization, and to embrace contradictions that normally divide us.

For this reason and to complement methodological doubt, Elbow (1986) offers "methodological belief: The equally systematic, disciplined and conscious attempt to *believe* everything, no matter how unlikely or repellent it may seem—to find virtues or strengths we might otherwise miss" (257). The conventional critical thinking process, exemplified in the classroom discussion of *Antigone*, "tends to imply a scarcity model of knowledge—namely, that one side can win and be right only at the expense of the other being wrong. The believing game, on the other hand, is essentially cooperative or collaborative. The central event is the act of affirming or entering into someone's thinking or perceiving. It tends to imply a pluralistic model of knowledge—namely that the truth is often complex and that different people often catch different aspects of it" (Elbow 1986, 289).

By helping us feel the power of unfamiliar, even objectionable ideas, methodological belief also helps us understand that "certainty is rarely if ever possible and that we increase the likelihood of getting things wrong if we succumb to the hunger for it" (Elbow 1986, 257). We have succumbed often. In past centuries, certainty has led to innumerable tortures and massacres in the name of religion, the burning of witches, and slavery. In our own times certainty, especially ideological certainty and the attendant inability to see with others' eyes, to experience others' worlds, to recognize and honor others' pieces of truth, has produced a testament of horror: the gulag, Auschwitz, Soweto, My Lai, Tiananmen Square.

Teachers in Educators for Social Responsibility[1] have found in methodological belief an antidote to certainty and a powerful teaching tool with which to promote the development of those qualities in thought and action that they see as essential for a more peaceful, just, and ecologically sound world. Among the most significant of those qualities is the ability to enter emotionally and intellectually into the worlds of others, to grasp, from the inside, what and how another feels and thinks—especially one whose views are very different from one's own, to open oneself to potentially transformative experiences, to move toward common ground and the greater possibility of joint efforts on crucial problems that the world so badly needs. Practice in methodological belief can offer a major contribution to this inner process as students consider the troubling issues that must arise in their reading, writing, and discussions.

Richard Falk (1986) addresses such an issue in his essay "Thinking about Terrorism." "By and large 'terrorism' is used to describe the tactics and methods of the weak," he writes, "while the indiscriminate violence of the strong is portrayed or glorified under labels such as 'patriotism' and 'national security,' which hide its true character" (Falk 1986, 888). Falk goes on to point out that "high-tech weaponry and tactics are not classified by the media as being terrorist, even when used against refugee camps or when women and children are the victims" (888). He calls for a counterterrorist program that includes a repudiation of both "terrorism against innocent people as an instrument of struggle" and "state-sponsored terrorism, especially by high-technology states against underdeveloped countries" (888). For Falk, "The graveyards of Hiroshima and Nagasaki are the number-one exhibits of state terrorism" (888). He excoriates "the hypocrisy of an Administration [the Reagan Administration] that portrays Quaddafi as barbaric while preparing to inflict terrorism on a far grander scale" (888) with nuclear weapons and that sponsors violence against the civilian populations of Nicaragua and Angola through its support of the Contras and Unita.

Is this "English"? The purposes of English classes include close examination of language, the study of techniques of persuasion and discussion of vital social issues—in short, the development of thoughtful readers, writers, speakers, and listeners. So yes, such topics are germane to the English classroom.

In "Thinking about Terrorism" key words include "terrorism," "patriotism," and "national security." What meanings does Falk give them? Why? What consequences follow from such meanings? How does Falk develop his essay? What techniques does he use to persuade the reader? How convincing are his arguments? How might a State Department official answer them? Falk's essay invites this kind of an examination of language and of the arts of persuasion.

As students in English classrooms read and discuss such novels, plays, and poems as *Huckleberry Finn*, *Julius Caesar* and "The Man He Killed," they must also consider major social issues: racism, the nature of power, why men fight. Provocative and controversial, "Thinking about Terrorism" calls for consideration of a global problem from a perspective that is rarely discussed on TV and that challenges the position regularly taken by government officials. Like the literary classics of Twain, Shakespeare, and Hardy, it raises questions that go to the heart of political and moral behavior.

In inviting a response to them, the English teacher reaches beyond the development of literacy skills, important as that is. For the English classroom at its best aims to enlighten and transform, to nurture the human person. Practice in methodological belief is a way to develop skills and insights contributing significantly to that goal; Falk's essay on a uniquely contemporary issue is a text with which to engage students.

The teacher can introduce methodological belief as the believing game and make the following points to students: They have probably noticed that, when we consider controversial issues like civil disobedience or the Arab-Israeli conflict, discussions tend quickly to become debates. Putting on blinders, we restrict our field of vision. We eagerly argue for our own opinions. We listen to opposing arguments mainly to find a flaw and when we do, interrupt and shoot them down. We are likely to be more interested in proving ourselves right than in considering seriously another point of view, in continuing to think. The idea behind the believing game is to promote continued thought by suspending judgment, opening oneself to the strengths and values of a perspective with which one does not agree in whole or in part, and working at believing that perspective.

The teacher should make it clear that the believing game is the first step in the critical thinking process. The second, the more familiar doubting game, offers the opportunity to ask probing questions, to cite inconsistencies, to provide information that rebuts. The third is to work toward judgment by integrating the insights gained by experiencing an idea from the inside and scrutinizing it from the outside.

Before reading "Thinking about Terrorism," and as an initial record of *their* thinking about terrorism, students might respond in writing to the following questions: What does the word *terrorism* mean to you? What are two examples of terroristic acts? What should be a few major elements in a counterterrorist program?

In assigning Falk's essay, the teacher will emphasize step one. That is, students are to work hard at believing as much of Falk's argument as possible and in particular his statement: "To sponsor violence against the civilian population of foreign countries is to adopt terrorism as a policy" (Falk 1986, 888). If, as is likely, they disagree substantially with his position, they should ask themselves: What does he see that I don't see? How might he be right? What can I agree with? Having read the essay, students should be divided into small discussion groups for fifteen minutes. They are to make only statements that support Falk. They are not role playing or pretending. They are finding and speaking from those places in themselves that genuinely connect with him. The groups may find helpful the questions Elbow (1986) suggests:

> "What's interesting or helpful about the view? What are some intriguing features that others might not have noticed?
> "What would you notice if you believed this view? If it were true?
> "In what sense or under what conditions might this idea be true?" (275)

Students are prohibited from making any negative or even challenging comments.

An acceptable statement might be: "I still remember how horrible I felt when I heard about the Pan-Am jet that was blown up over Scotland. Deliberately killing innocent civilians is terrorism. So I agree with what Falk says about U.S. jets bombing Libya. They killed innocent civilians. That's terrorism too." Unacceptable would be: "Quaddafi's responsible for the murder of U.S. citizens, so Libya's got to understand it has to pay for his behavior." During the small-group session the teacher's role is to monitor the discussions, moving from group to group to make sure students abide by the rules. Success, they need to understand, is not necessarily marked by believing everything Falk says but *by staying in the believing mode.*

When discussion flags after seven or eight minutes, as it well may, especially the first time students play the believing game, the teacher can interrupt and ask that they now work at formulating questions in the believing mode. These must aim at clarification and invite fuller understanding and acceptance. Perhaps other members of the group can answer them. They must not be loaded, rhetorical questions. An acceptable approach might be: "I'm having a problem about the Libya bombing. Was the U.S. deliberately trying to kill innocent civilians? Help me to understand why it should be considered terrorism if it wasn't." Unacceptable would be: "Isn't Falk twisting the meaning of 'terrorism' to fit his political views?"

Fifteen minutes on the believing game is probably enough for a first exercise. The remainder of the class can be used to process the students' experience through discussion of such questions as the following: What problems did you have? What resistances did you meet? How did you deal with them? To what extent were you able to make statements and ask questions that felt authentic? What did you notice about others' statements and questions? What effects, if any, has the believing game had on the beliefs you held about terrorism before you read Falk?

Students will have difficulty in early experiences with the believing game. In my own classes, students have said, "I don't like it. How do you expect me to believe something I don't believe and don't want to believe?" "I tried to believe but I couldn't. Something inside me kept saying no." As these two students suggest, believing can be uncomfortable, even threatening. Playing the game may challenge deeply held beliefs and the security that goes with them.

But, after a few experiences with the game, most students will at least begin to catch its spirit. "To my surprise, I believed some of it," said one after his third believing game. "It was like a light going on." This student was making progress, for the believing game does not ask one to surrender completely but rather to find truth in what someone else thinks, especially truth that contradicts to some degree what one has been thinking. When that happens, the student experiences complexity. Further, living with and thinking about it can yield a deeper understanding.

The next class session is the time for step two, the doubting game. Again the small group can be appropriate. The rule now will be to find flaws in Falk's position. Students might ask themselves such questions as these: What questions might point to weaknesses in his argument? Does the essay contain unwarranted assumptions or faulty logic? Does it lack evidence at any crucial points? Is there information Falk omits that would counter any of his arguments? Are there other evidences of bias? How might the President of the U.S. argue against Falk's views?

Having believed and doubted, students can turn to step three and the effort to integrate their thinking. Have the students' experiences of steps one and two opened the possibility of finding some common ground on the subject of terrorism? Are they feeling and thinking somewhat differently than they were originally? What does this mean for one's actions in a world where most social issues are complex and certainty about them "rarely if ever possible"? Following a discussion of these questions and as a conclusion to their work, students can subject themselves and the issue they have examined to some written analysis. What was their position on terrorism before they read Falk? What is their position now? What effects did the believing game have on their views? The doubting game? Efforts at integration? Why?

In such a self-assessment one student wrote: "Where is the truth? And what is the truth? The assessments and opinions are so widely varied that there is very little way of feeling confident that you have arrived at the truth. It is unsettling." It is unsettling. But that's what education should be—unsettling. As for the truth, education helps one learn how elusive it can be, that indeed most of the time we have to settle not for the truth but for truths.

If methodological belief, the element in the critical thinking process likely to be least familiar, is to become integrated into a student's way of thinking critically, it demands periodic classroom attention and should be infused into various activities. Play the believing game with Mr. Antolini's remark to Holden in *The Catcher in the Rye:* "I can very clearly see you dying nobly, one way or another, for some highly unworthy cause"; with the narrator's opening statement in *Invisible Man,* "I am an invisible man"; with the condemnation of Hester Prynne in *The Scarlet Letter;* with Biff's assessment of Willy in *Death of a Salesman* when he says that his father "had the wrong dreams. All, all wrong." Or with Happy's, "He had a good dream." With Creon's point of view; with Antigone's. The believing game is also appropriate when students have written essays arguing a point of view on a controversial issue. Small groups can listen in the believing mode as an author reads, then stay in that mode as they talk about the essay. It is worth noting that Elbow's development of methodological belief began in his own writing classes.

Another believing game opportunity can come when outside speakers at assemblies or in class argue issues. Students can ask questions of the speaker like those cited above to foster belief and have small-group believing-game discussions. The believing game has a special appropriateness when a student offers a view that others in the class find quirky or even stupid. The teacher can interrupt the session and class for ten minutes' worth of believing. What does that student feel and see? Am I sure I understand? What values underlie it? Which do I acknowledge as valid, as real? How can this point of view possibly be right?

Methodological belief calls for an open, safe classroom environment in which the most varied views are given not only a hearing but respect. It teaches recognition of limitations, openness to changing one's mind, delaying judgment, flexibility. It encourages continued thought. It enriches understandings. It has transformative power. It can be an integral part of one's way of being in the world.

In a famous passage of a letter to his brothers, John Keats wrote, "what quality went to form a Man of Achievement . . . I mean Negative Capability, that is, when a man is capable of being in uncertainties, mysteries, doubts, without any irritable reaching after fact and reason" (Pack 1974, 55). Walter Jackson Bate (1966) paraphrases Keats: "In our life of uncertainties, where no one system or formula can explain everything . . . what is needed is an imaginative openness of mind and heightened receptivity to reality in its full and diverse concreteness" (249).

What goal of the English classroom can be more important than the development of "Negative Capability" in every student? In a world where so many cannot tolerate ambiguity or their neighbors' perspectives, where so many hunger for certainty and are prepared to devour those whose certainties don't match their own, the English teacher's task is to cultivate "imaginative openness of mind and heightened receptivity to reality in its full and diverse concreteness." It is to cultivate a critical intelligence large enough and humane enough to "embrace contraries." It is to cultivate vision.

The believing game is soil for vision to grow in.

Notes

1. Educators for Social Responsibility (ESR) is a professional association of educators creating new ways to teach for active and responsible participation in an interdependent world. Its programs address controversial social, political,

and ecological issues. For additional information about ESR, contact the national office at 23 Garden Street, Cambridge, MA 02138.

References

Bate, W.J. 1986. *John Keats.* New York: Oxford University Press.

Elbow, P. 1986. "Methodological Doubting and Believing: Contraries to Inquiry." In P. Elbow's *Embracing Contraries: Explorations in Learning and Teaching.* New York: Oxford University Press.

Falk, R. June 28, 1986. "Thinking About Terrorism." *The Nation,* 888.

Grene, D., and R. Lattimore. (Eds.) 1954. *Sophocles I.* Chicago: University Press.

Pack, R. (Ed.) 1974. *Selected Letters of John Keats.* New York: New American Library.

Recommended Sources on Terrorism

Bender, D.L., and L. Bruno. (Eds.) 1986. *Terrorism.* St. Paul, MN: Greenhaven Press.

Bremer, L.P. May 1988. "Terrorism: Myths and Realities." *Department of State Bulletin.* Washington, DC: U.S. State Department.

Chomsky, N. 1988. *The Culture of Terrorism.* Boston: South End Press.

Crenshaw, M. (Ed.) 1983. *Terrorism, Legitimacy and Power: The Consequences of Political Violence.* Middletown, CT: Wesleyan University Press.

Dobson, C., and R. Payne. 1989. *The Terrorists: Their Weapons, Leaders, and Tactics.* New York: Facts on File.

Ford, F.L. 1985. *Political Murder: From Tyrannicide to Terrorism.* Cambridge, MA: Harvard University Press. 440.

Gutteridge, W. (Ed.) 1990. *Contemporary Terrorism.* New York: Facts on File.

Kronenwetter, M. 1989. *The War on Terrorism: Issues for the 90s.* New York: Messner.

Laqueur, W., and Y. Alexander. (Eds.) 1987. *The Terrorism Reader.* New York: Penguin.

Netanyahu, B. (Ed.) 1986. *Terrorism: How the West Can Win.* New York: Farrar, Straus and Giroux.

Schultz, G. April 1988. "The Struggle Against Terrorism." *Department of State Bulletin.* Washington, DC: U.S. State Department.

5 Learning to Be at Home: Oral Histories of a Black Community

Carol Stumbo
Wheelwright High School, Kentucky

> Discussions of issues such as these—the lives of presidents or the death of children—convey in almost every case the same experience of simulation; of seeming to be like some other thing we would call a *real* discussion. "The school's imitations, like fake fireplace logs, are not combustible," John Mann has written. "It's still a fake if it doesn't go outward to where the real fuel is."
>
> —Jonathan Kozol, *The Night Is Dark and I Am Far from Home* (51)

Last year, the Ku Klux Klan marched in the streets of a nearby town here in the mountains of eastern Kentucky. They marched in the presence of video cameras and print journalists, but without much protest from the average citizen. No voices were raised in Appalachia. A black author from downstate expressed his outrage that the demonstration could have taken place in such an apathetic atmosphere. "There are things that young people need to know," he told a group of students angrily after the incident. "You should know about James Meredith and Rosa Parks and the white freedom riders that were killed in the South. You have to know or we are all lost." We know and we do not know.

In the 1970s, Jonathan Kozol, the New England critic of education, asked a group of twelfth-grade students in an upper New York State school to define the purpose of studying history. The students responded with "History is everything that has happened in the past and is now over. History is cycles, processes, inevitable patterns. History is what is done by serious and important people." When Kozol inquired about whether history had anything to do with their own lives, they said that it didn't. History belonged to important people, not to the students in a high school or the average citizen. The educational system, Kozol argues, through its tendency to categorize, departmentalize, and label, cuts students off from history: "Why study history? The answer that we get is plain and uncomplex: in order to *teach* it, *total* it, *tell* it in writing, *cash* it in for profit, or *list* it alphabetically on index cards. It [the current method of teaching history] lifts children up from the present, denies them powerful access to the future and robs them of any ethical repossession of the past" (82–83). School also, according to Kozol, teaches us to use the third person in our approach to writing or knowledge, forgetting the "I" or the personal. "It seems almost impossible," Kozol asserts, "after twelve years of public school and four years of college to stand up and speak in the first-person present, undisguised [and assert]: 'I am alive right now. I see the world around me . . . I have power to change it' " (80).

This past year, I sat in a classroom with a group of college education students who were visiting the hills of eastern Kentucky to do some classroom observations. They had spent the day with several teachers and when school was dismissed, we all came together for a couple of hours on the second floor of an old elementary school built in the 1930s by the Works Progress Administration. We pulled battered student desks together to talk about what education should be. We talked about the region and some of its problems for a while, but at some point the conversation turned to life on their campus. I listened with some concern as students described the racial tension that exists on their campus. It was nothing like the incidents of racial hatred that have been reported recently at some respected ivy league colleges, but it was disturbing nevertheless. I was struck by the anger that I heard in their voices. One white student, in particular, talked about how tired he was of being made to feel that he had to atone for the fact that blacks had been slaves in this country or had suffered injustice at the hands of others. "I am not responsible," he said, "for what happened to people a hundred years ago or in the 1950s." In his opinion, nothing that happened in the civil rights movement in the 1950s was connected to his attitudes or the conflict taking place between blacks and whites on a college campus in 1989. He was angry that the past was even being mentioned. Others in the group felt the same way. I came away from the conversation shaken and disturbed. Was history something that did not have to be considered, as these young college students thought; did it have no relevance to their lives or situation?

The high school where I teach is the only one in our district with a sizeable black population. Because the enrollment has dropped to under three hundred students, our school is scheduled to be consolidated in the next year or so with another school which has never had any black students. Some parents oppose that consolidation. Even in the 1990s, there are those who don't want their children to go to school with black children. It is inconceivable to me that ten miles down the road from a school where blacks and whites have attended classes together for more than twenty years without major friction there is a group of people who find that totally unacceptable. I left the conversation with the student teachers realizing that one day they would occupy a place at the front of a classroom. I wondered what attitudes they would project to their students and how they would teach history. The Carnegie Foundation for the Advancement of Teaching issued the results of a college survey in May, 1990, reporting that the idyllic view that many held of college life "often masks disturbing realities" including "racism, sexism, homophobia, and anti-Semitism" ("Bigots" 1990, 104). It is as if we suffer from historical amnesia—college students wanting only to deal with today, forgetting the history of a group of people, and a group of parents hoping to turn the clock back completely to a different era. After that conversation, I was more convinced than ever of the necessity of connecting what we do in our classrooms with the real world and of finding ways in which our history means more than a couple of paragraphs in a textbook that are memorized and then forgotten.

For the past five years, another English teacher and I have been trying to create a different approach to learning with a group of students at Wheelwright, a small high school located in the hills of eastern Kentucky near the borders of West Virginia and Virginia. Our original intention was to find a way to motivate students to write and gain some sense of control over their own lives. When I first came to the town and the school in the late 1970s, the fortunes of Wheelwright had been on the decline for some time. Inland Steel Corporation had owned the town since the 1930s but had sold it in 1965, along with its mining operations, to another company that had no interest in continuing the paternalistic relationship created by Inland. For more than thirty years, Inland Steel had not only provided people with jobs; it had also maintained the homes it rented to workers, supplied the miners and their families with health care, entertainment, and recreation, took an interest in the schools—helping to construct buildings, even establishing college scholarships for the sons and daughters of their employees—and oversaw the operation of the city government—creating a city council, fire department, and maintenance department. When the company left in 1965, it did so without much warning, and the people of the town were devastated. After more than thirty years, the people of Wheelwright were free, but they didn't have the slightest notion of what to do with that freedom.

The first eight years that I taught at Wheelwright were probably the most difficult of my teaching career. I taught Chaucer and Shakespeare, sponsored the school newspaper, even directed the annual school play, and though I worked hard, I failed miserably as a teacher. Students saw little reason to be in school. Some came only because their parents were receiving some form of governmental assistance and they had to be there. Many of the people living in the town were older, retired miners. Most of the younger miners left when Inland did to take jobs in Illinois or at other locations in the region. People who stayed were often unemployed. The students in my classroom did not remember or care about the glory days of Wheelwright. They wandered the streets of the town, contributing to the graffiti on the boarded-up buildings, getting into trouble, and hating school. The older members of the community didn't take much interest in the school, and what they saw of the young people was not comforting to them. They were still trying to deal with the fact that the company was gone for good. Although I had students in my classroom at that time who did well in school and went on to college, most of them did not, and that had a great deal to do with what they were being exposed to in school and what they had to confront once they left the school. The lives of most of my students are hard ones. Some have been abandoned by parents to live with grandparents; others live with a divorced parent. Many of them are poor. As in most eastern Kentucky mining communities, there is a great gulf that separates people economically. We have students whose parents can afford to send them to school in expensive sports cars and others who can't buy a good, warm winter coat. In the light of all that, what was happening in the classroom—the study of participles and algebraic formulas—seemed like a waste of time to a large number of students, and they rebelled openly, becoming discipline problems in the school, or withdrew in a kind of sullen despair at the back of the classrooms, shutting off the voice of the teachers at the front of the room. It took me a while to realize that however much my training caused me to resist their judgment, they were right. School didn't make sense to them. What use could they make of what we were teaching in our classrooms?

Nothing in the schools in our area reflects the fact that we live in an area rich in the oral tradition of storytelling or history. If a student learns about the history of the Appalachian area or reads a piece of literature about the region, he or she does so at a college level or as part of a special course in Appalachian studies long after the student has left the public schools. Students, for the most part, do not know the history of their region. As disturbing as this fact is, it is not the most damaging thing that we do to students. We also fail to help them make connections between what they are learning in school and what they will be able to do with that knowledge once they leave our schools. Our region has had a long history connected to outsiders— beginning with the coal barons who developed the mining industry but chose to live elsewhere, and the groups, largely sponsored by churches and civic organizations, who created some of the first schools in the region, and ending with volunteers working for federal programs such as VISTA in the early 1960s and President Lyndon Johnson's "War on Poverty" program. One of those early educational efforts took place in 1898 when the Kentucky Federation of Women's Clubs sent four women into the hills of eastern Kentucky where they set up tents and taught a kindergarten class, passed out magazines, books, and newspapers, and taught local women how to make "beaten biscuits" and sew. That initial trip resulted in another excursion into the mountains the following year by five volunteers from Lexington and Louisville, Kentucky, and one from Philadelphia, Pennsylvania. In time, those visits led to the creation of the Hindman Settlement School which for many years was one of the most important schools in the region (Whisnant 1983, 24–25). Although the Settlement School seemed to be aware of the presence of a native culture and respectful of that, many of the schools created in the mountains were modeled after those found in larger urban areas and were responsible for introducing extensive changes in the Appalachian culture. As a result of the influence of these "outsiders," there was little difference between the schools in Pittsburgh or Detroit or those created in time in Appalachia. Information is delivered in forty-five minute blocks with little connection to other subject areas, much less to the real world. As educational reformer Theodore Sizer has pointed out, the model of the American school was determined by the assembly lines in the factories that we created in the early nineteenth century, and we have never really escaped from it.

That model is still in use today in schools in Appalachia. Some of our students are enrolled in advanced courses aimed at preparing them for college, but the vast majority of our students are either enrolled in a general education track or in a vocation track that is supposed to prepare them for jobs in the real world after graduation from high school. In most cases, the occupations are not present in our region, and students have to leave the area to find a job. The educated people who do return to work in the area find themselves working in a culture and region that they do not understand. They cannot bring about any changes. Teachers in our area, frustrated about the factors that they believe keep them from being successful in their classrooms (the disinterest of parents in education, the lack of jobs and hope in the region, the unemployment, the domination of local politics in almost every institution), continue to teach algebra, American history, and government, and kids continue to leave the school system.

Many of the problems that teachers are experiencing in Appalachia, however, are not unique to our region. Unfortunately, some of the problems with education seem to be nationwide. Reports such as *A Nation at Risk* have added to the public perception that schools are not doing what they should. A report issued by the National Association for the Assessment of Educational Progress in 1989 indicates that no significant gains have been made in this country in reading and writing over the past eighteen years. Students question why they need to learn grammar or complete a writing assignment that ends up, at best, in a writing folder after it has been revised or in a wastepaper basket as students leave the classroom, which happened so often in my first years of teaching at Wheelwright. As a teacher, I have had my own questions over the years about what was taking place in my classroom. What did I want students to leave my classroom with? What skills or abilities or knowledge did I want them to possess? When students lacked the basic skills, after hours of repeated drill, it seemed irrational to think that more hours of the same would help.

James Moffett has written in *Coming on Center* (1988, 208), "One reason young people are so hard to handle is that we are not doing what we profess but are using schools as mere holding tanks to keep them from exploring the world they never made but will some day have to live and work in. We must give them reading and writing as theirs, as human rights, not give with one hand and take back with the other." I believed there was a need to connect the learning and writing that was taking place in my classroom to what was happening to the students I taught. We were not teaching students anything about the history of the region, giving them little or no understanding of the problems that confront the area or the origins of those problems. We needed to give them the skills necessary to identify and analyze a problem, and to arrive at solutions that could be acted upon.

In 1985, another teacher and I began what we thought would be a six- or seven-week project in two of our English classes. Working with a senior and sophomore class, we began conducting interviews in the community around our school. What we hoped to do through a combination of oral history, literature, and traditional research was to look at such issues as the use and misuse of power, the dependence of a group of people upon a single industry such as coal mining, the effects on a people when they live under a paternalistic system too long, and the exploitation of the area by people within and outside the region. The class began as a special project in two traditional English classrooms, but because of the demands placed on the students in putting together a magazine, in 1986 we applied for and received permission to teach an enrichment course. It is a course that was, in the beginning, based on the model created by Eliot Wigginton and his students at Foxfire.

Students from grades 9–12 enroll in the course where they are expected to produce two issues of an oral history publication called *Mantrip*. The magazine takes its name from a term used by miners to identify the car that takes miners underground to work in the mines and is currently being sold in twenty-one states. Because we involve students heavily in the decision-making process, the basic structure of the class continues to evolve as we work with different groups of students. They are expected to make decisions not only about what kind of work is done, but how we go about that work.

Students choose the particular focus of the research that they will do. They conduct interviews in the community and prepare them, along with articles based on interviews, for publication. Although some college-bound students elect to take the class, most of our students are average or below average by the school's definition. More experienced students work with new students, teaching them how to interview and edit. When the students enter the class, many of them have had little experience in writing and practically no exposure to computers, but by the time they finish the course they have learned how to transcribe and edit an article using word processing and how to reduce an interview, in most cases, from seventy-some pages to eight or nine pages. Some fairly sophisticated reading and organizational skills are needed to make that reduction. Once the interview has been completed, an introduction to the article is written and photographs taken, and the students lay their work out on a computer using desktop publishing. It is not the kind of work that you would expect from students who attend a school with some of the lowest test scores in the district, but it is what they do. No other school in the district has a course that demands those skills from students—our students take some pride in that fact.

In addition to their work on the magazine, students are expected to design a final project that focuses on research and action in the community. Last year, a group of students studied the coal industry, researching the effect that the burning of fossil fuels has on the Earth's atmosphere. They talked to mine owners, engineers, and representatives from environmental agencies. Students wrote articles for the local newspaper and posted notes on a World Class conference as part of a telecommunications conference sponsored by Breadnet and the Bread Loaf School of English. Through a computer and modem, students were able to write notes and discuss the impact of burning coal on the world's forests with students from North Carolina and Alaska. They discussed the issue of absentee ownership with students from Peru and Chile and the effect that the destruction of rainforests will have on our world. From that, we moved on to a project in which students began to address some of the other environmental problems that confront our region. Students brought in outside speakers who talked about the quality of water in the region and solid waste problems, and wrote articles for the local paper about those problems and what was happening with global warming. They took photographs of local dump sites. They adopted a section of a creek that runs by the school. They mobilized members of the community and began clean-up efforts. Another group of students wanted to save a small library in our town that had been boarded up for two years, and in order to do that, they had to do an intensive study of land ownership. They built on the research that had been done earlier by a group of students, made telephone calls, and addressed the city council, which finally gave them control of the hundreds of books that were lying unused in the unlit building. Before school ended, the students had distributed most of those books to local schools that have very limited libraries.

One of the most important projects that we have undertaken in the class over the past five years is one that involved the black community near our school known as "Hall Hollow." Black miners and their families have lived in "hollows" or areas tucked between the hills of Appalachia since the early 1900s. Communities similar to the one in Hall Hollow can be found throughout eastern Kentucky and West Virginia in places such as "Shop Fork" at Wayland, "Jackson Hollow" at Jenkins, or at "Red Fox" in Letcher County. Named after one of the early families that settled the area (Wash Hall and his descendants), Hall Hollow is located in a narrow stretch of land between two hills, hidden away like many other black communities in the hills of Kentucky and West Virginia, away from the main highways and roads. Although these are places where miners and families of retired miners continue to carry out their daily lives, most people in the region seem unaware of their existence. Ed Cabell and William Turner, the authors of *Blacks in Appalachia,* believe that, in a sense, blacks in Appalachia have been invisible. Because their presence has not been acknowledged in the literature or the history of the region, black people have not really counted. It is almost, according to Cabell and Turner, as if the black people who live in those hollows do not exist, and to some extent that assertion is probably true. In the fall of 1986, however, the stretch of land in one of those hollows became a focal point for one group of students in our magazine class. The project was an attempt to understand how blacks had ended up in this part of the country, and what happened to them once they arrived here. As teachers, we began to realize that it wasn't just Appalachian history that we were failing to teach. The black students who attended our high school were not learning anything about their own history or culture either. One teacher was appalled when she discovered that some of her black students knew very little about the National Association for the Advancement of Colored People or what it had accomplished. It really shouldn't have been surprising though. We offered no courses in black history or black literature. We seemed to be offering education that was connected to everything, but in the end to nothing—at least nothing that was concrete or that touched their lives.

Even if we had offered a course in black history, it would not have dealt with the history that affected the lives of this particular group of students. Much of that history simply could not be found in textbooks. Dr. William Turner, a historian and the founder of a black newsletter called *Sojourner,* told students in an interview that much of what historians had written about black people in other areas did not fit the experience of the people in Appalachia. Turner, who was born in a county near ours, realized that even after years of formal study, there was a great deal he did not know about blacks in Appalachia, and if he wanted to know about them, he wouldn't be able to do so through traditional scholarly study: "It was like I was trying to take a cookie cutter—you know you take a cookie cutter and say, 'Here's some dough,' and you put your cookie cutter on it. I was cutting black people out of the mountains [with] a cookie cutter that had been made somewhere else." He put aside some of his preconceptions about black Appalachian history and talked to ordinary people in the community:

> My dad could tell you things about the mountains I can't tell you. He once told me when I first wrote about blacks in Appalachia— some little article that I had written—he said, "There's enough you don't know about the black people around here that would fill every abandoned coal mine in eastern Kentucky." And I took umbrage with that because I thought I was a lot smarter than him.

What Turner did was return to the oral history tradition, similar to William L. Montell's approach in *The Saga of Coe Ridge*, a study of a black community near the Kentucky-Tennessee border. To find the answers, Turner went back to the old black men and women who could remember stories of how it was. "They could tell you," he said. "And they'll tell you things you could never read anywhere." We hoped they could.

Assisted by a grant and tape recorders supplied by the Kentucky Oral History Commission, a group of students at our high school began the Hall Hollow Project in the fall of 1986. The grant was the first of its kind made by the commission to a group of students, and the trust demonstrated by the KOHC made us take our responsibilities seriously. Knowing that copies of our interviews would end up in the oral history archives of our state capital reaffirmed the belief that student work could have importance beyond the classroom. One of the first tasks that we took on was to define the scope of the project for the oral history commission. After some discussions, we arrived at the questions that we would try to answer over the course of the school year: (1) How did blacks come to Wheelwright? (2) What were the communities like that they came from? (3) Was there prejudice in the camps or underground, and what was the nature of it if it existed? (4) What happened to the black culture in the camps? Did black families retain their own culture or did it give way to the culture of the mountains? (5) What did the coal company do to strengthen the position of blacks, or were blacks used as a lever against white workers? (6) What role did blacks play in the formation of unions? (7) Were blacks aware of other black political movements (the civil rights or the black power movements)? (8) In what ways was the black experience different from that of the white coal miners? (9) Did the role of blacks change in the mining industry over the years? Were they moved into supervisory positions? Did their relationships in the community change? (10) What was life like for the blacks in the present-day town?

We had no way of knowing how difficult the project would be when we began it. First, we had to piece together what was known about blacks in Appalachia and learn what, if anything, had been written about the subject before we began. We discovered paragraphs and occasionally chapters that dealt with black miners in several of the books about the region. That reading gave us enough to start with, and as we conducted our interviews, we were able to fill in the picture more, acquiring a sense of how blacks had arrived in the region. Blacks first came to Wheelwright and other coal camps during the early 1900s. In the beginning, "agents" or "recruiters" went to the South, promising blacks a job and a free train ride if they would agree to come to the coal fields. This was known as the "transportation system." Agents for the coal companies traveled southward to such areas as Birmingham, Alabama, where blacks worked in both coal and ore mines, looking for laborers and promising free railroad tickets or "transportation" to the coal camps further north if blacks would sign up and agree to work in the coal mines. Later, as word spread, or when the companies had a sufficient manpower base, blacks came on their own and some were brought because they were good athletes and the coal companies wanted them for their baseball teams.

Once they arrived in the camps, blacks were assigned housing. These colored sections were not always exclusively black because white families sometimes lived in adjoining houses and sometimes, within the colored section itself, or in the "bottom," as the black section in Hall Hollow was called.

The important thing to me as an English teacher was the complexity of the research. In the past, I have worked with students on research papers and watched them—in consternation at times—as they unearthed contradictory pieces of information. Students seem to have no patience with conflicting data. So much of what we do in school, from the material that is read by students in textbooks to that presented to them by teachers in classrooms, seems to wrap all knowledge up in neat, little packages. It is only on the college or graduate level that students begin to understand what real research involves. Much of the information we were encountering added to the confusion rather than giving us simple truths, but there was some information that we could validate both through oral interviews and written sources, which seemed to be definite enough to give us a working base. The black camps themselves were located in "hollows" away from the main portion of the camp, and once the sections were designated as colored camps, they remained colored camps. Blacks did not settle into other areas.

Although we had black students in our class and the population of the town was small (approximately seven hundred people), gaining the trust of the blacks in Hall Hollow was not always easy. In spite of the fact that black families had been living in the area for a long time, there was some fear and uncertainty as we began our interviews. Blacks would talk to us, but the first interviews were difficult to interpret. In one of the early interviews that we did with the minister of the Baptist church, he told us the following about the early days in Wheelwright:

They [blacks and whites] hadn't had any big trouble before I
came. They still didn't have any trouble after I did come. We was
able to get with the officials and have a meeting on our problems
and solve them. . . . We had a little trouble once. It wasn't too
serious. The way I understand it—you know, children will clash
sometimes. It didn't mean anything. I think one of the bosses
took it [integration] up and caused a little trouble—a right smart
little stir about it. Our superintendent told him he could just go.
He said he could have nothing like that here's. . . . There was no
more serious trouble. I don't think there was any more racial
trouble to amount to anything. (Reverend E.H. Terry, 1986)

It's a simple paragraph, but it illustrates the type of learning that
students were being exposed to each time we went out on an interview.
What did this information mean? Although Reverend Terry worked
underground as a miner, there is no mention of any problems that
working men may have experienced. He downplays the notion of
trouble until he begins to talk in more detail about the picketing that
occurred when the school was integrated in the 1960s, and then he
uses the phrase "a right smart little stir about it." Finally, he raises the
issue of the role that the "company" played in bringing about integration. Men's jobs were apparently on the line if they went against
the new integration law and the company's position. What kind of
role had the company played in the earlier relationships between
blacks and whites in the community? How much of what Reverend
Terry was saying was determined by his own personality and religious
beliefs?

James Moffett has asserted that literature is dangerous because of
its ability to stimulate thinking and cause a reexamination of beliefs.
Although literature has the potential to do those things, in most high
school English courses, far too often "literature" consists of a reading
followed by a discussion and set of questions in which all the answers
are arrived at quickly and neatly. What my students were encountering
was material that was indeed "dangerous," requiring careful thought
and interpretation. The study also cut across curriculum lines so at
different points in the class the students were using reading, research,
and writing skills to examine their own lives in the context of their
history.

Kisha Cotton, one of the students in our magazine class, was a
member of Reverend Terry's congregation at the Friendship Baptist
Church. Her grandfather, William Smith, who was known as "Big
Track" to the people in Hall Hollow, was a deacon in that church. He
had died the year we began the project. Big Track's death reminded
all of us how important the information was that ordinary people

possessed and how easily that could be lost to all of us. Part of the work that Kisha did for the project was interviewing and preparing a map outlining the location of the houses and identifying who lived in them. Last year, she also did some personal writing about what it was like growing up in Hall Hollow.

One of Kisha's essays, called "A Matter of Heaviness," was written after a group of seminary students visited our classroom. Kisha had a long conversation with one of the students who was from Africa. He questioned her about whether she had encountered much prejudice living in eastern Kentucky. Ironically, she told him that much of the prejudice was not directed so much at her being black (that was comparatively light), but she felt more as a result of being termed an "Appalachian" or a hillbilly. Kisha posted the essay on Breadnet, the telecommunications network established for teachers who have attended the Bread Loaf School of English in Vermont, and she received responses from students in Iowa, Virginia, and Montana, many of whom had never gone to school with blacks. Others shared stories with her about friends who had also been discriminated against. It was an important moment of consciousness for Kisha. Although she had not been completely protected from racism in Hall Hollow, she seemed to feel that as a senior in high school, she was about ready to enter a world where she would have to deal with it more directly:

> For as long as I can remember, everyone in Hall Hollow has raised everyone's children in one way or another. Because my brother and I grew up in a single parent home, my mom tended to let us grow free of the rules. She didn't shelter us or try to make us something we weren't. I had baby-sitters until I started school. My brother, four other friends, and I were all taken care of by these people at the same time. We played, we fought, we cried and we all loved Plump and Theeny [the two baby-sitters].
>
> Living in Hall Hollow was great until I got old enough to recognize prejudices. That was when I was about ten years old and my mother put me in my first beauty pageant. A woman said that a Negro shouldn't have won over her baby. I knew then there were prejudices and I realized that there were even jokes about Hall Hollow. It was sometimes called "nigger hollow" but it still was home and I felt comfort in being there.
>
> Things are changing now. Theeny is gone. Plump doesn't remember those days and great grand-daddy is gone, but having those people in my life was the best childhood a little girl from Hall Hollow could have had.

Kisha's essay reflects some of the same ambiguity that we experienced when we looked at Reverend Terry's interview. Although she says that she did not experience much prejudice, the hollow itself was known as "nigger hollow," and she felt the direct impact of prejudice when she entered a contest that involved other children. We would discover, as we did more research into Hall Hollow, that the amount of prejudice depended on the people that we were interviewing and how close they were to the actual black community and the town. As students came into contact with children and adults from other communities, they encountered attitudes that were different, and they did have to deal with prejudice. It was important that all of us look at that more closely.

What we were doing in our class was also important to me as an English teacher. The language of school, in too many cases, is not the language of the students who enter my classroom. Removed, academic words often separate young people from what they know, and, in a real sense, inhibits their learning. Through interviews, my students have the opportunity to listen to people use language to talk about things that they care about, to use words that are emotional but have purpose. I have watched several retired miners talk to my students with tears in their eyes, and that has had a profound effect upon my own students' ability to write and communicate. They begin to use words in a more direct, meaningful way after working with these interviews. These students come from a rich oral tradition that has, at best, been a double-edged sword. On the one hand, that tradition has been responsible for producing many talented writers, but it has caused problems for many students when they have entered the school system. Dialect accounts for the richness and flavor of some of our best stories, but in many of our schools, that dialect is seen as a problem by teachers—one that must be corrected as soon as possible.

Reconnecting students to the spoken word in powerful ways is important. Students who work with interviews do not end up producing disembodied, empty pieces of writing. Much of their time is spent conducting and transcribing interviews with others, but they are also producing articles about those subjects, articles that are tied into their own world and experiences in a real way. Over the past five years, I have watched many teachers begin oral history projects and have seen some of the same things happen to those teachers and students as I have experienced: teachers who are touched in a personal way by the interaction between older people and their students, teachers whose teaching style undergoes subtle changes because they find themselves working *with* students rather than directing them—all of those teachers have found powerful reasons for using this technique, but I always find myself wanting to say, "But it can do more."

That "more" has a great deal to do with the language development of students. James Moffett recommends that students be taught to read on the secondary level by having students talk into a tape recorder and then, with the help of the teacher or other students, transcribe their own words and read them. "I think the voice has to act as an intermediary for the beginning or weak reader between his oral language, his nonverbal expression, and books" (45). The same thing can happen with writing. My students and I conducted a classroom research project two years ago, looking in some detail at what happens as students worked on editing articles for the magazine. Tona Rhea, one of the students who was part of that project and the Hall Hollow project, was a wonderful natural writer. One of the first pieces that she wrote that year was a personal narrative, called "A Sister's Goodbye," about the death of an older sister. Written at times in fragments and with a great deal of dialogue, her writing in that piece was as close to natural speech as it could possibly be. It was a beautiful piece of writing. Yet, when Tona wrote something formal, more involved, for the magazine or the class, her language became confusing, unclear. By the end of the year, after she had worked with oral interviews, there was a change in her writing. She was able to take on subjects and handle them in a clear manner. That happened only after Tona had spent the better part of a year—working first on an interview with a retired policeman who had certain attitudes towards blacks that Tona at first had trouble understanding, and then with an interview that she did with her aunt in Hall Hollow. It is important that language and its use is connected in a real way to subject matter. She was not only improving her writing skills but struggling with her attitudes about racial relations:

> While doing this interview, I found out that he [the former policeman] is not too bad of a person. He has a few problems— some of which I had not expected to encounter. He was born at a time when blacks were not thought of with much importance. You can't really blame him for thinking what he was taught to think. His environment sort of made him the way he was. The blame falls on him if he has taught his kids to think the way he does. I must say that I had trouble with him at first. It took some real trying on my part to understand and accept him.

Ten students were involved in the Hall Hollow project the first year. These students volunteered to work on this project while the rest of the class continued with the production of our magazine. We usually spent a couple of days each week out in the community conducting interviews. After we returned, we listened to the interviews and analyzed them in an attempt to evaluate the information that we had.

We also looked at questions that we were not finding answers to and were constantly creating new ones as a result of the information we were discovering. It was exactly the type of process that students would need as they worked on traditional research projects—forming a hypothesis, validating it, revising, and doing additional research.

Some of the students expressed frustration as we worked on the project, especially at some of the information we were hearing, the seeming contradictions that were occurring in the information that we were uncovering; others, at the fact that this history was not nearly as easy to understand as was the kind they had been accustomed to in textbooks. One student, in particular, was confused about the fact that one of our best contacts, a white storekeeper who had grown up in Hall Hollow and that we had interviewed on many occasions, said that blacks and whites had no problems at all, but who, on the other hand, described in some detail how, over a long period of time, each Sunday morning the people would find a black person dead in front of the church house in Hall Hollow. "This doesn't make sense," she told me on several different occasions. "People aren't killed that often unless there are some kind of bad feelings." The problem was, what we should do about it? How did we deal with that contradiction? Did we challenge his statements or simply wait and fill out the picture through more interviews with him or those of others? If we checked the back issues of our local paper, would that assist us or just further complicate the whole matter? Students and teachers were being confronted constantly with opportunities to make decisions.

The year ended and the student graduated without really resolving her questions about the contradiction, but she, like the rest of the students that worked on the project, knew that it was not finished, that another group would have to continue because we still had too many unanswered questions. In the interviews that followed, we began to hear stories of the "removal" of blacks from an adjoining coal camp. Those stories came because we had widened the circle of our interviews, going outside the community in Hall Hollow, and perhaps because people were now accustomed to having us in their homes asking questions. Persistence, the willingness to continue to ask the questions, in time led to a different set of facts. A murder had taken place at a store in the black community, one source told us. A white boy had been killed and whites who were angry pelted black homes with stones until the situation reached a crisis. Stories were told of crosses being laid in the yards of black people—crosses made out of broken twigs to remind people of the kind of crosses that were burned by the Ku Klux Klan. Blacks were given the message in no uncertain terms that they had better leave the camp. Some of them went to other black camps in surrounding counties. Many of them came to live in the black camp in Hall Hollow near our school. Soon we discovered other sources who confirmed that story. We had finally located individuals who would talk about those problems and in time those that occurred when the town's swimming pool and the high school were integrated in the 1960s. It was almost like discovering gold—we were beginning to move beyond the superficial. The information that we were discovering was disturbing. We talked about the reality of what we were discovering on the way home from those interviews, but, ironically, we were at the same time elated in a way that no amount of textbook study could have ever brought about. We had invested a great deal of time and patience in the research, and were beginning to have some of our "feelings" or hypotheses confirmed.

As we widened the circle of interviews, we began to make several important distinctions. The first of these was that we needed some kind of comparison between the information and attitudes that we were finding in the hollow itself and those outside it. Most of the people who lived in Hall Hollow have had an experience that those just a few miles down the road had not had. They had lived alongside blacks for years. Others had only seen them underground or in the town. When we talked to people, even miners, that lived farther away from the hollow, we heard statements about foreign workers (the Italians, Polish, Russian people) who had come to the coal fields to work, and about blacks, that were less sympathetic.

Another distinction that we made fairly quickly concerned the age of the people we were interviewing. There were definite differences between the attitudes of the older members of the community (those who had been there in the 1920s and 1930s) and the other black miners who had begun work in the 1940s and 1950s. Because we felt that we needed to reach back to an earlier time, we spent many hours listening to and reviewing the oral history archives at Alice Lloyd College. It was there that we discovered the transcripts of Hilton Garrett. Garrett, who is ninety-five years old and suffering from Alzheimer's, still lives in the two-story house that he shared for more than thirty years with his wife Ruby in the hills of eastern Kentucky. Ruby is dead; his son, a child that he adopted and raised, has grown up and moved away. Garrett lives in the boardinghouse that he operated for years and is cared for by his next-door neighbor. Despite the fact that memories he had of his life in the coal fields of Alabama and Kentucky when "Jim Crow" was a way of life are gone now, he became an important part of our study. Fortunately, what he knew about life in Alabama and the hills of Hall Hollow was recorded on tape by the oral history project at Alice Lloyd before he lost his memory. Garrett helped us understand the earlier days in the camp, when blacks were denied supervisory jobs and the right to sit down in white restaurants or movie theaters. One fall morning, a group of us traveled across a mountain to the community college where we located the oral history archives in the back of the college library. We spent two mornings rummaging through files and tape cabinets in a room not much bigger than a closet until we located Garrett's interview and were finally able to hear his voice for the first time:

> There's been some tough times in these coal camps. There was certain places I couldn't go in. It was like that fountain [the white drugstore] down there. I couldn't go in. That was for white folks. It wasn't for me. We had to live with it. That's all there was to it. We knowed it was an unfair deal. Different jobs in the mines, that was what I hated. If I could have got equal breaks in jobs, I wouldn't have cared nothing about the rest of it.

"They [the white man] just now took the foot off his neck," Garrett said. The important thing about his interview was the fact that it stood in stark contrast to what we had been hearing from people we had interviewed earlier, providing us with additional confirmation about our initial feeling that, in some way, we were not hearing the complete story. As a teacher, I appreciated it for the layer of complexity that it added to the work that we were doing. Students were almost forced to begin to think in different terms, learning to separate "fact" from interpretation of fact, coming to understand that the truth that they were looking for was often swirling around in a cauldron of conflicting information.

One of the other figures that played a prominent role in our research into the history of blacks in our area was a law official by the name of "Bad John" Hall. Because of the fear that he induced, blacks reportedly gave themselves up voluntarily when Bad John Hall sent word to them that he wanted them to come in. Although he was said to be on "friendly" relations with the black people in the town, there was an element of fear and intimidation because he represented white law and order and power. Some of our contacts spoke of an incident in which a man had been killed in an argument at a local gambling establishment. Blacks were involved in that. Two of the students in our class spent almost six weeks trying to understand Bad John Hall and the role that he played in our research. Much of that time was spent in just trying to sort out what they were uncovering:

Bad John Hall was more than a famous figure in our community. For us, he has been a semester long assignment which will continue through the spring of this year. Many people have different opinions about the kind of man Bad John Hall was. Some say he was a tragic hero while others say he was a merciless killer. Some believe that he killed in defense of himself and his friends while others believe that it was just a pastime for him. One side of his story has been told by his nephew and will be presented in the fall issue of our magazine.

Part of our research efforts dealt with weaving strands among the different stories we heard from the people that we had chosen to interview. At times, the pieces were like parts in a gigantic tapestry that we were trying to put together. During the course of the two years that we worked on the project, we interviewed pastors, coal miners, housewives, professionals, teachers, musicians, and a man who was doing an intensive research project of his own about a local black writer. We tried to correlate the information from those different sources. The stories that we heard from miners presented a picture quite different from that told by their wives. Because of the dangers that all miners faced underground, many of the white miners told us that they paid little attention to the color of skin, but one of the wives described the terror that she felt when she was first married and left alone in the hollow at night and how she had thrown away any gifts of food that black neighbors gave her. One other black miner remembered white men who wouldn't speak to him once he was above ground and encountered them on the street. Black preachers recalled services that they had preached in white churches, but others talked about "knowing their place" and what they could or couldn't do. As soon as we thought we had reached the point where we could begin to come to some kind of conclusion, a statement or interview came along that made that impossible.

Three students did a study of the local black cemetery, making lists of the people buried there along with dates, trying to discover why some of the graves had long wooden crosses stretched across them, if there were any significance in the fact that many of the blacks chose to have their dead relatives buried "back home" in Alabama and North Carolina. That study in turn led to an attempt to discover what had happened to other people who had lived and died in the hollow. At times, we hit a wall in trying to research a simple thing such as how the black school got its name. We suspected that the school known as Palmer-Dunbar took its name in part from the black poet Paul Laurence Dunbar, but we were never able to discover where the Palmer part had come from. When we learned that other black schools in the area also had the same name, that only added to the confusion. We studied records of the company for information about the number of black children that had received scholarships to college, the organizations that blacks and their children belonged to, and we also looked at the black school that had been built in the hollow for information about the number of children enrolled there, the way that the school was operated. Was it simply modeled on the white schools in the area? Once we discovered that the black church had been such a powerful force in the lives of people, we began to ask more questions about the choir and the musicians that performed there.

Throughout the course of this project and during the five years that we have worked on *Mantrip*, we have had visitors to our class and, on occasion, some of those people have questioned the skills that students are acquiring through such work. Because the course is an elective one, the questions are perhaps not as difficult to answer as they might be if we were attempting the project in a regular English course, but I remember one young man's clear disapproval when I spoke to a group of education students at a college in the central part of our state. He didn't think that students should receive high school credit for such work. It was not the proper kind of work for school. On the other hand, there are those individuals who approve of students doing such work in the community but conceive of it as a kind of wholesome but slightly simple process, not demanding any kind of rigorous academic skills. It is neither of those.

Several weeks after I talked to the students at the college, they made a trip to our classroom, where they had an opportunity to observe students working on the Hall Hollow project and our magazine firsthand. As the skeptical student watched students taking the raw material from those Hall Hollow interviews, often a massive amount of information—sometimes more than a hundred pages of written material that would be condensed to fit seven to ten pages in printed form—he began to change his opinion about what students were learning.

What judgments have to be made as students decide to omit certain material? The student has to evaluate information—what is at the heart of this interview? Looking at all the other interviews that we have conducted, what new information does this interview offer? Because this is material that has to be edited, shaped in a sense by the students, they are addressing all the skills that a writing class does and then some—paragraph unity, transitions and flow of information in a coherent way, correct usage and spelling. One important thing that seems to happen is that students learn to organize quickly. Given a pair of scissors, the student may decide to cut out sections of the interview and categorize them by stacking all the material about "work" in one pile and that about "childhood" in another. Some choose to do this with colored pens rather than scissors, but the results are the same. They soon recognize that words and sentences have to be sorted in the same way that you would a set of geometric shapes— squares in one section, circles in another—except that it is more complex when you are dealing with words.

We encourage first-year students in the class to use a chronological order when they work with structuring an interview proceeding from birth to present times so that they will not feel too overwhelmed as they try to give shape to their interviews. With other, more experienced students, we suggest that they begin with the most critical information in the interview, then work their way back to a chronological order, in much the same way that authors make use of a flashback or find ways to include simple autobiographical information (birthplaces, parents' or children's names) in the introduction. Some students are reluctant to revise their own writing. In this process, they are encouraged to experiment, to try out many different ways of ordering information as possible and they do not seem to find the process nearly as frightening as when they are working with their own writing.

At the end of each school year, when students in the magazine class are asked to design their own research projects that are not tied directly into the production of *Mantrip*, they do some important work. It is often exhausting. It is demanding, frustrating at times and rewarding at others, but it is never boring. In the past, students have combined oral interviews with more traditional forms of research, doing everything from a study of black writers to papers on subjects such as W.E.B. Du Bois's criticism of Booker T. Washington. Some students this past year engaged in a long writing exchange with students on a kibbutz in Israel. Students from the Ramot Heft School in Israel carried on a conversation through a telecommunications hookup with our students in eastern Kentucky. We learned about the "Children's House" at the kibbutz where students are cared for and educated from an early age, but we also discussed prejudice in all cultures. Those students at Ramot Heft School shared a dialogue with us, for example, that had been written between an Arab and a Jew. Our students were able to share with them information about racial relations in this country and what we had learned from our study in Hall Hollow. Both groups read pieces of literature, such as a selection from James Baldwin's *The Fire Next Time*, and used that as a springboard for further dialogue. It was one of the most powerful experiences that

I have ever had as a teacher—to watch the students in Israel and ours here confront some of the beliefs that they held about others, often without thinking about them very deeply, and then witness those same young people try to transcend those beliefs. Our students were able to draw on their knowledge of the black experience and use what they knew about the past in a thoughtful way in their discussions. When we read or saw news reports of people being killed in Israel, those deaths meant something to us because of our personal contact with students there. We were out there where the real "fuel" is, as John Mann has said we should be, and the discussions we had were anything but imitative. They were about real people and death.

At the heart of everything that we do in our classroom is an attempt on the part of young people to deal with the importance of this place in their lives. The Kentucky essayist Wendell Berry has said that "wisdom is not a journey of miles but a spiritual journey of an inch— very arduous, joyful and humbling, by which we arrive at the ground at our feet and learn to be at home." Our students are learning about their own community, how to be "at home," and, we hope, how to act on the knowledge they acquire. Some of them have assisted with the restoration of the black cemetery in our community. They have catalogued the names of the people buried there as well as helping with the efforts to maintain the cemetery. Over the years, the student projects have taken on different forms, but they all have one element in common—they are tied in an integral way to the world around the students.

One of the most encouraging aspects of the work is that it continues, and as it does, a kind of library of student work is left behind for others. One black student this year has chosen Hall Hollow as the subject of her research. She will start by reading the transcripts of those interviews published in *Mantrip* and listening to tapes. She will add to the body of research already there—student research, and she will go away, as most blacks do in time, because there is not much of a future for young people in this area, but she will leave with a better understanding of where she has come from, and she will have acquired writing and thinking skills that will serve her well, no matter where she chooses to live. She will learn to be at home with herself and her history. I cannot imagine this student or any of the others who have worked on the Hall Hollow project ever asserting that what has happened to people like Hilton Garrett has nothing to do with them. This black history belongs to both the black and white students in my classroom. These young white people may not have posted the "Whites Only" signs or refused to promote a man because of his color, but that history is part of who they are. Just as part of them can be found in men like the white storeowner who coached a little league team in Wheelwright and refused to eat in any restaurant on the road that did not serve both blacks and whites. In the classroom, through their work, we believe that students, both white and black, are reclaiming their past, making it an "ethical repossession" as Jonathan Kozol says we need to. We hope that students see history in human terms, that they will remember the voices of people like Hilton Garrett and what they have learned from them. I have to believe that is important.

One critic of modern life has said that we have lost sight of the genuine in everything that we do, and without that sense, we can do little that has any real meaning. I think he is right. The genuine can be found not only in the writings of people like Faulkner and Hemingway, but also in the voices of the people just beyond our classroom doors. The real fuel is out there—so is the learning. We just have to open the doors.

References

"Bigots in the Ivory Tower." May 7, 1990. *Time*, 104–06.

Cabell, E., and W. Turner. 1985. *Blacks in Appalachia*. Lexington: University Press of Kentucky.

Kozol, J. 1986. *The Night Is Dark and I Am Far from Home*. New York: Continuum.

Moffett, J. 1988. *Coming on Center: English Education in Evolution*. Portsmouth: Boynton.

Montell, W.L. 1970. *The Saga of Coe Ridge: A Study in Oral History*. Knoxville: University of Tennessee Press.

Whisnant, D. 1983. *All That Is Native and Fine: The Politics of Culture in an American Region*. Chapel Hill: University of North Carolina.

6 Telecomputing and Social Action

William W. Wright, Jr.
The BreadNet in the Schools Project

"Maybe this will lead to a grassroots student movement..."
—Greg Coverdale, biology teacher,
Lima, Peru

You have heard the stories about how, in the spring of 1989, Chinese students in Boston faxed clippings describing the Tianamen Square massacre back to their incredulous friends outside (and inside) Beijing. A few weeks before that horrible event that Ted Koppel beamed to our living rooms, former Secretary of the Treasury Blumenthal was on "This Week with David Brinkley." When asked about the democratic reform movement in China, the Soviet Union, and the Eastern Bloc countries, he said that it all stems back to one event: the invention of the computer chip.

Since the summer of 1984, at the Bread Loaf School of English in Middlebury, Vermont—and during the school years at various remote and not-so-remote schools—the computer chip has made it easier for people separated by time, distance, and academic disciplines to work together. Starting with one-to-one electronic links of students and classes, we have evolved to computer conferences that let groups of classrooms collaborate. In this essay, I will tell a little about that evolution—how we at Bread Loaf (and eventually an international group of teachers and students) organized ourselves so that writing and learning could become more of a social activity and lead to social action. Just as the Chinese students organized themselves using electronic mail and facsimile networks, concerned students and teachers in classrooms are beginning to shape themselves into what professor John Elder calls a "community of concern."

What Is Bread Loaf?

The Bread Loaf School of English is one of the ten summer graduate programs of Middlebury College in Vermont. Each summer around

122

250 people—mostly secondary English teachers—come to study literature, writing, and theater with first-rate faculty members. People usually take two courses each summer. In five summers (or fewer) they can get a master's degree. The six-week summer sessions are held at a mountain campus which adjoins the Green Mountain National Forest.

What Is BreadNet?

In 1984, with a grant from Apple Computer, Bread Loaf set up Apple Cellar, a computer writing center. When the Apple Cellar closed down at the end of the summer, computers and modems were mailed out to rural teachers. We wanted to see if (1) students would write more when the drudgery of revision was removed, (2) students would write in a different way if writing could be sent to new audiences across the country, (3) rural schools could benefit from online resources, and (4) teachers could share ideas on a network.

We now (as of the Summer 1990 session) have six school years of experience under our belts and we've come a long way since the first wobbly e-mail (electronic mail) exchanges. Here is a little of what we have learned:

A computer conference (BreadNet is a series of computer conferences) lets geographically dispersed people (or classrooms) use modems and a distance network to accomplish a task. (Modems, as most of you know, let you connect computers to information services through phone lines.) A moderator creates a topic. For example, the topic of one conference was "rain forests." People read notes put up by others and add pieces of writing of their own—at their convenience. (I want to make it clear that it is not like a telephone conference call or a video teleconference; participants do not have to be on at the same time.) Benefits are that you transcend distance and time and there is a written record of the discussion. A computer conference is more dynamic than electronic mail. While e-mail is just a faster version of the paper-and-stamp kind, a computer conference gives you the feel of a community of writers. It is not unlike having a group of people sit around a table and discuss an issue. The wonderful thing about this group is that one person might be in Jakarta, Indonesia, one in Idaho, and one in eastern Kentucky—all reading and writing at their convenience. The "people around the table" can also be classrooms broken into teams of students.

An International Discussion of Environmental Issues

BreadNet has sponsored several projects that let groups of classrooms work together. The most effective ones have had a person in charge (we call them moderators), guidelines so we won't have too much information, and a beginning and an ending. Groups of eight to ten classrooms seem to be about the right size.

In May, 1989, we started a project called "World Class." Participating classes all read an article in *National Geographic* about the destruction of tropical rain forests. A week-long discussion was held on the network. It ended with an essay contest organized by the overseas American Schools in Santiago and Lima, with essays graded by teachers and students in eastern Kentucky.

In November, 1989, we held the second "World Class." Students and teachers read articles about all aspects of the environment in a special issue of *Newsweek*. A major part of this event was an interview with Rick Adcock, U.S. Senator Albert Gore's global environmental specialist. We took selected student questions to his office, recorded his answers, transcribed the tape, and sent his words back to the network.

The most ambitious telecomputing project we set up came in March and April, 1990. It involved the linking of three teacher networks— two in the U.S. and one in London—for seven weeks prior to the twentieth anniversary of Earth Day. Twenty-five overseas schools took part, including ones in Dubai (the United Arab Emirates in the Persian Gulf area), Moscow, Bogota (Colombia), Lima (Peru), and the Shetland Islands (Scotland). We asked twenty teachers from the two other networks (Iris in the U.S., and Campus 2000 in London) to register and agree to certain guidelines. Thirty schools from BreadNet took part.

In the online event that ended on Earth Day 1990, the common reading material was ad-free reprints of *Time* magazine's planet-of-the-year issue (we mailed out over 2,500 copies to the seventy schools in the project). Also in the mailing were how-to-manage ideas for working in the classroom, ideas developed by teachers who had been part of previous online events. We had schools register for the limited number of slots in the seven-week online project. Participating teachers agreed to read and send notes to the conference at least twice a week. Working in a computer conference that started in the fall, a team of eight teachers planned the spring project. Here is the schedule that we mailed out in February:

February 1 [six weeks before classes went online]—BreadNet office mails reading materials to schools. This included tips for how to work with teams of students and manage information in the classroom.

First week—Each class sends to the main conference a half-page introduction. Send to your cluster [there were five clusters or groups of classrooms, called ECO 1, ECO 2, etc., as well as the main conference] one or two informal essays about environmental problems. Begin thinking of five questions that your class wants to ask an online expert, (in this case, the global environmental specialist in Senator Gore's office).

Second week—Moderator of each cluster selects two questions for online guest. Cluster discussion begins. During the week, the moderator sends excerpts to the main conference.

Third week—Clusters discuss global warming and rain forest destruction. Moderator sends excerpts to the main conference.

Fourth week—Clusters take a break. Main conference open to anyone. [We asked that notes be limited to 60 lines.]

Fifth week—Clusters continue. Focus on local problems and how these have national/international problems. Also, what can we do locally to solve the problems we've discussed so far?

Sixth week—Clusters focus on solutions to problems discussed earlier and on answers to questions raised earlier. Suggest ways to take action.

Seventh week—Each class sends two or three essays to a special conference that we set up.

The Opening Day in a Global Classroom

I want to emphasize that a team of teachers had been working online as a planning committee all fall. They debated what should be the common piece of reading, put together tips for teachers who were new at such events, and decided how the seven weeks should be organized.

The six weeks or so before we started the online conference were intense—not unlike the preparation for a big meeting of any kind. We put together materials, copied, stuffed packets, and mailed the reprints of *Time's* planet-of-the-year issue all over the globe. When the day arrived for people to put introductions on the main conference—then move to the smaller conferences (called clusters)—we had the fear that any host must have: that nobody would show up. But they did. Here are samples of the introductions:

1:3) Carol Stumbo   05-MAR-90   0:43

Hello, World Class, from the journalism class at Wheelwright High School. Wheelwright is a small town located in the Appalachian mountains of eastern Kentucky with a population of about seven hundred people. Nuclear power plants, major factories, and massive build-ups of traffic are absent from the lives of people in our community. The environmental problems that most affect the people of eastern Kentucky include the possibility that we may become the dumping ground for other states' solid and chemical waste, an act that promises to add to our landfills and pollute our water and air. Coal mining, the major industry in eastern Kentucky, has been responsible for the destruction of land and the loss of trees, the pollution of water supplies, and worst of all, the creation of acid rain. People in this area depend on coal mining and strong lobbyists have also fought governmental efforts to require the industry to produce "clean burning" coal. We are looking forward to being part of this important discussion on World Class.

1:4) John Forsyth   05-MAR-90   1:38

The 13 ninth graders in Wilsall, Montana say "hi" to all world classers. A brief introduction from the class follows. We'll have more to say in eco3. John Forsyth–teacher.

From the class—Wilsall, Montana is a small ranching community that is located along the Shields River in southwestern Montana. Over 75% of the people in Wilsall are ranchers. Wilsall is only 2 hours away from Yellowstone. So, like our beautiful park, we have blue skies, clear water, and tons of wildlife. But lately, our water hasn't been so clean, our skies not so blue, and our animals not so plentiful. We, like many other places, have an environmental problem of our own. Since this town is so small, people rarely think about such things as throwing garbage out car windows or putting filters on their chimneys to reduce the amount of smoke being thrown into the air from our wood burning stoves. When everyone in town (even if there are only 250 people) forgets about these things, our town can become quite a mess.

1:5) Mindy Moffatt   05-MAR-90   1:55

Hi Everybody!

I'm Mindy Moffatt, 6th grade teacher in Southern California, and the moderator for the cluster group known as eco4. My class and I are excited to be a part of World Class and we look forward to getting to know our friends around the world much better as we work together on this project.

Here is the introduction from my students:

Hello from Greentree Elementary School in Irvine, California! We're a 6th grade class (11 and 12 year olds) in Southern California. There are 30 students in our class representing many nationalities (Vietnamese, East Indian, Korean, Chinese, Iranian, Hispanic, and Peruvian to name a few). We are only 10 miles from the beach. Last month there was a big oil spill in the ocean and on our beaches. We went whale watching and saw a grey whale. We are concerned about the environment and hope to learn more about what we can do to make the world a better place.

1:6) Jakarta   05-MAR-90   2:19
Jakarta Introduction

Hello! We are a group of seventh graders at Jakarta International School who call ourselves the Telecommunicating Conservationists (or T.C.'s). We have chosen to be a part of this project because each one of us is concerned about the environment, and we think our opinions from here in Indonesia are important. Thinking back on our first impressions of Jakarta when we moved here, most of us remember being shocked at its hugeness, its pollution, its crowding, and its dirt. We often see people bathing or washing clothes in muddy, filthy-smelling canals, which are really open sewers. The streets are jammed with people, and there don't seem to be any traffic rules at all. And the smell, a combination of car exhaust, sewer odors, and durian (a fruit resembling carmelized garlic), just about knocks a newcomer out. But there are many beauties in the environment here. Even in the middle of the city, plants flower profusely, and on clear days we can see volcanoes in the distance. Just an hour from Jakarta's port are coral islands where you can forget the city entirely. We've all adjusted to life in Indonesia now. In fact, we like it! After all, who's going to complain about year-round summer? We realize that our first impressions were due to the fact that we were seeing a developing, Third World nation for the first time. Now that we've lived here for a while, some of us for most of our lives, and learned more (in science and now English class!) about conservation, we realize that Indonesia has serious environmental problems, and we'd like to help.

(T.C.'s: Kevin Rennie, Canada; Amanda Kirkham, Canada; Jane Gooding, Canada; Sean Malue, U.S.A.; Lea Ann Leatherwood, U.S.A.; Ayan Dasvarma, Australia) Ayan Dasvarma Jakarta

The good thing about working with other networks is that someone (Bob Shayler with the Iris network) figured out a way for us to include a class in the Soviet Union. That message, for those of us who had grown up during the Cold War, was thrilling. I have not edited the text. Some schools, we must remember, are working in a second language.

1:34) Bob Shayler   06-MAR-90   12:37

H E L L O FROM TROITSK ! ! !

We are members of Bytic youth center in Troitsk, Moscow reg., USSR. We are very happy to take part in the World Class project. This project is really interesting for us because we are worring about ecology situation on Earth and about our future.

Our town is situated near Moscow, it's small but very "green". Our town is not big and isn't old. It's only 15th years old. There are many nice forests around the town. You may say that our town is ecologicaly cleaned but we aren't sure because there are many industry enterprises in our town which soil environment. For example, textile factory which soiling our river.

There are 23 students in our group yet. Mostly our group consist of those students who have been in US or going to this trip. We are students from different schools, but we live in the same town. We splited our group on four parts and each of them consists of 5 or 6 students. The age of each student is from 14 to 16 years old. We all like sport, walk, listen to music, parties very much. We prefer Bytic to school although we must go to school because in Bytic we have opportunity to take part in events of our own interest and to get more information about our friends from other countries.

And some words exactly about Bytic. Bytic is computer center in our town and very many students spend a lot of free time working with computers and solve many different problems. We get a lot of knowledge about different kinds of science. Now we have three branches of Bytic. The first of them is only for using computers, the second one is for phisical experiments with computers and the third one is for ecology.

This is only small part information about us and our Bytic. We are waiting for more information about other classes.

Bytic students and Lena Dudochkin.

A Community of Writers Takes Action

The seven weeks which followed were filled with discussions that ranged from how CFCs (chlorofluorocarbons) cause ozone depletion to what impact some religions have on the environment. While some teachers reported that their students felt helpless when confronted with the bleak news about environmental problems, most in this online community of concern did more than whine. One class in eastern Kentucky went to the local officials and insisted that a cleanup week be declared. A class in Virginia set up a recycling center and pushed for the school to shape up. Their efforts made regional television. Several groups wrote letters to local, state, and national figures. A teacher from Alaska gave firsthand accounts of the oil spill, but did not stop there. She put up a list of resources, such as where to write to get recycled paper. Students added to the list.

The following samples from the network show some of the early exchanges in one of the clusters.

2:4) Donna Frink   13-MAR-90   14:23

Our students from Ligon Middle School in Raleigh, North Carolina, USA are interested in finding out more about our ECO-1 classmates. Here are some questions they have been wondering about.

To the students in the United Kingdom:

Is nuclear energy beginning to effect your lives? Do you have nuclear power plants in your area? How do you feel about nuclear power? If you are not using nuclear energy, what other sources of energy are you using? Sharif Durhams

To the students in Sun Valley, Idaho:

North Carolina is home to many different species of animals. I would like to become more knowledgable about the wildlife in your area and how their habitats are being maintained. Sam Parker

Have you had any acid rain in your area? If so, what are the effects? Tony Mattei

Do the tourists in your area pollute your community more than the citizens do? How large is the town where you live? Marcia Toms

To the students in South Carolina:

How do you feel about North Carolina dumping toxic waste in your state? What solutions do you see for the toxic waste problems in our area? Sharif Durhams

To the students in Toronto, Canada:

Since Toronto has grown rapidly in the past three years, what changes have you seen in pollution in your area? P. J. Puryear

Is your government assisting in the improving of the conditions of the environment in your area? If so, how and what does the government provide to help these problems? Heather Spears

Do you regularly have acid rain in your community and if so how it is effecting your lives? Marcia Toms

To the students in Surrey, BC, Canada:

When we look at the map of Vancouver it looks like you have a similar geography in your coastal area to ours in North Carolina. We have a system of intercoastal waterways and rivers. We are concerned about the pollution in our coastal area and wondered if you have the same concerns.—Telecommunications Class, Ligon Middle School, Raleigh, North Carolina

Do you have a problem with acid rain in your area? Sharif Durhams

To the students in Lima, Peru:

What stand is the government taking on the destruction of the rainforests? Are you near a rainforest? Jamie Taylor

2:8) Carrie Bashaw   15-MAR-90   16:16

Response from Carrie Bashaw's classroom in Sun Valley, Idaho

The rain forests are disappearing fast. One football field of rain forest is cut down every second. Fifty acres are ruined every minute.

People are using slash and burn techniques to destroy the forests. This destroys the ozone and the habitats of many animals. Inhabitants say they need more room for cattle graze, to make coffee fields, and to extend their towns and villages. Because of this, hundreds of different species of plants and animals are wiped out each day. The animals are losing their environment as are the rain forests' natives. The rain forests are very important because not only do they provide a home for half of the worlds' species, they also provide the cures for many diseases. Some people believe that the cure for cancer will be found in the rain forests. Some ideas that our class had for preserving the rain forests are: We have had several fundraisers (we sold one hundred heart-shaped Valentines' cookies) so we can buy rain forest acreage in Belize through an organization in Massachusetts (we have the information if anybody is interested). We are in the process of purchasing three acres thus far. We want others to participate in this so we can make a chain of privately owned acreage across Belize and other rain forest lands. By doing this, we will help to stop the steady progress of deforestation across the forests of South America.

2:9) Carrie Bashaw   15-MAR-90   16:25

Response to Donna Frink's class in North Carolina (Question 1) from The Community School in Sun Valley, Idaho—

There is a lot of wildlife and game in the Ketchum-Sun Valley area. Sun Valley depends on the Snake, Salmon, and Big Wood Rivers because there are all kinds of fish that live in these rivers. Because of overfishing and water pollution, we must restock the waters with fish eggs. Elk are hunted in the area. They are hunted for their meat and hide. Animals like elk, deer, and waterfowl are killed just for sport and food. There are only a certain amount of permits to be bought so people can legally hunt. We do have a small problem with poachers and when they are caught their names appear in the local newspapers. If the winters are rough the elk come down and there is not much food for them. There are cans set up in convenience stores where people can donate money for food for the elk. The Fish and Game Department stocks the areas with hay.

One other thought: our fishermen are very active in promoting the benefits of catch and release fishing—where you hook the fish, yet return them (alive) back to the water. Some people advocate Idaho as someday being a "catch and release" state. [Note: Some people feel that fishing is OK as long as you don't keep the fish; others disagree with this policy, saying that released fish usually do not live very long.]

Do you have a lot of wildlife in your area? How does hunting and pollution affect them?

2:12) Lima   16-MAR-90   14:27

Greetings from Peru! I'd like to reply to Karen Wessel [Karen, a teacher in Alaska started a "resources" discussion on the online service and suggested several ways to be a more responsible consumer; others added to her ideas] on the network and thank her for the excellent information shared recently with World Class. I have written away for the Seventh Generation catalogue and was inspired by the Iroquois quote. I'm using the quote as a topic in my creative writing club. I see our dialogue as having many spinoffs. It is great to feel that we are working positively through World Class to try to improve the environment but I have also been professionally enhanced by the sharing of ideas coming across the network. Again, thank you Karen! Greg Coverdale, Lima, Peru.

2:13) Bill Hay   17-MAR-90   13:02

To: the students in Raleigh, North Carolina:
From: Inter-A, Surrey, BC

We in Surrey have also been concerned with the amount of pollution in our water, especially in our major water ways such as the Fraser river and the coast between Vancouver island and the mainland. We are mostly concerned with oil spills because they damage so much. Scientists have predicted that a major oil spill will hit Washington state or B.C. [British Columbia] in the next five years. The Fraser river, which runs just about a mile north of our school, is in a major industrial area. Because of its position, it gets polluted easily. It does look a lot worse than it is because it stirs up a lot of silt on the river bottom and it runs several hundred miles through B.C. and past several pulp mills. We are doing a geography project to test the chemicals in the Fraser. Is the condition of the Neuse river the same? Howe sound was closed to shellfish fishing because of the two pulp mills dumping stuff into it. The main pollutants are dioxins. Yes, we do have a problem with acid rain, but it is much harder to find information on it because it is not a major environmental issue here. However, the provincial forestry branch had to move a seedling nursery out of this area because of acid rain but that is one of the only stories that I've heard. We believe that there is a major problem with acid rain but we students know too little about it. We would like to know what you know about your acid rain. Our major issues around here are recycling and the logging industry. Mike Watkins and Kevin Walton

2:14) Lima   19-MAR-90   11:46

TO: Donna Frink's students at Ligon MS in Raleigh, NC

The present government here in Peru is not concerned at all about the effects that the destruction of the rain forest will have. Instead of protecting this land, it is giving part of it to peasants in the area so they can grow crops. Fortunately, next month there is going to be a general election, and another government may replace this one, and it might stop the destruction of the Amazon forest in Peru. I do not live near a rain forest, since I live along Peru's coastline and the forest is located much farther inland.

FROM: Daniela Belmont, Colegio Roosevelt, Lima, Peru

2:15) Donna Frink   20-MAR-90   11:49

To the students in Sun Valley, Idaho:

We are very interested in finding out more information about buying rain forest land in Belize. Will you send me some information about this? Jamie Taylor, Ligon Middle School, Raleigh North Carolina

North Carolina is home to many different species of wildlife. I live in Wake County, one of the innermost counties in the state. It is highly industrial, therefore farm land is scarce. I live on a farm outside of the capital city. Since deer and foxes aren't too crazy about the roar of car engines they come and live in our farm community. My brother, father and I don't usually hunt around our farm but go to Bertie County where the deer are over populated. We haven't had much of a problem with poachers, but in Harnet County a man was caught and convicted on charges such as two counts of hunting at night and out of season.

I currently have four pairs of Bobwhite Quail, they are originally native to this part of North Carolina but are hard to find wild. Most hunting clubs raise their birds for shooting. Sam Parker, Ligon Middle School, Raleigh, North Carolina

The following essay from a student in Kentucky shows some of the struggles that took place out in the schools. Carol Stumbo, her teacher, was on the planning committee for the World Class conference, served as a moderator, and continues to make things happen.

Bill,

Up front, I apologize for the length of this note. It was written by a senior during the first week of my journalism class. I have never had this student in class. She was involved in our work last year only as a result of what students did, giving of her own time outside of class. Maybe it is important to post it here.

Carol

Although Wheelwright High School is located in a small community deep in the hills of Floyd County, Kentucky, it has several things to offer that people other than the students don't see. From the outside Wheelwright High School has the worst name of any school in this county. What everyone doesn't see is the real heart, our hard working team of students and faculty. We have worked together as one big team for the past few years. Together we have experienced several important things.

Ms. Carol Stumbo sponsored the Earth Day project that we were involved in most of the last school year. As a group we sat and thought out several ways in which we could clean up our community. Lots of ideas came to our mind but, of course, we could not accomplish them all without the help of others in the surrounding area. Concerned citizens volunteered to help with the clean up program.

Although we had the help of others, there were some students who couldn't have cared less about what happened to the environment.

As devoted environmentalists, we stuck together, no matter how tough it seemed to be getting. We ignored the students that didn't seem to care about what we were doing. We taught other students at our school and those at the local elementary schools about the environment. We visited other elementary schools and helped them get projects started. We became angry quite a few times at the apathy of some of our students and even started to call it quits. We even started to think that there was no use in going on with what we were trying to do but it wasn't that easy. Giving up would have been the worst thing to do, so as hard as it seemed, we kept up the struggle.

We sponsored a recycling drive which allowed students to bring in aluminium cans which would later be transferred to Prestonsburg, Kentucky. The money that we received was divided between the student or group of students that brought in the most cans and the school itself. We wrote articles for the local paper. We spoke to the city council and local civic organizations about the need to clean up our district.

On several occasions people passing by would glance over and wonder what are those children doing in the creek. Actually, we were cleaning the creek out. Wearing rubber gloves, boots, and pulling our hair back didn't bother us at all.

Our environmental group even planted several trees around our community. Not only did we thrive on the importance of our surrounding environment being clean but we looked at issues that affect the entire world. As a group we studied pollution across the nation such as the acid rain in Canada and the burning of the Amazon Forest in South America.

Together we thought out solutions to some of the problems that exist in our local area. We looked at other serious problems outside our community such as the smoke from factory smoke stacks or the oil spills in Alaska. We did something important together.

Tonya and her friends in Kentucky were part of seventy classrooms that did something important together. We hope that Greg Coverdale in Lima is right—that this will be the beginning of a global student movement, a global community of people who will learn from each other, write to the people who can make changes, and continue to take action.

III Teaching Writing for Social Responsibility

7 Empowering the Voiceless to Preserve the Earth

Daniel L. Zins
The Atlanta College of Art

Teaching Writing in an Age of Mass Death

I have been teaching three sections of Composition 101 in the Liberal Arts Department of The Atlanta College of Art each year since the fall of 1978. I have regularly made changes in these classes, but the most important transformation occurred in 1988 when I decided that "Preserving the Earth" would become the course theme.

Beginning with my first composition class more than a decade ago, I have allocated two to three weeks of each semester for discussing the threat of nuclear war. But, over the years, I have come to believe more and more strongly that none of our students should leave our colleges and universities without a higher level of "nuclear literacy" than is likely to result from experiencing merely a few class sessions on this issue. Thus, about two years ago I decided that I would devote about *two-thirds* of the semester to the indissolubly linked problems of nuclear war, militarism, and the making and unmaking of enemies. As it happens, soon after I made this major change in the course, it became more and more clear that—largely because of the bold leadership of Mikhail Gorbachev—the Cold War was finally ending. It would be most unfortunate, however, if members of our profession were to conclude that this superpower rapprochement and the subsequent collapse of the Soviet Union absolves them from having to grapple with these issues in their teaching.

Because in our century human beings have killed more than one hundred million of their fellow human beings, and because we now have the technology to dwarf even that number, educators have, perhaps, no more important task than to help their students to understand the various ways human beings dehumanize and demonize other human beings, and to explore with them how we might be able to end this now prohibitively dangerous practice. Thus, the central

137

text for my class is Sam Keen's *Faces of the Enemy: Reflections of the Hostile Imagination.*[1] Illustrated with hundreds of examples of poster art, cartoons, photographs, and other images of how enemies have been portrayed by various nations throughout this century, Keen's study also provides a perspicacious analysis of how and why enemies are created, dehumanized, and destroyed.

According to Keen, "the two major problems that will have to be solved if we are to survive long beyond the twentieth century—the habit of warfare and ecological pollution—are two sides of a single coin. When we define ourselves as superior to our neighbors and to nature, we inevitably create a hostile environment, an ecology of violence."[2] One of the most obvious manifestations of the demise of the Cold War is the striking metamorphosis of national security discourse, with superpower leaders and many other elites now suggesting that the possibility of *environmental* holocaust, and not the threat of nuclear war, is the cardinal danger facing humanity. Due primarily to increased mass media coverage of the topic, one finds little difficulty today convincing most students that environmental issues merit much greater attention in the classroom.

But with *glasnost, perestroika,* the marked amelioration of U.S.–Independent Commonwealth relations, and the stunning changes in Eastern Europe, our culture now seems to be pervaded with the complacent assumption that *ipso facto* the nuclear predicament itself has been forever resolved, and that we no longer need to be particularly concerned about the Bomb.[3] If the possibility of nuclear holocaust has never been an easy "subject" to teach—even when the Soviet Union appeared particularly menacing—those who believe that this issue must still be confronted are now faced with a much more formidable challenge. I fear that for all but a few educators "nuclear war" will again become a nonissue. Although, in *some* important ways, the danger of nuclear holocaust obviously has diminished, I submit that another cycle of cultural apathy toward the Bomb is unwarranted—and will surely have detrimental, and quite possibly grave, consequences.

Race, Class, Gender, and the Bomb

Much of the great canon controversy of recent years has centered around questions of class, race, and gender. Like many other educators, I have long lamented the shameful neglect of these issues in traditional humanities education. It behooves us to redouble our efforts to correct this problem. But, in the extensive canon debates decrying this omission, far too little attention has been given to another serious lacuna: the failure of humanists to focus a great deal more of their teaching and research on past, current, and possible future episodes of genocide.

Early in my course, I tell my students that they have probably heard, more than a few times, that the purpose of their education is to prepare them for the future. Acknowledging that this is *one* of the purposes of my teaching, I then stress that because we live in a century of mass extermination of human beings—and the relentless, and, recently, ominously accelerated, extinction of countless species of plants and animals—I have another, perhaps even more important, responsibility: helping them to investigate what can be done to increase the chances that they and other life forms on our planet will indeed *have* a future. I see no reason why educators cannot confront this ultimate concern and, at the same time, also address issues of class, race, and gender. In fact, most of the readings for my composition course (which, in future semesters, will continue to focus on enemies, militarism, and possible nuclear and environmental holocausts) have been selected precisely because they also deal with poverty, racism, and/or sexism.

For example, after thoroughly discussing Martin Luther King's "Letter From Birmingham Jail," we turn our attention to three essays which share a number of his central concerns. "The Other Side of the Trident Tracks," by Buck Jones and Jim Douglass, urges us to open our eyes to the enormous suffering resulting from the invisible *structural* violence of the negative peace which still prevails in much of the world, and in many parts of our own society. Robert Coles's "Children and the Bomb" focuses on how young people of various races and economic levels view the nuclear threat. Gary Smith's "Peace Warriors," a sympathetic but not uncritical examination of the continual civil disobedience of the Berrigan brothers and Elizabeth McAlister (and how the children of Philip Berrigan and his wife might be affected by the extraordinary sacrifices their parents make for peace), has elicited a wide range of often passionate responses from my students. Like Douglass and Jones, the Berrigans would like us to ask ourselves how we are able to "live quietly in a country spending *three-quarters of a billion dollars each day on armies and weapons while 40,000 of the world's children each day died of illness and malnutrition? Well, you are, you are!* The bomb is killing *right now!*"[4]

Because every human being is at least a potential victim of nuclear technology, I think it is still of great value for all of us to try to empathize with the first victims of the nuclear age. Thus, after having my students examine two powerful works of art inspired by the atomic bombings of Japan,[5] we read two moving short stories which focus on more recent, and possible future, victims of the nuclear age: Yves Theriault's "Akua Nuten (The South Wind)" and W. C. Bamberger's "The Last Fence."[6] Theriault, himself a descendant of Montagnais Indians, dramatizes the confrontation of an innocent bystander from the Third World and an affluent but desperate white family seemingly unaware that there might be nowhere to hide from a major nuclear war. Bamberger dramatizes how Native Americans in New Mexico who are dying from uranium mining convene a colloquy to debate whether it will be possible to ever end their victimization if they continue to grant officials in Washington the power to frame the issue.

"The Last Fence" nicely introduces a crucial topic that has always been one of my principal pedagogical concerns: the enormous power of language, and how easily it can be—and how often it *is*—used to manipulate and deceive us. Because so much of the language surrounding nuclear "war" and nuclear "weapons" is especially misleading, I encourage my students to put these two words in quotation marks, as a periodic reminder that what we are talking about here has very little in common with their received notions of war and weapons.

To illuminate why so much of the discourse on nuclear "war" and nuclear "weapons" is obsolete and insidious, I have my students read James J. Farrell's *The Nuclear Devil's Dictionary* and Carol Cohn's already frequently anthologized 1987 essay on nukespeak. Inspired by Ambrose Bierce and George Orwell, and illustrated with many apposite cartoons, Farrell's witty and satirical dictionary, the author informs us in his introduction, "merely translates the vulgar vocabulary of nuclear nukespeak into common English in order to keep us all from being lexi-conned by the powers that be."[7]

After spending a year of her life immersed in the world of America's defense intellectuals, Cohn became convinced not only of the value, but also of the hazards, of learning to speak "technostrategic" language: it is not merely an additive, but rather a transformative, process. As she learned and began using technostrategic discourse, which rarely considers the victims' point of view, Cohn found it difficult *not* to think like a "defense intellectual."

"Those of us who find U.S. nuclear policy desperately misguided," Cohn concludes in her feminist analysis, "appear to face a quandary. If we refuse to learn the language, we are virtually guaranteed that our voices will remain outside the 'politically relevant' spectrum of opinion. Yet, if we do learn and speak it, we not only severely limit what we can say but we also invite the transformation, the militarization, of our own thinking."[8] This dilemma is very real, and admits of no easy solution. I tell my own students that I believe it is a mistake not to achieve at least some mastery of technostrategic discourse, but I also caution them that if they fail to continuously, and very carefully, monitor their own thinking while they are reading, hearing, or using it, it is highly possible that they will end up acquiescing to ideas and policies that are not in accord with their own ideals and values.

Many of my students become both astonished and outraged as they, for the first time in their lives, actually begin decoding nuclear discourse. After reading Cohn's essay, one student wrote, ". . . there were several points brought up which annoyed me. 'Human death simply is collateral damage.' How can anyone say a human life is collateral? What are we, slaves? We as human beings are not property owned by our governments." Somewhat puzzled by one of Farrell's definitions, another student remarked, "I've become accustomed to euphemized language but isn't it illegal to speak of things as totally opposite what they truly are? Can our president lie to us that much? How he [Reagan] gets 'Peacekeeper' out of MX missiles is beyond me; then again, it would be real peaceful if everyone were dead." Like Farrell, more than a few of my students understand that it is best not to enter the bizarre world of nukespeak without a sense of humor.

I, too, try to keep this in mind when choosing other readings and films on this forbidding topic. In past years I have used Kurt Vonnegut's novel, *Cat's Cradle*, and Tim O'Brien's short story "Civil Defense," a humorous account of a young boy who does not find growing up in the 1950s near Montana's nuclear missile fields particularly amusing.[9] Of course, a number of darkly humorous films are also available on nuclear weapons. In addition to the brilliant *Dr. Strangelove*, I have also used, at various times, *Atomic Cafe*, and *When the Wind Blows*, an adaptation of Raymond Briggs's fine comic book about the futile attempts of a hapless elderly British couple to cope with the aftermath of nuclear war.

For the past several years I have also shown my students the "peace through strength" film *Countdown for America*, and various readings whose perspectives I do not share.[10] Given that the "Pentagon propaganda machine," the mass media, and most high schools ensure that students entering college classrooms are already quite familiar with mainstream arguments, it would not appear to be incumbent upon us to always provide "equal time" on important and controversial issues. Nonetheless, I think it is a good idea to help students to become critical readers of all kinds of texts, including verbal and visual mainstream texts on war and militarism. For example, one of my students, after reading a half-dozen short essays from very different perspectives on the question of whether humanity would "survive" a nuclear war,[11] wrote in her journal that one thing which really scared her

> was something I found out about myself. I read six different viewpoints, and at the end of each essay, I was just about convinced. My opinion was swayed between two polar opposites in a matter of 3 pages! I think (and hope) that it had something to do with the fact that I *wanted* to believe all the positive viewpoints. I hate to think that I'm *really* that vulnerable to everything I hear.

If most of our students *are* terribly vulnerable to the plethora of specious arguments that they read and hear about nuclear weapons, the only effective antidote is to help them to become much more critical readers of the entire range of discourse on this and other controversial issues.

Empowerment and Democracy

Throughout the nuclear age, unfortunately, we have never had anything even approaching a genuine public debate on issues of nuclear weapons or national security. All but a few citizens, and all but a few educators, have consistently deferred to the "experts," the nuclear priesthood, on these concerns. One particularly unfortunate result of widespread citizen indifference throughout the nuclear age has been unconscionable levels of "weaponry" and military spending. An equally baleful, but rarely acknowledged, consequence also needs to be underscored: when security policies are conceived and implemented with so little public involvement, our very democracy, which these policies are purportedly defending, is undermined in fundamental ways. Interestingly, two of my students *did* acknowledge this in their journals. "If we must keep nuclear weapons for freedom's sake," one student perceptively observed, "then we have already taken our own freedom. Truly free people do not live in the malignant shadow of destruction." And his classmate wrote that "as long as one person controls the button, ours is no longer a democracy."

Thus, I urge my students *not* to leave these issues to the "experts" who have never been able even to agree on what the central questions are,[12] let alone on how we might devise an international security regime which has a chance of engendering a stable, just, and durable peace. I try to convince my students that if they are willing to consistently give even a modest amount of their time to learning more about these issues, there is no reason that they should not be able to participate intelligently in national security debates. And I even suggest that perhaps they cannot be responsible citizens in a nuclear age if they *fail* to do this.

The pedagogy that I employ and the writing exercises that I require are intended to give my students sufficient confidence in the worth of their own voices so that never again will they feel comfortable leaving issues that profoundly affect their own lives and futures to others. Rather than doing a great deal of lecturing, I ask my students many questions on assigned readings (or the topic we are discussing), and I urge them to formulate their own questions. Because so much of our public discourse addresses only the symptoms of our most pressing problems, I am especially concerned that my students learn how to ask really *intelligent* questions, questions that penetrate to the very heart of the most important issues of our time. I believe that once students begin to do this, they are likely not only to have considerably less awe of many of our so-called experts, but will also apprehend that, when it comes to many national security and environmental issues, they will be much better served if they can become *their own* experts. In a culture that cries out for genuine leadership, there may be no more important purpose of education.

Although I require a number of formal essays and a research paper of my students, in an important sense it is the journal that is at the heart of my course. I have found that journals can be very effective in helping students to find and validate their own unique voices, and to exhume thoughts and feelings that have been partly or deeply buried. This is especially important with regard to nuclear issues, which, understandably, have often been almost wholly repressed.

I have had my composition students write nuclear journals for many years now, and I have received a wealth of fascinating material. At the very beginning of the semester, before my students hear my own views, I have them write several pages on "growing up in the nuclear age," or "living in the shadow of the bomb." Accentuating that, above all, I want an *honest* account of what they really think and feel, I inform them that they can write about *anything* that in any way touches on the assigned topic: books they have read on nuclear weapons issues, nuclear war films, music or art focusing on this problem, conversations with their family or friends, anything they've noticed in the mass media (and how the media framed and presented it), whether and to what extent the Bomb was discussed in any of their high school classes, and nuclear dreams. I also encourage students to jot down any questions they may have on this topic. As the course progresses, I ask them to use their journals to monitor how their thinking and feelings might be changing, and to respond to any films I show, or class discussions, or conversations they are having on nuclear issues. For some of the required readings, I have my students write short formal essays, but for others I allow them to comment in their journals. At the end of the semester I have them write a brief entry reflecting any final thoughts, conclusions, or comments on the course.

The first two semesters that I gave primacy to the nuclear threat, most of my students responded very favorably to the course. During the past two semesters, however, enthusiasm for the course has waned somewhat, with more than a few students expressing a desire to spend additional time on environmental issues. I have recently begun to devote more class time to our rapidly deteriorating biosphere, and in the future I intend to allocate about as much time for the threat of *environmental* holocaust as for the possibility of nuclear holocaust, enemy-making, war, and militarism.[13] Moreover, I will continue to try to make my students more aware of why militarism and environmental destruction are often very closely linked. In my class, we make the transition from nuclear and military issues to environmental ones by viewing the new film by Mark Mori and Susan Robinson, *Building Bombs*, a look inside the Savannah River nuclear weapons plant. In addition to examining the crises of conscience of individuals who work on thermonuclear weapons, *Building Bombs* also paints a chilling picture of the extensive poisoning of the land and water at and around the plant.

Thinking and Writing About the Unthinkable

The end of the Cold War notwithstanding, our students will perforce have to live out the rest of their lives in the nuclear age, and they should know something about it. Because high schools have largely neglected this issue, most of our students know very little about the history of the nuclear age, the quantity and quality of current arsenals, targeting plans, actual versus declared policies, the particulars of military spending and waste, or connections between interventionist foreign policies and nuclear strategy. Unless ordinary citizens become considerably more informed on these matters, we risk squandering an historic opportunity to reduce the risk of nuclear war much further yet, and to achieve much more reasonable Pentagon budgets.

Noting that she was curious about the development of the first nuclear weapons, one of my students wrote in her initial journal, "I am glad that I am finally getting an opportunity to learn about all this. Hopefully my questions will be answered. Can we compare nuclear wars to the wars of the past?" If many of our students have difficulty appreciating the inconceivable destructive power of the Bomb—I emphasize that however horribly destructive today's "conventional" weapons have become, thermonuclear weapons differ from them not merely in kind, but in degree—there are also a number of individuals who exaggerate their power. According to one of my students, Pat Frank's novel *Alas, Babylon* (which he had read the previous year), "wasn't very accurate because with the amount of weapons around today we could blow the earth out of orbit and into another solar system."

Although many of our students have heard that we have enough nuclear weapons to blow up the earth any number of times over, most of them still have difficulty visualizing just how many nuclear warheads actually exist. A student wrote, "One of the things that was brought to my attention was the number of nuclear weapons we have. I knew there were more than enough to blow the world up but I didn't know how much more. The dot chart[14] that was passed around the class had a dramatic effect on my conceptions and I think the whole class's. The quantity of nuclear weapons is absurd. What are we going to do with all these warheads?" Many of my students have expressed surprise, and, not infrequently, amazement, as they learn more and more details about the nuclear predicament. As one student observed at the end of the course, "This class has certainly opened my eyes to many subjects often hidden during my 'education' at high school."

In my teaching I am especially concerned with having my students confront issues that they would otherwise likely not engage. And, of course, few issues have been more assiduously eschewed in our culture than that of nuclear weapons. "The Bomb is a difficult subject for me to deal with," one of my students acknowledged. "In fact, it is one that I have *had* to push to the back of my mind." Another journal began: "Nuclear Stuff. I can't believe I'm sitting here about to write about nuclear stuff! If there's any issue I try to avoid thinking about, this is it. Until this point I've been quite successful at avoiding the issue. I've intentionally become very callous in regard to the subject."

It is hardly surprising, then, that not all of my students have been ecstatic upon learning what they will be studying in Composition 101. In her final entry one student wrote, "I remember what I wrote in my first journal. I was scared to death to take your class, but I'm glad I did. In fact, I probably would have been worse off had I *not* taken it.

I learned a lot about things that should have been told to me a *long* time ago." Well into the semester, another student shared these thoughts:

> When I first came into my composition class and listened to Mr. Zins speak, I felt a very hostile attitude toward him and his class. Everything that he spoke about had to do with ideas that I just simply don't care about one way or another. Spending an entire semester on the subject of nuclear war? I told myself this had to be a joke. There was no way that I was going to waste my time listening to some hippie speak about saving the world. However, as you can see, I am now spending my valuable time writing down my thoughts. I feel like I may have come to a revelation in my life.

This student, who wrote a number of very thoughtful papers during the semester, came to the realization that perhaps he had previously given very little thought to the issue of nuclear war because of *fear*. "Could this fear be so great," he asked himself, "that it sent a mental block when it came to thinking about nuclear war?"

But most of my students during the past two years, it should be noted, have not appeared to approach the course with undue trepidation. "I don't really know enough about this topic," one student admitted. "I wish I did. I hope to learn a lot more about not only English but your theme to the course." And another student announced in her first entry: "I am very excited about this class. I want to learn more about this threat my generation has been saddled with. The sins of the parents are definitely visited upon the children."

On the first day of class, as students look over the course syllabus, they read: "The nuclear age has been called the age of anxiety. It is also, unfortunately, an age of pervasive cynicism. Because I am convinced that this cynicism has very harmful and dangerous consequences, I believe it is imperative that we discuss possible reasons for the sense of helplessness, powerlessness, and fatalism we see all around us." What I find particularly distressing is that so many of today's *youth* are already profoundly cynical. Over the years, an alarming number of my students have articulated sentiments like these:

> I'm just one peon in this massive, over-populated, junk-infested earth. I feel I cannot do anything to help the world. Call me a pessimist. I just get angry thinking about it. We are raised in a society that says, 'Look out for yourself and then worry about others.' I haven't even found myself yet, so what am I supposed to do? I think someone who cares a lot more than me will do something. At least I hope.

Many young people seem to believe that about the only way things might be improved is by protesting; yet they are convinced that even protesting is ultimately pointless. "I have seen how difficult it is for radicals or protesters to change the minds of those in government," lamented one student. "On Merritt Island (where Kennedy Space Center is located) people protest 'blast-offs' left and right. They get arrested, and the rockets go off. The protesters seem to fail every time they seem to make a difference. Protesting seems like a complete waste of time to me."

If many students dismiss the value of peaceful protest out of hand, others are apparently unaware even of the *existence* of the massive antinuclear protests that erupted little more than a decade ago. One student, for example, assumed that "no one really does anything about this ominous threat," while another, after our discussion of Martin Luther King's "Letter From a Birmingham Jail," concluded that

> if we could only find a man that would fight that hard for the end of nuclear arms, we could very well have hope in ending the arms race. If we could just find one man that would put his life on the line, then maybe we would realize just how important the issue is. America needs someone who will stand up against the government for the things that are right. The problem is that no one wants to do it. . . . until at least one person does this, I'm afraid I can find no hope.[15]

My students have expressed their sense of despondency, despair, and fatalism in many different ways. One wrote, "My hopelessness and frustration and plain fear cause me to doubt the wisdom of bringing children into the world. I cannot, practically, believe man will wake up before he destroys himself." Another student, fearing that human beings "are the next dinosaurs," added that occasionally she does "feel optimistic, when I feel that maybe people will change, but the number of people who want change is too small. I hope one day soon our future on this planet will become important enough to save it. But I doubt it." Even more grimly resigned was the freshman who declared, "I really don't care if the bomb was planned for take off today or tomorrow. Why fear for your life if you have no control over what takes place in your life?"

Over the years, a disturbingly large number of my students have persuaded themselves that they really do have "no control" over major social and political issues. And that this must always be the case. A not uncommon form of this fashionable fatalism was expressed by the student who wrote, "If it is God's will that a nuclear war happens, one will happen. If not, there will be no war." But, for another student, the issue was not necessarily quite this simple:

> I don't think that there will be an all-out nuclear war. I don't
> think we or any other big country are that stupid. Still, if that's
> the way God wants the world to end, then that's probably what
> will happen. That doesn't mean we should sit around and see
> what is going to happen. We should do what we can to avoid it.
> I don't know of a lot to do, however. I'm open to suggestions.

While some students have convinced themselves that there is nothing
they can do about such issues as unbridled militarism or environmental
destruction because they would rather not have to in any way
inconvenience themselves or make the commitment and sacrifices
required to combat these evils, I am sure that more than a few others
would be willing to work to make the world a better and more just
place if they could be persuaded that the actions of ordinary citizens
really *do* make a difference. Thus, it is crucial that we do more to
enlighten our students about what *is* being done, and what else *could*
be done—individually, locally, nationally, and globally—to prevent
needless suffering and the killing of human beings and other life
forms.

Making a sharp distinction between a healthy skepticism, which I
urge my students to cultivate, and cynicism,[16] which, I suggest, is not
only corrosive of the human spirit but has very deleterious practical
consequences, I discuss possible reasons why so many of my students
over the years have convinced themselves that they, and their society,
are without viable alternatives. And I also suggest that it is important
to interrogate who might *benefit* from this widespread passivity, ac-
quiescence, and resignation.[17] I discuss cynicism at considerable length
with my students because I believe that such an attitude exacerbates
many of our most pressing problems and virtually ensures that solutions
to them will continue to elude us. And, more importantly, I am
convinced that *cynicism itself* is one of the major problems of our time.
"Power corrupts," writes Sam Keen, "but so does powerlessness."[18] I
think we scarcely realize just how much both real—and imagined—
powerlessness has already corrupted our students. Or how much it
may have corrupted their educators as well.

It is especially gratifying to me, then, when I see students transcend-
ing their learned helplessness and powerlessness, and renouncing their
roles as passive victims. "I've come to understand that I matter," one
student asseverated. "I am no special wonder in this world but I do
have a voice. Just existing as a single human being allows me to have
some say, however small it may be, in what goes on in the world. . . .
I can make a difference in this world." Another student thanked me
for making her "aware of the nuclear difficulties in our world" and

"for opening [her] eyes to the changes that can be made." And an individual who chose to focus on what she perceived as the more immediate environmental threat remarked, "I know things can be done. I also know not to buy styrofoam cups anymore, not to use aerosol hairspray, to never start my car again. . . ." Or, perhaps, at least to start it somewhat less often.

One of my students, who found the time we spent on nuclear war "interesting," added that she still preferred not to think about the issue and had not changed her mind "about what can be done: not much." But she pointed out that the time we devoted to "nuke war" probably "was beneficial to some people; I'm talking about those who wouldn't ever give much thought to those issues otherwise. You definitely got the class thinking." She also complained that she was unable to get one of her classmates "to shut up about nuclear war. He kept doing all these war themes for our projects in studio classes."

In fact, over the years many of my students have limned nuclear themes in their studio work, and more than a few of them have expressed their increased concern about this issue in various other ways. Some have joined Greenpeace and other antiwar and environmental organizations. Two of my students took a semester-long independent study course with me on nuclear war to enhance their understanding of the subject. One of my students completed the transcontinental Great Peace March. Others have been involved in a peace camp and have engaged in nonviolent civil disobedience. Two of my first-year students produced a hilarious video about the availability (and quality) of bomb shelters near our school, and another individual made a significant contribution to an award-winning film on the manufacture of nuclear weapons. While all of these actions are the result of a congeries of factors, quite a number of my students have made it clear to me that it has been my own concern which has encouraged them to become actively involved with antinuclear and, especially more recently, environmental issues.

Environmental Holocaust

As previously mentioned, it is the destruction of the environment that is concerning more and more of my students.[19] Ruminating on the possibility of nuclear war, one student wrote, "I often wonder if the day will ever come. But worrying never solved anything so why not get on with it and try to solve some more pressing problems, i.e., starvation, overpopulation, or environment to name only a few. Let's just stop worrying about what we cannot control." The suggestion here, of course, is that, unlike the possibility of nuclear war, an environmental holocaust *can* be prevented by concerted human action. Similarly, another student found it

> strange how part of the population is so concerned about the nuclear age which is upon us. The reason: every day this wonderful, advanced creature called man, is polluting and slowly but surely destroying our society. With the waste, harmful pollutants and the barbaric slaughter of forests (our main source of oxygen) the world will eventually turn out the same as if there were a nuclear holocaust.

Two other students expressed appreciation for becoming much more enlightened about nuclear weapons issues, but indicated that they would have preferred more class time on the environment. "I am really appalled by the destruction of our earth and the reasons for it," wrote one student, while his classmate observed that "the environment is really to me the pressing issue." And another student, like more than a few of his peers, found it "very difficult . . . to believe that the money put into the nuclear arms race is not being invested in the restoration of our quickly deteriorating environment." "Apart from the nukes," he added, "I'm glad to see someone who cares about our ecology. . . . From this point on I will try my hardest to be aware of my environment and to keep it clean and healthy."

I am confident that this individual, and many other students who take my writing classes, will entertain the possibility that constructing a well-written paragraph, or essay, or research paper, is not necessarily the only, or perhaps even the most important, mission of "Composition 101."

Notes

1. Even if the Cold War *is* over, this is still a book that everyone should read. I would also highly recommend John W. Dower's *War Without Mercy: Race and Power in the Pacific War,* an extended meditation on Keen's theme. With the ending of the Cold War, most Americans (according to a recent poll) believe that Japan is now the greatest threat to the United States. Thus the lessons of Dower's incisive study have become even more important.

2. 135.

3. Three antidotes for complacency might be William A. Schwartz and Charles Derber, *The Nuclear Seduction: Why the Arms Race Doesn't Matter and What Does;* Desmond Ball and Robert C. Toth, "Revising the STOP: Taking War-Fighting to Dangerous Extremes"; and a recently publicized event: Iraq's clear intention to acquire or produce nuclear weapons.

4. Jones and Douglas, *Fellowship* (December, 1988), 5–6, 21; Coles, *New York Times Magazine* (December 8, 1985), 44ff.; and Smith, *The Washington Post Magazine* (June 5, 1988), 22ff. (The quote is from page 26.)

5. Japanese Broadcasting Corporation. 1977; and John W. Dower and John Junkerman.

6. Theriault in H. Bruce Franklin, 1984, *Countdown to Midnight: Twelve Great Stories About Nuclear War;* and Bamberger in John Witte, 1984, *Warnings: An Anthology of the Nuclear Peril.* In both stories we see how the bomb, social class, and racism are indissolubly linked. (The bomb and racism also intersect in another short story we read, Langston Hughes's "Radioactive Redcaps.")

7. James J. Farrell, *The Nuclear Devil's Dictionary,* 3.

8. Carol Cohn. "Sex and Death in the Rational World of Defense Intellectuals," 716.

9. Originally published in *Esquire* (August, 1980), this story now appears in somewhat altered form as chapter two of O'Brien's novel *The Nuclear Age* (New York: Alfred A. Knopf, 1985).

10. Also worth considering for classroom use is the film *To What End?,* which very fairly presents the following four viewpoints: peace through strength, strategic defense, arms control, and disarmament.

11. In Bonnie Szumski.

12. See Paul Bracken and Martin Shubik.

13. But in this essay I will focus primarily on the nuclear threat which, I would like to reiterate, still merits more than a marginal slot in all college curriculums.

14. This chart has 121 squares; the single dot in the center square represents all of the firepower of World War II; all of the other squares, which are nearly filled with dots, represent the firepower in existing nuclear arsenals. "Nuclear Weapons Chart" obtained from Promoting Enduring Peace, P.O. Box 5103, Woodmont, CT 06460.

15. After reading Gary Smith's essay on the Berrigans, this student realized that some citizens *have* made an extraordinary effort to combat nuclearism and militarism. Of course I made it clear that the Berrigans have hardly been alone in this struggle, even if their sacrifices are indeed much greater than most are willing to make.

16. Just as I point out that, for me, a healthy skepticism and cynicism are two profoundly different things, I also discuss at some length why, in a culture where we see so much blind and militaristic "nationalism" masquerading as "patriotism," it is most unfortunate that these two very different terms are also often used interchangeably. See Wendell Berry's superb essay, "Property, Patriotism, and National Defense."

17. On the difference between *superstitious* helplessness and *learned* helplessness, see Nicholas Humphrey and Robert Jay Lifton.

18. Keen, see note 1, 154.

19. Our major text on the environment was Bill Devall and George Sessions. I also shared with my students the views of a number of deep ecology's critics, including Tim Luke, and Murray Bookchin. We next read selections from Judith Plant's excellent anthology, *Healing the Wounds: The Promise of*

Ecofeminism. A number of contributors to this anthology very efficaciously link environmental destruction with other major social problems and issues. We concluded the course by perusing the final section of John Robbins, *Diet for a New America,* which exposes the staggering environmental costs of the meat industry and Americans' carnivorous eating habits.

References

Ball, D., and R. Toth. 1990. "Revising the SIDP: Taking War-Fighting to Dangerous Extremes." *International Security,* 14:4.

Bamberger, W. 1984. "The Last Fence." In J. Witte *Warnings: An Anthology of the Nuclear Peril.* Eugene: Northwest Review Books, 74–80.

Berry, W. *Home Economics.* San Francisco: North Point Press.

Bracken, P., and M. Shubik. 1982. "Strategic War: What Are the Questions and Who Should Ask Them?" *Technology in Society,* 4(3): 155–79.

Bookchin, M. 1988. "Social Ecology Versus Deep Ecology." *Socialist Review,* 88(3): 10–29.

Cohn, C. 1987. "Sex and Death in the Rational World of Defense Intellectuals." *Signs,* 12:4.

Coles, R. 1985. "Children and the Bomb." *New York Times Magazine* (December): 44ff.

Devall, B., and G. Sessions. 1985. *Deep Ecology: Living as if Nature Mattered.* Salt Lake City: Gibbs M. Smith, Inc.

Dower, J. 1986. *War Without Mercy: Race and Power in the Pacific War.* New York: Pantheon Books.

Dower, J., and J. Junkerman. 1985. *The Hiroshima Murals of Iri and Toshi Maruki.* New York: Kodansha International.

Farrell, J. 1985. *The Nuclear Devil's Dictionary.* Minneapolis: Usonia Press.

Franklin, H. 1984. *Countdown to Midnight: Twelve Great Stories about Nuclear War.* New York: Daw Books.

Humphrey, N., and R. Lifton. 1984. *In a Dark Time.* Cambridge: Harvard University Press.

Japanese Broadcasting Corporation. 1977. *Unforgettable Fire: Pictures Drawn by Atomic Bomb Survivors.* New York: Pantheon.

Jones, B., and J. Douglas. 1988. "The Other Side of the Trident Tracks." *Fellowship* (December, 1988): 5–6, 21.

Keen, S. 1986. *Faces of the Enemy: Reflections of the Hostile Imagination.* New York: Harper and Row.

Luke, T. 1988. "The Dreams of Deep Ecology." *Telos,* 76: 65–92.

O'Brien, T. 1985. *The Nuclear Age.* New York: Alfred A. Knopf.

Plant, J. 1989. *Healing the Wounds: The Promise of Ecofeminism.* Santa Cruz: New Society Publishers.

Robbins, J. *Diet for a New America.* Walpole, N.H.: Stillpoint Publishing.

Schwartz, W., and C. Derber. 1990. *The Nuclear Seduction: Why the Arms Race Doesn't Matter and What Does.* Berkeley: University of California Press.

Smith, G. 1988. "Peace Warriors." *The Washington Post Magazine* (June 5): 22ff.

Szumski. 1986. *Nuclear War: Opposing Viewpoints*. St. Paul: Greenhaven Press.

Theriault, Y. "Akua Nuten (The South Wind)" in H. Franklin (ed.). *Countdown to Midnight: Twelve Great Stories about Nuclear War.* New York: Daw Books, 134–45.

8 "Writing in the Margins": A Lesbian- and Gay-Inclusive Course

Ellen Louise Hart with Sarah-Hope Parmeter
University of California at Santa Cruz

"Everybody would be a better student in this whole country if they were taught to write how they felt and not what they thought they were supposed to say."[1] These observations grew out of a student's experience in my intermediate writing course on research methodology called "Lesbian and Gay Research Matters!" Gillian had used the course to write about her father, who is gay, and to begin research for a book she plans to write on gay fathers. Later, she was asked in an interview why she thought lesbian and gay issues should be discussed in a writing course rather than being left to literature, or political science, or sociology courses. A writing course is the first place lesbian and gay issues belong, she responded, because writing about lesbian and gay experience and about homophobia, the fear of lesbians and gays, requires students to put themselves into their papers, and this means learning that personal writing is a legitimate form of academic writing.

I was taught to teach students to write about how they felt and not what they thought they were supposed to say, ten years ago in an adult literacy program at an urban community college.[2] I worked as a tutor in a classroom where personal writing, putting yourself into the paper, was the key: "Introduce yourself." "Tell us about your family." "That happened to you? Do you want to write about it?" "When you saw that movie, what did it make you think about and how did you feel?" When I came to teach at the university I brought the narrative approach with me. I continue to encourage students to think of personal narrative not simply as a beginner's tool, but as a form integral to all

I would like to thank my "Writing in the Margins" students for their generosity in allowing me to quote from their writing, and Sarah-Hope Parmeter and I would like to thank the following friends and colleagues who read the first draft of this chapter and whose comments and suggestions contributed substantially to its development: our frequent co-collaborator Anza Stein; Megan Boler, Carol Freeman, and Don Rothman at UCSC; and Marlene Griffith, retired from Laney College.

genres of the academic essay. My teaching has taught me that students must be able to tell their stories if they are to learn to write from their own point of view. Furthermore, students have particular stories to tell, silences to break, and if at some point in their development as writers they do not find the opportunity to do so, they suffer the consequences—their writing becomes stunted, they get blocked and stuck, and additional problems with motivation, critical thinking, and learning will inevitably occur. Lesbian and gay students are especially vulnerable since rarely have they seen themselves represented in a class or been encouraged to speak freely about their lives. Raised in a culture that fears and hates them, they have been taught to fear and hate themselves, to hide themselves, and to censor their writing. At every grade level, lesbian and gay students are forced to circumvent the drive for self-assertion and self-revelation, resulting in patterns that disable them as writers and, in turn, affect their education in untold ways.

In this essay, I will show that lesbians and gays in a writing course where most students are not lesbian or gay can learn to explore their issues, find their voices, gain confidence, stop censoring themselves, think more critically, and write more persuasively, if the course values personal experience writing and provides an environment where it is safe for all students to write authentically. For lesbian and gay students to make these advances with writing means that an entire class must search out the roots of personal and cultural homophobia. What I have found, and will later discuss, is that confronting homophobia is challenging and rewarding work that can contribute significantly to the progress each student in the course makes with writing. My point of reference is the section I teach of a required composition course at the University of California at Santa Cruz (UCSC), and my focus is the unit on lesbian and gay issues.

"Writing in the Margins" places lesbians and gays in the context of groups who are literally and figuratively "homeless" in American society. By exploiting the pun that is the title of the course, I do not mean to imply that the groups represented—people of color, women and men challenging traditional gender roles, lesbians and gays, poor people and the homeless—actually are marginal. As Judy Grahn, poet and lesbian cultural worker, reminds us, the culture of any group of people may seem marginal to others, but it is certainly central to that group.[3] This is the point educator Smokey Wilson makes when she deconstructs the metaphor: "really there are no margins, only a variety of centers."[4] Those who choose to enroll in my section include students of color, students of various religious backgrounds, working-class students, women and men challenging traditional gender roles, and white students interested in exploring their ethnic and cultural backgrounds. The average class size is about eighteen students. The pattern of enrollment I have observed is that in each class there are usually one or two students who "come out," that is, identify themselves as lesbians or gays, and two or three who explain that they have lesbian or gay family members. The majority, who do not identify themselves as lesbian or gay or as having close relationships with lesbians or gay men, often describe themselves at the beginning of the course as curious about lesbian and gay issues and concerned about homophobia.

Premises

Before I turn to a discussion of writing by students in the course, I want to offer some premises that inform this essay:

1. "Lesbian" and "gay" are the terms of choice for lesbians and gay men because of their historical derivations and cultural contexts. "Gay" can apply to both women and men, although women often prefer to use "lesbian." I refer to "homosexuality" only when quoting students, or when I specifically want to characterize sexuality, since the word is a clinical term that creates a misleading emphasis, feeding into the myth and stereotype that anything lesbian and gay has something to do with sex. Sexuality is an important part of identity, but not its totality. Lesbians and gays are a group of people for whom sexual, affectional orientation is one aspect of living and loving and being in the world. Therefore, to include these voices does not mean "sexualizing" a course; it means that as teachers we are creating a space in our classrooms for a group of people and their culture.

2. Lesbians and gays, who originate from every ethnic and religious background, and every economic class, have a rich and diverse culture that includes partnerships, families, friendship circles, households, neighborhoods, clubs, community groups, business and professional associations, athletic events, religious organizations, rituals, holidays, ceremonies, political movements, an alternative press, historical landmarks, archives, art, music, theater, film, literature, scholarship, ways of using language. This culture enters a writing course when we teach lesbian and gay texts.

3. We have lesbian and gay students in our classrooms whether we

realize it or not; extrapolating from estimates of the general population, ten percent of our students are lesbian or gay. Twenty-five percent have an immediate family member who is lesbian or gay. When we ignore these students, we help perpetuate homophobia, perhaps our society's last socially sanctioned taboo.

4. As teachers of writing, we are learning to pay increasing attention to the representation of traditionally marginalized and excluded groups. We teach in a multi-ethnic, multicultural society, and we wouldn't dream of not teaching texts by women writers, African Americans, Native Americans, Chicanos, Asian Americans, Jewish Americans, working-class writers, writers who are differently abled. But many of us resist teaching clearly identified lesbian and gay writers, who must be included if a course is to be representative rather than exclusionary.

5. When we bring lesbian and gay subject matter into our classrooms, it cannot be reduced to the model of the controversial issue, some version of "Lesbians and Gay Men: Pro or Con?"—a dehumanizing, fundamentally illogical approach. Lesbian and gay existence is a fact, not a controversy, and therefore not a subject for debate.

Establishing a Context for the Material

It is essential that material concerning lesbians and gays be strategically presented and not dropped randomly into a writing course. The subject is likely to be new, perhaps confusing or uncomfortable, and students need time to get settled. In a course such as this one—as in many of the writing courses we teach—we want students to identify topics that especially interest them and to become engaged with writing as a process—to use free writing, write rough drafts, receive responses, and revise. We want them to start finding "trusted readers"—the teacher, the writing assistant, and each other—as they work together in writing groups and as a whole group commenting on each other's papers. Lesbian and gay students, in particular, benefit from the opportunity to become comfortable writing for the course before they are encouraged to explore their experience as lesbians and gays. For these reasons it is best to start the course with material for discussion that is at least somewhat familiar: my opening readings are on the interconnections of writing, race, and identity.[5] However, I use writing by lesbians on this topic because students need to be exposed to clearly identified lesbians and gays writing about all subjects. Our first class discussion is on Audre Lorde's essay "The Transformation of Silence into Language and Action," the story of "a Black lesbian warrior poet," as Lorde describes herself, who is facing breast cancer, fighting fear, and calling on all writers to examine their own silences.[6]

We continue reading work by women of color, and a discussion of racism and ethnic jokes leads us to consider sexism in the language— "the great person-hole cover debate."[7] We talk about "the social geography of childhood"[8]: what does it mean to grow up as a girl or a boy in our various ethnic, cultural, religious traditions? We read essays written by men on "the myth of masculine mystique"[9] and why "American men don't cry."[10] Students write about gender roles, examining images in advertisements or in television series. They write about sexism in their families and in their romances: the women responding to Virginia Woolf "killing the angel in the house,"[11] the men writing about ridding themselves of "the knight in shining armor." They write stories about female and male role models, and describe friendships between women and friendships between men. Papers examining gender roles and celebrating same-sex friendships prepare the way for the section on lesbian and gay concerns.

We begin this unit by reading interviews with lesbian and gay teenagers and adults,[12] people talking and telling their stories; for many of the students this is the first contact with lesbians and gays they have ever had. Then we read an AIDS memoir,[13] an essay by a lesbian teacher,[14] articles on homosexuality and religion.[15] At this point, we are in the sixth or seventh week of the quarter; the students know each other and they know me, they are used to examining issues relevant to their lives and to the lives of others, and they are prepared for the assignment to write on some aspect of lesbian and gay culture and experience, or to write about homophobia.

Lesbian and Gay Students Write about Lesbian and Gay Experience

In our society, lesbian and gay issues are so loaded that, as teachers of writing, we cannot simply assume that "if I tell my students it's OK to write personally and they need to write about this, they'll do it." Placing lesbian and gay material on the reading list still may not be enough. If lesbian and gay students are going to put themselves into their papers, they need to be able to write without being afraid, and this means that peers in writing groups must truly be "trusted readers," and teachers must be ready for conferences or conversations in which we reassure students that they really are welcome to be

themselves. For example, lesbian and gay students at UCSC report
that when they find out there is a writing course that deals with
lesbian and gay issues, they are, in the words of one student, Rick,
"ecstatic—thrilled beyond belief." Renee, interviewed after completing
"Writing in the Margins," recalled how she felt when she first heard
about it. "I was really excited. I got the Reader. I read all the lesbian,
gay, bisexual stuff right away. It was really, really exciting." Yet this
excitement did not show when she was asked on the first day to write
about why she had chosen the class:

> I was interested by this section's description and by the fact that
> we would be reading and discussing issues of homelessness and
> homosexuality. These are two issues that are all too often put "in
> the margins," and these people are so often unfairly discriminated
> against in so many ways. I was glad to see that, for once, these
> people would be looked at with respect and as a learning expe-
> rience.

"These people"—in her early essays, as in her first-day writing, Renee
seemed to be removing herself from the page. Her discussion of a
friendship with a woman was vague, full of convoluted sentences
written in language that was awkward and remote. She sounded as
if she were half writing for herself in a kind of journal style, and half
for someone she hoped would not be able to understand what she
was saying.

I wondered if Renee might be gay. While lesbian and gay students
are often "invisible," lesbian and gay teachers, as well as teachers who
have been sensitized to lesbian and gay issues, can sometimes identify
these students, sometimes through their writing. On several occasions,
Renee had walked me to my office after class, talking casually about
papers she was writing for this course and others, and I had a sense
there was something on her mind. One afternoon we stood outside
the classroom, and she told me she was really enjoying the course—
because she was a lesbian. I happened to be in a hurry at that moment,
but took the opportunity to say, briefly, that I was a lesbian, too; that
I was aware that lesbian and gay students often had a difficult time
writing about their experiences; and, with her vague draft in mind,
that I hoped she would be able to be herself in her writing for the
course. She looked amazed, and relieved, and we parted. Her revised
draft showed that my invitation had made a difference. She began:

> "My silences had not protected me. Your silence will not protect
> you."—Audre Lorde. "Lying is done with words, and also with
> silence."—Adrienne Rich. I can relate so well with what these
> two women are saying, because I too am gay. When Lorde and

> Rich talk about being afraid, lying to cover up women's love for
> women, and the institutionalization of heterosexuality, I have seen
> and experienced exactly the same things.[16]

Here Renee is bold and much more clear. In her next paper, she sounds
even more comfortable with writing; her language is rhythmical and
playful as she sets up her topic by describing a recent talk with Rick:

> As the conversation continued, he told me that he had taken
> "Writing in the Margins" last year, and had loved it. He talked
> about some of his experiences in the class, and I shared some of
> mine. He asked me about the homophobia paper, to which I
> replied that we were working on that very paper this week. He
> said that he had written his on internalized homophobia. "What
> a good idea," I thought as my mind started to work double time
> so that I could both carry on a conversation with him and think
> about what I was going to say in my paper.

Renee wrote about "internalized homophobia," the fear and hatred
lesbians and gays are socialized into having toward each other and
themselves. For her final project she researched a student movement
working to establish a lesbian and gay studies program on campus.
At the same time that she was exploring deeply felt issues, she was
developing writing strategies and learning to write for an audience. In
an interview, she evaluated her progress:

> Writing before was a chore that I had to do to pass classes. Now
> it is still a chore that I have to do to pass classes, although taking
> this class has opened up a new form of writing for me, a more
> personal form, a more audience-directed form.
> Rather than just—"God, I have to think of a theme, I have to
> write five pages on this theme, I have to bring in quotes"—it can
> be more my personal reflections, a more relaxed style rather than
> a traditional academic paper. I was really glad to see that I can
> still write a good paper. In fact I have a friend who says my
> writing has really improved since taking the class and I believe
> it has.

Ting, a member of Renee's writing group, also picked up on the
change in her writing. When asked in an interview whether she
remembered any particular papers from her writing group on this
subject, Ting described Renee's circuitous draft. "It sounded kind of
weird," she said, "like she wasn't really touching on the real issue."
Ting explained to the interviewer that the next time the group met,
Renee told them she was a lesbian. "I'm just glad she felt safe—secure
enough to tell us," Ting said. "I'm just glad she was comfortable
enough." What happened in the writing group was essential for lesbian
or gay students working with their peers: Renee's "trusted readers"

proved they really could be trusted. Because students in the group were engaged in reading about lesbian and gay issues, and attempting to understand their own homophobia, they were able to create an atmosphere in which Renee felt safe enough to put herself into her paper. "The more we educate ourselves about homosexuality it will be less of a scary, mysterious unknown," Ting concluded in her paper.

Another student's story highlights the isolation a lesbian or gay writer can feel "in a class full of straight people," no matter how safe the environment, and reveals the indecision and blankness that can result even when a student is a confident and talented writer. Ellen opened her first-day writing by explaining that she was taking "Writing in the Margins" because she was a lesbian and "would be writing in the margins all of [her] life." "I have always found writing relatively easy and I enjoy it immensely," she added. During one of our first discussions on lesbian and gay issues she came out to the class, a group of students she described as neither hostile nor homophobic. And yet this is what happened when she tried to discuss her topic with the group and then sat down to write:

> I didn't know where to start. The class went around talking about the ideas people were thinking about. As I heard the ideas I began to feel more isolated. I knew I was probably the only lesbian in the class, but suddenly I really felt it. Frustration was silently pulsing through my veins as my turn to speak was coming close. As the words came out of my mouth, my shoulders were knotting up and my once clear idea started to get fuzzy as I heard my voice.
>
> My first reaction was: make a good impression. Soon after I realized the absurdity of this. I decided to talk about a topic that really interested me to write about, and I tried not to care about making any impression. As I spoke about internalized homophobia I felt like I couldn't articulate what I was wanting to say.
>
> When the discussion was over I felt like I was even more confused about what I was going to write about. I wasn't thinking about writing something for myself, instead I was thinking about how I would represent a gay perspective in a class full of straight people.
>
> When I finally sat down to write, my brain felt like a blank slate.

Ellen's narrative points out the problems for a student who feels she is a representative voice obligated to educate others.

Clearly, "minority" writers must not be made to feel that they are there to explain or prove themselves to the "majority." In my classes I would never say "we will now have the lesbian or gay point of view" and call on the lesbian or gay student. But short of not making things worse, there wasn't a lot I felt I could do to help alleviate Ellen's sense of isolation. I do not announce to a class that I am a lesbian, but I always come out in conversations with students who come out to me. And I think I sound like an authority on lesbian and gay issues in class discussions, so I assume every one will figure out that I'm gay if they wonder about it. In one discussion, someone mentioned that Ellen was the only gay person in the class. I said that they weren't including me, and people nodded, but it was clear to me that, as the teacher, I am in a separate category, and one lesbian student is still alone.

What can make a difference is the open-minded behavior of the group of students engaged in the process of informing themselves about lesbian and gay issues. In the process of revising, Ellen asked the class for responses to the draft of her paper, the description of sitting down to write that was part of a layered coming-out story. In her self-evaluation, she commented, "It was important for me to share my work with other students. This was very helpful in developing confidence in my writing." When an audience of educated readers is in the making, lesbian and gay students can make progress at moving through difficult moments to emerge as more confident writers who are writing personally and developing academically. Rick described his progress with writing in this way:

> This was the first time I could write about what we were reading and be myself at the same time. It was a wonderful experience.
> During the quarter my writing became more personal in nature rather than just academic. What it's done is open up a whole new area of writing for me that's really helped me a lot in all of my classes.

Non-Lesbian and Gay Students Write about Homophobia

A successful writing course leaves students with a sense of accomplishment: it gives them an opportunity to write well, and students write well about subjects that challenge them and touch them personally. Again and again, "Writing in the Margins" students note in their self-evaluations: "During this course I feel like I have grown and learned a lot." "I feel like this class was not only a writing class, but it also helped me develop myself." "I feel I have grown as a writer and as a person." Writing about homophobia is often cited as particularly difficult, it is a "tricky" issue, a "touchy" subject, but it is also regularly mentioned as an assignment that becomes a catalyst for personal growth. In his self-evaluation, Walter described the value of writing this paper as he reflected on the progress he made in the course:

> My writing skills have no doubt improved during this quarter.
> They improved with every assignment. The papers on homophobia
> and gender roles helped me grow as a writer because they made
> me search deep inside myself to write about personal experiences.
> Writing about homophobia was not easy. It made me realize that
> I was homophobic and made me face this fear.

In their writing, students repeatedly show how willing they are to face their fears, and how quickly their alienation and hostility can change once they have a chance to read and to realize that lesbians and gays have feelings like their own. I have discovered that students in the course have a highly developed sense of fairness: as they read, they object to the cruelty and discrimination lesbians and gays have experienced. For many, the common bond of being misunderstood, of suffering unfair treatment—from parents, peers, teachers, as well as from the society at large—becomes a bridge to identification and understanding.

Certain themes emerge in the writing of non-lesbian and gay students as they make these connections. Some link homophobia with racism, or relate lesbian and gay experience to their own process of exploring and claiming an ethnic identity. For example, Walter, who is Asian, was influenced by ideas he encountered as he read an interview with a gay Asian:

> Reading several articles written by homosexuals gave me insight
> into their everyday lives, what they had to go through, and how
> they felt about rejection by society. The interview with Dennis, a
> gay Asian, also provided insight on how minority homosexuals
> had to deal with "double discrimination." "A minority within a
> minority" was how Dennis described it. It helped me to understand
> that treating homosexuals differently is just as bad as being a
> racist.

In a paper called "Wall of Homophobia"—which she concludes with the line: "As I encounter new people and books, you can see that I'm slowly, and slightly cautiously, knocking down my wall"—Tracy wrote:

> The internalized oppression a homosexual must feel in a hetero-
> sexual world would be overwhelming. I can empathize to a certain
> extent with this suffering. You see, my father is Jewish, though I
> never considered myself a Jew. The fact is I always thought of
> Judaism as solely a religion; if you don't practice it, you are not
> Jewish. But, as my society has shown me, this is not true. Judaism
> is a race and Jews are discriminated against.

AnnaLyn, a Filipina American, came into the course with the idea that lesbians and gays constitute a minority group and that as a woman of color she could identify with them. Still, in a paper called "I Am a Homophobic," she wrote: "homosexuality is a very uncomfortable topic for me," and "I find that I'm very ignorant about homosexuality." But she made a connection with a teenager named Joanne, whose story she read in an interview. AnnaLyn explained that she had once "lived in a community filled with white, Anglo-Saxon Americans. In my neighborhood and school I was the only Filipino; other minority races were scarce." Later, at a different school, she found that "Asians and other minority races were the majority":

> I made friends with people of my race. I didn't feel different thereafter. I found my missing link, my true identity. It was similar to what Joanne had said in her interview, "I think if it had not been for the other lesbians I knew, my life would have been unbearable."

At the end of the course, AnnaLyn evaluated her work:

> I've seen myself grow as a writer in this class. I feel doubly more confident and I'm not scared to approach a topic of a paper with my own ideas. I feel that I've written more thoroughly, clearly, and specifically. I've noticed that my own voice now comes to life within my papers, I have a lot more things to say, and I say them as clearly as I can.

"Writing from the heart," which was her stated goal for the course, led AnnaLyn to compassion and insight, and to new skill with writing.

Like students with a background of minority religions and students of color, another group with a certain kind of connection to lesbian and gay material are those students who have lesbian and gay family members. Often these students feel stigmatized, are reluctant to reveal that they have a lesbian or gay in their family, and eventually in the course they "come out" for family members in a way that is similar to a lesbian or gay student's process of coming out. "I never thought much about homosexuality until my sister Chloe came home for Christmas after her first quarter at college," wrote one student, and another: "My family's awful, unspoken disgrace was that my brother is gay. At first I thought that the secret was better kept in the family, but now I am relieved that my brother's secret did not turn into the silencing of his life." While there is a small but growing literature on the topic of lesbian and gay parents, I have no reading to make available to students about lesbian and gay siblings. The moving stories my students have told convince me that there is a significant need for research and writing in this area.

In the writing of the non-lesbian and gay students in the course, friendship with a lesbian or a gay is a common theme. Here's the beginning of one story:

> Seniors were the coolest because they had the privilege of going out to lunch. Everyday the lunch bell would ring and all the seniors would gossip on their way out to the parking lot, with their keys on display, and speed to the closest frozen yogurt shop. It was on a day not unlike the one I just described when Phil came out to me. We were in my car on our way to Numero Uno's Pizzeria where they guarantee "your pizza in ten minutes or it's free." I had just made a left hand turn into freedom (out of the school parking lot) when a serious look came over Phil's face. "Rachel, I have to tell you something," a dreadfully long pause, "now, I'm not sure . . . and I've been debating back and forth . . . , but I think that maybe . . . I might be . . . sort of gay."
>
> BOOM!!!! The bomb had been dropped. My mouth dropped open as my heart skipped a couple of beats.

Another subject frequently discussed is homophobic language. One woman wrote: "I have always been able to joke freely about homosexuality, but I'm not sure if this is a healthy thing to do. I have never thought of what a joke might do to someone and I used to use words such as 'fag' and 'queer' very often." When she discovered that a favorite teacher was a lesbian, she changed her attitude: "From that point on, whenever I heard someone use the word 'faggot' or 'dyke' I would jump on them like a vicious cat."

In another paper on this theme, "The Porter College Code of Conduct Opened My Eyes,"—which refers to a UCSC college community's antidiscrimination code—Jack tells the story of a time when he constantly used the term "fag" as a joke and a generic insult. When he uses the word on movie night at his college, and this is "kindly yet strictly" brought to his attention by a fellow viewer, he looks back and recalls "sitting in one of the bathroom stalls on the first day of school, and there it was: The Porter College Code of Conduct. I paid no attention to it at all." On movie night, he returns "to the same bathroom where I knew it was posted to reread it, taking it seriously this time." But, he asks, "you know how it takes a traumatic experience to get you to change your ways?" Several weeks later at a party in a dorm lounge, he yells at a friend at the top of his lungs, "Ralph's a fag!"

> It was just like a movie: the party was silent, the music stopped, people stopped dancing. Everyone was looking at me. It had popped out again: the "f" word, and everyone heard it. It wasn't meant to be a discriminating comment, but only I knew that. I

> told everyone as best I could that I was deeply sorry and I didn't
> mean to hurt anyone and became so confused that I left the room
> very quickly trying to hide my face. I was so humiliated. I went
> to my old thinking spot: the bathroom stalls. When I looked up
> from my crouched position, there it was, staring at me with an
> evil eye: The Porter College Code of Conduct.

Jack goes on to explain that he "no longer uses the 'f' word" because
of the impact the Code of Conduct finally made on him. I distribute
this paper each quarter for discussion and to introduce the topic of
homophobic language, and it always succeeds at making students
laugh as they consider Jack's example.

There are students who do not want to write about homophobia.
In my course, they are aware that a writing assignment can always
be changed to meet their needs, so sometimes they opt to return to
the previous assignment and write a second paper on gender issues.
Brian was a weak writer, disengaged from the course, and he seemed
especially uncomfortable with lesbian and gay material. He met with
me and we looked for a subject he really wanted to write about, which
turned out to be the story of a friendship with someone he had known
since childhood. "As Close as Brothers" was the best writing Brian
did all quarter. The next in the series of assignments for the course is
an essay that uses research. One lesbian student wrote a paper called
"How Do Lesbians See Themselves?" and a gay man wrote on
"Personal and Political Visions of Gayness." Students who are not
lesbian and gay have written papers such as: "What the Silence Does
to Us" (on Chicana lesbians), "The Secrecy of Sexuality in the
Classroom" (on lesbian teachers), "Gays, Film, and Homophobia."
Without any discussion with me, or explanation for his change of
mind, Brian wrote a paper called "Homophobia and How It Is Relevant
in Our Lives." His research might have been more substantial, but he
did use personal narrative as effective evidence for his argument, and
he completed the course, which had been in question before he wrote
"As Close as Brothers." My point here is that homophobia is not a
topic to be forced on anyone, but it can be compelling, and sometimes
even reluctant writers overcome their resistance to it and are motivated
to write well.

Another reluctant writer, Linda, was nervous about the "political"
content of the entire course. Unwilling to more than minimally revise,
she wrote in a terse style, and if she spoke at all during class discussions
she was drawn to defend a man who was usually at odds with any
number of people in the group because of his conservative views. But
in her papers she began to consider new ideas. Writing about homo-

phobia, she took on "a strong pro-choice attitude for sexual preference," a position she described as "quite a novelty," explaining that an essay by a lesbian teacher unable to come out, and reach out, to her students because of the fear of losing her job had "touched her heart" and helped to give her "a new outlook on homosexuality." However, she was blunt about the limits of her new outlook: "I still have not overcome my repulsive feelings completely. I guess, like most things, it takes time." "Repulsive" is a strong word. Linda is not proving to anyone that she's become "political" overnight. But she is being honest, and she is taking risks with writing. She wrote in her self-evaluation:

> As a result of this class, I learned quite a bit about things I was considerably uninformed about. This was my goal, in addition to improving my writing. I am gradually losing my fear of writing assignments. . . . I feel that my papers took thought and effort, and honesty. I am improving in the revision process. However, I think my greatest improvement, as a result of the readings, the discussions and the feedback, was the expansion of my mind.

Risk Taking

Our goal as teachers—to expand our students' minds—requires that, like our students, we take risks. A concern many teachers may have is that working with lesbian and gay subject matter will lead students to do "inappropriate" writing—writing that is overtly sexual or that seems to be a cry for help, writing we feel we can't "teach to." I have found that there are some students who want to focus on the sexual aspect of gay experience, and these are the non-gay men who write about the difficulty they have getting beyond their "repulsion" at the images in their heads of two people of the same gender, especially men, having sex with each other. But these students have not "sexualized" the writing assignment. One man began:

> My friends and I would be quick to point out what we thought was homosexual behavior in other people at the beach and at social gatherings. Our discussion of their behavior would eventually lead us to a conversation based on criticizing the disgusting nature of lesbian and gay sex.

Then he described how the picture changed for him:

> I have always thought of the heterosexual love-making that I have experienced as something more than just physical attraction. I now see homosexual sex in the same light. When I think about gay and lesbian sex, I am no longer concentrating on the sexual practices themselves. Instead, I am concentrating on the feelings

> of love and emotional bonding that can go along with any sexual
> experience between two human beings.

Another man wrote:

> I have always equated homosexuality with only the sexual side
> of a relationship, and have never tried to see any other facet of
> a homosexual relationship. I was very uncomfortable with the
> thought of sex between homosexuals, and so I never looked
> beyond what I ridiculed, mostly due to what I didn't understand.

Then he focused on how the course reading had affected him:

> I have learned the most about homosexuality from Paul Monette's
> *Borrowed Time: An AIDS Memoir,* and very similarly from a
> relationship between two gay men that I have known for years.
> It took the *Borrowed Time* piece to make me go back and analyze
> the relationship between the couple at home, and to see how that
> was so much like the one between Paul and Roger. From their
> feelings of loneliness before they met to the bond that grew
> between them, I could see the strength in their companionship.
> There is so much more than just the sexual side of their relationship
> that I could now begin to visualize.

These students are not writing "inappropriately." They are tracking an
intellectual process, and describing and analyzing their own shifts in
point of view.

In one instance, a "Writing in the Margins" student wrote a piece
focusing on sexual confusion and alluding to sexual fantasies. First, I
asked Roberta to make an appointment to see me, and I made sure
that she knew about the many campus resources for lesbian, gay,
bisexual, and "questioning" students. In fact, she did know about a
support group and had started going to meetings. Then the challenge
became how best to work with her writing. Rather than asking her to
revise, I asked her to contextualize the piece she had written, to
examine the process of writing it and of sharing it with her writing
group. This seemed a bit risky to suggest, but Roberta bravely agreed
to try it. Her next draft began:

> Last week I was asked to describe an encounter I have had with
> an issue related to the subject of homosexuality. Since I have just
> recently had a strong attraction to the same sex, I decided to
> explore my own sexuality. This was a very difficult task because
> I had never written or spoken about it to anyone.

She includes the original piece, then goes on to describe reading it to
her writing group:

> I was surprised to find tears come to my eyes, and my voice
> quiver when I began reading out loud. I presume it was a result

of fear, admitting these feelings to others, and further confirming them. As Bradley Artson describes in his essay, "Judaism and Homosexuality," I am a victim of Western culture that "actively supports heterosexuality and condemns homosexuality, thereby encouraging those who discover their homosexuality to repress it." I did not receive the shocked response that I was expecting. They were all very respectful, and even grateful that I shared my feelings with them.

Roberta's assessment of her writing group's response was right on target. After she read them the original paper, a member of the group approached me to ask if she could change her topic because "something incredible had happened in her group." In her new paper, she wrote that "what Roberta did was one of the most courageous acts I've ever witnessed."

Students often intuitively handle situations I worry about being able to prepare them for. Rick identified himself as a drag queen, a man who wears women's clothes, and he often wore dresses and high heels to class. I recognized the tension in the room when Rick arrived in drag, but I felt it would be wrong for me to initiate a discussion, and Rick never brought it up, although he did write about it. Three men in the course also wrote about it. One titled his paper "Should Men Wear Dresses?" and he begins:

> One day a classmate of mine began dressing like a female. This posed a whole new set of problems for me. How could I treat a guy wearing dresses the same as my buddy wearing blue jeans? Once again the conservatism left over from high school played a role and thoughts such as "What a fag!" entered my mind. People began talking around campus and many people I talked to said that he had just plain flipped out. But, was he flipping out or were we?

He concludes with a discussion of his "semi-homophobia" and this statement: "I am hopeful that I will eventually be able to cleanse myself of these irrational fears, and someday be able to confidently say, 'Yea, there is nothing wrong with a man who wears a dress,' with conviction and self-assuredness that I am saying what I feel." Here are the words of two other students:

> My gay friend Rick likes to wear skirts, high heels, and other women's clothing. If I refuse to accept Rick because he does not conform to the heterosexual standards of male clothing, I am adding to his oppression by making him feel bad about his gay "Drag Queen" identity.

> When I first saw Rick in a dress, I didn't want anything to do with the "fag." After I got to know him, my feelings of anger and

prejudice changed. I now respect him, not as a heterosexual or a homosexual male, but as Rick, a kind and sensitive friend.

Teaching Against Violence

The last passage was written by Brian, which is particularly striking because a student who at first did not want to write about homophobia at all ended up writing about his own homophobia, and a new-found sensitivity, in the context of his potential for committing violence. Lesbians and gays are the cultural group in the United States most targeted for hate crimes and acts of violence. Students write about their participation in acts of hate and violence, and this is very difficult to read, but it is something teachers must be willing to face. Brian told this story:

> Everytime I saw a man or men, whom I believed to be gay, I would feel a strong sense of anger toward them, almost to a measure of violence. I especially remember this one occasion when some friends and I were in Los Angeles. One night we were literally looking for gays to bother. After a while we found one, he had a wig and heels on. He looked as if he was ready for a night on the town. As we pulled closer to him, we slowed the car to a mere crawl. As soon as we were in range, we began yelling comments, which are too rude for me to repeat. When we drove away, a couple of my friends actually wanted to go back and, as they put it, "beat the fag's ass."

A woman wrote:

> I began to realize things about my boyfriend and our friends that caused me to rethink the respect I had for their dare to be different, rebellious attitudes. One day at lunch, I overheard them talking about "fag bashing." This appalled me, but I held my silence for a while. My desire to be accepted, in what was probably the most insecure period of my life, was at war with my knowledge that there was definitely something wrong with their actions.

Acts of violence against lesbians and gays are the "norm" in this country. As teachers of writing, we may not see stopping violence as part of our jobs, but a lesbian- and gay-inclusive writing course can have this kind of influence, as in the case of Brian, who concludes, "The readings had such a great impact upon me ... I was moved in such a way that I felt like a damn fool."

Another kind of violence teachers can prevent is allowing students to write the kind of hate-filled diatribes produced in some well-meaning writing courses I have heard about, where lesbian and gay material has not been introduced in sensitive and strategic ways. Paul was a student who, in another setting, might have produced violent writing that other students would have been obliged to read. Explaining that he had enrolled in the course only because it fit into his schedule, his first-day writing, which only I read, included these thoughts:

> I am very homophobic, I can't stand gays, and am very prejudiced against them. I feel that my upbringing brought these negative feelings upon me. The community which I lived in was very conservative. Being a fag was considered the worst thing you could be. I am not prejudiced toward anything else, and I would like to learn more about this race of people. I don't feel that these feelings will ever leave me, but maybe my hate will lessen.

It was clear from this writing that, despite his hatred, Paul was still open to learn. As his self-evaluation shows, for some people "a little bit of real knowledge" goes a long way:

> The reader and the class have been the first information I have heard in support of homosexuals. I am still very ignorant, but this little knowledge I have gained through taking this class is already beginning to influence my opinion. I was discussing this matter recently with a few of my housemates, and they expressed the same attitude I had before this class. When I asked them what they think of homosexuals they said first of all they try not to think of them. When I persisted, their feelings were to the effect that homosexuals didn't have any right to live. Even though I would have said the same thing two months ago, what they were saying sounded so stupid to me. It's not that they're stupid, it's that they know nothing about homosexuals. A little bit of real knowledge could change a lot of people's minds toward this subject.

The following year Paul sent one of his friends to enroll in the course.

Transforming Silence into Language and Action

I hope this essay can serve as a starting point for those who want to make classrooms more representative of diverse student populations. As teachers, we talk about writing as empowerment; we talk about students placing themselves in their texts. If we want our lesbian and gay students to place themselves in their texts, we need to invite them into our courses. As the saying goes, "silence is not neutral: silence is straight."[17] I take heart from Audre Lorde who, in urging us to transform silence into language and action, reminds us:

> [We must not] hide behind the mockeries of separations that have been imposed on us and which so often we accept as our own.

For instance, "I can't possibly teach Black women's writing—their experience is so different from mine." Yet how many years have you spent teaching Plato and Shakespeare and Proust? Or another, "She's a white woman and what could she possibly have to say to me?" Or, "She's a lesbian, what would my husband say, or my chairman?"[18]

Teaching lesbian- and gay-inclusive courses means facing and overcoming these fears. Lorde advises us: "We can learn to work and speak when we are afraid in the same way we have learned to work and speak when we are tired. For we have been socialized to respect fear more than our own needs for language and definition."[19] Aarti, an Indian-American student, writes about overcoming her fear: "When I was choosing a Writing 1 class, I was kind of scared to take 'Writing in the Margins' because this class would cover the topic of gays and lesbians. I feel just by signing up I have begun the process of becoming more educated." As teachers, let the courage and determination of students be a lesson to us.

Notes

1. We are indebted to Ellen Newberry, who was a student in Sarah-Hope Parmeter's intermediate writing course "Writing Ourselves: Toward a Lesbian and Gay Identity" and a writing assistant for "Writing in the Margins." A graduate student at San Francisco State University working on a Master's in composition, Ellen interviewed Gillian, along with a group of former "Writing in the Margins" students, as a part of her own research on lesbian- and gay-inclusive writing courses. Whenever there is a reference to a student interview, it is to Ellen Newberry's work, which is central to this chapter.

2. For a description of the literacy program, Project Bridge at Laney College in Oakland, California, see Mike Rose. 1989. *Lives on the Boundary: The Struggles and Achievements of America's Underprepared.* New York: The Free Press: 213–23.

3. Judy Grahn. 1985. *The Highest Apple: Sappho and the Lesbian Poetic Tradition.* San Francisco: Spinsters, Ink: xvi.

4. Smokey Wilson. Personal communication. Laney College.

5. In their first quarter at the university most UCSC students take college Core Courses; UCSC is made up of a number of individual colleges. Core Courses often include a focus on race and gender.

6. Audre Lorde, 41–42.

7. Lindsy Van Gelder, 120.

8. Ruth Frankenburg. 1988. "Growing Up White: Feminism, Racism and the Social Geography of Childhood," "White Women, Race Matters: the Social Construction of Whiteness," diss., University of California at Santa Cruz.

9. Gloria Steinem. 1972. "The Myth of Masculine Mystique."

10. Ashley Montagu, 243.

11. Virginia Woolf, "Professions for Women."

12. See Ann Heron, ed. 1986. *One Teenager in Ten: Testimony by Gay and Lesbian Youth* (New York: Warner Books) and Nancy Adair and Casey Adair, eds. 1978. *Word Is Out: Stories of Some of Our Lives.* New York: Delacorte Press and San Francisco: New Glide Publications.

13. See Paul Monette. 1988. *Borrowed Time: An AIDS Memoir.*

14. See Anza Stein. 1988. "What's A Lesbian Teacher to Do?"

15. See Bradley Shavit Artson. 1988.

16. Renee's references are to the previously cited essay by Lorde (41) and to Adrienne Rich. 1979. "Women and Honor: Some Notes on Lying." *On Lies, Secrets and Silence: Selected Prose 1966–1978,* 186.

17. Sarah-Hope Parmeter is the originator of this "saying."

18. Lorde, 43–44.

19. Lorde, 44.

References

Adair, N., and C. Adair. 1978. *Word Is Out: Stories of Some of Our Lives.* New York: Delacorte Press.

Artson, B. 1988. "Judaism and Homosexuality." *Tikkun* 3(2): 52–54, 92–93.

Frankenburg, R. 1988. "Growing Up White: Femininism, Racism and the Social Geography of Childhood." Diss. University of California at Santa Cruz.

Gelder, L. 1980. "The Great Person-hole Cover Debate." *Ms. Magazine,* April: 120.

Grahn, J. 1985. *The Highest Apple: Sappho and the Lesbian Poetic Tradition.* San Francisco: Spinsters, Ink.

Heron, A. 1986. *One Teenager in Ten: Testimony by Gay and Lesbian Youth.* New York: Warner Books.

Lorde, A. 1984. *Sister Outsider: Essays and Speeches.* Trumansburg, N.Y.: The Crossing Press.

Monette, P. 1988. *Borrowed Time: An AIDS Memoir.* San Diego: Harcourt, Brace, Jovanovich.

Montagu. 1967. *The American Way of Life.* New York: G.P. Putnam's Sons.

Rose, M. 1989. *Lives on the Boundary: The Struggles and Achievements of America's Underprepared.* New York: The Free Press.

Stein, A. 1988. "What's a Lesbian Teacher to Do?" In S. Parmeter and I. Reti, (Eds.). *The Lesbian in Front of the Classroom: Writings by Lesbian Teachers.* Santa Cruz: HerBooks: 4–16.

Steinem, G. 1972. "The Myth of Masculine Mystique." *International Education,* 1: 30–35.

Woolf, V. 1988. "Professions for Women." In C. Muscatine and M. Griffith, (eds.). *The Borzoi College Reader.* New York: Alfred A. Knopf: 256–61.

9 Public School and University Compañeros: Changing Lives

Debbie Bell
Ohlone Elementary School, Watsonville, California

"These letters are *wonderful!*" beamed Mariana[1] after receiving her first letters from her new university partners. "They are the *best* thing, the *best* thing!" She smiled, hugging her purple UCSC (University of California, Santa Cruz) folder to her chest as she skipped back to her desk to finish responding to her new friends.

Mariana entered the fifth grade with a history of being a fairly gloomy child who felt she had no friends. Spending a great deal of her time whining and tattling, she had been perfecting the role of victim and outsider for most of her school career. As she tried to articulate her happiness and her new sense of belonging, I smiled and knew that she was right. These letters *are* the *best thing*, and so is this Partnership. The best thing.

Then Ramón shoved his letter back under my nose and said, "Léame mi carta, maestra" ("Read me my letter, teacher"). Soon we were off in a corner, writing like mad.

This essay describes a university/public school Partnership between students in my bilingual fifth-grade class at Ohlone Elementary School in Watsonville, California, and students at the University of California, Santa Cruz (UCSC). The Partnership, which is now in its third year, involves four different UCSC writing, core, and research courses taught by Sarah-Hope Parmeter.

Social Issues in the English Classroom?

I do not actually teach in "the English classroom." You see, I am a bilingual teacher. Simplified, that means that I use two languages—English and Spanish—for instruction.

This Partnership is supported by a grant from Campus Compact's Campus Partners in Learning Programs, by Merrill and Oakes Colleges and the Writing Program at the University of California, Santa Cruz, and by the Central California Writing Project (CCWP). Additionally, because of this Partnership, Ohlone School has been named an NCTE (National Council of Teachers of English) Center of Excellence for Students At-Risk.

In my self-contained, bilingual fifth-grade classroom, I simultaneously teach students who are progressing through myriad shades of bilingualism and biliteracy, from monolingual in either English or Spanish and sometimes pre-literate, to completely bilingual/biliterate. Thus, the role of language and literacy is complex and means many things within the context of "the bilingual classroom," or, more generally, "the language arts classroom."

Additionally, I am not solely "a Language Arts teacher," bilingual or otherwise. I teach *all* subjects to my students. Certainly, language arts are a primary focus in my classroom. All my students need to develop high-level communication skills, and biliteracy is our highest standard. Reading, writing, translation, second-language development, and many forms of communication and thinking are guided by work in the language arts.

Furthermore, in every other subject that I teach, from social studies to art, from science to physical education, from math to family life, language arts are an essential component of the teaching, the learning, and the thinking that go on in my classroom.

Fighting the Odds: Addressing and Overcoming Social Issues

As a bilingual teacher working in an impoverished and fairly segregated community, I find the very nature of what I do to be immersed in social issues. Social issues are also at the core of what statistics might predict for my students in terms of school "success."

Through our writing partnership with university students, my fifth graders have challenged the educational status quo. Because of political, economic, linguistic, cultural, and educational "realities"—all social issues—nearly all of my students are (or have been perceived as) at risk of dropping out of school and/or low academic achievement, or at least are very unlikely to go on to higher education, especially above the community college level. Those that do make it into the four-year university system are statistically unlikely to graduate. Nonetheless, this Partnership has started to redefine my students as "college bound."

"College Bound" or "At Risk": Statistical Reality, School Definition, or Self-Perception?

When I was about eight years old, I started saving money for college. I perceived myself as "college bound." My parents, all of my grandparents, and several of my great grandparents were college educated, and although I may not have consciously known that, it impacted my view of what people *do*. My father was a college administrator, and I had grown up on university campuses. I learned to read before kindergarten, and, all through school, my mother was very involved in my education, assuring that my academic needs were being met.

I was a "good fit" with the school system. Not only did I perceive myself as college bound, so did my parents, my teachers, my relatives, my parents' friends, and my friends' parents. The possibility of *not* going to college never entered my head, and I certainly didn't dream that anyone I knew could have perceived me as other than "college bound." In fact, I thought *everyone* went to college . . . that it was just what people *do*.

Almost none of my students know anyone in their families who has gone to college. Many strive to be the first in their family to graduate from high school. Some are the first to learn to read. Who am I to say to my students, "*Of course* you'll go to college"? And who am I to say, "*Perhaps you won't* go to college"? I feel that it is inherent in my job as a teacher to inspire and assist all of my students to "succeed" within the academic setting. I do not want to say to them "go to college or you will be a failure," but I feel that to offer them anything less is to limit their access to the full spectrum of opportunities within our educational system.

Bridging the (Perceived?) Gap: Fifth Graders Go to College

> I really love the program with the UCSC students. I hope we do something like that in Jr. High. I've never done something this fun in school. It teaches us how to make friends fast, and how to get along with each other. It's probably not going to be so fun in Jr. High. I really like it when we go (to UCSC) five times a year. I really like this program.
>
> —Elvia

Currently, the Partnership involves weekly letter exchanges between partners from each school, several visits per quarter of UCSC students to Ohlone and Ohlone students to UCSC, potluck dinners for parents to meet the UCSC students, graduation ceremonies, and several field placements of UCSC students in Ohlone classrooms throughout the year. Additionally, Sarah-Hope Parmeter, the UCSC writing instructor involved, spends ample time in my classroom getting to know my students. This year, we have expanded the program to include the other fifth-grade class at Ohlone.

The Watsonville community of Pájaro, where my school is located, is an impoverished, and primarily Mexicano, agricultural and industrial area, crisscrossed by railroad tracks, and separated from the rest of Watsonville by the Pájaro River. The gang affiliated with Pájaro is the "Poor Siders."

The student population at Ohlone is 98% Hispanic, 89% Limited English Proficient, 75% Chapter 1 (below the 45th percentile on state achievement tests and district-defined as "at risk") and 90% come from families that qualify for Aid to Families with Dependent Children (AFDC).[2]

About twenty-five miles and several light-years away is UCSC. The university is nestled among the redwoods, overlooking the Monterey Bay, in a very affluent part of Santa Cruz.

The primary focus of this collaboration is to develop strong academic and social ties between elementary and university students, particularly Chicano/Mexicano students, especially through the medium of writing. Through this Partnership, we wish to create for both student groups something personally meaningful within their education to keep them in school; we want them to believe in themselves and school in a way that will not exclude them from the educational system.

For the elementary students, we are trying to make school meaningful and to create an environment and an experience base that includes them in a "college bound" definition in a strong and natural way. Maybe if they define themselves as college bound, then the system will not decide for them that they are not. We are trying to give them *ownership* of the university so that it feels like it is there for *them*.

Because of this partnership, throughout the school year my students learn about how the university quarter system works, what finals and essays are, what dorms are like, how financial aid works, what "college-bound" high school classes are, what is required to get into college, and what is required once you get there, and much more about the workings of the university. Also, they learn about the freedom and responsibility of choosing your own classes, setting your own schedule, eating in the dining hall, having girlfriends and boyfriends, working and going to school, attending protests and sit-ins, and getting narrative evaluations (the UCSC option to grades). They not only know that university students have to buy their own books, but they also know where the bookstore is. They casually and with authority talk about going to McHenry Library or the West Field House or the recreation room at Crown. Most know about "Elf-land," a magical place in the woods on campus that many UCSC students may not even know about.

And they learn all this not through "lessons" about university life, but through their friends—their partners at UCSC. The university is a place they know and feel comfortable in, not because I took them there on a tour, but because their buddies live there and that is where much of their fun together takes place. Information about college matters because it is about real people, not just something to think about in ninth grade during career week when many of them may *not* be counselled into college-prep courses anyhow, but rather because it has to do with the part of school that almost every one of them comes to call the "best thing."

Many of the university students involved in the partnership have chosen to participate because, in the words of their teacher, "they are students who have a strong desire to serve the communities that they came from, and are seeking an education for that purpose." One of the university courses built around the partnership is a university composition course called *"Escribiendo para Transformamos/Writing to Change Our Lives,"* which has the stated goal of influencing the future makeup of the university student population through early outreach to under-represented communities.

The university students who have chosen to participate in the program represent an unusually high percentage of minority students as compared to the university population at large. In the first year, 40% of the UCSC students in the program were Chicano/Latino (as compared to about 9% of all UCSC undergraduates[3]), and another 27% came from other minority groups (as compared to about 15% of all UCSC undergraduates). The percentages were even higher in the second year, with at least a 75% minority enrollment in the majority of Partnership courses. The high minority, and especially Latino, enrollment reflects the value that this partnership has for students of color at the university.

In addition, over half of the UCSC students involved, and 100% in some of the writing classes, could be considered initially underprepared for university-level work, based on their statewide Subject-A exam scores, which tests basic writing skills and plays a major role in their continued university enrollment. Although they have initially beaten "the statistics" by making it into the university, at least some of the college students involved in this partnership could be described as "at risk" of not graduating.

This partnership attempts to offer both student groups enough to help them persevere, stay in school, and be empowered participants in their education.

Writing Letters: Literacy and Relationships—Mariana, Vanessa, Naomi, and Others

The first time my students wrote letters, we brainstormed questions that they might have for university students and things in their lives that their "pen-pals" might want to know about them. Many of the letters were formal and uncomfortable. But a week later, when letters came back addressed to particular students, something magical began to happen. Writing letters started to be about relationships. Knowing that they would eventually meet their partners face-to-face added to the excitement of getting to know one another personally through the letters:

> . . . We get to meet new people we never met in our life. We can get to know what kind of things they like. It's like a mystery . . . you have to wait to see what they look like, if they like to play games, if you will be embarrassed. And maybe the UCSC students have some things in common with the Ohlone students. . . . I like it a lot. We can write to them by letters, they answer back and we answer back to them and it gives us writing time . . . if we have to write a story and we do not want to we can write to our UCSC students. We spend one hour of writing to the UCSC (students). We have all the time to write.

> —Mariana

In addition to the friends that she gained, Mariana's attitude about writing was affected by the letter writing. At the beginning of the year Mariana repeatedly told me that she did not like to write. By the end of the year she was not only excited about writing letters, but also was very involved in being an author.

As the program gained some history, the format of letter writing as a means of developing relationships went through various stages. The fifth graders got a firsthand understanding of the university quarter system when they came back from winter break and had to accept that many of their partners were no longer enrolled in one of Sarah-Hope's classes. Many had to get to know new partners, while still trying to maintain some contact with old partners who were now busy with other university classes.

But, despite the frustration of losing regular contact with their original partners, my students' first letters to their new partners were more confident: they knew what letter writing and the Partnership were all about. They could explain to their university partners how it worked, and many of them already were putting in requests for what they wanted to do and see on their next visit to the university. By the time Spring quarter came around, they were old hands at introducing their new UCSC compañeros to the ins and outs of the Partnership. One of the most exciting things for my students, however, was when some of the UCSC students took a variety of Sarah-Hope's Partnership courses over the year to maintain contact with their buddies.

> I love our thing we are doing with Sarah-Hope Parmeter, Debb. My new partner is the same guy from the beginning of the year, but I want to see who my other partner, Joe, is. . . . Oh, my other partner's name is Lou. I never got his address. Now is my chance. Elvia is also Lou's partner and Anna is Joe's partner. Joe has a Thunderbird. I hope my partners both come (to Ohlone) tomorrow.
>
> —Sancho

> With the students I am doing pretty good and again I got one of the partners I started with first writing letters and I am glad I got him again to see how he has been doing these days. I am going to give him a letter because he gave me the Ninja Turtle book and it is a neat book and I am looking forward to meet my other partner even though I forgot his name, but I think he is a very, very cool dude.
>
> —Milo

By the second year of the Partnership, even the introductory letters at the beginning of the year were much less stilted. This time we all had a larger context for what this letter writing meant. Sarah-Hope and I were more enthusiastic and helpful, and my students were aware of some of the magic that was tied to these letters: they had seen university students pouring out of my classroom last year, had heard about our five trips to UCSC, had had brothers, sisters, friends, and cousins in my class, and they had the library of books written by Sarah-Hope's students the previous year to give them a taste of what was to come. [For more information about these books, see the forthcoming section entitled "What's the Most Important Thing You Have to Say to These Kids?"]

Once the Partnership got underway, letter writing became such an essential part of what we *do* at school that all of my students were, and continue to be, completely engaged in reading and writing every Friday after recess, and, quite frankly, it has very little to do with me. Within moments of receiving them, these "at-risk" students scurry off to pore over every detail of their precious letters. There is an atmosphere of collaboration, sharing, oohs and aahhs, triumphant outbursts, and lots of literate activity.

Some students who only understand Spanish receive letters in

English and don't even notice the "barrier" to communication; they simply find someone to help translate the letter. Other students overlook obvious errors in the university partners' Spanish writing skills because they know that maybe their partner didn't get to use Spanish in school. Students who can barely read carefully work their way through what is sometimes nearly illegible handwriting, drawing in their friends and table-mates to decipher every last word. Non-writers dictate long, detailed letters to classmates, the teacher, or anybody they can find. Beatriz, who was just beginning to write in English, felt totally comfortable writing to her non-Spanish-speaking university partner in English, and was aware of the power of biliteracy. Thus, along with wanting to extend their relationship to include photos and phone calls, she embarked on the task of teaching her partner Spanish:

> Thank you. for the pictur But I dont. have a pictur But al go and te mi sister to give me a pictur of my if she stil havet so im fain in school can you cant bring ur cámara if you com to tec a pictur Two getor Two copies if you have a camara and al call you at a stor bicous I cant get a telepon tocal gust mye sister But Im goin to tech you Spanech for y can lornd espanesh school is escuela hause is casa invitation is invitacion partie is fiesta and dest is escritorio and Book is Libro and shoes is sapatos and Plant is planta and close is serado das ol for today and dis is a present fomi youl siet. From Beatriz hasta lavista

During letter-writing time, no one sits around waiting to be prodded into action. If they need help, or just want to share something, they find someone who will sit with them. Most of them just write: no instructions, no explanations—everyone knows what he or she wants to do and gets right to it.

The hardest thing is getting them to stop writing—to finish up and get back to "school." But they are motivated to finish on time because if their letters don't leave with Sarah-Hope—who brings the letters herself and spends letter-writing time with us—then their UCSC partner won't receive a letter in class on Tuesday. Nonetheless, they would like me to allot more time, because the letter writing is important to *them* and because the *relationships* are important to them.

Vanessa wrote very little for school. In her journal, she would occasionally drop one or two word clues about some deep, personal issues—her parents getting a divorce, problems with wanting desperately for the boys to like her, being overweight and starting to get acne: teen issues, self-confidence issues, scary issues. But it was letter writing that really opened Vanessa up. Her partners were people she could count on to understand her without the fickleness of early adolescence. They would be there and understand when she felt like the rest of her friends had deserted her. When writing letters, she seemed to blossom. She treasured the letters they sent to her, and when she wrote letters or wrote about the University, her partners, and the Partnership, writing was suddenly not such a terribly difficult thing to do. But so much depended upon feelings. With the partners she felt completely loved and unconditionally accepted. So, she poured time and effort into her letter writing.

Relationships and the power of these friendships comes up again and again in my students' writing. Naomi, who was going through a lot at home, wrote:

> Yo sí quiero ver a mis estudiantes nuevos. Y quiero que jueguen conmigo bien y que nunca me olvide ni yo a ella y todo el tiempo cuando agarro nuevos estudiantes yo no me quiero separar de ellos o ellas. Y sí los quiero mucho pero bien mucho hasta lloro de tanto genio que no están a mi lado o estar platicando con ella o él. Lo que hacemos con los estudiantes es fantastico y es una buena cosa . . . me gusta mucho con toda mi vida.

> [Yes, I like to see my new (UCSC) students, and I like that they play so well with me and I don't ever want her to forget me nor me her. And every time that I get new students I don't want to be apart from them, and I always ask for photos to remind me of them. And yes, I love them so much, so very much that sometimes I cry when they can't be at my side or if I can't be talking with him or her. What we do with the students is fantastic and is a good thing . . . I like it very much with all my life.]

>   —Naomi

Non-Writers and Tough Guys ("Talk about 'At Risk'")—Berto, Manuel, and Ramón

The first year of the Partnership, I had two students who were not able to read, and who could barely even write their names. Berto had only been in school for a little over a year, and, being very street-wise, had a hard time adapting to simply *being* in school with all these other students. When he came to me, he had not quite finished getting a mountain of anti-social and illegal behavior out of his system. The other student, Manuel, had been in school in Mexico and in the U.S., but had moved from school to school and country to country so much that no one really knew what he knew, or why he wasn't reading.

We began working with them in a very nontraditional, nonremedial way. The Partnership involved them indiscriminately in an entire class of "college-bound" fifth graders: students who, instead of being taught only remedial skills and being tracked into "low" groups, were learning what college is all about and what it takes to get there. And they were learning it from real university students, many of whom were the first in their families to go on to higher education, many of whom had beaten the odds.

Though Berto and Manuel were unable to read and had missed a great deal of school, this Partnership made it clear that they were "college material" if they wanted it badly enough. After all, they now knew some college students who were cool, street-wise, tough, who had not necessarily always done well in school, and who had made it anyway. Within this definition, Berto and Manuel were not automatically excluded from what it might mean to be "college bound." Additionally, they were immediately called upon to be authors. They discovered that they *needed* literacy for personal reasons, not just because I said so. They were soon reading their journals aloud with the class, collaborating on authoring stories, and waiting with anticipation for the letters from their UCSC partners.

For the non- or pre-writer, dictation is the most effective way to get his or her thoughts and words onto paper. It is the students' first taste of the power of the written word, of their *own* written words. Dictation was integral to letter writing for Berto and Manuel. They could neither read the letters they received nor respond to them without someone acting as an intermediary between them and print. One day during letter writing, a UCSC student—who had been in Sarah-Hope's class the previous quarter and who was now doing an independent field study in my classroom to maintain her ties with my students—came in and took dictation from Manuel and Berto in Spanish. She was still learning Spanish, so, as she wrote what they dictated, two of the most talented writers in my class looked over her shoulder. Rather than hassling their classmates for having someone write for them (we call it "hiring a secretary"), they just looked on and helped the UCSC "secretary" with her spelling.

Many students love to "hire a secretary" during letter-writing time if they can. Even the newest writers become much more involved in correcting spelling, grammar, or punctuation when an adult is writing for them. *Many* times I am corrected by students as I try to keep pace with their thoughts. Sometimes it is the best writers who seek out one of the adults to write for them, just because it is fun to supervise someone, and to watch their words flow across the paper with the accuracy that they know they are very close to achieving. This diffuses the focus on those students who *need* the extra help in order to write at all.

The following year, Ramón and I developed our relationship primarily through my secretarial service to him during letter writing. He, too, was a street-wise and sort of tough kid. Although he was extremely intelligent, his academic skills were low, his writing was frustratingly slow and painful, and he was dyslexic.

One Friday, Ramón wrote to his partner that he better watch out when they come to visit because his teacher (me!) is a great goalie in soccer and will not let him score even one goal. As I wrote this, Ramón and I smiled. We both knew what a lie it was, but it was Ramón's way of acknowledging our many conversations about his championship soccer games, conversations that had come about when he wrote about them to his partner with me as his scribe. Because the rest of my students were truly engaged in their own letter writing, I actually had the time to write with Ramón. It became a ritual that we both counted on.

Unlike Berto and Manuel, Ramón *could* have read and written these letters himself, but he knew it would slow him down and limit what he had to say. He also knew that his university partner, a Mexicano whose schooling had not helped him develop and maintain his native language skills, made enough mistakes in his Spanish that, for Ramón, reading the letters himself would have been confusing even if he could bypass letter reversals and figure out all the words. By hiring me as his secretary, he was able to see the value of being able to read and write fluently; to side-step spelling and usage errors and get to meaning.

As I wrote for him, often two or three jam-packed pages, he read along and was very patient about correcting me when I got it wrong. Clearly, his Spanish was better than mine, and better than his university partner's, and yet Ramón had been considered a "low" student for most of his life. This was one opportunity for him to feel the power of his own knowledge. And he was doing it for himself, not for me.

The letters are one way in which the Partnership is about reading and writing. They are also about gaining ownership of the university, fighting the odds, developing relationships, making decisions, and a whole lot more—but *literacy* is the key. Students experience literacy in a personally meaningful way. They learn about audience, format, and conventions of writing because it matters.

What's the Most Important Thing You Have to Say to These Kids—Enrique and Berto

Another way that the Partnership uses literacy is through the books that the UCSC students write for my students. In her university writing courses, Sarah-Hope asks her students to create a book for the fifth graders as their final project. Her instructions are that they find the most important thing they have to say to these ten-, eleven-, and twelve-year-olds, and say it in the most effective way. She also asks that the books be bilingual.

In an English-dominant university, in an English-dominant society, how can a university writing teacher require that her students produce some of their coursework in a language which some of them do not know at all, which others may speak but barely write, or may be learning slowly as a foreign language? Some others may be literate in Spanish but they have also worked their entire school career to master English so that they could get to the university where they are supposed to be continuing to master English in this writing course so that they can pass a writing test in English.

Of course, since these university students are trying to say something important, they want their words to have meaning for my students, many of whom are not yet literate in English. This gives Spanish a powerful position in a university writing course—for many Latino students, Spanish has never been given such status. It is a chance for them to find a voice that they have rarely been asked to bring into their education. Spanish as a valued and treasured voice, bilingualism and biliteracy as power, culture, and right, are the core of my bilingual program—perhaps this is a way in which the university students gain an understanding of some of these social issues. (Certainly, the requirement does not make the course unattractive to university students: for winter quarter in our third year, all of Sarah-Hope's Partnership courses were completely filled *before* the *pre*-enrollment period and had waiting lists twenty students long).

The UCSC authors decide what it means to create bilingual books: whether that means that everything in the book appears in both languages, that some pieces are in English and some in Spanish, or that the languages spiral in and out of one another in a single piece. They usually work in groups, which is sometimes the only way they can meet the bilingual requirement. They negotiate and help one another and struggle. The biliterate students are in high demand and often have to do more work, but then, this has been the case with the letter writing all along and has something to do with what they get out of the course. To Sarah-Hope's students, it is worth the extra effort to negotiate a biliterate environment, because effective communication with the fifth graders *matters* to them as well as to my students. Enrique, another of my very "at-risk" young "Home Boys,"[4] was a street dancer, not a writer; a dude, not a student. Writing nearly killed him. That's why he never did it. In fact, he pretty much didn't do any schoolwork. He wasn't a tough, mean, or defiant person. He'd really have liked to do well in school. But he'd had so little success in school. It just didn't work for him. Dancing was where it was at. He was *good* at that. He got respect.

But letter writing was pretty cool—because Angel, Enrique's partner, was *really* cool. He wasn't a phony "Home Boy." Angel was from L.A. and he'd been in a gang. So, when he wrote his book for the fifth graders, they knew he knew what he was talking about. *The Problems of Gangs and Drugs* is not just some adult-sponsored, anti-gang propaganda to ignore. It's a beautiful book; it's an honest book, with true stories and incredible art work. And right there on the inside cover, it's dedicated to Enrique.

> This story will deal with the bad effects of gangs, including the harm they cause in the community. Many of the gang members join violent street gangs at a young age, between ages 13–15 years old. . . . The kids start to believe that gangs will make them safe, make them seem tougher or "BAD" and more popular. Young kids see gang violence in movies, t.v., and in the streets. They think that the gang life is exciting, fun, and never-ending. Death is something that will never be real until it happens to them.
>
> The truth is if you are in a gang, you will either get killed or go to jail. If you don't die, then your brother, mother, sister, or father will someday get killed by a gang. The gang life is full of pain and suffering. Many people have to suffer because they live in a gang ruled neighborhood or because they're wearing a certain color.
>
> . . . Bullet was a gang member . . . he was shot two times. The back of his head had two bullet holes. He was killed by a "Blood" because of the color blue. Gangs are for losers.
>
> —from *The Problems of Gangs and Drugs*

The part about Bullet surrounds an incredible illustration of a "cool" gang type. The message is very powerful.

Berto, my street-wise non-reader, was equally drawn to the power of written language through many of the books written by the university students for my class. Books that speak straightforwardly about the risks and temptations of gangs, drugs, getting drunk at parties, getting (someone) pregnant, getting AIDS, and other issues that are in the forefront of his life gave him yet another link into the power of literacy.

> In the chapters of this book, you will read several anecdotes regarding different people's experiences. The stories address topics of peer pressure, pregnancy, ditching, and drugs . . . We would like you to think about how each story might relate to your own life, and what it would mean to you, taking into account your own values, if any of these things happened in your lifetime.
>
> —from *Four to Grow On*

Berto eventually coauthored a book called *Di "NO" a Drogas* (Say "NO" to Drugs) which he donated to the class library so that other students could read it. He felt like he could share a message with other students. After all, he's a cool *vato*,[5] and like the cool vatos at UCSC who had written books on these subjects had reached him, so, too, might he reach other fifth-grade vatos who were on their way to the life of drugs and gangs.

Remember, this was a street-tough twelve-year-old who could not read or write and whose antisocial and illegal behaviors made it very difficult for him to function in school, where he had been for only a little over a year. He was still in school two years later, which was quite a victory, and he is probably still in school now. Perhaps the Partnership had something to do with it. By the end of his year in my class, he had seen the university and loved going there. He had developed close friendships with several university students. He had begun to understand what university students do and think and write. And he was expressing a strong desire to be able to go to college some day.

The power and variety of the messages that are now in my ever-growing library of university-made books can really only be fully appreciated by spending days reading them, as well as appreciating the beautiful artwork and the bows and glitter and photographs that adorn them. Or better yet, to be there when my students and their partners read and review these books together or when the new batch of books are presented to them as gifts.

In the Partnership's second year, the UC students sat with my students at Ohlone and reviewed some of the previous year's books *before* they wrote their books. They got into "pre-writing response groups" and were able to see which books most appealed to their fifth-grade buddies—their audience. My students were able to look at the books with a critical eye—assessing what they liked about them to help actual authors. When the new batch of books arrived, they got to see the impact of their advice and criticism. There was nothing contrived about this process approach to writing. Next year, I hope for my students to write books for their second-grade buddies as well. I hope that they can get valuable feedback from the seven-year-olds and experience the process from both ends.

More About Writing and Being a Teenager—Ronaldo, Freddy, and Laurie

For Ronaldo, writing was a waste of time. He was certain he had no stories to tell. But the letters to and from UCSC were different. They had nothing to do with school or me. They were about things that mattered—sports, being cool, and not being bugged by adults. Through his relationship with the UCSC students, Ronaldo was able to channel some of his teen frustrations with the adult overlords in his life (you know, teachers, parents, *us*) into an outspoken political activeness. So many college students are into changing the world through political activism. Who better to take Ronaldo's complaints about school and unfair policies and turn them into political stances on societal issues? And who better to model to Ronaldo that staying in school was the best way to truly be able to effect real change?

When we studied civil disobedience and nonviolent change in my class, Ronaldo wanted to know how we could get rid of two adults at the school who were making his life miserable. He felt that they violated his rights and was beginning to articulate that maybe being at an impoverished school in an impoverished community where disenfranchised parents rarely made a fuss about keeping the school accountable might have something to do with why we were supposed to put up and shut up about people who did not meet his standards—and those the school professed to demand—for the way people should treat students. He was right. They were unfair and not really an asset to the school. But I couldn't even discuss it with him. They were my colleagues. He could, however, discuss it honestly with some of the university students, especially those who had been at various school events and who shared some of his opinions, or who had been involved in sit-ins, hunger-strikes, and protests to change university policies.

When we got a new principal during the year, she invited my class to come to her office and get to know her. "Do you have any questions?" she asked. Ronaldo put up his hand, "When are we getting a new P.E. teacher?" he asked. He was trying to make sense of his world and gain some power in it. It may have been an awkward question, but he felt he had a right to ask it. Interestingly, the teacher in question was eventually ousted from classroom teaching—in fact, less than a month after Ronaldo's request.

> "You're ready to be in college right now, where students can at least try to really change what they don't like, aren't you?" I joked with Ronaldo one day when it was time to return to Ohlone from UCSC.
> "Yeah, just leave me here," he smiled.

Similarly, Freddie liked the secrets he shared with his partners. "No, don't tell her!" he warned a friend after a trip to UCSC. He didn't want me to find out that they had played Nintendo for most of the day, because he knew how I felt about *that*.

"Well," I told him, "I still have the same opinion about you wasting your intelligence, but I know that what makes this Partnership work is that you get a little freedom from my judgments . . . that's all part of taking responsibility for your own education." He rolled his eyes at his friend.

Another time, Freddie wanted me to read his letter aloud to him. Just as I was about to begin, he kind of smiled at me. "You know," he warned me, "they swear in these letters."

"I know, and that's part of why this works, why you love it. Communication uncensored by me and the school, just like when you and your friends are out from under my radar-hearing. But it gets you to write, doesn't it?" I smiled. "Who knows? Maybe it will even make you want to go to college."

Laurie also found a haven in the politics of the university students. Raised primarily in Georgia, she was extremely outspoken when we studied slavery, Martin Luther King, Jr., and the civil rights movement. "I know lots of racists," she would say, "and sexist pigs, too!" She soaked up stories about the UCSC students at a sit-in to protest institutionalized racism in the University system, vigils for AIDS victims, and Nelson Mandela's release. She wore "Stop Apartheid" buttons (given to her by one of her UC friends) and went with me to the Earth Day festival in Santa Cruz where she saw several of her university buddies. She even got to speak on the university radio station on one of our field trips to solicit subscribers to public radio. When some of Sarah-Hope's students worked in my class on field placements—independent study courses which give them credit for continuing to work with the fifth graders—Laurie wanted to collaborate with them on writing a book about injustice.

Sometimes, because of her vehement and outspoken opinions, but primarily because of some very negative and self-destructive social behavior, Laurie had an intolerably difficult time fitting in with her peers. Through the Partnership, she had access to a whole different— and much less judgmental—group of friends, many of whom adored her fierce declarations for her various causes, and many of whom had similar passions. Unlike the daily difficulty she had at school even with her "best" friends, Laurie often expressed strong, self-confident feelings about her relationships with her university partners—many of whom she had adopted simply by beginning to write to them after meeting them during UCSC visits to Ohlone or Ohlone visits to UCSC.

> Me and my partners had the best of times. I have so many partners. Their names are Nancy, Tracy, Rebecca, Albert, Alysha, Diane, Danielle, Lynne. It will be nice to write to all these people . . . I had fun on the field trip (to UCSC). We are going to have fun next time . . . this was the best day I've had all year. It was exciting, too. I love going to UCSC. It is like, so great. Thank you, thank you, thank you very, very, very, very, very much. I wish I could have stayed longer, because it is very, very, very, very, very fun.
>
> —Laurie

Involving the Family: Turning Risk Around—Crispin, Yamilet, Maribel, Lucía, and Asusena

Crispin's parents came to everything. They came to the potlucks where parents and their children's UCSC partners got to meet one another. They went on several field trips to UCSC. They were even interviewed and photographed for an article in the Central California Writing Project Newsletter:

> As they walked around campus, one of the UC students told Crispin's parents, "Sus hijos tienen el mismo derecho de una educación como cualquiera otra persona."—"Your son or daughter has as much right to an education in California as anyone else does."
> "A lo méjor ésto podría ser real," Crispin's mother says. "Dicen que es el país de oportunidad y es cierto,"—"Maybe this could come true. They call this the land of opportunity, and it's true." Yet many of the parents don't feel they can help their kids understand what a university is about. In class the next week, Crispin says, "Mis padres me dijeron que, 'Así no tendrás que ser como nosotros y trabajar en los fils.'"—"My parents told me, 'This way you won't have to be like us and work in the fields.'"
> He went on to say, "Se puede asistir a la universidad aunque no tenga dinero. Algunos no van por falta de dinero, pero no es

necesario. Yo quiero ir a la universidad para ser alguien en la vida."—"You can go to the university even if you don't have money. Some people don't go to the university for lack of money, but that's not necessary. I want to go to the university to be someone in life."

—Roger Bunch, *Student Mentors*, CCWP Newsletter, v.2, no.1

Crispin's parents are now certain that he will be able to go to college because they know what it's all about. They have begun to become informed about the application procedures, entrance requirements, financial aid availability, etc. They have gotten to know so many wonderful UCSC students in whom they can see their son one day. I visited them nearly a year later, and they still spoke of Crispin's partners by name, and everyone in the family knew where he keeps his Partnership letters. Additionally, their daughter was at that time in the first grade. She also had been to the university and had had older pen-pals last year because her teacher had begun a similar partnership with high school students after hearing about our project. Not only was the whole family involved, but now this letter writing and university visits were becoming a norm.

The year before the Partnership began, one of my very gifted students told me that college wasn't for Mexicanos and that he would not betray his people. Last year I had the pleasure to have his sister as a student. Yamilet wrote many times of how her parents wanted both of them to go to college, and she wrote as though perhaps her brother were reconsidering the idea. Their parents were fairly involved in the Partnership, especially through the enthusiasm and seriousness with which Yamilet shared it with them.

A mí me encanta escribirles a los estudiantes de la universidad y estoy bien contenta con Sarah-Hope y con usted, maestra. El viernes para mi es un encanto, y también cuando vienen los estudiantes es un encanto, y cuando nosotros vamos para allá también es un encanto para mí.

A mi mamá le gusta esa idea porque así nosotros nos empeñabamos más en ir a la universidad. También me dijo mi mamá que ojalá que nosotros téngamos empeño en ir a la universidad y que ellos iban a pagar todo el dinero que se necesitara, no más para que nosotros vayamos a la universidad y aprendemos lo que quieramos nosotros.

[I love writing to the university students and I am very happy with Sarah-Hope and with you, teacher. For me, Friday (letter day) is magical, and it is magical when the students come here and when we go there (to UCSC) is also magical for me.

My mother likes this idea (the Partnership) because this way

we will work harder and be more determined to go to college.
She also says that hopefully we will have the perseverance to go
to college and that they will pay all of the money necessary, just
so that we go to college and learn what we want.]

—Yamilet

Maribel's mother also came to all Partnership activities. She remembered how she had once dreamed of a college education for herself,
and then for her oldest daughter, without the dream becoming real.
As she saw all of the UCSC memorabilia, letters, and photographs of
university students begin to cover Maribel's bedroom walls, she began
to feel like this time, for Maribel, the dream of college might finally
come true.

The last time I talked to them, Maribel and her mom were talking
about going to college together, and taking Maribel's sister (who had
her first child at the age of seventeen) with them. College became a
family dream because of the Partnership.

Lucía might be the most outstanding student I have ever had. She
is every teacher's dream: an avid reader who has worked her way
through every library in town; an outstanding, completely biliterate
writer who was ready to publish; a student delighted with the magic
of math and science . . . in love with learning of any kind. One day
she said to me, "Ms. Bell, is it possible to have *two* careers? Could I
be both an astronomer *and* an author?" She was so relieved! She
wrote:

Power: To me, power doesn't just mean being able to beat people
up. Power is something much more serious.

When people have discipline and education, they have power.
Education is important because when you grow up you will need
to have a job, because money doesn't grow on trees. And you
need to have an education also because it makes you feel good
about yourself and you discover many different things. I discovered
reading, and now I want to be an Author. When you learn a
subject, and you like it, you might want to be that when you
grow up.

Power also means that you have to believe in yourself and to
think positive. If you just give up in life, you will be like a nobody.
You have to try and try something all over again until you learn
it. Never give up.

Power also means fighting for your rights. If you just stay
quiet all the time, and you don't understand something, you're
never going to learn it. So SPEAK up!

—Lucía

And yet, Lucía's mother expressed only a moderate opinion of her daughter's chances of succeeding in school. Lucía missed most of our field trips to the university because her mother kept her home. I visited their tiny apartment many times to see if I could influence her mother's decision. Sarah-Hope came with me a few times. I talked about the Partnership, the letters, and the field trips, and I pointed out Lucía's goals and her academic excellence. Her mother responded dubiously. Lucía was delicate and needed to stay at home, and well, college was such a question . . . money, and living away from home, and it was so far away. Usually, when I visited, Lucía hid out in the other room, only reluctantly coming out to join us, although always with a smile. They had no phone, and her best friend who lived in the next apartment said Lucía never came out at all on the weekends or in the summer. She seemed to be subdued and quiet at home, except when showing me her latest cache of library books, her cat, or describing the latest science special she had seen on the public television channel.

Finally, despite her bus sickness (which did not seem to affect her that day) and her asthma and her possible cold, not only did Lucía come with us to UCSC (one time out of five), but her mother came as well. We got her mother all of the admission and financial aid forms in Spanish to study. She got to see what a university and university students are like, and she got to see her daughter in action. I believe that visiting the university probably had a greater influence on her mother's attitude about the university than on Lucía's. Lucía already knew she wanted to go. But now, her mother at least had some idea of what it was all about.

I recently visited Lucía and her mom. After chatting for awhile, I asked her mother if she thought the Partnership had helped make college seem like a more realistic goal for Lucía. She looked at me like I was crazy. "What Partnership?" she wanted to know. Then she asserted, "We've always intended for Lucía to go to college." Maybe it wasn't the accolades I was hoping for, but regardless of what she attributed it to, her mother was talking about college as a given.

Sometimes, as in the case of Asusena, the impact of the Partnership on the family was not as direct, but perhaps will prove equally powerful. Asusena's mother worked two jobs to support her children. She could not come to any school events, and was almost never home. Asusena's academic skills are very high, and she's an excellent artist, but she rarely came to school, and when she did, she nearly always arrived late and often without her homework. Nonetheless, she was one of the most conscientious letter writers. She would write five or six long, detailed letters to her many partners every week, spending a good two hours deeply involved in reading and writing every Friday morning. The only time any adult in her family came to school was at one of the potlucks with the UC students. Her aunt came and spent the evening in deep conversation with some of Asusena's partners.

One day, Asusena brought her family pictures to show me. We had talked a lot about how difficult it was to be the first in your family, especially for a lot of the girls (primarily because of teen pregnancy, child-care responsibilities, etc.), to do something like go to college.

> "This is my sister, Adriana."
> "Oh, she's pretty. How old is she? Has she graduated from high school?" I asked.
> "No, she stopped going to school." We looked at each other.
> "Will that make it harder for you?"
> We looked through more pictures—more older sisters, brothers, and cousins, some who had graduated or who planned to graduate, but none who were talking about college.
> "This is *Gloria*."
> "Is she your oldest sister?"
> "No, this is *Gloria*. She's my [UCSC] student!"

So, now Asusena has someone who is a college student among her family photos.

From "At Risk" to "College Bound"

I believe the Partnership has really made a difference for many of my students, especially by including them in the "college-bound" club. They gain ownership of the university. They are beginning to develop literacy in the language of academia on which to build later when it comes time to ask about financial aid, or dorms and dining halls, or final exams, term papers, and taking the SAT. At least some of these might be words they've heard or things they've seen. These fifth graders are starting to talk about college—starting to envision themselves as "college bound," starting to say "When I go to college."

They now have a context in which to imagine themselves as college students because they have been wrapped up with college for a year. They have seen other Latinos who have made it to college despite the odds: despite having to master English as a second language; despite financial difficulties; despite a school system that consistently fails to prepare Latinos for college; despite lack of exposure to, experience with, and guidance from family members who know the ins and outs of the university system; despite these and other factors that so often cause "at-risk," LEP (Limited English Proficient), Hispanic, impoverished, or migrant students to opt out of the educational system at an early age.

Through this Partnership, my students begin to gain this exposure, experience, guidance, vocabulary, and ownership of the educational system and what it takes to get to college. Along with their personal experiences and relationships through the Partnership, they have a beautiful, bilingual guide for college-bound students in one of the UCSC student-written books that is consistently a favorite: *The Road to College.* This book ties specific information about getting into college, college life, and photographs of the university, dorms, and dining halls with the authors' personal stories of growing up in Watsonville, Guatemala, Vietnam, San Francisco, and South Korea. It even includes one of the UC student's financial aid statements. My students also have many other books that speak to them honestly and supportively about the choices they will have to make during adolescence—about friends, drugs, sex, gangs, and staying in school—and about the impact that those decisions will have on their lives and on their opportunities to get to college.

I hope that this Partnership and all that it embodies combines to give my students the self-image that says, *"Even if it's hard, I can do it, too, because I know what it's all about and I know that the university is there for me!"* It may also empower Sarah-Hope's students to see how continuing their educations and graduating from college will help their Ohlone compañeros beat the odds, influence the make-up of the future university population, and take a part in changing the world.

Notes

1. All names (except the author's, Sarah-Hope Parmeter's, and Roger Bunch's) have been changed for reasons of privacy.

2. These figures are from the 1989–90 school year.

3. These figures are from the 1989–90 academic year.

4. "Home Boy" or "Home Girl" are terms gang members often use to refer to fellow gang members, and which "wannabe's"—younger kids who glorify and emulate gang life, even claiming affiliation with specific gangs—use to refer to "cool dudes." In fact, the term is popular among many students, even those who openly oppose gang activity. Often "Home Boy" is used as the opposite of the term "School Boy," an often derogatory term for someone who does "too" well in school.

5. "Vato" is a term used very much like "Home Boy," although it almost implies that one is cool without necessarily implying gang membership; it is more like a "wannabe." A gang member would more likely be called a "cholo."

10 Ethnographic Writing for Critical Consciousness

James Zebroski
Syracuse University

Nancy Mack
Wright State University

The English Teacher in the Twenty-First Century

As we English teachers prepare to enter the twenty-first century, we are discovering that our classrooms are at the forefront of the changes beginning to sweep the world. We see new student populations entering our classes, coming from varied cultures and ethnic communities, often speaking other languages. We realize that the literacy instruction we are charged with passing along to the next generation cannot be separated from the lives of these students. And yet the lived experience of our students often differs radically from our own. The lives of our students increasingly put to test the assumptions about race, class, gender, and sexuality that have over the past hundred years informed the making of the traditional English curriculum.

Ethnographic writing provides one of the best methods that we have discovered for connecting classroom instruction in literacy with the lived experience of our students. Shirley Brice Heath defines ethnography as a writing "genre which results from a set of methods which include long-term residence within a group, knowledge of the language of the group, and selection of methods of data collection" (94). Ethnographic writing makes the social and political nature of language (and language instruction) explicit to the writer. The dialogic dimension of ethnography in which the ethnographer returns to the people at the site and discusses his or her interpretations with the people is especially crucial. Ethnographic writing, then, reports on reality, the reality of our students and the people important in their lives, but it does so from the perspective of the insider in the community. The writer tries to understand how these people construct their world and their knowledge of it.

Over the last decade, we have used this activity with diverse student populations which have included inner-city seventh graders, prison inmates, first-generation college students, education majors, and graduate students who are classroom teachers. We also believe that doing our own ethnographic writing has helped us to view our classrooms in a different way and has made it possible for us to think more critically about our own reasons for teaching students to write.

We believe that education is not a spectator sport and that students are not only capable of, but, due to their differing experiences and perspectives, are especially well positioned to *produce* knowledge, not simply consume it. Ethnographic writing provides the English teacher with a genre and a set of related language processes that work with the materials of our students' lives. Ethnographic writing potentially breaks open the traditional curriculum to the worlds outside.

The Ethnographic Alternative

All of this is, of course, not new. John Dewey long ago argued for the centrality of student experience in the school curriculum. More recently, in the early 1960s, Paulo Freire worked with literacy teachers in Brazil using ethnographic methods to teach peasants to read and write. Anthropologists on his team presented the peasants with some tentative findings about the community. These findings were put forward in pictures and in talk, posed as questions for the "culture circles." The peasants in these "culture circles" were asked to talk about their lives, to participate in revising these findings and in creating their own understanding of their community from their own perspectives. Literacy was then introduced into this rich set of contexts as an instrument for further community- and self-reflection. Literacy became the peasants' instrument for producing knowledge, because, in Freire's view, literacy, as a visible product of the "culture," is the perfect instrument for studying "culture." Reading and writing in Freire's process were taught for critical consciousness, not as one-dimensional, passive "skills" for the inculcation of elite values.

Freire's use of ethnography to teach peasants in Brazil to read and write dovetails with some of the alternatives to literacy education that have arisen in the United States. Eliot Wigginton used a related approach in the rural South starting in the late sixties. After trying out the traditional English curriculum in his Georgia classrooms and having it fail miserably, Wigginton decided to ask his students to interview people in the community to gather folklore and "traditional" knowledge. His students, of course, went on to create the widely known, highly successful, and greatly respected Foxfire project and have over the past twenty years published many volumes on the life and lore of their people. Wigginton discovered that his students, in the process of composing *Foxfire*, not only used and improved their reading and writing abilities, but also gained a measure of pride in their own culture. They came to value the knowledge of tradition bearers who might otherwise have been ignored. And his students came to see more clearly their place in the local communities and the value of resisting national forces that would erase local and regional difference.

In the cases of both Freire and Wigginton, the people in the community are seen to be co-teachers. They are viewed as experts, as creators of knowledge. Students, when asked to do ethnographic writing, become, in a certain sense, apprentices to the tradition bearers in the community, and, after learning from these people, are asked to teach their classmates and their teacher about what they have found and written up. Thus, ethnographic writing has the potential to give students the opportunity of making their lives in various communities the subject of classroom talk, study, reading, and writing.

Practices and Principles

What, precisely, do we mean by ethnographic writing? There are a range of ethnographic practices coming out of different traditions of knowledge making, deriving from totally different conceptions of knowledge. For example, in the English classroom, it seems singularly inappropriate to teach ethnography as a "scientific" practice. We are not interested in having students play at being scientists, distancing themselves even further from knowledge and knowledge making. We do not want our students seeing the people they interview as "subjects." We do not want students to feel the need to emulate a false objectivity. To teach this sort of ethnography in the English classroom is, at the very least, to put another set of methodological obstacles in front of our students. At worst, it unthinkingly reproduces ruling power relations.

But then again neither are we interested in having students do a purely interpretive ethnography that privileges for its own sake a phenomenological concern with recreating the categories of experiences of those at the site. This "slice of life" ethnography too often is ahistorical and ignores the very sorts of social concerns of importance and interest to our students.

Instead, we ask students to do what we call critical ethnography, writing that foregrounds the lives of our students and their use of critical thinking, reading, and writing processes. We want students to connect school with society, to see more clearly the relations between them. Students are already involved in many communities. The English classroom becomes one place where knowledge of these communities can be created and shared.

So, ethnographic writing often

- gives a reader a glimpse of the daily activities at the site.
- tries to present motives as viewed by the people at the site.
- provides the words of the people through direct quotation.
- provides telling dialoque.
- gathers information collected through observation and interviewing.
- attends to how all activities at a site work together as a whole.
- attends to overt and hidden conflicts that pull the community apart.
- details the ways people at the site act, talk, and think.
- looks at what people at the site do, say, and make.
- investigates how people at the site produce knowledge.
- studies the ways knowledge is related to language and power.

Our students work on their ethnographic projects over a longer period of time than is usual for other writing assignments—anywhere from four weeks to an entire term. Ethnographic writing is always a part of a broader unit rather than a decontextualized writing assignment. Because failure is likely if the teacher does not understand the larger class context out of which this assignment arises, we sketch out below one course. This sketch is *not* meant to be prescriptive, but it is meant to highlight the importance of seeing the ethnographic writing project holistically and in context. The surest guarantee of failure is to make ethnographic writing into a set piece, into a formula which can be broken down into component skills, and one which has not been carefully prepared by and integrated into the English curriculum.

In one research-writing course, the second in the sequence of required college writing courses, students investigated "working." All assignments were in some way related to this theme of working. The class read selections from Studs Terkel's book *Working*, from Henry David Thoreau's essay "Life Without Principle," from Tillie Olsen's *Silences*, from John Steinbeck's *Grapes of Wrath*. Students listened to the Woody Guthrie song "Pastures of Plenty," and compared that song with songs by Bruce Springsteen on the closing down of factories and the resulting devastation. Many of these students knew about such economic devastation first hand and were encouraged to write and talk about the difficulties friends and relatives in the region were having as the mills shut down. Significantly enough, these students discovered from other students in the class that similar economic hard times were occurring for the farmers in the region. Students read parts of Donald Trump's *The Art of the Deal* and related self-help writing, but also began looking at the vast critique of work in twentieth-century industrial society as exemplified by Eric Fromm's discussion from *The Sane Society.*

The readings and recordings of the first part of the course were always parallel to activities that asked students to write about their own working experiences and those of people they knew. Students were also asked to look at how work was portrayed in the media—in television dramas and in TV commercials, in magazine ads, in our language and way of thinking about and categorizing our world (the obsession we observe with "the weekend" as opposed to the relative silence about the week, for example). The class concluded that working in the United States seemed to be portrayed as a negative, powerless, violent experience. Students found that this conflicted with their ideology of work, their vision of the American dream. So, *only at this point*, did students go out into the world and investigate their subject by writing ethnographically about it. Are the worlds we inhabit different from the worlds portrayed in the literature we have been reading? If so, how? If not, then why not?

Only after the context had been carefully set did we ask students to select a "site," a group of people who "work" and are willing to talk about it. Because so many of our students these days often hold down jobs on their own in addition to going to school, this became a way for them to make that life a subject of their school life if they wanted. Students were asked to keep detailed field notes of their observations. A bit later on they were also asked to interview some people in depth, and to keep notes of that. All the while, students were coming to class with their notes and were writing and sharing reflections on their observations and interviews. Finally, students were asked to select, from this mass of specifics, that information that seemed thematically connected with, that supported or contradicted, the themes they had noted in their study of work. This was written up in several drafts as a report on the site. These ethnographic essays were published together as a class book that all students then carefully read. As a class, we generalized from the essays in front of us, comparing and contrasting the worlds presented in them with the worlds presented in the literature we had been reading. We then assigned follow-up papers that quoted and cited the students' ethnographic essays to prove a thesis about working. The final volumes of ethnographic essays were bound and placed in the library and distributed to audiences outside of the class.

One student, who wrote the essay titled "Stepping Stone" for the class book *Collected Ethnographies: Spring 1986,* studied the work and workers at a local McDonald's fast food restaurant. The writer noted:

> ... Wilma and Jenny, the up till now congenial assistant managers, are beginning to show the strain from the barrage of questions and rumors. Wilma, a college graduate with a Masters degree in music, had settled for this position after being unable to find employment in her own field. Wilma is constantly saying that McDonalds "is only a stepping stone until something better comes up. If I get something better, I'm getting out of here." Jenny, the other assistant manager, considers McDonalds a stepping stone to the future. "Just let that bank call me and see how quick I get out of here," Jenny was often heard to say. Jenny is on the list to be considered for employment by a well-known bank in the area but has been told that it could be as long as three years until her application will be considered. A Bachelors degree in business has not insured Jenny's dreamed-of future upon graduation from the university.

The writer describes the seeming contradiction between the American work ethic and the reality of work at this job.

> "Getting out" is the greatest obsession of virtually every worker at McDonalds. To the workers, "getting out" is another way of saying going on to a better future. Tatiana is sure she only needs to work until December and she will have enough saved for business school. Crystal needs at least another year for tuition money, then she can afford to take a job with less hours. The employees are mutually bound together by their desparate need for the only jobs they are able to get in the depressed local economy and their overwhelming desire to "get out."

This essay goes on to narrate the arrival of a new manager at the fast food restaurant:

> In mid-February Fred arrived in all his magnificent three hundred and twenty pounds of fatty flubbering flesh. ... It is apparent from the first schedule he made which employees Fred liked and which ones he didn't. Several employees who previously had seven hour shifts with thirty-five to forty hours a week find that

their schedules are now containing a total of sixteen hours a week with two and three hour shifts. Quiet, soft spoken, twenty-year-old Katrina seems to be a target for many of Fred's sarcastic remarks. "Speak up," he snaps at Katrina as she tries to serve a dining room full of customers. "I swear, she walks around like she doesn't know where she's at." Fred continues in a loud voice with a sneerful expression on his face.

The essay moves towards its climax by carefully providing the reader with detail—the complete essay is over two thousand words long—giving the facts involved in this emerging situation. The writer selects and arranges materials carefully to achieve an effect. The writer critically examines the situation and appears to achieve some degree of what Freire calls "critical consciousness" toward the situation.

The next morning, Jenny reported to work as usual. She had chosen to accept the demotion, at least until the district manager could intervene on her behalf. After all, what was her crime? She had always told everyone that she was applying for other jobs, and that if she ever got another job she would be able to "get out." McDonalds was only a "stepping stone" after all. She was only trying to better herself. A couple of hours into Jenny's shift, the telephone rang. Fred answered it in his office. "Jenny I want to see YOU NOW," bellowed Fred. "You will," Fred started as soon as Jenny walked into the door, "learn not to try to go over my head again! You have proven your disloyalty to me again by trying to go to the district manager, but I OWN fifty percent of this place and you no longer work here as of right now! You will never work for me or this restaurant again!" As Jenny walked through the frontline in tears, Fred emerged from his office with a smug satisfied smile on his rotund face. . . . The shift finished in a cheerless atmosphere. Everyone knew what had happened. Jenny had finally "got out." Their shift over, the employees walked out together.

We offer these snippets from the longer student text not simply to give the reader a sense of the kind of writing that the ethnographic project tends to produce. We are particularly impressed with the chance offered to connect school (and literacy) with experience outside of school. We are excited by the potential that ethnographic writing has for breaking open the school curriculum to the social issues closest to the students.

Ethnographic Possibilities

The account given above is obviously just one scenario. Ethnographic writing is highly adaptable. We have used ethnographic writing in a more focused look at social class, as a method to help middle school students examine the rich languages they speak, and as a means for prison inmates to collect parole board stories. Ethnographic writing has been central to folklore collection projects (urban legends of the sort Brunvand describes), language study projects (slang studies, analyses of work jargon), and local cultural projects (the history and role of local institutions—churches, youth groups, ethnic clubs and festivals). The point is that, in each case, ethnographic writing bridges school and the society, literacy and life. Most importantly, we accept ethnographic writing as authentic knowledge making, on par with any of the popular and elite literature studied in our courses.

Procedures and Problems

Undertaking ethnographic writing in the classroom requires careful planning and clear direction. Having dealt with various teacher and student frustrations when others have tried it, we recommend the following procedures when using ethnographic writing in the English classroom.

1. Begin with reading about the thematic topic before students select their field sites. Also, talk briefly on a need-to-know basis about methods used by ethnographers: observation, questioning, interviewing, keeping field notes.

2. Require that students select a specific site by a particular date.

3. Talk about the ethics of ethnographic writing and the need in most cases to inform and involve people at the site.

4. Ask students to make at least one field notebook entry for each visit. Also ask students to make one reflective response for each visit.

5. Encourage students to do very detailed field notes, since they should not know beforehand exactly what they will select to include in the final essay.

6. After several weeks of fieldwork, many pages of written observations, and lots of classroom discussion of the sites, ask students to declare a clear focus for their reports.

7. Encourage students to make sense out of their data through critical analysis. Larger social issues should be considered. The reader of the ethnographic essay needs to understand why studying a specific group can be useful to society at large.

Benefits of Ethnographic Writing

As a classroom activity, ethnographic writing unfolds in interesting ways. Students assume authority as the experts on their sites, taking this commitment seriously. They often demand the skills that they need to assure effective and well-written texts. In one case documented in ethnographic detail by Sharon Dorsey, middle school students decided they wanted their manuscripts typed. This decision led to their mastery of several word-processing programs that their teacher didn't even understand. Skills become a necessity to maintain the integrity of the enterprise. Thus, these middle school students, even though dismissed early, decided to remain in school on the last day of classes in order to ensure that each chapter of their publication was proofread by the group as a whole. Watching middle school students squabble over the rhetoric of comma placement while their peers were flooding from the school for summer vacation was a remarkable sight.

It would obviously be foolish to imply that all students would be this committed to ethnographic research. The point is that ethnographic writing can be used to teach almost any literacy skill in context. Students tend to approach these tasks with greater enthusiasm and mastery than when these same skills are taught through drills and pop quizzes. Ethnographic writing is a whole language learning experience par excellence. The parts of the literacy process are taught in a context that accepts the student's need and ability to create knowledge that is important, useful, and oftentimes, aesthetically pleasing.

But, as English teachers, we are concerned with more than just mastery of minimal literacy skills. We are also committed to recognizing the central place social issues have in the English curriculum. Studying social issues in the context of everyday life can be much more meaningful to students than studying the same issues in trumped-up classroom debates. Ethnographic writing provides students with specific cases from everyday life which can be carefully examined.

Ira Shor, in his book *Critical Teaching and Everyday Life*, shows us how often we are alienated from recognizing and understanding more deeply the conflicts in our own lives. Shor suggests some ways of making the English classroom the place where we can begin to think critically about our world. Our classroom practices extend Shor's observations. Our class discussions have become more focused and productive when they moved from vapid generalization to specifics drawn from the lives of teachers and students. The English classroom can be and must be the place for dialogue about the relations in effect between language, knowledge, and power. We seek to examine and open up for discussion student observations of the life that surrounds them, rather than indoctrinating students with either the teacher's beliefs or those of the dominant ideology. We want our students to develop their *own* critical consciousness, not simply parrot their teachers' views or reproduce the ruling class ideology. This is the most important ability that students could take from our class, from our ethnographic writing projects—to begin to make sense of their everyday worlds, of their own words, and to feel that understanding is possible and can lead to transformation of those worlds and words.

References

Anaftof, E. with J. Levin. 1983. *Twixt: Teens Yesterday and Today.* NY: Franklin Watts.

Brake, M. 1980. *The Sociology of Youth Culture and Youth Subcultures: Sex and Drugs and Rock n Roll.* NY: Routledge, Kegan, Paul.

Brown, C. 1978. *Literacy in Thirty Hours: Paulo Freire's Process in North East Brazil.* Chicago: Alternative Schools Network.

Brunvand, J. 1981. *The Vanishing Hitchhiker: American Urban Legends and Their Meanings.* NY: Norton.

Dorsey, S.R. 1985. "An Ethnography of a Middle School Language Arts Class." Diss. The Ohio State University.

Freire, P. 1973. *Education for Critical Consciousness.* NY: Seabury.

Heath, S.B. 1987. "The Literate Essay: Using Ethnography to Explode Myths." Judith Langer (Ed.). *Language, Literacy and Culture: Issues of Society and Schooling.* Norwood, NJ: Ablex.

Jacobs, J. 1984. *The Mall: An Attempted Escape from Everyday Life.* Prospect Heights, IL: Waveland Press.

Lloyd-Jones, R. and A. Lunsford. (Eds.) 1989. *The English Coalition Conference: Democracy through Language.* Urbana, IL: NCTE and MLA.

LeMasters, E.E. 1975. *Blue-Collar Aristocrat: Life-styles at a Working-Class Tavern.* Madison: University of Wisconsin.

Palmer, P. 1990. "Good Teaching: A Matter of Living the Mystery." *Change Magazine,* January/February, 11–16.

Rubin, L.B. 1978. *Worlds of Pain: Life in the Working Class Family.* NY: Basic.

Spradley, J. 1980. *Participant Observation.* NY: Holt, Rinehart, Winston.

Spradley, J. and B. Mann. 1975. *The Cocktail Waitress: Women's Work in a Male World.* NY: Wiley.

Spradley, J. and D.W. McCurdy. 1972. *The Cultural Experience: Ethnography in Complex Society.* Chicago: SRA.

Terkel, S. 1972. *Working.* NY: Avon.

Wigginton, E. (Ed.) 1972. *Foxfire: 1.* Garden City, NY: Doubleday.

11 A Ghostly Chorus: AIDS in the English Classroom

M. Daphne Kutzer
State University of New York at Plattsburgh

An English Department colleague of mine says, only half-jokingly, that students need not be psychology or sociology or any other sort of -ology major: they need only take English courses; need only read, write, and think to learn about human nature. I tend to agree with him. Yes, I want my students to leave my classroom better writers and better thinkers, to know the rules governing punctuation or the difference between synecdoche and metonymy, but I also want them to leave knowing more about themselves and the world they live in. Literature and composition not only reflect the world, but like Alice's looking glass can help students enter new worlds, worlds important but unknown or unexplored by college students. In the past three years, I have developed a strategy for using various social issues, and especially AIDS, as subject matter in both writing and literature classrooms, with an overwhelmingly positive response from the students.

I should say that this project developed itself, with the help of the students. I began as a frustrated process-oriented teacher of composition, someone in search of appropriate writing models for both beginning and advanced composition students. Some semesters I chose a standard rhetoric/reader, others I resorted to packages of xeroxed articles that struck me as interesting, and once I assigned *Time* magazine as the basis of short, weekly, written assignments on current political and social issues. These approaches had mixed results, and at last I asked the students (by means of an anonymous survey they filled out at the first class meeting) what contemporary social topics they would enjoy reading and writing about.

When I first used the questionnaire, in 1987, one of the questions was "What do you think is the most important social issue facing America today?" Nearly every student responded with "AIDS." This surprised me, since I teach at a medium-sized university campus in a rural area, where at least a third of our students have grown up in small towns far away from such "urban" issues as AIDS. But I had promised these first-semester freshmen that they would be writing on subjects they cared about, and that I would write an essay along with them, so I told them they had one week to give me three typewritten pages on the subject of AIDS. The only further advice I gave them was that I wanted honest reactions to the disease, not a research paper—I forbade them to use the library, which they didn't mind at all. I also promised them that they would have a chance to see and comment on my drafts of an AIDS essay while they were working on their own.

Writing my own essay on the subject of AIDS was at least as frightening to me as writing was to my students. I'm in a low-risk group, but most of my friends are not, and by 1987 I was seeing the first AIDS-related deaths among friends. Dealing with my grief on paper, and then sharing that grief with twenty-some unknown young adults, was something I wasn't sure I could cope with. On the other hand, I remember telling myself, here was an opportunity to do something for myself while I educated my students not only about writing but also about a life-threatening disease that they were all at risk for, so I took a deep breath and plunged into my essay.

Two days after they received their assignment, the students saw my first draft, which began, "AIDS crept up on me, a mere whisper of a strange new virus at first, but now a loud and ghostly chorus chanting always in my ears. Two friends have died, and a third was just readmitted to the hospital a year and a day after his first admission and diagnosis of AIDS." I had never had a classroom as intently quiet as the one in which the students read my draft prior to discussing it, nor was I prepared for the intensity of the analysis of the draft. I don't know what I had been expecting from class discussion, but I knew I was nervous enough about sharing the writing that I chose not to read it aloud to the students. As they read silently, there was no shifting in chairs, no staring out the windows, no doodling in the margins. They were more involved in what they were reading than I have ever seen students be, and not because they were reading great writing. They were absorbed because I had been honest about my promise to let them write about issues they cared about, because I risked showing myself to them as a fellow, feeling human being rather than a goddess with a red pen, and because they were reading and writing about sex and mortality, two subjects that, at their age, are intensely interesting and frightening and now, in these times, more closely linked than ever.

That I presented myself as an open and caring fellow human being, one willing to take risks with a room full of strangers, in turn made my students more comfortable in working with my essay and with their own. I didn't yet know their names, and they were freshmen in only the second week of class, yet they were willing to tell me that most of my examples of AIDS victims focused on "special" people like actors and dancers and not on ordinary people; to point out that if I wanted to reach them as my audience I ought to stay away from such "fancy" words as "futile" and "bereavement"; that my title was boring; and that many of my sentences were too long and difficult for them to follow. I incorporated much of their advice in my next draft.

When, the next class period, they turned in *their* first drafts, I was more astonished than I have ever been as a teacher of writing. Here were freshman students in the fall semester, students who didn't know me at all or have much reason to trust me with their feelings, students who knew their essays were likely to be dittoed and passed around for the class to discuss, and they turned in essays containing passages like the following:

> I'm a virgin. I have been refraining from sex for a specific purpose. I really want to be in love with the "right" guy. Everyone thinks, "Oh, she is waiting until she gets married." I believe in premarital sex, much to the surprise of people who know I'm a virgin. The truth is, I haven't found anyone to share sex with who is worth the sacrifice.

> When AIDS was first widely discovered amongst the homosexual population I remember the words of my neighbor while in deep discussion with my father. "Serves those queers right, god is trying to scare them straight!" How could someone believe that a disease that only kills could be a blessing? I can't remember what my father said but I'm surprised he didn't slug him. My father is a strong man, both physically and mentally. He never shunned me or my brothers, not even after my oldest brother told my father he was gay.

> As each day passes by my fears grow stronger and stronger for I know that soon someone close to me will tell me that he or she is dying of AIDS. I am so sure that this will happen because I happen to be of the gay community; I am a lesbian.

These are not exceptional examples—every one of my students was equally frank and honest. Their writing still had problems with punctuation, grammar, sentence structure, paragraph organization, and all those other difficulties in freshman writing, but every essay had a thesis statement and every essay had a personal voice. I did not receive a single draft that was the equivalent of "My sister is like my best friend" or "I admire my father more than anyone in the world" or "The woods in winter are like a wonderland" or any of those other generic student essays that too many of us face too often.

Beginning the semester this way had a number of positive effects. Students quickly learned to trust the classroom as a writing environment, and me and their peers as guides through it. They couldn't yet define a thesis statement, but they could certainly produce one. They came to understand very quickly what "voice" means when applied to writing, as well as the importance of audience. They watched me struggle through seven drafts of my own essay and learned that writing is not magic, that it is hard work even for professionals. They learned that writers collaborate with and depend upon editors, and that this process differs substantially from plagiarism. Most important, perhaps, they and I learned how writing helps us order the world, helps raise a "momentary stay against confusion" as Frost once wrote, and how writing can help heal.

But the students learned more than the mechanics of writing—they learned something about themselves and the complexities of the world they live in. They were full of questions about the disease itself, and, although I am not a health educator, I know a great deal about AIDS and found myself fielding questions about transmission, symptoms, prevention, and treatment. There was a gasp when, in response to a student question, I told them that there are at least five students on our campus who have tested HIV positive. There were further gasps when I gave them copies of Kinsey's statistics on the incidence of homosexual behavior and adultery among men.

After such a dramatic start, I wasn't sure the remainder of the semester would be quite so interesting, but I was wrong. Students had learned that those "boring" headlines in *The New York Times* actually had something to do with their lives, and we had a lively time writing about advertising, drugs, rock and roll, government funding of education, feminism, and other contemporary issues that interested them. None of these were research topics, although gradually students began to use the library on their own, which made the mandated "documented essay" of the semester a much more pleasant task than usual. I didn't always write an essay along with them, but workshop sessions and peer editing became a much more natural part of the classroom than they had before my experience in using AIDS as a topic.

I learned at least as much from this project as my students did. My own writing improved dramatically because I was forcing myself to write for an audience not of Ph.D.s or subscribers to *The New York Times*, but of ordinary American middle-class young adults. This is, after all, the primary audience of my teaching life, and I got to know them and their lives much better during this project, which helped me continue to connect better with them during the course of the semester. I learned something about honesty in writing, and I certainly learned how to begin to deal with grief and loss through words and not only through tears.

The AIDS project was a risky one, and for me personally got riskier over the next few semesters as the disease hit closer and closer to home. By the spring of 1988, my own first draft of an AIDS essay (which, to be honest, was really about the third draft, though the first I shared with the students) began "I saw a ghost last night. Avoiding grading final exams, I tuned in *Nova*. Halfway through the show, medical students were interviewing patients, one of whom was my dear friend Mark. He had died of AIDS two weeks before the show aired" (see Appendix). That was an awful evening for me. Mark had given a lot of interviews in the last year of his life, but in August he had told me he'd sent the *Nova* people away because they were too intrusive. Apparently he had changed his mind, because there he was, looking so healthy and yet so close to death.

Had I never used AIDS as a subject for student writing before, I might not have been able to write about Mark and share his life and death and my love for him with my students. Two years later, as I rewrite this chapter and think about him, I'm still crying and still miss him, and two weeks after his death I could barely hear the name "Mark" without bursting into tears. A number of things gave me the courage to go on with the assignment, however. First is my insistence on honest writing from students, and hence from myself. Writing about any other aspect of AIDS that semester would have been a dishonest act on my part, and would have been revealed by limp prose. Second was my certainty that Mark, an educator himself, would have wanted me to share his life with young people. In his last letter to me, he wrote, "Promise me that you will always carry a bit of my anger, and, a lot of my love. Challenge hate with love, a flood of Light. Please know that In Spite of Everything, YES. As the Latin saying has it, 'Dum vivimus, vivamus'—while we're alive, let us live." Third was my great desire to write something worthy of the life Mark did live. This I think I suceeded in—and the essay I eventually finished was Mark's last gift to me.

The essay about Mark also gave me the courage to expand my use of AIDS as a topic, to take it out of the composition classroom and see if it could be used in the literature classroom in similar ways, with similar effects. I began by assigning Larry Kramer's *The Normal Heart* in an honors seminar entitled "Men, Women and Love," a course that included *Wuthering Heights, The Good Soldier, Othello,* and more contemporary works by Adrienne Rich (some of the "Twenty-One Love Poems"), Jane Rule ("Middle Children"), and others. My goal in developing the reading list was to give students good literature to read, as well as literature that explored the variety of love human beings experience. Lulled, perhaps, by my experiences in the writing classroom and by the fact that my twelve students were "honors" students, I expected greater knowledge and less anxiety about the disease in this classroom. I therefore began our discussion of the play the way I might begin any discussion of drama, with an exploration of structure and character.

I immediately found myself in trouble. The students were very resistant to the play, not so much because of the subject matter of AIDS, but because of the forthright treatment of gay characters. In composition classes, homophobia had not caused a problem; here it seemed likely to. The students knew a great deal about the disease of AIDS (although not enough), but little about gay-male lifestyles, and were too troubled by camp humor and gay "bitchiness" to focus on the play as drama, or AIDS as subject and metaphor. Halfway through the first class discussion, I abandoned my notes and asked the students what they were having trouble with. We spent over an hour discussing so-called "deviant" populations, and especially the gay population, the preconceptions and misconceptions the dominant society might have about such "outsiders," and the problems this might cause in one's personal life. Some of them made interesting connections to Othello and his problems in Shakespeare's play, or to the Catholic questions raised in *The Good Soldier,* but the majority of students found themselves uneasy (and uneasy because they were uneasy and felt they ought not to be) about such passages as the following, a discussion some of the AIDS activists are having while stuffing envelopes:

> BRUCE: Are you a transvestite?
>
> MICKEY: No, but I'll fight for your right to be one.
>
> BRUCE: I don't want to be one!
>
> MICKEY: I'm worried this organization might only attract white bread and middle-class. We need blacks . . .
>
> TOMMY: Right on!
>
> MICKEY: . . . and . . . how do you feel about Lesbians?
>
> BRUCE: Not very much. I mean, they're . . . something else.
>
> MICKEY: I wonder what they're going to think about all this? If past history is any guide, there's never been much support by either half of us for the other. Tommy, are you a Lesbian?

TOMMY: (As he exits into the kitchen.) I have done and seen
    everything. (55)

As one student said, "Do gay men really talk like this?" This launched
us into a discussion not only of gay lifestyles and gay sensibilities, but
also into the various uses of language. Some students were uneasy
when one gay character called another "faggot," until a fellow student
said, "But isn't it the same as one black calling another 'nigger'? They
can do it because they're equals—but a white person can't." The
students gradually became more comfortable with the characters, and
their discussion of the play began to dip below the surface of the
action to explore such issues as the reappropriation of language by
minorities, the nature of black humor, and the meaning of "normal"
when applied to the heart and its loves. Students still needed a road
map through certain aspects of the play—references to Stonewall and
other important events in the history of American gays went right
past them, but by the end nearly all of them found themselves moved
by Felix and Ned's love and Felix's inevitable death. Several admitted
to crying through the last scenes of the play, and further admitted
that they would never have believed they could cry over doomed
homosexual love.

Class discussion of this play was some of the most intense I have
ever engaged in—we often went over the class period and ended up
discussing the play and its issues out in the hallway. Still, I was
surprised at the number of students—over half—who chose to write
about this play for their final essay. One of them was one of my more
macho male students who had begun as the most resistant of readers,
who said to me after class one day, "I've decided to write on Kramer's
play, because I figure if it bugs me so much I'd like to know why."
This is precisely the kind of risk I want students to take, and this
particular young man ended up writing an insightful essay in which
he praised the play for being a moving love story, one that rises above
the polemical notes and occasional set speeches.

On the whole, however, I was disappointed with the essays on *The
Normal Heart*. They were not nearly as open and honest as the essays
my relatively untutored composition students had been writing. In
large part I think this was because the conventions of literary analysis
allowed the students—if not actually forced them—to distance themselves from the subject matter in a way impossible in the personal
essays my composition students were writing. Too many of the essays
on Kramer contained passages such as the following:

> Ned Weeks and Felix Turner are a gay couple who truly fall in love with each other. This play makes one realize that it is possible for two men to share deep, romantic, and caring emotions. Ned has had many affairs in his life, but Felix is the first person he allows himself to love. Ned's devotion to Felix becomes apparent when Felix is diagnosed with AIDS. Ned takes care of Felix, supports him, encourages him, and stands by him until Felix finally dies. In the scene where Ned throws the groceries on the kitchen floor, the power of Ned's feelings for Felix emerges.

The scene in question is the emotional climax of the play, wrenching and moving, yet the reader of this dispassionate student prose would never guess as much. The literature students engaged in more sophisticated and emotional discussion than the composition students, but in safer approaches to graded exercises.

Part of this, I think, has to do with the fact that I was merely changing content, not approach, in using AIDS in the literature classroom. I didn't approach Kramer any differently than I approached Stephen Crane. AIDS (and sexuality in general) is of such imperative importance to students, so closely linked to their own hopes and fears, that I have begun to realize it can't be taught the way other topics in literature are taught. AIDS is a gut-level issue, and it is a mistake for a professor to distance herself from this fact by starting out with a discussion of structure or theme or character development. In retrospect, I should have started that particular discussion—and perhaps all discussion in literature classes—on a more personal level. The better question to start with would have been "What troubles you about this play?" or "What do you have in common with these characters?" In the composition classroom, I had gone out of my way to make such personal connections; in the literature classroom, perhaps due to graduate-school conditioning, I had not been so forthcoming.

I have not had much opportunity to use AIDS in other literature classes that I teach, although this past semester it arose rather unexpectedly in my course on Women Writers. We were discussing some of Audre Lorde's erotic lesbian poetry (the students' choice, incidentally—they could have chosen to discuss safer poems on African heritage) when someone mentioned AIDS, and, before I knew it, questions and comments were flying right and left. Even in 1990, among upperclassmen, there were misconceptions about the disease. We did eventually get back to Audre Lorde, but not before one student shared her experiences working with AIDS babies in a hospital setting, another told of her cousin who had died of AIDS, another of a fellow student whose boyfriend was HIV positive, and not before I had given an extremely straightforward lecture on risk, transmission, and prevention. Half the class personally thanked me for taking the time out from literature to talk about AIDS and told me that they weren't getting this information any place else on campus. This was also a class where students kept reading journals that I commented on periodically, journals where thoughtfulness counts and neatness, organization, and grammar do not. Journal entries on the issues of sexuality and on the class time we spent on AIDS were much more open and honest and engaged than the writing the honors students had done on *The Normal Heart*. When next I teach a literature class that lends itself to using AIDS or some other important contemporary issue, I plan on keeping a reading journal myself and sharing it with the students, the same way I share drafts of essays with composition students. I suspect this will help engage students with the literature, rather than presenting them with Great Writing that seems like some sort of ancient Sumeric code to be deciphered.

All of my literature classes deal at least peripherally with social issues, because literature itself often confronts social issues. Using controversial social issues as subject matter in writing and literature classes may leave one open to accusations of teaching a "political agenda," but in most cases such accusations are false. By and large, my students are the ones who choose the subject matter, and they learn early on that in my classroom, at least, they are free to disagree with the professor's viewpoints: I grade them not on their political opinions but on the competency of their writing and lucidity of their thinking.

The reason AIDS works so well as a topic is because of its essential and immediate value to the students. Essays on other social issues such as the homeless or welfare mothers are never as provocative or evocative for my students as the ones on AIDS. My students are not afraid of becoming homeless or having to accept welfare—they are afraid of AIDS, which strikes not only at their own sense of mortality, but also at their sense of morality. Students are afraid, and rightly so, that they are at risk for AIDS, or that someone they love is. At the age when they are discovering and experimenting with sexuality and when they are looking forward to and preparing for their futures, they are faced with the reality of their own mortality, the fragility of human life, and the limits of medicine and science. Writing about such a subject makes it impossible for students to write false, dishonest "college student prose," and also forces them to confront the world they have been born into.

Appendix: Celebrating Death

I saw a ghost last night. Avoiding grading final exams, I tuned in *Nova*. Halfway through the show, medical students were interviewing patients, one of whom was my dear friend Mark. He had died of AIDS two weeks before the show aired.

In retrospect, I shouldn't have been so shocked to see his videotaped image. I knew Mark had been interviewed for a number of television shows, primarily because he cared about health education. In fact, our passion about teaching well was a large part of our friendship. Nonetheless, seeing a vibrant and seemingly-healthy Mark on television when he had been cremated two weeks earlier left me tearful for hours. I had known for two years that he would die, and thought I had reconciled myself to his death. I was wrong. I will never be reconciled to his death, and part of the reason I'm writing this essay is to help keep him alive, at least in memory.

I wish you could have known Mark. He was funny, widely read, and had the same eclectic taste in art I do. He wore his hair a bit long and had John Lennon glasses, and he spoke with a kind of staccato rhythm. He loved the North Country and came back often to hike the High Peaks and see old friends. He was a terrific cook—I spent my first Thanksgiving in Plattsburgh with him and ate far too much chestnut stuffing. We once spent an evening at the college president's house giggling and drinking too much and causing much local gossip. Mark was the kind of man who, while dying, regularly sent illustrated letters in his spiky handwriting to friends, telling them to cheer up and not feel sorry for him.

Mark wasn't perfect, of course—who of us is? He could be absolutely exasperating, especially when in his earnest mood. Then he could be as serious as a priest, and as unrelenting. He could be stubborn, and he could demand too much attention from his friends, asking them to listen to endless hours of what was wrong with his life. But even in his worst moments, he cared about others, and he always wanted to help people understand themselves, himself, art, and especially health care.

Mark took awhile to find work he cared about, and health administration was his eventual choice. He moved to Boston and got a succession of good jobs and was becoming a highly respected professional, widely quoted in the press and published in scholarly journals. He'd found a life-partner and just bought a condominium when he developed a cough that wouldn't quit. In the hospital, he knew the diagnosis even before he was told, because the doctor showed up masked and gloved.

Mark responded to AIDS with anger, but also with grace. Instead of concentrating on himself, he concentrated on others, allowing film crews and photographers and interviewers to follow him around. He'd always been an educator, and he devoted the last two years of his life to educating about AIDS. He wanted people to know that promiscuity is not the only route to the disease—he himself had had very few lovers. He wanted heterosexuals who don't inject drugs to understand that they, too, are at risk. He wanted people to understand the enormous social cost of AIDS, not just in terms of medical costs, but in the talent and potential being lost. One in six babies in the Bronx is born with AIDS, and most don't live past the age of four or five.

I think Mark would be pleased to know that I am writing about him and sharing his life with my students, though probably not so pleased that I am still grieving his death. Mark always wanted to celebrate life, both his own and that of others, even while he was dying. He insisted that his memorial service be a celebration, not a mourning, and requested that his ashes be scattered at Lake Clear, a place associated with good memories of friendship, dark summer nights, too much wine, and much laughter.

So I don't want to end this on a sad note, because Mark wouldn't have liked that. We all die eventually, and Mark was fortunate in that he lived so well. He may not have lived long, but he brought joy to his friends, and I hope that by sharing his story I can help continue what he no longer can do—educate others. I learned a lot from Mark, not only about AIDS but about life. I'm glad he'll never be gone completely. His image and words will appear in films and help people understand AIDS. His face and his voice will always be in my mind— and the minds of all his friends and family. If only one person learns compassion about AIDS from reading this, from having some small contact with Mark's life, his life won't have been in vain. The best way I know to celebrate Mark's brief existence is to do what I do best—teach—and I hope I can teach about both writing and about AIDS in the process. I owe it to Mark, whom I miss and will always miss. You would too, if you'd known him.

References

Kramer, L. 1985. *The Normal Heart*. New York: NAL.

IV Teaching Literature for Social Responsibility

12 Breaking the Silence: Addressing Homophobia with *The Color Purple*

Vincent A. Lankewish
Pope John XXIII High School, Sparta, New Jersey

> Very rarely do we see anything [in the media] about gays that is not making fun of them or exaggerating stereotypic qualities they are all supposed to possess.
>
> —Jennifer, high school senior

These words, written by a student in my senior English honors class, reflect all too accurately the negative ways in which gay people are depicted by the American media and, consequently, perceived by the American public. Yet nowhere are these perceptions propagated more strongly, it seems, than in the high school classroom, where the word "gay," as well as derisive terms such as "homo," "fag," or "queer," is used repeatedly as the ultimate insult or form of degradation. In fact, some students have even come to use "gay" to criticize *anything* that does not meet the standards of style, taste, or "acceptability" established by their social circles. When a student, for example, exclaims, "That movie was so *gay!*", he or she may be indicating that the film, though not necessarily homosexual in its content, was in some way unsatisfactory—boring, juvenile, or simply "un-cool." Used in this context, the word "gay," to some degree, is stripped of its associations with homosexuality, becoming just another word in the young adult dictionary of pejoratives. Yet despite this "new" usage, it seems doubtful that the word ever *really* loses the negative homosexual connotations it has for many teenagers. In fact, this may well explain its adoption as a generic put-down.

Although one might assume that the increasing *exposure* to gay culture due to the spread of AIDS would have forced some of our students to rethink their attitudes toward gay people, many teenagers have remained surprisingly insensitive to gays and ignorant of the injustices they suffer. One need only glance at newspaper reports of rising anti-gay violence and of the increasing number of AIDS discrimination cases for evidence of the contempt with which gays are still regarded by a significant segment of American society.

My English class, however, has served as a place in which to help students acknowledge and, ideally, transcend some of their prejudices towards gays and minorities in general. Admittedly, some educators may debate the appropriateness of trying to effect such social change through the curriculum. In his book *Tenured Radicals*, Roger Kimball, for instance, has argued forcefully against the "politicization" of the study of the humanities and adamantly objects to the use of the classroom as a forum for the advancement of specific political agendas.[1]

Yet the inculcation of respect for individual difference and of compassion for the oppressed, while indeed a political act, strikes me as part of a teacher's job. Although I do not feel it is my place to compel students to adopt a particular view as their own, I do believe that I have a responsibility to encourage young people to respect the rights of others to live as they choose.

In this context, I have found Alice Walker's *The Color Purple* a highly accessible epistolary novel through which teenagers may encounter and consider more fully the legitimacy of gay relationships while, at the same time, gaining insight into the experience of African Americans during the first half of the twentieth century. Perhaps it is the sensitivity and candor of the narrator, Celie, a young girl of color, which permits this. Beginning with her first letter, in which she discloses to God that she has been a victim of incest by the man she believes is her father, Celie endears herself to the reader. "I have always been a good girl," she writes, evidently holding herself accountable for what has happened.[2] As she unfolds the story of the brutal treatment she also receives from her husband, Albert, whom she refers to as Mr. _____, and of her painful separation from her beloved sister, Nettie, it is difficult for the reader not to accept and respect the love she eventually receives from the woman Shug Avery. Shug, Albert's former lover, comes to convalesce at Albert's home, where she is nursed back to health by Celie. During her stay, Shug becomes Celie's salvation as she showers Celie with affection and encourages Celie's discovery of her own independence and strength as a woman. Their relationship, in turn, serves as a model of the support *all* women—lesbian, heterosexual, and bisexual—may offer one another. The impact of their partnership on those around them also reveals the liberating effects women may have on a male-dominated society.

Perhaps because lesbianism is only one facet of this controversial story involving misogyny, racism, and British imperialism, the relationship between Celie and Shug may seem a little less threatening to students; there are many other issues to divert their attention from it. In fact, those who wish to do so may ignore altogether the true nature of these women's love, viewing it only as a "good friendship," rather than a deeper union. This denial can be avoided, however, by directly addressing the issue of lesbianism. Admittedly, some students may be unable to accept the sexual dimension of the relationship. Even so, studying the novel may motivate students to reevaluate long-held beliefs and wonder if romantic and sexual relationships between members of the same gender are wrong, as they have been conditioned to think. Students obviously will not change their minds overnight. The classes to which I have taught the novel over the past three years attest to this fact: one boy, for instance, eagerly defended his assault of a gay man who was attracted to him, while some girls were "revolted" by Celie and Shug's sexual experiences. Nonetheless, reading *The Color Purple* prompts questioning of the social tradition of homophobia—that is, the fear of homosexuals.

During my first year of teaching, I was extremely alarmed by the frequency with which my seniors' everyday conversations included ridiculing of gays. Initially, I did not realize that I could use literature as a vehicle for challenging their prejudices. However, our study of a different novel eventually led me to include Alice Walker's book in my syllabus. After teaching James Dickey's *Deliverance*, in which two men are raped by male "hillbillies" in the deep south, I found myself disturbed by the conclusions about gay life that my students might come to from the novel. Some critics might argue persuasively that the word "gay" is not even applicable to the hillbillies; still, I could not help feeling that my students were left with the impression that these backwoods criminals were examples of "typical" gay men— grotesque degenerates who secretly sodomize innocent victims. Quite coincidentally, the following year, while searching for a novel to juxtapose against *The Taming of the Shrew*, I decided upon *The Color Purple*, and discovered that Celie not only differed markedly from Katherine in her emancipation from the patriarchal world in which she existed, but that she also conveyed, perhaps unconsciously, a highly positive attitude towards her gayness, as well as toward her African American heritage.

It was not without some anxiety that I assigned the novel for the first time, particularly because I was teaching in a Catholic school in a fairly conservative area of New Jersey. Fortunately, my department chairperson had given me a great deal of academic freedom, which enabled me to teach not only *The Color Purple* but other potentially controversial works such as Toni Morrison's *Song of Solomon* and Bobbie

Ann Mason's *In Country*. I also suspect that a good number of my students' parents must have recognized that, regardless of their religious convictions, their children could not be sheltered from the issues raised by these novels: In teaching *The Color Purple* for three years, I have had only one complaint from parents who objected to the novel's "graphic descriptions of sex abuse" and criticized its language as "crude and obscene." These parents also argued that despite its literary merit, the novel failed to "uplift" their child's Christian values. This response appears to have been an exception, however, and does not seem to reflect my students' largely positive reaction to the book.

Still, when I introduced the novel, I was rather unsure about the way my seniors would respond. After discussing Celie's first letter and considering the novelty of Walker's use of the epistolary format, I left my students to read on their own. Throughout the two weeks I allotted them to finish the book, my colleagues repeatedly told me that they had observed my students engrossed by the story. The day the assignment was to have been completed, I sensed that nearly everyone in the class had actually done the reading.

I spent the first class period eliciting overall reactions and tried to steer the conversation away from exclusive discussion of lesbianism, which I planned to address later, along with lessons on African American English and on the roles of secondary characters in literary works. The lesson on Celie and Shug's relationship, however, seemed pivotal to my students' appreciation of the work.

I began the lesson by zeroing in on my students' overall perceptions of gays and asked my class to describe in a short freewriting exercise the stereotypes of gays that permeate our society and the ways those stereotypes have been or continue to be spread. When I taught the same lesson the following year, I amended the question and also asked my students to identify ways in which these stereotypes were now being broken down and replaced by more realistic images. Retrospectively, I realize that, without the amendment, my question served to elicit mainly negative images; yet, even with this addition, very few students were able to discuss the breakdown of stereotypes since so few positive portrayals can be found in our popular culture. As one student put it, stereotypes "are reinforced by skits on shows such as *Saturday Night Live* and *Three's Company*." Only recently has this begun to change as a result of films about AIDS such as *An Early Frost* and *Longtime Companion*, both of which feature three-dimensional gay men who gain our admiration and respect.

When asked to describe traditional images of gays, however, most students were able to do so with little difficulty. In a single paragraph, one student captured the class's prevailing impression:

> Gays are often stereotyped by behavior, language, and dress. Men who are not athletic or who seem "feminine" are labelled gay. Men who speak with a high voice also come under this label. Females are labelled gay if they show any traits of males. Many women who are athletic, muscular, or have a deep voice are labelled as homosexuals. Women who are tough and stand up for themselves in some instances are labelled in this way.

This student went on to explain that social convention has led to identifying as gay anyone who does not conform to a preconceived notion of masculinity or femininity. Although this student admirably challenges the practice of stereotyping, inherent in her analysis is the belief that there is still something wrong with being gay, that to be perceived as gay would somehow be humiliating.

Perhaps, then, the most significant questions to be answered are these: Why is our society still so afraid of gay people? Why are we particularly troubled or threatened by gay men who *are* effeminate and lesbians who *are* masculine? And why are we so fearful of crossing gender barriers? Students' most common answers to these questions focus on society's intense fear of difference and its desire for homogeneity, individual insecurity about one's own sexual identity, and the threat of AIDS.

In attempting to explain the prevalence of homophobia, one student argued that "people shun what they don't understand." She also pointed to insecurity as a deep source of prejudice when she explained that "men, especially, try to show that they aren't gay by putting down men who are and trying to be as masculine as possible." Another student maintained that gays "are looked down upon because society feels they will definitely have AIDS or some kind of disease. People are afraid of them because they are different and not of the 'normal' lifestyle." Yet the most sensitive and eloquent analysis came from a young man with a relative who had been diagnosed with AIDS. He wrote:

> These stereotypes are permeated in a society that lives in constant fear, fear of the unknown, fear of the different. As the adage goes, fear breeds hate and this is exactly what we do. We collectively judge the actions and morals of a chosen few when we ourselves have no right to. . . . AIDS also has a big part in this since it was first seen as 'the gay plague.' Fear of gays has been dominant in society for quite a while. Some can't stand to see someone whom we perceive as wrong wield any sort of power, and we will go to any means to keep them from authority, such as the tragic case

[of Harvey Milk] in 1970 in San Francisco. There will be no end
soon to this cycle so long as we, as a society, are ignorant of the
views of those who differ from the mainstream.

Admittedly, not every student's writing is as enlightened as this;
however, the writing assignment may expose the class to the view of
an open-minded peer who accepts gays as they are—a view which
may have far greater impact than that of the teacher.

In addition to prompting students to explore their own attitudes
toward gay people, this exercise may lead to a more general discussion
of gender roles. Which qualities, I ask, do we identify as masculine,
and which as feminine? Why, in 1990, are a large number of men, for
instance, still "suspect" if they are "emotional," enter careers traditionally designated as "women's," or enjoy supposedly "feminine"
hobbies like sewing or knitting? Why are women, for that matter,
"expected" to be more sensitive than men and to enter service careers?
Why are women often considered "pushy" if they assert their power
in the business world? For many students, exhibiting traits not "characteristic" of their own gender seems tantamount to being gay, and
that is still seen as socially unacceptable.

Even talking about gays is, for many, still taboo. So that students
will feel freer to tackle this potentially threatening topic, I do not
collect or grade the writing. In the post-writing discussion, I also don't
force anyone to read his or her observations, especially since there
may be some gay students in the class who may or may not yet have
revealed their own orientation. Even if some students do not participate
at all in the discussion, at the very least they will have had to
acknowledge the existence of gay people and the mechanisms of
homophobia. Although no absolute conclusion may be reached in my
class, the writing and discussion prepare the way for examining
lesbianism in *The Color Purple*.

I begin the next day's lesson by asking my students to talk about
their responses to Celie and Shug's relationship. Never has there been
a uniform reaction. Some view the relationship as healthy and nurturing
and have little or no difficulty accepting its sexual dimension. Others
recognize the importance of Shug's love for Celie, since it prompts
Celie's journey toward self- discovery, but are still uncomfortable with
the relationship's physicality. Some are completely disturbed by the
relationship, and are virtually unable to discuss it. Other students
maintain that Celie is a lesbian only because she has been abused by
men like Fonso and Albert. Although there *is* evidence to suggest that
Celie's experiences with men may have been responsible for her
lesbianism, this view seems based more on the common belief that

gayness is "caused" by external factors rather than internal ones, though not necessarily, that it is "biologically," determined. Still others seem to deny or explain away the women's intimacy and try to construe the relationship simply as a platonic friendship. True, Walker never has Celie, Shug, nor any other character use the word "lesbian" to describe the women's love, but this does not seem to be because Walker is afraid of same-sex intimacy. Rather, the noticeable absence of the word may reflect a deeper concern about the potency of language: labeling people and relationships in simple, familiar terms not only limits those people and relationships, but also dictates other people's expectations of and responses to them. Perhaps, then, Walker rejects the use of labels to avoid these limitations and prevent snap judgments, as well as to remind us that we are dealing with individuals, rather than types.

As my students grapple with such issues, I refrain, as much as possible, from commenting, and instead encourage them to establish a dialogue with one another. If a particular viewpoint begins to dominate, I may occasionally intervene and solicit an opposing opinion, particularly if the discussion is degenerating into a diatribe against gays.

Once various reactions have been shared, I ask my second key question: How does Celie and Shug's relationship transcend stereotypic images of lesbianism? The previous day's discussion makes this question relatively easy to answer. If the assumptions are that gay people are noticeably "different" from heterosexuals, that they usually exhibit behavioral patterns associated with their opposite sex, and that, if they engage in relationships at all, those relationships are either insubstantial or exclusively sexual, then Celie and Shug serve to invalidate such beliefs, for neither woman fits this mold. Both, for instance, have had relationships with men, Celie by force and Shug by choice, and both have had children. In addition, neither woman is portrayed or perceived by her community as masculine. Although some might view the control the women take over their own lives as masculine, Celie emphatically identifies this power as "womanly." Since we are presented with lovable, sensitive, intelligent women who might not "look" like they could be involved in a lesbian relationship, Walker helps us to see that appearance does not necessarily reflect a person's sexual orientation or capacity to love. That the women are both African Americans also helps to illustrate that sexual orientation is not a matter of color.

Once students have evaluated the ways the women, as individuals, transcend stereotypes, the class may next consider their characteristics as a couple. The most important and most frequent observation students make is that their relationship is loving—a quality that teenagers might not readily associate with gay partnerships. Although Shug does lead Celie to a powerful and fulfilling sexual awakening, the love between these women goes beyond the body. As Celie restores Shug back to health, for example, she finds herself mesmerized by Shug's beauty, yet even as she bathes Shug, Celie feels more than sexual desire. "I wash her body," she writes, "it feel like I'm praying," (53) thereby suggesting a spiritual dimension to her attraction.

At this point in the lesson, I think it is valuable to inform my students that, despite my stress on the importance of acknowledging the lesbianism in the novel, I believe that Walker's greatest thematic concern is the positive impact love can have on any person's life. Regardless of its source, love is a universal force with the power to heal, to nourish, and to facilitate self-respect. To some extent, then, attempts to label different forms of love in the novel may seem restrictive. Such attempts may even conflict with the story's recurrent idea that love is free, boundless, and beyond definition. To pigeon-hole the novel as a "gay book," some might argue, divests it of its broader message about the value of all kinds of love.[3] One need only consider the enduring bond between Celie and Nettie, who write to each other for years before their reunion, for evidence to support this view. Still, I think Walker *is* deliberately encouraging acceptance of forms of loving that we might not be accustomed to accepting.

After discussing these possibilities, my students then describe the evolution of Celie's attachment to Shug and usually have little difficulty seeing that Shug provides Celie with a constant source of strength and support. Upon learning that Albert beats Celie, for instance, Shug holds Celie, kisses her, and promises to stay until he stops abusing her, a promise which sets the stage for Celie's further growth. Students may also point out that Shug plays a key role in helping Celie come to terms with her rape and with the loveless life she has led thus far. If no student does so, I draw the class's attention to the crucial passage in which Celie explains, "Nobody ever love me. [Shug] say, I love you, Miss Celie. And then she haul off and kiss me on the mouth" (109).

This passage reveals Celie's first experience with love since Nettie's departure; it is also one of several descriptions which may make some students uncomfortable since it brings them face to face with the reality that the women do relate to one another sexually. I can vividly recall, for example, one girl literally shuddering at the thought of this kind of intimacy between women. While it might be easier to skip or quickly gloss over the scene to avoid having to deal with such reactions, doing so may undermine the lesson since it enables students to ignore that gay people, like heterosexuals, can be physical.

Although this truth may be difficult for some students to accept, others are equally, if not more, troubled by the inequity they perceive in the relationship. Some students believe that Shug is not as committed to Celie as Celie is to Shug and see Shug's attraction to Celie as somewhat transient, particularly because Shug has had previous and coexisting relationships with men. "I think Shug is just using her!" I can remember a student saying. "She led Celie on!" Other students recognize the intensity of each woman's feelings for the other, along with the many benefits Celie derives from Shug's love, but question whether Shug receives anything from Celie.

Challenging this perception and helping students see that Celie does, in fact, nurture Shug requires close examination of later scenes in the book. Perhaps the clearest evidence of the ways Celie "gives" to Shug can be found when Shug decides to leave Celie to have a "last fling," as Shug calls it, with the nineteen-year-old musician, Germaine. Not surprisingly, students sympathize with Celie after she loses the person she loves most; some even resent Shug for abandoning Celie. "How could Shug do this to her!" one student asked. Yet Celie's willingness to let Shug go demonstrates to Shug (and to my students) that Celie's love has no strings. Shug's separation from Celie while traveling with Germaine also helps Shug realize that Celie not only provides her with stability and security, but that Celie is also the center of her universe. To illustrate this point, I ask my students to look at the passage describing Shug's homecoming. Celie states that upon Shug's return, "[Shug] smile, come put her head on my breast. Let out a long breath" (248). The implication here—that the relationship has matured into something permanent—may surprise students who believe that long-term commitment between gay people is impossible.

Once my students have finished examining Celie and Shug's relationship, I ask them to explore the ways it functions within the novel's overall structure. How, for example, is the love and support that Celie and Shug give to each other reflected in other relationships between women in the book? How are the men in the novel affected by Celie and Shug? What role do Celie and Shug play in restructuring the world in which they live?

In order to begin answering these questions, I ask my students to select and analyze in a paragraph a relationship between any pair of women in the novel who, like Celie and Shug, support and nurture one another and facilitate the transcendence of male power structures. I emphasize at the outset that these relationships need not be lesbian in nature. The parallels students discover are usually significant. One student, for example, observed that Celie's daughter, Olivia, and her African friend, Tashi, mirror the Celie/Shug relationship since "Olivia wants Tashi to go to school with her so [Tashi] can learn; she doesn't want [Tashi] to become the typical [Olinka] tribeswoman." Just as Shug encourages Celie to free herself from Albert's power, so too does Olivia urge Tashi to overcome the restrictions that the Olinka men place on their women. Another student saw the bond between Celie and Shug reflected in the friendship that develops between Sofia and Squeak, the wife and lover, respectively, of Albert's son, Harpo. "When Squeak has the opportunity to go away with Shug to sing," the student wrote, "Sofia offered to take care of Squeak's daughter." Despite their initial dislike for each other, the two women "come to care for one another and each other's children." A third student focused on a less obvious pair, Corinne and Nettie, who both work as missionaries in Africa with Samuel, Corinne's husband. The student observed,

> Corinne and Nettie parallel Celie and Shug. Corinne allowed Nettie to come and live with her and her family, just as Celie allowed Shug to come into her home. When Corinne and Nettie go over to Africa as missionaries, they realize that they need each other tremendously in order to survive within the Olinka tribe. They get along as if they are sisters and Corinne allows Nettie to borrow her clothes. Corinne also serves as a mother figure to Nettie.

Admittedly, the comparison may not be quite as pertinent as that of, say, Olivia and Tashi, since Corinne's suspicion that Nettie and Samuel are the real parents of her adopted children eventually leads her to alienate Nettie. (The children's resemblance to Nettie is otherwise inexplicable to Corinne since she does not know that Nettie *is* actually their aunt.) Nonetheless, Corinne and Nettie do represent, at least in the earlier portion of the novel, another example of a strong tie between women that serves as a challenge to patriarchy.

Despite the way these and other relationships illustrate the positive effects of female bonding, some girls in my classes have remained quite skeptical about the concept of "sisterhood" which governs the novel. "In the real world," they tell me, "women aren't always as supportive of one another as Walker implies." The abundance of close relationships between women also prompts some students to ask, "Does Alice Walker think all women should be lesbians?"

I try to point out that Walker is neither advocating "a world without men," nor holding up lesbianism as the best or only way for women to live happily. When I ask students to locate examples of positive heterosexual relationships in the novel, for instance, they are easily able to find several happy couples, including Nettie and Samuel (who marry after Corinne's death) and Tashi and Adam, and can see that Walker, in fact, illustrates that a variety of relationships—gay, heterosexual, married, unmarried—can work as long as each partner is willing to respect the other's individuality and need for freedom. Perhaps homophobia accounts for students' anxieties that one of the strongest relationships in the novel—if not *the* strongest—is lesbian. That Celie and Shug's love should be a model for others may be threatening to some students.

Perhaps just as alarming to others may be Walker's often harsh portrayal of males, many of whom rely on violence and aggression as means of dominating women. When asked to cite examples of likeable men in the novel who do not fulfill the traditional male role of "oppressor," students may have difficulty. Although they may suggest Adam, Samuel, or even Jack, the husband of Sophia's sister, Odessa, these men are clearly the exceptions rather than the rule. Students have a much easier time finding examples of men who try to preserve their long-held power over women: Fonso, Albert, and Harpo, for instance, are all obviously guilty of abusing women. Yet, I ask my students, do any of these men change in the course of the book? If so, what factors are responsible for the change?

The most common replies focus on Albert, who becomes more sensitive to the needs of others and more appreciative of his own life as he observes the love that Celie and Shug share. Students are often startled by—if not to some extent incredulous of—Albert's transformation, and find it ironic that he begins to take care of his own house, to cook yam dishes for Sophia and Harpo's ailing daughter, Henrietta, and to design and sew shirts. Once these actions have been discussed, I direct the class to a moving passage which reveals a fundamental change in Albert's understanding of love. While sitting with Celie, Albert explains:

> When it come to what folks do together with they bodies . . . anybody's guess is as good as mine. But when you talk bout love I don't have to guess. I have love and I have been love. And I thank God he let me gain understanding enough to know love can't be halted just cause some peoples moan and groan. It don't surprise me you love Shug Avery. . . . I have love Shug Avery all my life. (236–37)

Observing this change in Albert's worldview is rewarding not only because it suggests that he has found a richer, happier life, but because it may also serve as a sign of hope that our students, too, may someday come to the realization that we need not judge the ways people love one another. Although teaching this lesson is a challenge, perhaps doing so will make obsolete the student's words that begin this essay and help more young people experience Albert's enlightenment.

Notes

1. Roger Kimball. 1990. *Tenured Radicals: How Politics Has Corrupted Our Higher Education.* New York: Harper and Row. Preface, esp. xv–xvi.

2. Alice Walker. 1982. *The Color Purple.* paperback ed. New York: Simon and Schuster, 11. All further citations appear in the text.

3. For further consideration of this concept, see reviews of *The Color Purple* by Rita Mae Brown in *The San Francisco Chronicle* (July 4, 1982), and by Kerita Black in *The Philadelphia Enquirer* (Aug. 1, 1982).

13 Using *Native Son* to Explore Language and Stereotype

Jimmie Mason
John Muir High School, Pasadena, California

With the ever-changing ethnic make-up of classrooms today, it becomes imperative that educators deal with social issues, especially ones focusing on race relations. English teachers, particularly, have an opportunity and a responsibility to encourage students to approach literature from both a historical perspective and a personal one; otherwise, too many students will not only remain unresponsive to a particular work, but will continue to wonder what real meaning it has for their own lives.

This essay is designed to present, in abbreviated form, the manner in which I have utilized literature—in this case, Richard Wright's *Native Son*—as a means of educating students about racial stereotyping, while at the same time enhancing their enjoyment and appreciation of literature. What follows is a "lesson plan" that works for me. I hasten to emphasize that the technique I use with this book can, with appropriate modifications, be adapted to the teaching of other literary works, Mark Twain's *The Adventures of Huckleberry Finn* for example.

I teach at John Muir High School, in Pasadena, California, the home of the Rose Parade and Rose Bowl Game. The school is located within a predominantly black community. Its student body is 49 percent black, 30 percent Hispanic, 17 percent white, and 4 1/2 percent Asian/ Filipino. We draw from a diverse population, with both wealthy and poverty-level students and a growing population of foster children. Although our Hispanic population is steadily increasing, the fastest growing group of students, new to this country, are Armenians. And the number of students who are continuously moving from school to school is greater than we would like.

As a black woman who grew up in the South and attended all-black schools through high school, with no experience with other racial groups, I consider myself fortunate to be able to work in such a diverse environment. Our students are enriched through their opportunity to

231

interact with different races from different economic and social backgrounds.

The Importance of Preparing Students to Study "Social Issues" or Potentially Controversial Subject Matter

There are several approaches one can use in preparing students for a particular work, but included in these should be helping students understand how their personal experiences relate to a work of art. Richard Wright's *Native Son* is one of my most successful sources for approaching issues such as stereotyping, prejudice, and racism. Before I begin to deal with these issues, however, I make sure my students are reasonably comfortable with me and with each other. From the start, students know that I, as their teacher, will not tolerate the use of any derogatory terms directed at others, or themselves. I gently, but firmly, confront the epithets they use or are familiar with. We discuss such derogatory terms as "chink," "ofay," "honkey," "coon," "nigger," "spick," "beaner," "wop," "dago," and so forth. For some, to acknowledge these terms is humorous—at first. For others, these terms are offensive or make them feel uncomfortable.

What is curious about derogatory terms is that many minorities, particularly blacks, tend to direct these terms at each other. I try to get students to understand that it is unreasonable to take words that have the potential for suggesting that one is less than human and assign them to themselves. We then discuss some historical facts relating to the terms "coon" and "nigger," along the following lines.

It is, of course, probably impossible to trace the precise origins of such terms, but absolute certainty is not required in this kind of lesson. The derivation of "nigger" and "coon" are sufficiently described by H. L. Mencken (1977) in *The American Language: Supplement I*. Mencken suggests that "nigger" is derived from the Spanish word for black, "negro," and that the use of "nigger" was not widespread in America until the nineteenth century, which, of course, coincided with slavery. Unlike "negro," the word "nigger," offensive to many, is part of the baggage of slavery that has lasted to this day.[1]

The term "coon," according to Mencken, was derived from the word "raccoon," and has been in use since the 1880s. Its usage was greatly abetted by a black man who wrote a song using the term. While his intent was innocent, the derogatory use caught on, much to his dismay. This information can be useful with students, since, as Mencken confirms, these words are deemed insulting when used by other races, but some—especially "nigger"—have often been used among blacks without such offense. Students' reactions upon learning this history are a vivid example of how the educational process can work: once they are confronted with the words and the history (as opposed to ignoring the subject), students uniformly confess that they never knew the origins of the terms, never truly appreciated the offensiveness, and are amazed that they would unthinkingly use them.

Before we begin to study the work in question, we hold open class discussions to examine (1) why people would call someone of their own race, themselves, or someone of another race offensive or derogatory names; (2) why they may become upset if someone of another race directs an offensive or derogatory word at them even though they may have previously used the word about themselves; and (3) how other ethnic groups feel when they hear a group use these derogatory terms.

Black people do not use the word "coon" in referring to themselves or other blacks, but many too frequently use the word "nigger." They say that they basically use the word to denote brotherhood. They do not connote the historical use of the word. I ask students why they publicly use the word in reference to themselves, thereby giving a license for others to do the same, yet become angry when other groups do so. The response is generally that they don't give much thought to their use of the word. Many say they have grown up hearing the word from family members and friends and had not had it brought to their attention that they should take offense or be offended by its use by members of their own race. Many students say it is the first time they have been challenged to think about how they refer to themselves, why they do it, when they do it, and some of the consequences of their doing it. Almost always, black students acknowledge that they "have helped to perpetuate stereotypical views through [their] use of the word 'nigger.' " However, many also say that, while they now realize the inappropriateness of their personal use of the word and will attempt to stop using it, "it is still difficult to convince friends and family members" to do so.

White students say they "do not understand why blacks call themselves 'nigger,' yet get angry if whites do the same." They come to understand that black students' use of the word has a different connotation than it would if white students were to use it. I often ask my white students if they ever call each other "honkey" or "ofay." More often than not, they say no. I then ask my black students if they have ever heard whites refer to themselves in such derogatory terms, and they, too, say no. We then discuss reasons why blacks do and whites do not use such terms for themselves. Many conclude that "blacks have not yet been able to discard this baggage from slavery days." The majority of my black students say that if more teachers would make an issue out of their use of the word "nigger," maybe that would help to eradicate its free usage. I may ask them how they think they would respond if a white teacher told them of its inappropriateness. Some say they have never been told by white teachers not to use the word, although they have often witnessed it being used in the teachers' presence. Others say they "don't know if a white teacher would, or could, have the same influence" as I do, because I am black. Still others say that "since whites were the originators of the word's derogatory usage, they have no right to sermonize on blacks' usage of the word." I ask them if truth depended on the race of the person. Of course all respond by saying "truth is truth." "If that is a fact," I ask, "why then do you disregard truth because it happens to come from someone white?" This type of dialogue is fruitful, because it starts students thinking about their own prejudices: "I never thought about it that way."

We also discuss the media's portrayal of blacks. Black students are adamant in their distaste at being viewed as "thugs with big radios," "thieves," "pimps," etc. Some protest that "the portrayal of blacks who commit crimes is different from that of whites who commit the same crimes, and that blacks also tend to be given heavier jail sentences for the same crimes committed by whites."

Students relate incidents of vandalism by students of both races. Some say, "more often than not white kids are released to their parents faster than blacks are," and "the media portray black and Hispanic males more negatively than they do any other group of people." Many students ask, "why are the majority of our jails filled with black and Hispanic males if they make up such a small percentage of our population?" "Are these males really that much worse than males of other races?" "Why are most unemployed males black or Hispanic?"

These perceptions are widely shared among minority students and many white students: it is a perceptual framework that must be dealt with in any multicultural setting. These types of questions and discussions help pave the way for the reading, discussion, and understanding of Richard Wright's *Native Son*.

Reading, Understanding, Discussing, and Applying Literature

Students are assigned a certain number of pages to read each night, followed by a discussion of them the next day. I do not hesitate to give pop quizzes if only a few students participate orally in the discussion. This is done to encourage students to read and participate in daily discussions. Nothing is more boring to me than to have only me and one or a few students discussing an issue. I attempt to get all students to participate in some way in order to check for understanding of the work. I generally ask students if they have any questions or comments related to the assigned work. If they do, those are addressed first. Some examples of questions students might have:

1. Why does Bigger have to beat the head of the rat after it is dead?
2. Why does Bigger scare his sister with the dead rat when it is obvious that she is terrified of it?
3. Why does Bigger feel the need to act tough, even with his family?
4. Why does Bigger think poor whites are harder on blacks than rich whites?

After responding to students' questions, I ask questions to check for understanding or to stimulate discussion. While I have some set questions to stimulate discussion, I often find that I have to be flexible in the questions I ask, depending on the reaction of the students. I might ask these questions:

1. How would you react if you felt, as Bigger does, that you "did not have a wider choice of action," and were forced to take a job you believed demeaned you?
2. How many of you live in a one-room apartment with three other people? How do you think you would feel if you had to live that way?
3. How did it make you feel to see Bigger and his friend, Gus, play at being white?
4. Why is it that Bigger was afraid of robbing from whites, yet had no fear of robbing other poor blacks?

In each discussion, I attempt to challenge students, often playing the devil's advocate. For example, I might ask students how many of them would take a menial job, such as dishwashing, and work for less than minimum wage in order to help support their family. Most say they would not. I then ask them why are they so critical of Bigger's reluctance to take a job that he felt was beneath him. Some say, "If I was on welfare, as Bigger's family was, and was forced to work, I would do so, but resent it, as Bigger did." I also ask, "If you, because of being black or Hispanic, thought you would not get a better job than you now have, regardless of finishing high school or college, would you continue going to school?" Almost all say no. "Then you think you are better than Bigger?" I inquire. Often students are embarrassed to admit that they either feel that they are better than Bigger, or that they might respond as Bigger had, by resenting being forced to work because their welfare support was to be terminated.

Through open discussions, most students come to see that, by demeaning themselves and others, they perpetuate various prejudices. All discussions follow a similar pattern. I may ask students what they feel or think about certain things, and this generally gets them to open up. For example, I may ask how they felt about the court's treatment of Bessie's death as compared to its treatment of the death of Mary. Almost all students are offended that Bessie's death was not as important to the court as Mary's. Some remarks may be, "Bigger intentionally killed her"; "They only mentioned Bessie's death to prove what Bigger did to Mary, even though Mary's death was accidental." Others become concerned that the judge allows Buckley to call Bigger such names as "half-human black ape," "mad black dog," "sub-human killer," "human scum," "black cur," and "treacherous beast," yet warns Max, Bigger's attorney, when he refers to Bigger as "poor boy." Instead of providing students with my opinion on such questions, I, more than likely, ask them why they think the judge allowed Attorney General Buckley more freedom than Max. After such discussions, students often come to see that most of us have some type of prejudice about another group, and it is important to examine why—understanding that any ethnic group can have some of the same negative and positive characteristics. I explain to students that Richard Wright tried to make this evident in his essay "How 'Bigger' Was Born," which serves as a preface to the novel. I then summarize the essay so that students will have a deeper understanding of Wright's motive(s) and concerns in writing the novel. I explain to students that Wright wanted to dispel some critics' views that he was advocating violence by blacks against whites because of white society's oppression. I emphasize that Wright says that he wanted to show the violent potential of one oppressed—that any society can breed Bigger Thomases. I proceed to give them specific examples from the essay:

> . . . Bigger Thomas was not black all the time; he was white, too, and there were literally millions of him, everywhere. . . . It was as though I had put on a pair of spectacles whose power was that of an x-ray enabling me to see deeper into the lives of men. (xiv)

Students are asked to think of any individual they know of, black or white, who had reacted violently against others. Some students relate domestic violence they have witnessed. Others recall events they may have read about: the Manson killings, the MacDonald killings, the Hillside Strangler, Ted Bundy, the Watts riots, the Detroit riot, etc. After brainstorming different types of violent reaction, students generally conclude that whites tend to react more violently and more viciously on a larger scale than blacks, yet blacks get more negative publicity. Students admit their disdain for gangs and their violent wanton assaults, not only against other gangs, but on innocent people. Black and Hispanic students see these gangs as more negatively represented by the media than they do a Ted Bundy representing the white race. Students ask, "Would black gangs be allowed to go to white neighborhoods and kill as freely as they do in minority neighborhoods?" I tell them that they probably would not. Then, they ask, "Why is it allowed to continue happening in minority communities?" I tell them it is partly political, and partly because the minority community would complain of harrassment by law enforcement officers. I also tell them that the media loves sensationalism and tends, unfortunately, to overstress crimes by minorities. I encourage them to watch the news or read the papers and make up their own minds.

I further explain to students that, despite his belief that Bigger could be of any race, Wright concentrates upon the disenfranchised native Negro American and the potential consequences of being denied an opportunity to develop one's humanity. I read from Wright himself: "that the environment supplies the instrumentalities through which the organism expresses itself, and that environment is warped or tranquil, the mode and manner of behavior will be affected toward deadlocking tensions or orderly fulfillment and satisfaction" (xvi).

Some students want to know why Wright chose to focus on a black, rather than a white, if Bigger could be any race. I tell them that he does so because he was black, had experienced some of the inequities of society, and could, therefore, personally relate to the black experience. I remind them of Wright's *Black Boy*, which they had read the previous year, and of how Wright had depicted his years of growing up in the South and the underlying fear of blacks, particularly black males, being accused of a crime by a white. Wright tells of a friend's brother who had been hanged because he slept with a white prostitute. Wright, himself, was threatened because he found himself staring at one of the prostitutes when he delivered something to her room and she was lying naked with a white man.

I then ask students if they believe their environment is mainly responsible for their behavior. None say their environment is totally responsible for their behavior, although they admit its influences. Most of the students say that, of the elements of the environment, their family and friends have a deeper impact on their actions than other outside forces. While most students see themselves as worthy individuals, almost all of my minority students relate that they have felt the sting of prejudice because of their color and where they live. For many, escaping the projects is the impetus for striving to get an education.

Notwithstanding the fact that some students live in environments where violence and drugs are common, these students say that most of them are not violent and don't use drugs. They resent the stereotypical view, held not only by some whites but also by some blacks, that just because they live in such an environment, they are assumed to be a participant in such negative reactions to poverty.

To confirm students' belief that all races have oppressed people in them, I relate some of Wright's feelings upon the writing of the novel. Wright says he reflected upon reading of the oppression in old Russia, Hitler's oppression of the Jews, and the oppression of the Negro in America. He "was fascinated by the similarity of the emotional tensions of Bigger in America and Bigger in Nazi Germany and Bigger in old Russia. All Bigger Thomases, white and black, felt tense, afraid, nervous, hysterical, and restless" (xix). The sufferings of these oppressed people gave Wright "the idea of writing a novel in which a Negro Bigger Thomas would loom as a symbolic figure of American life, a figure who would hold within him the prophecy of our future" (xxi).

Students are called upon to give examples of how, negatively or positively, different individuals (fictional or real) have reacted to their environments. One student said that despite being born when her mother was only sixteen, she will not become pregnant at such a young age, as too many of her acquaintances have. Her environment is the impetus for her striving for something better. Students recall more recent acts of rebellion as a result of oppression, particularly in Africa, China, and Germany, as well as individual rebellion on their part when they feel that their parents, or teachers, attempt to oppress them too much. One student said that he resented the double standards of adults. His coach, he said, uses profanity with players, yet they cannot use it at him. "If he wants respect, he should give it."

A few students relate how some of their friends distrust whites because they perceive whites as thinking them inferior or thieves. For example, one black male student related how he and two friends had gone to a major department store and were looking through different items of clothing when a security guard came up to them to ask why they were there; yet, the guard did not ask the same question of some white kids who were also looking through clothing. The student says he became very angry and felt degraded. Because of this experience, he says he could understand one wanting to react violently to such distrust.

Some minority students say they sometimes feel the difference in the way some teachers treat them. These students say they often do not feel that teachers expect them to excel as much as their Asian or white peers. I ask them why they don't try to prove the teacher(s) wrong by doing well in school. Most respond that, "You don't understand how hard it is to try to do well when someone treats you like you are idiots, or do not think you capable of performing at a higher academic level." One eleventh-grade black student recounted being in first grade and being told by her white teacher that she could not do as well as a white classmate because she was black. She says that she has always done well in school, yet the sting of that remark has stayed with her, sometimes causing her to doubt her ability to compete academically with whites. She further states that she can understand why some blacks do not do well in school because they may also have experienced negative comments about their learning potential at an early age.

I try to get students to understand that Bigger, like them, has been conditioned, to a large extent, by society's view of him. A negative result of Bigger's oppression is evident from the beginning of *Native Son* when he and his friend, Gus, play at being white. This specific quotation is acted out by students.

> "Hello."
> "Hello," Gus answered. "Who's this?"
> "This is the President of the United States speaking," Bigger said.
> "Oh, yessuh, Mr. President," Gus said. "I'm calling a cabinet meeting this afternoon at four o'clock and you, as Secretary of State, *must* be there."
> "Well, now Mr. President," Gus said, "I'm pretty busy. They raising sand over there in Germany and I got to send 'em a note. . . ."
> "But this is important," Bigger said.
> "What you going to take up at this cabinet meeting?" Gus asked.
> "Well, you see, the niggers is raising sand all over the country," Bigger said, struggling to keep back his laughter. "We've got to do something with these black folks. . . ."

"Oh, if it's about the niggers, I'll be right there, Mr. President,"
Gus said. (22)

The quoted passage, with its use of the word "nigger," serves as a
good example of how blindly we can demean ourselves without
examining why.

Besides serving as a means for discussing derogatory terms, *Native
Son* also serves as a means of discussing some of the inequities in our
society. I tell students that most violent crimes committed by blacks
are against other blacks. I give an example of why this is often the
case: Bigger and his friends had often robbed from other blacks, but
were afraid to rob from whites:

> They felt that it was much easier and safer to rob their own
> people, for they knew that white policemen never really searched
> diligently for Negroes who committed crimes against other Ne-
> groes. For months they had talked of robbing Blum's, but had not
> been able to bring themselves to do it. They had the feeling that
> the robbing of Blum's would be a violation of ultimate taboo; it
> would be a trespassing into territory where the full wrath of an
> alien white world would be turned loose upon them; in short, it
> would be a symbolic challenge of the white world's rule over
> them; a challenge which they yearned to make, but were afraid
> to. Yes; if they could rob Blum's it would be a real hold-up, in
> more senses than one. In comparison, all of their other jobs had
> been play. (18–19)

Students agree with Wright's depiction of Bigger's reaction to robbing
whites. They relate instances of fights in their community where the
police have taken seemingly forever to get there, even when it had
been reported that a life was in jeopardy. They also relate instances
where blacks have fought other blacks at school and not much was
done about it—if a black and a white fought, a heavier penalty was
given to the black. They say that disruption in the classroom by a
minority is often treated more sternly than a disruption by a white.
This perception of unfairness, they say, can sometimes cause a minority
to give a teacher a rough time. While I attempt to avoid students'
"bashing" particular teachers, whether or not I agree with students'
perception of unfairness is not an issue—the important thing is to
allow them the freedom of dialogue.

Other inequities in our society can also be discussed by using student
examples. The novel is rich in the ways it introduces social issues such
as stereotyping, prejudice, and racism. It is important that students
see that they can take personal responsibility in helping to dispel these
inequities: by not demeaning themselves or others; by striving to see

people as individuals, regardless of color; and by realizing that oppression has the potential for creating violence in any people.

I ask students what they think they can do to dispel negative views of themselves and others. Some of the responses are "We need to first respect ourselves"; "One way to do this is to not refer to ourselves in negative ways, nor to allow our friends to do so"; "We can try to make our friends more conscious of how we may cause others to view us negatively"; "We can attempt to eliminate some of the slang or profanity from our vocabulary, or if we do use it, to choose the right setting"; "We can always try to do our best in school, regardless of how we may perceive that a teacher thinks us incapable of doing well academically"; "We can stop acting the negative part expected of us."

Once students begin to understand that they have little or no control over others, but they do have some control over how they conduct their own lives, I begin to see a change in how they relate to each other: they start to view themselves in a more positive light. Whether or not the changes I see are permanent ones, I cannot tell. The important thing is that the seed of self-worth has been planted. They will have to keep watering it. I believe most will, based upon comments they make to each other when someone attempts to put another person or group down. For example, if black or white classmates refer to someone of another race negatively, saying "they always do this or that," someone will always challenge them to explain who "they" are, attempting to make the individual realize that he/she is stereotyping or categorizing. Students realize that there can be positive results of rebellion against and/or questioning injustices. The civil rights movement is the result of such reactions.

Students should, however, also understand that racism often brings about negative results. This effect is reflected in Bigger's trial and going to the electric chair for murder. His conviction is based on the murder of only Mary, a white girl, and not also on the murder of Bessie, his black girlfriend. The jury was not concerned that Mary's death was accidental while Bessie's was premeditated. Their major focus was that a black male had killed a white girl, presumably after raping her. Students are disturbed that the jury mistakenly assumes that Bigger raped Mary, yet is not concerned that he raped Bessie before killing her.

While the novel illustrates our society's racism, I always try to emphasize that although our society may be racist, the charge does not apply to all white people. It is important to emphasize this so that white students will not have to feel the burden of what some of their forefathers may have done. To confirm this, I tell my classes that

Harriet Tubman would not have been successful with her deliverance of blacks from slavery through the underground railroad if it had not been for Quakers, who were white. I also note that Wright's depiction of two whites (Jan and Max) in the novel demonstrates this idea: Jan attempted to make Bigger feel his equal, and Max, an attorney, fought for Bigger's life.

White students feel relieved that they do not have to carry the burden of some of their forefathers' injustices to minorities. Many acknowledge that they have been criticized by other whites for having black friends, or for going to a school where minorities predominate. They say that because of their exposure to Muir's environment, they will be better able to face the real world than their counterparts, whose only exposure has been to others like themselves.

My experience with black/white relationships in my classroom is positive. I remember one discussion we were having about blacks calling each other "nigger" as a sign of brotherhood. One black male said that he would not allow a white to call him that. A white student, who happened to be a friend, asked him why he couldn't call him "nigger" if he was as much a friend as another black. The black student said it had nothing to do with him, he just wouldn't take it the same way. The discussion that followed was one of the best I have ever experienced in the classroom. I just sat and let the students work it out themselves. The black students came to the defense of the white student, emphasizing that friends should be treated the same; that the black student should not allow anyone, black or white, to call him "nigger," because he had a given name. What a delight it was for me to silently witness kids' ability to respectfully discuss a sensitive issue and to resolve it positively. The black conceded that he had not given his remark much thought and that he shouldn't allow anyone to call him a derogatory name. The black and white friends left class together, amiably discussing the issue.[2]

Throughout the reading of the novel, students may discuss black-white interrelationships: (1) how they feel about having a friend of another race; (2) how their parents feel about their friendship with someone of another race; (3) how they feel when they are the only race represented at a gathering; and (4) how they can help eliminate stereotyping, prejudice, and racism. An appropriate time for this type of discussion is when Bigger is coerced into taking Mary and Jan to eat at a black café where he's ashamed to be seen with them.

Many of the students say they like having friends of another race, yet they sometimes get negative reactions from family and friends of their own race. For example, blacks may be told that they are trying to "act white," while whites may be told they are trying to "act black," just because they may associate more with a group of another race. Most say their parents accept friends from another race, but tend to become anxious if they date someone of another race, often fearing the reactions of family and friends for their allowing their child to do so. One white girl relates the bigotry of a neighbor over the fact that a friend of hers was dating a black kid. Although this happened a year ago, this student is still angry and ashamed that her neighbor would show such bigotry. Students also say that if they are at a party and people are friendly it doesn't matter if they are the only one of their race represented. Students feel that the only ways they can help eliminate stereotyping, prejudice, and racism are to first focus on their own behavior and how they view others unlike themselves; to try to see people as human beings with some of the same frailties, motives, ambitions, likes and dislikes, and to try not to participate in the bashing of another race. One white student, who comes to Muir despite his living in an upper-middle-class white community, relates how he often has to confront his white friends because of negative comments about black students at Muir. The student says that he was at a party and was talking with a group of students from other schools about the sports they played. When he said that he was on Muir's football team, they were shocked because he is in honor classes—Muir has a reputation for being top-rate in football, and here was a white student saying that he was a member of a black team that is assumed to consist of underachievers. This student challenged his friends about their false perception of those who go to Muir and play sports there.

White students say whites generally view blacks as the media portrays them because they have had no personal dealings with blacks. If blacks do not fit the negative stereotype, they are set apart as being "different" from the norm. Those who are not "different" are seen as illiterate, poverty-stricken, violent, irresponsible, drug addicts, or a combination of these negatives. These students say it is only after being exposed to a multicultural environment that many of their negative views of blacks have been dispelled.

After students have discussed their own experiences with people of another race, they have a clear understanding of why Bigger felt uncomfortable with Jan and Mary, and why he did not want to go into a black diner with them for fear that his friends would see him with two white people and later tease him about being with them. It also provides a means for discussing Mary and Jan's lack of knowledge about blacks, and how, because of their ignorance and best intentions, they made Bigger feel even more inferior and uncomfortable. One student was angry that Mary tried to coerce Bigger to go into the diner. He wanted to know why, if they wanted to make Bigger feel comfortable, they didn't take him to one of the white diners—why does the black person always have to be put to the disadvantage? I explain that it was not their intention to make Bigger feel uncomfortable; they were merely trying to prove to him that they were in earnest when they said they wanted to be his friend. We then read Mary's comments about wanting to get to know blacks better:

> "You know, Bigger, I've long wanted to go into those houses," she said, pointing to the tall, dark apartment buildings looming to either side of them, "and just *see* how your people live. You know what I mean? I've been to England, France and Mexico, but I don't know how people live ten blocks from me. We know so *little* about each other. I just want to *see*. I want to *know* these people. Never in my life have I seen inside of a Negro home. Yet they *must* live like we live. They're *human*. . . . There are twelve million of them. . . . They live in our country. . . . In the same city with us. . . ." her voice trailed off wistfully. (70)

This quotation provides an opportunity to discuss how blacks might be perceived by white society, particularly upper-middle-class society. Black students tend to be outraged that Mary would even make the statement that blacks are "human," too, and that "[t]hey live in our country," which is an indication that she really believes that Bigger, as well as other native-born blacks, are aliens of this country, and are somewhat misplaced. One black honor student was so furious at Mary's comments that when I asked, as I always do, if there were any questions or comments about the previous night's assignment, she said quite strongly, "When are we going to be recognized as being as much a part of this country as the Europeans who came here? Why are we the only people not recognized as full-fledged citizens?" It is important that the teacher lead this part of the discussion sensitively; otherwise, both white and black students may become antagonistic toward each other and lose sight of the objective of seeing how *Native Son* serves as an example of what can happen to one oppressed, and how it also provides an opportunity for constructively dealing with stereotyping, prejudice, and racism.

The discussion of this novel also involves other social issues or potentially controversial subject matter (e.g., how society views sexual relationships between black males and white women differently than it does sex between white males and black females; how white society feels threatened by the black male; how the media and police treat blacks differently from whites; whites' and blacks' views of each other;

the inequities in rent, food, and clothing in black communities; fear of communism). My experience has been that open, honest, uninhibited discussions provide fresh approaches to these issues. While the subject may make students and teachers initially uncomfortable, it is a necessary discussion if we are to break down some of the stereotypical barriers which can separate students and teachers, and impede their appreciation and understanding of literature and how it relates to their own lives.

One positive way to end the novel is to present to students James Baldwin's suggestion in *The Fire Next Time* (1963):

> [If the] relatively conscious whites and the relatively conscious blacks, who must like lovers, insist on, or create, the consciousness of the others—do not falter in our duty now, we may be able, handful that we are, to end the racial nightmare, and achieve our country, and change the history of the world. (119)

Notes

1. Mencken, H.L. (1977). *The American Language: Supplement I.* New York: Alfred A. Knopf.

2. A number of my colleagues wonder how I get my students to be so open in class discussion. I have to admit that I have no formula, except to try to be as open and honest with them as I possibly can. I do think that my initial rule of "no profanity or derogatory terms are allowed at any time," emphasized on the first day of school, sets the tone for the class. I explain to students what offends me; namely, all words that are derogatory and tend to put someone or a group down. I list a number of words, and explain why I find them offensive. I then ask them to let me know what offends them, as I would never want to do anything to offend them. I emphasize that if I ever did I would appreciate their coming up to me after class and letting me know. It is important that they know that I will not accept disrespectfulness from them at any time. Another rule is that if I offend one of them they cannot attack or confront me in class: they must deal with me on an individual basis, as I will deal with them. Whenever I discover that I have been in error, I do not hesitate to apologize to them. One technique I have is to bow to them and ask to "kiss their ring," in humble submissiveness. They love it!

In the discussion of any work, I attempt to get students to relate it to their own experiences, often role playing. Through sharing their own experiences and role playing, they learn that, while they may have different experiences, they also share common ones. Learning of commonalities helps set the tone for open, honest discussions.

I emphasize that, while they may not agree with each other, they must be courteous and show respect to one another. I set an example for them through my dialogue with them, always endeavoring to respect their opinions, even if I don't agree with them.

14 Racism and the Marvelous Real

Cecilia Rodríguez Milanés
Indiana University of Pennsylvania

Being a Latina instructor of alternative pedagogy, I am always interested in social issues. During a literature/composition course I taught (as part of my teaching assistantship) at the State University of New York at Albany, some of my white, middle-class students associated my ethnicity with the reason why I am preoccupied with social issues, stating that they understood (or rather they could justify) my "obsession." For them, a conscientious concern for a more representative and balanced reading list (gender and race) constituted obsessive behavior. When we read the works of writers such as James Baldwin, Ralph Ellison, Toni Cade Bambara, and Toni Morrison and discussed the impact and significance of racism in North America, for instance, they complained that we were reading too many disturbing texts:

> I'd like to read fun books instead of social awareness stories. Not that I don't like social books but it would be a nice change of pace.

> I found much of the reading to be depressing. I think that I would've enjoyed reading more joyous works than prejudice works.

> My only complaint is what we have read. I know you feel it is important to read social commentaries, especially dealing with minorities.

> There was *way* too much emphasis on minorities and feminism.

The great majority of my students were Long Islanders, with the typical racially sheltered lives one associates with the suburbs of the dominant culture; a minority were from white working-class areas in the "upstate" region. Another handful came from racially diverse, depressed, and violent areas of New York City. It was interesting to see that when my students, particularly those who were members of the dominant culture, found themselves no longer the predominant focus of study, they considered their culture and themselves in jeopardy.

Although most of the texts I chose dealt with some social issue, not all of them did. In fact, students selected two of the three novels we read as a class; however, many still objected, resisted, and put up barriers against my selections for the reading list. Perhaps it is also related to the fact that I ran my course in as democratic a fashion as I could and therefore sanctioned their resistance. By deconstructing institutional authority, that is, describing and demystifying the inter-locking systems of oppression which foster and depend on racism, sexism, and classism, I gave them room to question my authority. After all, they were students, and students are oppressed by the institution; so my task was to make explicit the connection between their oppression and the system which oppresses us all. This questioning made it easier for my students to be creative, to take chances, and to assert themselves, particularly in regard to their responses to noncanonical texts. By requiring their input in the running of the class and by making collaboration and revision the normal mode of operation, the students moved away from being passive receptors toward being active partic-ipants.

Although a socially conscious agenda informed my considerations in selecting texts for an intergrated reading list, I also had to consider that most North American students, whatever their backgrounds (and especially first- and second-year students), would not have much experience reading literature outside of the western European/North American "classic" tradition. For an introductory fiction/composition course I taught recently, I started the list with some nineteenth-century women writers such as Sarah Orne Jewett and Mary E. Wilkins Freeman because of their focus on women struggling against male-dominated society. From there we worked forward in time toward modern writers such as Louise Erdrich, Yukio Mishima, and Ray Bradbury, dealing with issues such as the rights of Native Americans, capitalism, and nuclear war. I also included some Latin American writers, particularly writers of the "marvelous real," or "magic realism," which may be loosely defined as an allegorical style where the imaginary and the fantastic are "weighted down by drab and sordid reality" (Charters 984). The beauty of much Latin American writing is that while it is often fanciful and humorous, it also frequently deals with crucial social problems and issues. These works would be presented later in the semester, after students had tackled the works of contemporary African American writers.

In trying to break through some of the barriers students put up when discussing social issues, I find it necessary to use nontraditional strategies such as "rotating chair," problematization of texts, collaborative learning, memo writing, and others drawn from radical and feminist pedagogy. A cornerstone of my teaching is conversation—dialogic discussion informed by the work of Paolo Freire. I also strive to be a practitioner of a facilitative, caring pedagogy as described in the work of feminists Margo Culley, Catherine Portuges, Elizabeth Flynn, Barbara Smith, and others. These strategies help break down structures of the patriarchal hierarchy of North American education and make the way for a more engaging mode of learning. While focusing on how I eased student apprehension and resistance in dealing with an unfamiliar genre (magic realism) and a social issue (racism, in this case), I will illustrate some of the alternative strategies which helped in this process.

One of the strategies I routinely use for large-group discussion, a "go-around," provides the opportunity for every student to speak. One day I asked my "Introduction to Fiction" students to have a go-around with Toni Cade Bambara's story, "Hammer Man." Each person was to choose a sentence, phrase, or paragraph and read it out loud and make a comment about why she or he chose it until everyone in the circle had had a turn. One young woman from the upper Westside of Manhattan, Debi, read the following from the text:

> After a while a center opened up and mother said she'd increase my allowance if I went and joined because I'd have to get out of my pants and stay in skirts, on account of the way things were at the center. So I joined and . . . I sneaked into the office, that's when I really got turned on. I looked into one of those not-quite-white folders and saw that I was from a deviant family in a deviant neighborhood. I showed my mother the word in the dictionary, but she didn't pay me no mind. It was my favorite word after that. (1144)

Debi said that this quote proved that the young girl in the story was really bad, and since she had misbehaved and her parents hadn't disciplined her, then they were being irresponsible and were shirking their familial duties. Debi was particularly disturbed that the girl's parents would let her go out and play after dark in the schoolyard. I personally hadn't considered this portion of the story unusual since I very much identified with the girl's experience as similar to my own rearing in urban New Jersey, but I did not offer this observation because I had a feeling that at least one of the two or three students who were from "the city" would attest to the "truth" of Bambara's piece. After she finished making her point, the student sitting next to her, Chuck, offered the following quote:

> . . . a squad car pulled up and a short cop with hair like one of the Marx Brothers came out hitching his pants. . . . [Manny] wasn't paying no mind to the cop. So, quite, naturally, when the cop slapped him upside his head it was a surprise. (1145)

Chuck was extremely disturbed over Bambara's choice of the word "cop" over "police" or "police officer." He was even angrier that Bambara would show the police abusing the young man and said, "My dad's a police officer, and they just don't do that." Well, where I grew up, some did, and so when no one volunteered, I asked a young African American man to comment. James had written an essay describing his life, "Growing Up in New York City." He squirmed a bit when I called on him out of turn, but he quietly told the class that when he was growing up police were always referred to as "cops." No disrespect was intended—"it was just what we kids called them." He added that children as young as seven routinely stayed out at night to play in the street or schoolyard. I added that while the vast majority of police officers were fair and just people, police brutality against minority persons was, unfortunately, a fact of life. Debi went on to say that it was her belief that the type of lifestyle described by Bambara was nontraditional and "not right." Another student, Sonya, from a far less privileged background than Debi, asked her pointedly if any lifestyle different from her own was "incorrect or morally inferior." Debi was stunned, as were others in the class. She probably did not expect anyone to challenge her, especially Sonya, who had not talked much during discussions. Debi never responded, but the whole class seemed to shift its attention to a visibly angry Sonya who would have just as soon diverted it back to Debi. Sonya's and James's contributions in this exchange between students of different backgrounds, I feel, is much more powerful than any lecture about differences in culture and class I could have given. The upshot of this and other discussions in that class was that Debi and others like her were able to glean a better understanding of the lives of those who weren't born into middle- and upper-class comfort and security. Another repercussion of this exchange is that James's paper came to be read and shared by the entire class, especially this haunting section:

> The summer of 1982, however, was a time of turmoil and pain for me. That summer I was a witness of two murders. Both of the victims were friends of mine . . . Roy never hated anyone, nor was he by any means a trouble maker. Roy was the star point guard of my junior high school's team. He was going to attend

Thurman High School in the Bronx and was heavily recruited by high schools and colleges. He was killed at 4 o'clock on July 10, 1982. We were playing hoops that Saturday when he was struck by a stray bullet. The bullet came from across the street where two gangs, the Warlords and the Bronx Warriors, were shootin[g] it out over drug turf.

Another of my friends was murdered that summer. George Lucas was stabbed in the heart . . .

The rest of my high school career was full of violence. My mother taught me not to take part in or initiate violence unless violence should find me. . . .

I hardly return to the old neighborhood [Washington Heights]. My mom moved after someone got shot in the elevator of our building. . . .

James was generally reserved during class discussions, but his papers spoke out quite eloquently about the kind of life he had known growing up in the same state, sometimes the same city, that many of the class members called home.

Before going on to discuss more of the literature, I need to make note of the practice of "rotating chair." The purpose of using rotating chair for large- and small-group discussions is to prevent one person from dominating the discussion by "rotating" the speaker after she or he has finished speaking. The way it works is that one person begins the discussion; it's almost always me (partially this is due to my impatience, but it has more to do with focusing the discussion). After I've said my piece there may or may not be hands raised in response, but, either way, I choose one person to take over. When finished, the speaker then chooses another person to "chair," and the process is repeated until everyone in the class has had a chance to speak. One of the stipulations for rotating chair is that the speaker may never call on someone who has already spoken if there is another who is yet to be heard. If everyone has spoken at least once, then the current speaker is to call on the person who spoke the earliest on during our discussion (farthest away in turn). When this procedure for discussion is established early in the semester, it makes the rest of the term's work more egalitarian. Problems may arise when students lapse into calling on one or two who are more vocal than others, so I occasionally have to intercede in order to return the discussion to the rotation system.

Treating the works of popular North American writers such as Woody Allen and Ray Bradbury before going on to writers such as Gabriel García Márquez and Julio Cortázar helps to ease student resistance to the genre of magic realism. I found that if the class has read and discussed Allen's "The Kugelmass Episode," with its New York locale and magical box, before we read García Márquez's "A Very Old Man with Enormous Wings," for example, then the students are more likely to accept the realm of the marvelous real as a suitable setting. Of course, there will usually be some students who will declare García Márquez's story ridiculous and unbelievable, but when it comes to my turn at rotating chair, I mention that Woody Allen's magician and exploding box did not seem to detract from their enjoyment of that story.

Some of the writers of the marvelous real often use humor—biting, ironic, and sometimes absurd—to treat "heavy" or loaded issues such as imperialism, sexism, or racism,[1] but I was quite surprised to find a way into these issues without provoking as much hostility. This realization came while I was teaching Reinaldo Arenas's *The Graveyard of the Angels*, which treats the issue of racism with enlightenment and astuteness while presenting it in such an entertaining way that students are charmed and then disarmed by its depiction and treatment of racism in colonial Cuba. In Arenas's hands, Cirilo Villaverde's novel *Cecilia Valdés*, often considered an abolitionist tract not unlike Stowe's *Uncle Tom's Cabin*, is transformed into a comical farce, but with far-reaching results. In the preface Arenas calls Villaverde's work

> a moral mirror of a society perverted and made wealthy by slavery, and while it does describe the trials and tribulations of slaves in Cuba during the last century, it is also a "summa of irreverence," an attack on the conventions and mores of that century—which, by and large, are those of our own age. (1)

This is reason enough for Arenas to use all of his substantial powers of exaggeration in his revision of *Cecilia Valdés*.

The difference between the classroom discussions treating the texts of African American writers and those of the Latin Americans was startling. The mood of the classroom during a discussion of Ralph Ellison's "Battle Royal," for example, was somber, troubled, and angry; this is not necessarily bad, but there were times when the mood of some students was so defensive that it verged on the volatile, and, too often, this is counterproductive. While "white guilt" plays a part in some students' defensiveness, many may feel that I (a minority) am implicating them (the dominant culture) in the sin of racism. (On the surface, it is true that I am implicating them, but I am also implicating myself, for I, too, share in the oppressive system. My point is that my agenda is not hidden and is, therefore, open to scrutiny.) Discussions of Arenas's *Graveyard of the Angels*, on the other hand, were characterized by lightheartedness and gaiety. I was surprised at this shift in mood. In particular, I remember one student, Jon, during the class on a Langston Hughes story; he called both Simple and the narrator "stupid and incredible," so, for him, "the story [didn't] work" in fighting racism. Later that semester, Jon was eagerly offering up examples of racism from Arenas's text. I also found a similar change in the way students responded to the issue of racism in their reading journals.[2]

By reading selected works of African American writers such as Naylor, Bambara, and others early in the semester, students were primed for picking up the theme of racism in other texts. As a matter of a fact, most students couldn't wait to get away from these works of "social awareness." By the end of the semester, they enter a text such as *Graveyard of the Angels* beguiled by the humor and outrageousness of the writing but able to read beyond these elements to the issue of relations between the races. Arenas's text allowed my students to discuss some of the roots of racism in slavery and European cosmology by removing them from the often touchy modern focus of racism. It is far easier for many white, middle-class students to discuss racism if it is not related to their time, their corner of the world, or their people. While it is extremely challenging to return racism (or any social issue) to the present moment, it is also my responsibility. If I don't make the connection between racism in the nineteenth century and racism in the twentieth, then the adage "If you're not part of the solution, you're part of the problem" is still appropriate.

I suppose I should not have been amazed to see my students offering up so many humorous and horrendous quotations to share in large-group discussion. The following lines, a passage many students brought up, contain a taste of Arenas's sardonic humor in dealing with the cruelty of the slaveowners. Here, the white Gamboa family and their guests are gathered on the first floor awaiting the young master, Leonardo:

> Don Cándido, in a powerful voice, ordered an adolescent black, Toto, who was Leonardo's lackey, to wake him up. In a twinkling of an eye, the black was up in the young master's suite. He came back down even more quickly, even though he was dead: He landed right in the center of the hall where everyone was animatedly chatting . . .
> "Oh, that Leonardo!" complained doña Rosa in mock exasperation as she contemplated the black boy's cadaver. "He's always in such a bad mood when he first wakes up." It was true: Leonardo had killed several of the slaves who awakened him, even though the order had come, as always from don Cándido.

"Don't think that's one of his better qualities," don Cándido, visibly upset, barked at doña Rosa. "I've lost some of my best servants that way. And you know very well," he said now to don Pedro and Isabel, "that those dogs the English grow more stubborn every day about letting us unload sacks of African coal." (46)

The students laugh about Leonardo's ill temper, but when they stop smiling they realize that slaves were disposable "sacks of African coal." One day, during discussion on the novel, Jon, one of the most resistant students, said, "They really thought slaves were expendable commodities, huh?" Jon's new experience taught him that he could no longer easily dismiss a story, character, or issue. A young man who had bitterly critiqued my focus on racism earlier in the semester added, "Life was so cheap." We then referred back to James's paper and talked about the violence born of institutional racism he encountered daily in his "neighborhood." These realizations came, not suddenly, but as a result of dealing with the issue (and other related issues) over the semester: reading works treating it, writing about it, and talking about it with others.

One of the scenes students love to read aloud and joke about is the one where Leonardo's lover, Cecilia, is trying to hide her African ancestry:

"Good heavens!" exclaimed Cecilia Valdés, looking up at the old clock on the wall. "It's almost five and I still haven't finished painting you up! Leonardo will be here any minute."

Cecilia was not speaking, despite appearances, to the old clock on the wall, but to her great-grandmother, doña Amalia. Cecilia, dipping her brush in a pot of white paint, was changing doña Amalia's black skin into ivory. And she went right on painting the old lady as she spoke to her.

"White! That's right! The whitest! . . . That's how Leonardo must see you. Leonardo must never know that you're a retouched Negress. If he were to find out, he'd never marry me. White! White! Not even mulatta! . . ."

"Cecilia, chile, ah alays been black an' ah lak it dat way. Cain't you at leas' let me die wit' my right culuh?"

"What?" exclaimed the suddenly serious great-granddaughter. "That's the limit! I turn you into a *human being* and that's the thanks I get? Complaints? Do you know how it was for me to get this barrel of white paint . . ."

"Ah wanna be black. Leave me mah own culuh." The Negress, or rather the white woman, since only one of her withered breasts was still black, and that too, would be white in a moment, again protested in a low voice.

"So you want to be black, eh? But don't you understand that in this world a black is worth less than a dog? Even if you work and get free, even if you get money—which is almost impossible.

> Look what happened with Dolores Santa Cruz. They never forgave
> her for wanting to sleep in a comfortable bed like a white person,
> or for having her own carriage. The whites tripped her up in their
> white laws until they stripped her bare. If she'd been white none
> of that would have happened. . . ." (63–64) [emphasis mine]

The ridiculousness of Cecilia painting her great-grandmother white is
heavily underscored by the tragedy of the truth of her words. Many
of my students come to see that much of what she says in the last
paragraph is still true today. A first-year student who was intrigued
by the issue of color—light- and dark-skinned peoples and social
stigma of such—decided to write a paper on Spike Lee's film *School
Daze*. One young woman was indignant that "Santa Cruz had earned
her freedom and the whites still found a way to enslave her." Dolores
Santa Cruz had been captured in Africa and sold as a slave but
"[t]hanks to her incessant work, trickery, and saving, she had purchased
her freedom . . . and became the owner of several gambling houses, a
bakery, and a shoemaker shop" (60). She was "picked clean" by
lawyers and judges who "legally" stripped her of her rights, deeds,
and properties. Moved by the character's struggle, another student
decided to write an essay on the reversal of civil rights legislation
during the last and present administrations. Some, unfortunately, may
never come to these kinds of realizations, and as much as I'd like to
open their minds to what I and many others see, I have learned to
accept that. I can only hope to be as tolerant as I can as I set a
dialogic/feminist example for my students. After all, tolerance is a
virtue many of them are lacking.

When students express the opinion that the type of racism described
in Arenas's text no longer exists, I ask them why the KKK is still going
strong and growing; why the Howard Beach killing took place; why
minority students on campuses across the country are continuously
harassed and/or physically assaulted? Sometimes returning the issue
of racism to the present is what is most indelicate about my pedagogy.
A day that remains very vivid in my mind is when a very large young
man, incensed over a scene in Alice Walker's *Meridian* where a character
lambasts government "help" for African Americans, stood up, and
over me, and began loudly criticizing SUNY/Albany's minority hiring
quotas and minority student grants (which inevitably come up whenever racism is discussed). I had to ask him to sit down because he
was towering over me; I was calm when I responded that if it weren't
for a minority student teaching assistantship, I wouldn't be their
instructor. He seemed genuinely surprised.

I feel encouraged about my work whenever I hear African American or Latino students ask themselves or their professors why their experience and culture are omitted from the focus of study, as a recent student of mine expressed in a midterm evaluation.

> Since I am Hispanic [I] would like to read a book related to 'our' struggles . . . It hasn't been easy for Hispanics either, especially since a lot of us are categorized under black. . . . A lot of students tend to complain about the stories and that they are sick of them. (I like them.) I have also learned that a lot of 'white' students are not as biased as I stereotyped them to be.

This student's last statement expresses the suspicion many Latinos feel toward white North Americans; a general distrust based on the discrimination they or their people have experienced in the United States. After discussing racism during class and in writing groups, she came to see that bigotry is colorblind.

Sadly, some students may not be able to "hear" us, though we speak articulately and illustrate clearly these social ills. There are students who believe in their heart of hearts, for example, that "white racism is as bad as black racism," as one first-year student expressed in his paper entitled "Racism is a Two-Way Street." His premise was based on the assumption that the ramifications, intensity, and efficiency of racism by African Americans was "as bad" and therefore equal to that systemic and systematic racism by white patriarchal North America. I read an article recently by Bill Perry, a Miami activist, which distinguished racism from prejudice:

> Racism, as I define it, is systematic denial, defamation and interruption of a people's history, humanity and right to freedom based exclusively on race. Racism is distinguished from prejudice inasmuch as it carries the power to impose—to carry out as a matter of policy and/or legislation. Consequently, African Americans cannot be racist, but, yes, they can be racially prejudiced. (*Miami Herald* 30 Dec. 1990: C1)

I wish I had had those words to share with my student when we exchanged these several lengthy memos about his paper.

> *Student:* I really feel that this paper touches an important topic. Racism against the white majority is something out there and really not examined . . . I feel the major strength of my paper is the truth behind it and my strong belief in it!
>
> *Milanés:* I feel the truth in the essay . . . I really was impressed with how you tell about being the object of racism and what a horrible feeling that is. Many Anglo people never know what that awful feeling/position is like. . . . I trust your anger and outrage. . . . I'll be glad to see you on this, especially about the difference between these kinds of racism.

Student: I'm really glad you approve of this paper's content. When I wrote it, I felt strongly about it and was able to write smoothly and quickly. When I showed it to the writing group one person really liked it and one other said I was nuts for choosing the topic and also that I had guts. I must admit I wasn't sure how you—not being a white Anglo male—would react. Your comments have helped, I think.

Milanés: It's tiring isn't it? Dealing with racism? It makes me tired—watching it, listening to it, reading about it. Your paper and its focus on detail draws out (painfully) painful experiences. I just finished James's paper before yours and think you two should exchange drafts and talk to one another. He talked about growing up in NYC and how he watched three friends die right in front of his eyes. The contrast between your topic and his is significant because, for me, they are related. I ran out of room [in the memo] the last time but now I want to address the differences between white racism and black racism . . . When blacks are racist against whites they usually have only a limited power over dominant culture in the US. Blacks *usually* don't have economic power over whites and let's face it, in this country economic power is what counts. Most blacks or Latinos don't have the power to exclude you from a job, apartment, or anything . . .

Student: . . . Anyhow, I'd like to know if this paper reaches you in any way. I want to know if this is delivering a message I'm trying to send—that is how terrible a thing racism is and how it *can hit both sides of the quarrel.* Could I have expressed myself more clearly? Please tell me how you feel about the paper.

Milanés: Perhaps this was a bad day for me to read your essay. I'll tell you why. I spent 3 1/2 hours of my day in meetings trying to find ways of making SUNY/A more hospitable to minorities. Since I'm the only Hispanic grad student in the dept, I need to be on these committees . . .

About your paper—what I felt this time was that you have experienced an incredible amount of frustration here at SUNY/A. This paper worked the best for me when you talked about your own experience with racism.

I'm really wondering what you think about my last memo to you. I feel even more strongly now that you need to think about the issue of difference with respect to the manifestations of racism. While both sides are intolerable—white racism against *any* minority group holds such an incredible amount of weight, power, privilege that I feel very sure in saying that the two can't compare.

This student never did address the issue of difference between white and black racism; he could not "hear" me. But for all the students who choose to ignore my comments or questions there are other students who are all too willing to abandon their structures, plots, or arguments to "please" me, such as Leslie, for example. Her essay on families presumed that all families were like hers—two loving parents and three happy, well-adjusted kids. She postulated that bad parenting was the root of all society's problems and when I problematized her assumption Leslie caved in. She completely rewrote her paper to reflect my thoughts.[3] The times when I sense this type of miscommunication happening during discussion sessions I go to my students in search of "testimony" to remedy the situation, as in the time I asked James and Sonya to comment on Toni Cade Bambara's story.

Dealing with social issues is never easy or always pleasant, but it is very important to me. Literature and literacy are also important, and through an alternative pedagogy I have been able to combine these, involving students more actively in learning to read (interpret), write, and question. In addition, using texts by writers of the marvelous real eases many of the volatile tensions that may arise when dealing with social issues such as racism. I hope that through sharing my story and experience, I can give other socially committed teachers ways into the important issues of our time.

Notes

1. Other teachers may experiment with texts such as Isabel Allende's *House of Spirits* for dealing with sexism, Manuel Puig's *The Kiss of the Spiderwoman* for tackling homophobia, and Gabriel García Márquez's *The Autumn of the Patriarch* for treating fascism. In fact, all of these texts critique facism in different ways and readers of the marvelous real know that that is one subject which always looms large in many Latin American texts.

2. It has been my practice to return journals at the end of the semester and therefore I cannot quote from them.

3. I'm happy to say that Leslie and I were able to more profoundly engage one another on the issues in her paper.

References

Arenas, R. 1987. *Graveyard of the Angels*. Trans. by A.J. MacAdam. New York: Avon.

Charters, A. Ed. 1987. *The Story and Its Writer: An Introduction to Short Fiction.* New York: St. Martin's Press.

Perry, B. 1990. "The Problem in Miami: Tacit Racism." *The Miami Herald* (30 December): 1C.

15 "I'm Not a Poor Slave": Student-Generated Curricula and Race Relations

Gail Tayko and John Tassoni
Indiana University of Pennsylvania

While discussing African American topics, we've found ourselves avoiding eye contact with African American students in our classes. We had assumed this reaction arises from our own inexperience as teachers, from our lack of exposure to African American culture, and from our attempts to compensate for situations where African American students, outnumbered 13–1 in our classrooms, have unwillingly become the focus of attention. Our white students' periodic references to African Americans as "the colored people" or simply as "they" during class discussion compound these situations. Greatly outnumbered and, perhaps even more, used to such alienating rhetoric, our African American students generally remain silent when topics affecting the lives of African Americans are raised. More and more, we feared addressing certain vital issues because of the awkwardness such discussions provoked.

We had *at least* two problems to confront: our own uneasiness, and the broader issue of race relations in the classroom. Knowing that we should act on the issues at hand, we decided to ask African American students in our classes to compose topic questions for the study of Harriet Jacobs's *Incidents in the Life of a Slave Girl: Written by Herself*, an assigned reading.[1] Our purpose was to open dialogue on African American issues by having these students, in a sense, offer us license to explore topics we had found ourselves avoiding. Looking our African American students in the eye, we thought, would not be so difficult once we had learned of their own concerns and expectations regarding Jacobs.

For our chapter, we planned to write about the list of questions the African American students created and to suggest ways that discussions

We thank David Downing, C. Mark Hurlbert, Samuel Totten, Marissa Tayko, and Michael Williamson for reading and commenting on this chapter throughout its composition. We thank especially those students who participated in our project.

258

of race could be conducted both tactfully and incisively. What we discovered was the complexity of relations—gender- and class-based, racial, pedagogical—that had all along pervaded our approaches to African American concerns. Having received our students' lists, we felt more comfortable broaching questions about *Incidents* and about discussing other African American topics. But, perhaps, the questions we solicited showed more of a movement away from, rather than a delving into, racial issues. As a result, this chapter delineates the factors that constrain dialogue as much as it suggests ways we might deal with these impediments.

In 1989, during our first semester as teaching associates at Indiana University of Pennsylvania, one African American, a male and a female, was enrolled in each of Tassoni's two English 101 classes. Two African American women were enrolled in each of Tayko's two 101 courses. When we (Tayko, who is a Filipina American, and Tassoni, who is white) suggested this project to our students, we related our concerns over the silence that had accompanied previous class "discussions." We told these students we were interested in knowing what questions or problems they had with the text, questions or problems we could raise to others in the class. Our students approached us several times throughout the exercise because they were unsure of what we wanted from them, and we explained that we were interested not in what was wanted *of them,* but in what *they* wanted.

We realized we hadn't "trained" our students for the assignment and had also given them little, if any, say in designing it. We had simply told them what we wanted when we described our project and its goals. From the project's onset, then, we unwittingly evoked our authority as teachers, creating an environment where our expectations—not our students' concerns—would remain the implicit targets of any questions we received. As an alternative, we should have arranged a session where our project could have been revised according to their own aims.

By singling out African American students for this assignment, we might have, in fact, intensified the alienation we hoped to decrease, and deepened the divisions that racial issues already exposed in the classroom. But such exposures represented one of our major aims in including Jacobs on our syllabi: by privileging the work of an African American woman in a course whose subject matter has principally been the tool of white men, we hoped to show how language itself functions to discriminate and alienate. At the same time, we saw the benefits of the exercise, since it would both draw us into direct and personal communication with our African American students over racial concerns and allow us to critically address such concerns to our classes as a whole. Although we never wanted to alienate individual students, our perception of the project's "advantages" somehow prevented us from seeing the implications involved in even approaching our African American students in the first place.

Each of us handled the issue of alienation differently. Tayko decided, at the time of the Jacobs discussion, to publicly acknowledge her students' participation to her classes. She felt they deserved recognition for their contributions, and she did not want these students to assume their instructor would simply pass off their work as her own. On the other hand, Tassoni concealed from his classes the African American students' contributions. He did so because each was the only African American member in his section, and he sensed that drawing attention to the individual student might actually defeat the purpose of the project.

We could have asked the entire class to compose agendas. This way, at least our authority over the text—as teachers, though not explicitly as non-blacks—would be qualified, and we would still get direct input from African American students. We might have also better perceived our non-black students as readers of race; that is, we might have better understood the assumptions brought into our classrooms about African Americans. It seems to us that this alternative would work well in exercises involving other issues and other texts where instructors would like to become familiar with their students' views and their degrees of cultural understanding.[2] By devising the project without our students, however, we actually reasserted our own rules as to what agenda was appropriate for our classrooms.

We hadn't facilitated our students' own understanding of the project, and this factor may have combined with the feminist qualities of Jacobs's work to limit the contribution of Ernest Joint (the African American male in Tassoni's class), although the project itself did open dialogue between him and Tassoni on some sensitive issues. For example, in some conferences Ernest initiated discussion, at one time talking about the African American usage of "nigger" and asking Tassoni how whites responded to the word "honkey." But despite Ernest's efforts, he just could not generate many questions in regard to *Incidents*. In fact, he offered only two questions: "Why was there slavery?" and a question about a passage in which Jacobs states "that slavery is a curse to the whites as well as to the blacks" (52). This latter question is significant because it is perhaps the only one we received that explicitly addresses race relations. Ernest's limited production alerted us to other factors that could affect this assignment:

the student's particular capability as a reader—the assumptions that led us to single out students in the first place apparently led us to assume them to be experts on nineteenth-century slave culture—and the nature of the work itself, which in this case expressly addresses a female audience.

Jacobs's text may not address male readers, particularly male freshman readers, to the extent that it does women. This is suggested by the questions created by the female students in Gail's classes, questions that show more a concern with gender, or even feminist issues. *Incidents* was meant to intensify the feminist dimensions of our courses, but with our assignment Jacobs's work could perhaps hamper as much as invite input from novice, male readers. A work like Frederick Douglass's *Narrative of the Life of Frederick Douglass, an American Slave: Written by Himself* might be more conducive to male readers if instructors, after reading the remainder of this chapter, are still interested in working with slave narratives in the manner we suggest. Douglass's text deals with attributes that are often associated with masculinity, an inadversion to physical confrontation, for example, so his *Narrative* might be—if we can allow ourselves another assumption—more accessible to male freshman readers. However, we're not saying that *Incidents* completely repelled Ernest. In a conversation some nine months after the project, we were surprised to hear him still talking about *Incidents*, considering the ways other characters, both white and African American, may have affected interaction between Jacobs and her mistresses.

Where *Incidents'* female narrator and audience might have limited Ernest's reading of the text, we also realized that the nature of the work could also affect—perhaps did affect—the rapport between student and teacher: a short time before Tassoni's section was scheduled to discuss Jacobs, the African American female student in his class decided not to participate in the exercise. Her withdrawal alerted us to yet another key issue in our project, our own gender and racial makeups. He felt he'd had a good rapport with this student, but discomfort she may have felt in discussing the issues in *Incidents* with a male, let alone a male of a different race, could have played a role in her withdrawal from the exercise. This withdrawal emphasized the illusiveness of our wished-for decenteredness. We hadn't, after all, surrendered full authority; we had still created a situation where an African American woman's concerns about a text written by an African American woman for a female audience would be mediated by a white man in a position of power.

Tayko's situation with her students differed from Tassoni's, since her exercise involved the interaction of a woman with female students (that she is a minority may also be of significance). When she initially asked them to take part in the project, they decided to meet together outside of class to discuss *Incidents*. As a result of these meetings, the questions provided by her students were often identical and were quantitatively successful in that they provided enough questions to comprise at least one session's agenda. The following paragraphs combine the list of issues, as written, that Christina Richardson, Antoinette (Toni) Jefferson, Tracina McCook, and Crystal McKnight raised.

Some questions concern more general issues about slavery: "Did slave owners think slavery was the will of God?" "What happened when the Fugitive Slave Law was passed?" "What did Aunt Martha mean when she told Benjamin, 'Be humble and your master will forgive you'? Why did she say that?" "Do you think Slavery increased the slaves' awareness, i.e., common sense?" "Do you feel that Jacobs's story is a true account of what actually took place during slavery times?" "Linda's [Jacobs's pseudonym in the text is Linda Brent] story is different from other slaves, most stories deal with the slave running to the North, but she stays in the South. Why?"

The following questions involve the impact Jacobs's gender had on issues dealing with personal relationships: "Could it be possible that Dr. Flint really had feelings for Linda?" "How does she explain her relationship with the white lawyer?" And one question combined concerns of gender and family: "Is Linda Brent a cruel mother for wanting her children dead?"

The last set of questions deals more specifically with Linda as a female slave: "What do you feel is the 'typical' slave girl? Do you see Linda Brent as the typical slave woman? Do you feel that Brent manipulated Dr. Flint?" "What about the sexual abuse of the slave women compared to the slave men?" "In the book she says that I feel that the slave woman ought not to be judged by the same standards as others. Is she saying that upon mature reflection, that women like herself should be judged (like men) on complex moral grounds—rather than (like women) on the single issue of their conformity to the sexual behavior mandated by the white patriarchy?"

When we reviewed two of the above questions, the one concluding the first set ("Linda's story is different from other slaves . . .") and the one concluding the final set ("Is she saying that upon mature reflec- tion . . ."), we realized that the student who submitted them relied to some extent on the "Introduction to *Incidents*," written by Jean Fagan Yellin, the book's editor. For the latter question, for instance, the student did explicitly indicate that her statement was "Taken from Intro." Although she may have been interested in these issues, these borrowed questions suggest her lack of confidence as a reader: despite our explicit emphasis on students' attention to their own interests, this student was still writing with her instructor's expectations in mind, as perhaps many of them were. In a later interview, Tracina even stated that the project was "easy" because the students had to just "see what you [Tayko] wanted." Our positions as teachers remained obstacles throughout the assignment: given that the agenda failed to address (more) incisive racial issues, we were not, *per se*, offered guidelines by the students by which to delve more deeply into these issues. Instead of giving us a list of topics that represented their own concerns, these students may have composed their questions according to past classroom agendas. In other words, by offering our classes these student-generated curricula, we inadvertently may have offered students curricula geared to reinforce the status quo.

What *other* assumptions could we have reinforced? Probably the most troubling one involves an unwarranted association between race and socio-economic class. Were we placing additional pressures on these students by assuming them to be authorities on their own race? And, even more, were we assuming that such a consciousness of race automatically made them experts on slavery as well? How *did* Tayko's white students read her acknowledgment of the African American students' contributions? Or, did we send the message that African Americans were invariably unbiased readers of racial conflict while whites were inevitably flawed? And we think of what might have happened if the questions provided by the African American students and, in turn, the answers offered by the white students, proved too provocative for the environment the class had developed. For example, what if a student had asked: "Why do white men always lust after black girls?" And what if a white student retorted with an equally biased remark about the sexuality of African American women?

The more we think about our project, the more we see the need for the entire class's involvement in developing agendas and, where courses allow, for including additional works dealing with a wider array of class, racial, and ethnic concerns. Exercises like these would allow students to participate on the basis of their own filiations: would allow, for example, an African American student, who is more conscious of her gender than her race, to compose questions based on feminist concerns, rather than have herself singled out so that a racial identity can be imposed upon her by someone whose race is not her own.

Additional meetings between groups of students may be necessary.

Before students are asked for their own individual questions, any offensive or provocative questions could be previewed by a small group of students, preferably the authors of the topics. With the instructor, they could evaluate the agenda in the context of potential reactions and—if they so choose—revise questions to suit the particular classroom environments. The aim in forming such a group is not to censor the material at hand in order to avoid controversial topics, but to have students think and talk about how particular questions might be controversial in their classroom and whether these questions were significant enough to be raised. (Might students actually find some value in asking why "white men always lust after black girls"?) On the other hand, if an agenda tended to skew racial concerns, the instructor could introduce a vocabulary to students, one that might increase the chances of such issues being raised during class discussions. In this way, particular students with whom instructors meet will have emerged from the students' responses as readers, rather than as representatives of their presumed racial or class filiations.

We didn't consciously presume our African American students to be experts on their race. However, Tracina McCook and Crystal McKnight felt that Tayko had indeed made such assumptions. In an interview, Tracina told her "that because we were black you did think we knew how it was back then." Crystal also wondered why Tayko had chosen them for the assignment since she believed "anyone else in the class" could have created the questions. Half jokingly and half seriously, she had even commented to Tracina: "I'm not a poor slave of the 1800s and my perception of the book doesn't necessarily have to be correct." Another student's comment was more ambiguous, though perhaps just as suggestive: Christina Richardson didn't feel Tayko was presumptuous, but qualified her reaction, saying her instructor had asked African American students to initiate questions "because [she] thought we could relate to the book better." And, while Christina thought the project "interesting," she also commented that "anybody could have done it, though."

On the other hand, from the beginning Ernest Joint felt the project was "a bright idea"; and Toni Jefferson later stated, "It was interesting to make up the questions rather than have the teacher make them up, so that the other students might understand better." When Tayko asked Toni if she felt the instructor had presumed her to be an authority on her race, she responded, "Not really," and reemphasized that the project's most valuable aspect for her was the idea of student-initiated topics. The notion of presumptuousness wasn't an issue for Ernest either. In fact, he appreciated the project because, as he stated, "most teachers are too scared to ask" African Americans about African American topics. Ernest's view suggests a willingness on his part to take part in a dialogue and also something disturbing about the way teachers are being perceived.

After presentation of the agenda, Tayko's students pursued an interactive dialogue. But we realize that the students' dialogue and their enthusiasm followed not so much from the fact that the questions were generated by African American students, but perhaps simply from the issues evoked, issues not explicitly racial, and perhaps as well from the fact that students (rather than the teacher) had generated the questions. Tassoni (who with Ernest's permission, supplemented his student's questions with those of Tayko's) did feel more comfortable in pursuing *Incidents* than he might have, had he not had an idea as to the African American students' readings of the text. But his white students were apparently uncomfortable, since they were inordinately silent on the day *Incidents* was discussed. In fact, after the session two white female students approached Tassoni and, seemingly apologetic for the silence that had preceded, confessed that they did not feel at ease discussing *Incidents* with Ernest in the room.

The image of these two white students, combined with the other variables that seem to dictate the failure of projects such as ours, alert us to just how complicated the racial and power relations in our classrooms are. We do feel that the existence of such impediments makes efforts like ours necessary, efforts that would take students' racial, gender, ethnic, and socio-economic filiations into consideration.

Notes

1. Jacobs's slave narrative combines issues of race, class, gender, and language, topics we frequently include on our English 101 syllabi, so that the gears of dominance and the role that language plays in such contexts may be better illustrated. Explicitly addressed to the North's white women abolitionists, *Incidents* details the desperation of a young African American woman fleeing an obsessed master who contrives to dominate her mentally and sexually. Not only does the narrative display how the rhetoric of slavery blurs lines between racial identity and socioeconomic class, but it also shows how gender differences attract their own unique forms of abuse. Jacobs's predicament illustrates the particular ordeal of African American women within the slave system and offers a critique of the institution itself. In key passages, Jacobs conceals herself for seven years in an attic within the vicinity of her master's own neighborhood. From this vantage point she contrives letters to confound her master's attempts to reclaim his "property" and at times delightfully observes his unscrupulous behavior. *Incidents* exhibits language

in both its oppressive and critical capacities, capacities to which we hope to make our students sensitive.

2. A YA work that could evoke class issues may be Norma Fox Mazer's *Silver*, which recounts the experiences of a girl from a trailer park who transfers to a high school attended principally by rich kids. Another YA work, one addressing ethnic issues, is Barbara Cohen's *People Like Us*. This story relates the complications a Jewish girl faces when her parents show prejudice toward her non-Jewish boyfriend. Additionally, African American works such as Paula Fox's *The Slave Dancer* and Irwin Hadley's *I Be Somebody* show the African American's introduction into white culture. Fox's text deals with a boy's experiences on a slave ship, while Hadley's portrays a boy who moves from a black community into the white world.

References

Cohen, B. 1987. *People Like Us*. New York: Bantam.

Douglass, F. 1845. *Narrative of the Life of Frederick Douglass, an American Slave: Written by Himself*. New York: Signet.

Fox, P. 1973. *The Slave Dancer*. New York: Dell.

Hadley, I. 1984. *I Be Somebody*. New York: Signet.

Jacobs, H. 1861. *Incidents in the Life of a Slave Girl: Written by Herself*. Ed. Jean Fagan Yellin. Cambridge: Harvard University Press, 1987.

Mazer, N.F. 1988. *Silver*. New York: Avon.

Yellin, J.F. 1987. "Introduction to *Incidents in the Life of a Slave Girl*. In Jacobs.

V Politics, Change, and Social Responsibility

16 Rumors of Change: *The* Classroom, *Our* Classrooms, and *Big* Business

C. Mark Hurlbert
Indiana University of Pennsylvania

Michael Blitz
John Jay College, City University of New York

> You're on the wrong side
> Of a rumor this time.
>
> —The Neighborhoods

As we write this, English educators across America are teaching about social issues in their classrooms. But despite our best efforts, the conditions in which we teach—the social issues we teach about and the actual *state* of education—don't change much. This astonishes and scares us. We keep asking each other, if so many teachers, such as the ones contributing to this book, are so tirelessly working for a better world, why don't we live in one?

What have we plugged into here? For one thing, the professional circuitry through which knowledge about the teaching of social issues in the English classroom is disseminated.

A quick, historical scan of the tables of contents of just one NCTE journal, the English Journal, *yields dozens and dozens of articles demonstrating that English teachers consider the teaching of social issues central to the teaching of English. One can find articles on censorship, the hidden curriculum, language legislation, multiculturalism, teaching English on Native American reservations and in African American ghettos and in Hispanic barrios, teaching the disadvantaged and students at risk, as well as articles on teaching high school students about racism, feminism, human rights, the environment, homophobia, AIDS, teenage pregnancy, drugs, peace, values, propaganda, war, politics, suicide, and the list goes on.*

A computer DIALOG search of teaching and social issues will locate over one hundred thousand citations to articles, position papers, conference papers, private foundation reports, federal government task force reports, federal government institution reports, federal government commission reports, state board of regents and commission reports, state government office reports, teachers' and school officers' council reports, teachers' association papers, university association reports, school board reports, workshop documents, ERIC publications, university press publications, school association reports, national and regional conference proceedings, national assessment agency proceedings and reports, reprints of related federal laws, surveys of community college teachers, instructional model publications, editions of journals, guides to the ERIC collection—and more.

Thousands and thousands and thousands of educators are talking and thinking and writing *and teaching about the teaching* of social issues—that means there may be hundreds of thousands, maybe millions of students involved. We have a history in which to ground our teaching. Unfortunately, this history is too large to be silent and too inchoate to be articulate. When considering the meaning of this mountain of suggestions, theories, models, research, ideas, and plans, we can't help feeling that somehow we aren't able to produce classrooms that respond either with a power equal to the psychic drain of the problems we face or to the volume of solutions that we have been offered.[1] At the same time, there is no other choice.

> In 1986, there were 2,086,000 reported cases of child maltreatment in the United States.[2]

Several years ago, "liberatory pedagogy" and "emancipatory classrooms" were the operative terms for the various publications, panels, and papers of a Conference on College Composition and Communication. When we attended the 1991 CCCC meeting in Boston, we noticed a number of the conference panels, papers, and publications had adopted new words, such as "cultural critique" and "resistance." With terms like these quite literally dominating the conference (and the discipline), an outsider might wonder that composition studies had become quite revolutionary, that, indeed, a cultural revolution was taking place in America (italics indicates our emphasis):

Thursday

"Writing and Intellectual Ownership, Part II: *Reconsidering* Intellectual Property and Written Texts"

"The First Forty Years of CCC: Looking Back, Taking Stock, and Planning for the Future"

"*Rethinking* Our Theoretical Constructs"

"Against Our Better Judgment: *Rethinking* Proficiency Testing"

"*Reorienting* Ourselves: *Reconsidering* Women's Role in the Rhetorical Tradition"

Reorienting Writing Centers: *Reconsidering* the Generation, Application, and Testing of Theory Through Research"

"*Reconsidering* John Dewey"

"*Reconsidering* the Disciplines Through Critical Thinking"

"Politics, Ideology, Pedagogy: A *Reconsideration* of Social Rhetoric"

"*Recharting* the Terrain: The Place of English in the New University"

"*Rethinking* Our Roles: School/College Collaboration as a Model for Our Future"

"*Restructuring* Writing Across and in the Disciplines: Historical, Political and Pedagogical Views of the 'Rhetorics of Inquiry' "

"*Reconsidering* the Issues of Gender, Race, Ethnicity, and Class in the Curriculum: The Bergen Community College Project"

"*Reassessing* Social Factors in the Development of Language Skills"

"*Reconsidering* the Classical Rhetorical Tradition: Contemporary Approaches to Aristotle"

Friday

"What Comes After Post? The *Rethinking* of a Future Pedagogy"

"*Reconsidering* Students and Their Writing on Computer Networks"

"*Redefining* Academic Discourse: A Feminization"

"*Reorienting* Technical Communications: Internal and External Perspectives"

"*Reconsidering* TA Training from Graduate Students' Perspectives"

"*Reconsidering* Methods: Enabling Diverse Student Populations To Play and Win the Game in Freshman Composition"

"*Reexamining* the Writing Center's Philosophy and Pedagogy"

"*Rethinking* Basic Writing"

"*Re-visions* of Basic Writing"

"*Reconsidering* the Discipline: Three Perspectives on the History and Present Situation of Rhetoric and Composition"

"*Reconsidering* Freshman Composition: Four Sophomores Look Back"

"*Reconsidering* the Conference Experience"

"*Reorientation:* How a Hypertext Tool Enhances and Changes the Way We Teach Composition"

"*Reconsidering* the Roles of Part-time and Temporary Faculty: Recommendations for Change"

"*Rethinking* the Writer's Journal"

"The Sophists in Historical Contexts: *Rereading* the Margins"

Saturday

"Journals as Bridges: A *Reconsideration* of Student Journals"

"*Rethinking* M.A. Studies in Composition"

"Against the Sophists: *Rethinking* Opposition"

"*Reconsidering* Research Methods in Reading: Promising Methods and Models"

"*Rethinking* TA Training"

"*Reconsidering* Collaboration: New Models for Freshman English"

Certainly, there is some reinventing going on at CCCC and in the profession. But the majority of English teachers aren't even members of NCTE and don't—or can't—take advantage of those innovations that NCTE offers. In *our* classrooms? We want to say "yes." But we've also been reading Jean-Noël Kapferer's recent social network analysis, *Rumors: Uses, Interpretations, and Images* (1990). In it, Kapferer argues that what makes a rumor interesting is the way it "mobilizes" a group both to believe its veracity and to circulate it. Certainly the call for change that gets passed around and through the profession has reached us, and you, and also the contributors for this book. And certainly we have passed on our own calls for change because we, too, believe that our writing and speaking and teaching will make a difference. But have we *really* made our classrooms different; that is, have we made them places where students get inspired to go out to do work of social consequence? Do our classes actually provoke people to concerned action—not only while they are in the class, but after? Is there any conveyance of energy? Yes, and no.

For the past three years, the two of us have been fortunate enough to meet and talk with teachers whose work we respect very much. These conversations became part of the material for our book entitled *Composition and Resistance* (1991). During these roundtables, we listened to teachers such as James Berlin, Nancy Mack, and Donna Singleton talk about how disillusioning it is to prepare students for the better lives they probably won't be having. The participants in *Composition and Resistance* spent considerable time, money, and effort in order to discuss alternatives to teaching the literacies and thinking that support the deceptions upon which the American dream is predicated—such as the promise of comfortable, happy lives to all ambitious Americans. We fretted together over the very notion of "a happy life" in a society that defines happiness in terms of wealth and power. We wondered whether our teaching practices, our practiced theories, were contributing to a hazardous mythology of progress. Specifically, the contributors shared how they teach students to use their abilities to create ways of intervening in the oppressive tactics of those who would exploit them.

And us! The administrative uproar that resulted at the University of Texas when a committee of teachers tried to redesign a first-year writing course, English 306, as a composition course dealing with gender issues, created more rumors than George Bush's appointment of a CEO at Xerox to the post of Deputy Secretary of Education (DeLoughry 1991). That these rumors were reported in *The Chronicle of Higher Education* and disseminated and augmented in faculty lounges around the country shows just how much we are all at risk. We have heard that the entire committee resigned. We wonder about the professional futures of its members. We have heard that the course, instead of becoming a progressive gesture toward change, has become yet another writing course in which grammar instruction is featured and a "melting pot" approach to teaching social issues is employed. (And we all know how well melting pots work in America!) But then the whole "politically correct" issue is like a rumor: great emotion— which we, too, feel—little critical consciousness, and too much misinformation. In fact, issues of "political correctness" and N.A.S. are less intellectual and political problems—though they are still both— than problems of management for a given institution infected with this particularly viral controversy. To be satisfied with the division between PC and, we guess, not-PC is to content one's self with a form of cynicism that attempts to shut the issues down rather than to understand much about real human differences. The question that educators sometimes forget to ask in the heat of such academic grudge matches is, are we *all* really committed to righting social wrongs? Are we all in agreement about even a few of these wrongs? If we are— however many "we" are—we will have to join with more and more of our colleagues and encourage still others to do just the sort of work done by the English 306 committee. We will have to question those in the profession who claim to be teaching for social responsibility while, at the same time, refusing to question the political implications of their teaching. We will have to question those who refuse responsibility for the political consequences of their teaching. We will have to question those who believe that "middle ground" curricula—the inclusive, not too conservative, not too radical, liberal studies program—is the most socially responsible. We will have to ask very difficult questions because at the heart of all of these positions is a belief that classrooms and curricula are only about content, that class procedures are not about the management of time and bodies and human consciousness. We talk about our classrooms as emancipatory, liberated spaces, but such talk is, finally, too decontextualized from the political, economic, racial, and sexual realities of the classroom *and* the street. All over the profession, small rumors combine to produce this one, great, overarching rumor: that our classrooms need to become *the* classroom. But our classrooms can't be as innocently ideal as *the* classroom. We can't leave the home(less) outside our doors. (Isn't it ironic that the one thing that people without homes ask on the street is, "Can you spare some *change*?" And the most common responses are, of course, "No," or, perhaps worse, silence.) And to expect our students to be so idealistic is both nostalgic and destructive. (*This* is a source of teacher and student tension and burnout that hasn't yet received the attention it deserves.)

And so we ask ourselves: What does it mean to try to make our classrooms become *the* classroom we have read about in journals and heard about at CCCC? We have yet to determine the answer or full significance of that last question, but here's what we think. The 1991 CCCC Convention featured, along with "liberatory pedagogy," "cultural critique," and "diversity," the term "change" as one of the more common impact words.[3] One panel, "Negotiating Changes," featured papers on Freire's notion of dialogue as the basis for a talk about "curriculum change and academic freedom." Another panel, "Changing Needs in Composition Programs," offered a paper with a puzzling theme: "Trial, Reorientation, and Reconsideration: The New 'Traditional' English Program."[4] Still another panel, "Instituting Changes, Changing Institutions: Rethinking WAC in a New Decade," suggests, in the strange, parallel form of its title, that when you institute changes, rather than change the institution, you fortify students to write and think for the future—a *rethought* future.

There is, as far as we can tell, a disparity in all of this between the classroom, in its various states of health and progressiveness as represented in the profession's public pageantry, and the classrooms in which we, as well as our friends, colleagues, and students, work. Teachers take ideas about teaching on a social issue, for example, from books, journals, workshops, and conferences, and bring them home to modify and adopt them into their classroom practices. This is done in good faith and often with genuine excitement for the innovative activities these teachers design and the socially responsible pedagogies they feel they are creating. But how often do/can these same teachers actually take the political agenda, especially radical political agenda, that teaching about a social issue may entail into their schools and universities? It seems that English teachers have a choice. They can ignore social issues in their teaching altogether—something many do (despite the mountain of diverse publications suggesting that English teachers don't). They can bleed the radical politics out of teaching about social issues and take the liberal approach of "doing what I can to help" (we wonder if liberal teachers such as these might be said to join the ranks of what Peter Elbow has called the "bamboozled"—a state of mind where one's pedagogy doesn't "match" one's ideology, a state of mind from which no one, certainly not us, is immune). Or they can decide, as Kathleen Weiler says in her essay in this collection, to work to change things in America even when meaningful change seems so impossible. They can work to become what Henry Giroux, in his essay, calls moral voices in the classroom and in the community.

Such commitments are not, to be sure, easy to make. But they are necessary if we English teachers really want to help the homeless or people suffering with AIDS, if we are ever to protect the environment, or *even* to ensure the fair treatment of substitute and part-time faculty in our schools and departments. Such commitments entail hard work for the already overworked and underpaid. In fact, we believe that committing ourselves to change means that we begin to turn the researchers' eyes we currently use in our classrooms toward Washington and state and local governments. James Sledd has been arguing for years that English educators need to pay attention to the interest that big business is currently exerting in education. As professionals, and as a profession, we need to start investigating just what American business is doing in our classrooms, just how entrenched corporate control of education already is. We need to find out where and when education fell further and further into the hands of those who have an explicit, vested interest in a particular, narrowly conceived breed of citizen as the server of the needs of the nation (Blitz and Hurlbert 1989; Hurlbert and Blitz, forthcoming). How and why did the nation become more and more defined by megaconglomerates whose main qualification is that they survive recession?

> In 1988, there were 31,900,000 Americans reported to be living below the poverty level.

When David T. Kearns of Xerox Corporation was quoted in one of a series of the "Inside the Mind of Management" ads in *The New York Times Magazine* as saying, "Education should not compete with national defense, the trade deficit, drugs or A.I.D.S. Instead, think of it as a solution to these problems," we got nervous (Blitz and Hurlbert, forthcoming). On the surface, Kearns echoes at least one powerful national mood. Education solves problems. And since education is, itself, an abstraction, schools must solve problems. Teachers must solve them. Students, ultimately, must "grow up" and solve them. How? By becoming part of the arms and legs of an industry that will wrestle with these problems? What makes us think this? For starters, Kearns has been nominated by George Bush to be Deputy Secretary of the Department of Education. As noted in *The Chronicle of Higher Education,* Kearns "is expected to concentrate on encouraging school districts to allow parents to choose the schools their children attend—a major theme of the Bush administration's education agenda" (DeLoughry 1991).

Musical students—shuffling from school to school, district to district, ethnic purity to ghetto to grotto. This choice is not about education, but about management. That's why we go "inside the mind of management." That's why schools must become more closely tied to industry. That's why Bush's agenda, his mandate, provides for a bureaucracy laden with corporate moguls who will influence, if not institute, policy and pedagogy (and if you have any doubts about this, just read what's being said by various captains of industry about the connection between literacy and good deportment—that is, competitiveness—and intellectual inability and tardiness during any number of Congressional hearings on the future of American education [Blitz and Hurlbert, forthcoming]). The message, in all of this testimony, is that students and teachers need only fine tune their classroom experiences to the tunes of free enterprise and to create simulations of the good life in its inevitability. *"If,"* the leaders of business seem to be saying, *"teachers could only teach the right things in the right ways!"*

We have reached a pivotal point in history in which we are at once on the precipice of global destruction and abuse and also in the race to one-up, to out-produce, to "bale out" sinking ships of capital so that new luxury liners of industry and waste can take to the seas. Education now means crafty management. CCCC may make a fetish of emancipation, liberation, critical consciousness, and cultural critique, but such a stance seems wistful. We are spreading rumors, rumors of change, of the well-being that will be the *product* of the proper procedures (if we can only establish them), of purposefulness, of the efficaciousness of our actions within our schools and the academy, of the wisdom of a discipline, of a profession rapidly becoming a population of ombudspeople who, as we are doing here, must arbitrate among an array of tense choices. From the looks of official business as it conducts itself into the affairs of education, the choice most likely to be made is the one which, for example, recognizes the need to maintain at least a high school educated minority student population. Otherwise, as Lodwrick Cook, Chairman and CEO of ARCO, asks,

"What is the future of our work force?" He says, "Our elementary schools are filled with minority students who have already decided to drop out of high school. Our mission isn't to hold them captive. It's to change their minds." Change their minds into what? Surely they would not welcome the kind of minds that ask, "What do David Kearns, Robert Allen, Lodwrick Cook, and for that matter, John Sculley, all have in common?"

David Kearns, Robert Allen, Lodwrick Cook, and John Sculley are all wealthy, powerful, politically connected—and definitely not "politically correct"—white males. All are CEOs and chairs of super-large corporations: Xerox, AT&T, ARCO, and Apple Computer respectively. They all possess the "minds of management" inside of which, as the Fortune Education Series of ads indicates, we can find the solutions to our culture's educational difficulties, its literacy problems. These are the minds which have planned a physical and emotional preparation for "our nation's future."

> In 1988, there were 738 reported applications for judicially authorized intercepts of wire or oral communications.

As an example of a rumor of change and the static reality such a rumor often represents, and as an example of how rumors are instigated by the media and conveyed to a conditioned audience, take the instance of how New York State Education Commissioner Thomas Sobol appointed a "high powered state advisory panel" of twenty-four scholars, school teachers, and administrators in July of 1990 (Hildebrand 1991). This committee, the New York State Social Studies Review and Development Committee, was charged with reviewing the state guidelines for curricula for history and social studies courses and to review the guidebooks that are used in primary and secondary classrooms. Essentially, the panel talked about the language—for instance, changing the word "slave" to "enslaved person"—and the rhetoric—how historical reality should be represented—of history.

Of the twenty-four members of the panel, several members were dissenting contributors to the report: "Dissenting panelists argued ... that the group's recommendations for adding more lessons on the history and culture of blacks, Hispanics, and other groups could result in 'ethnic fragmentation' of the sort now wracking India and the Soviet Union." (All following references to this panel and its report are from Hildebrand 1991.)

But what, we ask, instead of ethnic fragmentation, do we have now? Ethnic purity and unity? Ethnic consciousness, consciousness of cultural differences, can be astonishing and splendid. It is an awareness that the concept of "other groups" always includes one's own group—

that one is always influenced and nurtured by more than one's own group—that one doesn't *have* one's *own* group so much as one constitutes and is constituted by the *impurities* of diverse groups and diverse individuals.

Several committee members, including Arthur Schlesinger, Jr., complained that the report paid too much attention to ethnic differences and too little to "common values."

The "common values" are, we argue, too often the values of those who are in positions to set values. Are we talking about ethical values, or about the valuable as it is instituted and reinforced by those with socioeconomic power?

Columbia University Professor Kenneth Jackson commented that "'The people of the United States will recognize, even if this committee does not, that every viable nation has to have a common culture to survive.' He identified that dominant culture as one based upon 'Anglo' political traditions" (3).

Yet every "viable" nation has to depend, to great and small extents, on the viability of dozens of other cultures and values and ideas. Charles Howett, Amityville, Long Island, district director of social studies: "Clearly there is a greater need for awareness to multiculturalism so long as we don't lose sight of western civilization's contributions. . . . implementing these recommendations will be an enormous expense on top of the enormous budget crisis we're in right now" (3).

Why do so many educators seem to *fear* that by turning one's attention to new knowledge, we will "lose sight" of ideas which have literally dominated us for centuries? And why do so many educators forget to cite the enormous financial and *social* cost of *not* studying and learning from the experiences of others?

The report suggests, for instance, that the settlement of the American West be taught from several perspectives. One would be that of white settlers; the other of native Americans and Hispanic settlers who regarded the movement as an invasion from the east. This prompted the state Board of Regents chairman, Martin Barell, of Muttontown, to ask, "If you're going to tell them [students] General Custer was a butcher rather than a competent soldier, do you think they're going to believe you?" (19).

So, is the point that we ought not revise the curriculum because we'd have a credibility problem? We can't think of a more malignant resistance to change.

Edmund Gordon, a Yale professor who was cochairman of the committee, replied that teachers should provide a balanced view, pointing out that some regard Custer as competent and some do not. "I hope we won't have any teachers telling kids Custer was a butcher, even though I think he was," Gordon said (19).

That is, Gordon doubts teachers would be so irresponsible as to essentialize a civil-war general's character. He also reaffirms the view that teachers ought to find ways of leaving their own thoughts out of the classroom. One need not *say* Custer was a butcher. One *can* present the kind of anecdotal information—and encourage the kinds of investigative scholarship—that would make such a conclusion at least as available as one which finds Custer a great war hero. Since Gordon himself admits that he has come to the former conclusion, would he be willing to institute the curricular changes that would allow students access to information from which they might draw similar inferences?

The report recommends that students be encouraged to "see themselves as active makers and changers of culture and society" (19). Schlesinger responded, "I will be satisfied if we can teach children to read, write and calculate" (19).

Why would Schlesinger "be satisfied" with reading, writing, and 'rithmeticking? Because he recognizes that students are no more willing to hunker down to the "basics" of his type of scholarly habits than they ever were? If students are to be the social reformers of the future, they are in need of *re*-formed curricula in the present. Have our present methods for teaching "children to read, write, and calculate" contributed to the development of students' already established desires and capacities to reform society? Or have the prevailing methods helped to produce and maintain the society in which Schlesinger and others can rise to power and influence and comfort at the expense of the educated masses? The question remains, what must our students read, what must they write, and what, exactly, should it all add up to?

> In 1988, there were 92,490 reported cases of forcible and attempted rape in the United States.

In *Rumors,* Jean-Noël Kapferer comes to at least two significant conclusions. First, "Rumors reconfirm something that is self-evident: we do not believe what we know because it is true, founded, or proven. With all due measure we can affirm the opposite: it is true because we believe it. Rumors demonstrate once again, as if it were necessary to do so, that all certainty is social: what the group to which we belong considers to be true *is* true" (1990, 264). And second, we can intervene in the life of rumors and literally change what people believe and, therefore, do.

There is hope for change. We need to find new ways of helping more and more colleagues and students to believe that they do make a difference (even their indifference makes a difference, but we're talking about the quality of the difference one makes). We need to learn to resist the structure of the circuity of the profession when its corporate lack of efficiency would turn belief in the value of teaching about social issues into rumors of impropriety and propaganda. And we have to turn off the ways in which schools and universities are run like/by businesses. As we found out when attending the round-tables that became *Composition and Resistance*, we don't, in many respects, know what shapes the resistance to oppression can take, but we do know—and surely we are not alone—that the time we have for finding them has run out.

> In 1988, there were 15,463 reported AIDS deaths in the United States.

We heard a rumor that a small group of educators based in the Northeast is planning to create schools alongside and in the middle of busy metropolitan streets. The "schools" will have no walls and no regular faculty. People driving, walking, and cycling through will collaborate on projects designed to study the feasibility of cutting fossil fuel consumption, the prospect of providing shelter and food for the homeless and hungry, the need for community and cooperative literacy education, and the most effective strategies for getting the work of our society "done," without exhausting human creativity and desire and value.

We were also told about a rumor circulating on the West Coast that a radically new kind of university is in the secondary stage of planning. The primary stage, conducted by an organization that sees itself as an alternative to organizations like the MLA or NCTE, consisted mainly of the purchase of large numbers of foreclosure properties (with the money coming from a combination of benefactors, bartering, and bread and puppet performances) with the idea that these properties would become the sites of the new polyversity. In the secondary stage, the group proposes to create educational "installations," rather than buildings and institutional edifices. These installations, to be designed and created by artists, musicians, philosophers, scientists, and children, would constitute the first generation of sites in which the new higher education would take place. Subsequent generations would involve the revision and/or dismantling of any or all of the installations.

We recently learned about another project, already underway in several select institutions, in which undergraduate students are producing supplemental textbooks based on their own carefully directed research. These books will be used in conjunction with those normally ordered by professors for their courses. (One example we know about is a book intended to be used with David Bartholomae and Anthony Petrosky's *Ways of Reading* [1987]. The supplemental text is entitled *These Are Just Some Ways of Reading.*)

We have heard about several state university systems that now require that at least one chapter in all dissertations be written collaboratively.

We have read drafts of a proposed network of courses to be offered in colleges, universities, and high schools, and on computer mail services, which will consider types of literacy as various forms of institutional control. One such course is entitled "What This Literacy Will Allow You To Forget." Another is "Literacy as the Law." The content of the courses will be clusters of institutional documents ranging from books and articles to memos to syllabi to exams to mission statements to contracts to love notes to warning labels to students' writings to teachers' writings to. . . .

We hear a rumor that "the" classroom has never existed except *as* a rumor. We hear a rumor that many of the social and political and economic and educational changes that educators say we are making are also rumors. But we also hear a rumor that the rumors of change we keep hearing and talking about will themselves become changes in the rumors we spread about the well-being of our classrooms, our students, and ourselves. We need to tell new stories because we are living stories. They are real and must be told.

Notes

1. What makes *Social Issues in the English Classroom* unique within the hum of the profession is that it brings together the meaningful work of English teachers from various grade levels with the common purpose of encouraging others to work for social change, and within a structure that will, hopefully, promote further thinking about the teaching of social issues and further creative critique of the profession and the work of English professionals.

2. In this article we take our statistics from the 1990 *Statistical Abstract of the United States.* We are not statisticians, but even we realize that these numbers are often only estimates of the terrible reality of the social issues America faces. To put it another way, we know that there is little consensus

about census data. We cite these figures, then, archly, and with fear, and in order to sketch the imperative we feel to write this article.

3. Pursuant to the 1990 NCTE Board of Directors vote to hold hearings on the matter, members met in an open hearing to consider the question, "Should NCTE Change Its Name?"

4. Among others who have also closely examined conference programs and panel/paper titles, we recall that Patrice Fleck of the University of Pittsburgh, gave a paper at the '91 CCCC, entitled, "The Rhetoric of the Conference Pamphlet: A Dialect of Discoveries."

References

Bartholomae, D. and A. Petrosky, eds. 1987. *Ways of Reading: An Anthology for Writers.* New York: St. Martin's.

Blitz, M. and C.M. Hurlbert. (Forthcoming). "Cults of Culture." *Cultural Studies in the English Classroom: Theory/Practice.* Eds. J.A. Berlin and M. Vivion. Portsmouth, NH: Boynton/Cook Heinemann.

———. 1989. "To: You, From: Michael Blitz and C. Mark Hurlbert, Re: Literacy Demands and Institutional Autobiography." *Works and Days: Essays in the Socio-Historical Dimension of Literature and the Arts* 13 7.1: 7–33.

DeLoughry, T.J. 1991. "Bush Asks Education Department Officials to Quit; Xerox Chief Nominated as Deputy." *The Chronicle of Higher Education* 3 Apr.: A21, 25.

Elbow, P. 1986. "The Pedagogy of the Bamboozled." *Embracing Contraries: Explorations in Learning and Teaching.* New York: Oxford: 85–98.

Fortune Foundation Series Advertisement. 1990. *The New York Times Magazine* 2 Dec.: 62–63.

Fortune Foundation Series Advertisement. 1990. *The New York Times Magazine* 23 Dec.: 20–21.

Fortune Foundation Series Advertisement. 1991. *The New York Times Magazine* 17 Mar.: 24–25.

Fortune Foundation Series Advertisement. 1991. *The New York Times Magazine* 7 Apr.: 32–33.

Hildebrand, J. 1991. "History Revisited: Amid dissent, social-studies panel seeks greater focus on minorities." *Newsday* 21 June: 3, 19.

Hurlbert, C.M. and M. Blitz, eds. 1991. *Composition and Resistance.* Portsmouth, NH: Boynton/Cook Heinemann.

———. Forthcoming. "The Institution(s) Lives!" *Marxism and Rhetoric.* Spec. issue of *PRE/TEXT: A Journal of Rhetorical Theory.* Eds. James A. Berlin and John Trimbur.

Kapferer, J. 1990. *Rumors: Uses, Interpretations, and Images.* New Brunswick, NJ: Transaction.

U.S. Bureau of the Census. 1990. *Statistical Abstract of the United States: 1990.* (110th edition.) Washington, DC.

17 Ethical Guidelines for Writing Assignments

Sandra Stotsky
Harvard University

More than ever before, English teachers at all levels of education are being encouraged to have students discuss and write about contemporary social or political issues. How much class time English teachers choose to give their students for discussing and writing about contemporary issues will depend, of course, on the academic objectives they have set for their courses and the extent to which specific issues relate naturally to their academic content. But there are at least two good reasons why students should have some opportunities to discuss and write about current political or social issues in their English classes. First, English teachers are as responsible as social studies teachers for fulfilling the civic purposes of the schools—for developing informed and responsible citizens capable of representative self-government. Today's young adults have an extremely poor record as voters, despite the extension of the franchise to eighteen-year-olds two decades ago, and opportunities to discuss local, national, and international concerns in English as well as social studies classes might increase their understanding of public affairs, their interest in participating in public life, and their motivation to vote when they are able to do so. Second, effective citizenship depends heavily on speaking and writing skills, and the English class is the most appropriate place, if not often (and unfortunately) the only place, for students to practice speaking and writing skills. Today students need to be able to talk and write intelligently about many current political and social issues, as some affect them directly as students or strongly influence their school curriculum.

About six years ago, because of my many years of involvement in local community affairs, for the most part as a member of the League of Women Voters, but more recently as a member of the board of trustees of my public library and as a town-meeting member, I began to seek out and write up examples of classroom projects and writing

283

activities that sprang from discussions of current events, problems, or issues. My pedagogical purpose was to show both English and social studies teachers how they could legitimately engage students from grade 1 through the college years in a wide variety of participatory writing activities that could achieve both academic and civic objectives. The focus of my interests as a researcher was to identify and analyze the different types of purposes and audiences for the writing that students did. The monograph I eventually wrote, entitled *Civic Writing in the Classroom* (Stotsky 1987a), offers numerous examples of participatory writing (and speaking) activities by students whose purposes almost exactly parallel those for which adults regularly write.

In the course of my research, I came across a few classroom projects or writing assignments that seemed to me to be in conflict with a teacher's professional ethics. Some features of these assignments seemed to contradict professional knowledge about how writing should be used for developing thinking and learning, and in fact seemed designed to inhibit thinking and learning. Other features seemed to reflect a teacher's efforts to foster ethnic divisiveness, not common ground, among her students. However, I could not find a discussion of the ethical issues raised by these assignments in *The Ethics of Teaching,* by Kenneth A. Strike and Jonas F. Soltis (1985), a textbook that presents a number of cases and disputes as material for discussions of ethical dilemmas in teaching. Nor did these issues appear to be dealt with clearly in the Code of Ethics of the Education Profession, adopted by the 1975 NEA Representative Assembly and printed by the National Education Association in the *NEA Handbook, 1977–78.* Nor could I find any discussion of ethical issues that writing teachers in particular should consider in the context of their own classrooms. This was not too surprising, for discussions of ethical issues entailed by the teaching of writing in general are extremely limited in scope, as I have discussed at greater length elsewhere (Stotsky 1991), centering almost completely around the topic of plagiarism and thus focusing only on the ethics of students, not teachers.

The purpose of this article is to spell out several ethical ground rules for writing assignments that proceed from classroom discussions of current events, problems, or issues. I also offer two sets of writing assignments that I believe demonstrate an abuse of professional ethics. I explain why they are incompatible with the best pedagogical knowledge we have of the way in which writing instruction should proceed, or with the development of the intellectual qualities and moral character that all teachers should seek to develop in their students. Our own integrity as teachers requires us to be aware of the often fine dividing line between education and indoctrination, or between respect for "the student's intellectual integrity and capacity for independent judgment" and the effort "at all costs to avoid a genuine engagement of [the student's] judgment on underlying issues," as Israel Scheffler (1967, 120) states in an essay on philosophical models of teaching. Before we turn to these ground rules, we look at some guidelines for discussion itself.

First, under normal circumstances, the current event, problem, or issue that a teacher chooses to raise for class discussion (or that a teacher allows students to raise for class discussion) should be related integrally to the academic content of the course. Otherwise, the teacher may be suspected of trying to disguise a lack of preparation for a class lesson and to "kill time." Many works of literature may serve legitimately and naturally as a springboard for class discussion of a social concern. For example, classroom study of *Of Mice and Men* can lead to a discussion of the mentally retarded—in what ways the treatment of the mentally retarded and attitudes towards them have changed since the time Steinbeck wrote the novel and what problems still remain. However, teachers need to guard against selecting a work of literature for classroom study in order to discuss a social issue embedded in it. Selecting literature for its possible informational content rather than for its aesthetic qualities denigrates the literary imagination and subverts the primary purpose of literary study: to teach students how to understand a literary work. To select *Bleak House*, for example, in order to discuss the problem that the primary beneficiaries of lawsuits or legal entanglements may be the lawyers, not one of the litigants, is to do a disservice to the issue itself—*Bleak House* is not by its very nature a reliable and comprehensive exposition of the issue—to relegate Dickens' literary talents to secondary attention, and to negate the notion that literature is something we want students to read for pleasure. Further, to use a social issue as the organizing principle in a literature curriculum is to bias selection against works that do not raise social issues, like adventure stories such as *Kon-Tiki*.

Second, as wise teachers have always known, the most intellectually satisfying classroom discussions of current events, problems, or issues spring from a comprehensive and accurate base of information on the topic. An essential ingredient in an educationally useful discussion is not so much whether all "points of view" are represented but whether students have accurate and sufficiently comprehensive information on the topic for an informed discussion; significant facts for a topic may not necessarily be a part of anyone's "point of view."

Third, to guarantee that free inquiry has indeed occurred, students need to be prepared for discussion with information that *they* have sought out and brought in, in addition to any information the teacher has given them to read. Teachers have an obligation to protect themselves from any charge that they may be steering discussion in a particular direction as well as to show their students that free inquiry requires the students' independent efforts. This means, of course, that students need the research skills for independently seeking out information in a variety of ways and from a variety of sources.

Finally, and of particular importance today, students should be held accountable for their own thinking as individuals and should not be viewed as token members or representatives of particular social, ethnic, religious, racial, or gender groups. For example, the viewpoint of a student of Lithuanian descent does not necessarily represent the views of all Lithuanians or Lithuanian-Americans if a teacher chooses to engage the class in a discussion about the brutality of the Soviet government's attempted suppression of the Lithuanian independence movement. Nor does a child of the Hindu or Moslem faith necessarily speak for all Hindus or Moslems, here or elsewhere, in a discussion of the failure of the United Nations to direct its concern to the massacre of Moslems at the disputed Temple site in India. Students need to be reminded over and over again, at a time when they are consistently being categorized officially and unofficially into a variety of inconsistently defined racial, ethnic, and religious groups, that they do not think or speak for others, only for themselves as individual citizens, and that they have not been elected by anyone to think, speak, or write on behalf of others.

Guidelines for Writing on Current Events or Issues

As most teachers today know, once a discussion of a current event or controversial issue is underway, writing activities can play a significant role in the learning process. However, there are a few guidelines teachers should observe with respect to both the informal journal writing they often assign to help students work out their ideas more clearly and the more formal writing they assign for audiences inside or outside the classroom. The guidelines presented here are based on my analysis of the research projects and/or participatory writing activities I analyzed as part of the research for my monograph (Stotsky 1987a), on interviews with a variety of public officials (Stotsky 1987b), and on many conversations with parents and teachers over the past several years. These guidelines assume that the best professional knowledge we have on writing instruction should inform the directions teachers give their students and the procedures their students follow in composing this writing.

1. *Students should address topics appropriate for their level of intellectual and emotional maturity.* The event, problem, or issue should be one whose complexities can be adequately grasped by the students, intellectually and emotionally. For this reason, most foreign policy issues and topics like nuclear disarmament, abortion, or the sexual habits associated with the spread or confinement of AIDS are not appropriate in the elementary school. Even at the secondary school level, many local, national, or international issues are not appropriate for educational discussions if students have not already studied their historical background and/or developed some understanding of the many variables and technical concepts that may be central to intelligent discussion. As Theodore Sizer comments in *Horace's Compromise* (1984):

> If a student is asked to deal with concepts beyond his level of abstraction, he fumbles or gets frustrated or fakes it. One sees the last reaction at its most grotesque in social studies classes— for example, where students who do not have the remotest idea of the political concept of sovereignty bombastically debate the rights of Arabs, Jews, and Christians to Jerusalem and the West Bank of Jordan. Such superficial "debate" carries with it no sense of competence. . . . The exercise is spurious.
>
> Jerome Bruner's oft-quoted and liberating assertion that "any subject can be taught effectively in some intellectually honest form to any child at any stage of development" carries with it the obligation for the teacher to ascertain at what level of intellectual abstraction a student is and how to move him forward. (167)

Clearly, if the teacher is trying to help the class develop some understanding of the complexities, students *should* grapple with complex issues. But not if the teacher's goal is simply spontaneous discussion, and students lack sufficient substantive knowledge and conceptual understanding for an educational discussion about the issue.

For example, to discuss alternative rent-control policies for a local community, students need to be able to grasp subtle details about the various methodologies for assessing property and their short-term and long-term effects on a community's tax base. To discuss desirable national health care policies, students need to understand the nature of contemporary medical technology, demographic factors, and the host of ethical, financial, and emotional issues confronting medical personnel, patients, their families, and taxpayers in general. And to discuss, for example, the Israeli-Palestinian conflict—which is only one part of an exceedingly complex and larger area of international conflict today—students still need detailed historical knowledge of the twenty or so Arab or Moslem countries surrounding the State of Israel, as well as Israel's 3000-year-old history. Why is detailed knowledge necessary for an educational discussion of such issues? Because complex issues usually require complex solutions, and a classroom discussion that is little more than an expression of emotional stances based on clichés, vague information, or outright misinformation prevents students from developing the habits of the mind necessary for contributing to their solutions. Indeed, simplistic approaches and solutions to complex problems are apt to lead to even more serious political or social problems than the original problems they appear to solve.

Complexity and moral ambiguity are not easy for young minds to grasp, and teachers have an obligation to use class time for teaching students how to understand and deal with complexities, not for practice in ignoring them. If English teachers wish to discuss complex contemporary issues, they need to decide whether the amount of time needed for preparing students for an educational discussion is justifiable in their classes. If students are intellectually and emotionally incapable of addressing a topic with sufficient depth of understanding, then English teachers may be accused, either by parents with academic concerns or by taxpayers critical of school budgets, of wasting students' time or of manipulating them psychologically. While such charges may not be provable, they nevertheless (and inevitably) reduce student and parent respect for teachers. They also damage the professional image that all teachers are striving to regain after many years of being charged by academic scholars and other writers with the responsibility for their students' academic failures (see Stotsky 1989, for a discussion of this issue).

English teachers still need to exercise professional judgment about the use of class time for some less complex issues as well, even if these issues seem to be suitable for short-term study or extemporaneous discussion, and even if they are clearly related to a literary work the class has just studied. For example, the study of Anne Frank's *Diary of a Young Girl* or Elie Wiesel's *Night* (both popular books in the junior high school) might easily serve as a natural springboard for discussing whether Saddam Hussein should be tried for war crimes by a Nuremberg-like tribunal (Hussein's threat to turn Jewish cities into crematoria provides the salient thematic link), and whether Iraq should be required to pay war reparations to Kuwait, Saudi Arabia, and Israel. However, it is not clear to me how much students could gain from a short, informal discussion of the issue if they had no understanding of the legal concepts involved, nor am I sure that it is appropriate to ask eighth or ninth graders to write a letter to the president or secretary of state expressing their point of view on this issue.

2. *Students should not be asked to respond to writing assignments that stimulate hostility to others.* Although informal journal writing on social issues can serve useful personal and academic purposes for students, teachers need to exercise careful professional judgment about the way in which they direct students to explore an issue in the context of their own experience. For example, in a discussion of public ethics and the recent hearings of the House or Senate Ethics Committee (perhaps proceeding from a study of *All the King's Men, Bartleby the Scrivener,* or *The Last Hurrah*), students might be asked to write down their thoughts and feelings about the effect that improper conduct by public officials has on their sense of trust in public officials. Such a question stimulates moral thinking, but it does not elicit hostility to particular people or particular social groups.

On the other hand, if, after the study of such works as *Raisin in the Sun, Nisei Daughter,* or *Gentlemen's Agreement,* teachers invite students to recall acts of prejudice or other morally unacceptable forms of behavior directed towards them or their families as members of a particular social group, such assignments, of necessity, reinforce group stereotypes and may easily foster animosity between those students who consider their families or ancestors as victimized and those students whose families or ancestors are considered as the victimizers, especially if such assignments are not embedded in discussions about the social changes that have taken place or the political reforms that have been enacted to reduce these unacceptable forms of behavior. Such assignments may also create a psychologically unhealthy sense of moral superiority in those students who can claim victimhood, and encourage equally unhealthy feelings of envy or hatred in those who can't claim the privileged status of victim toward those who can. Teachers have a moral obligation to

reduce, not incite, inter-group hostility among the citizens of
their own civic communities, as well as a professional obligation
to place issues in their proper historical contexts. If teachers find
a compelling reason to ask their students about prejudice directed
toward them, they should also ask these students to think about
acts of friendship displayed toward them by members of the
same group to which the prejudiced persons belong, to reduce
or avoid stereotyping.

3. *Students should be able to formulate their own point of view.* The
   strongest and most positive motivation for writing springs from
   the writer's sense of ownership of his or her topic. This is as
   true for a research paper on a controversial issue and for a letter
   to a public official as it is for an experience-based essay. If teachers
   ask their students to follow up a discussion of an issue or event
   with research in order to compose a report or a position paper,
   they need to let students decide how they wish to formulate
   their specific points of view. The result will most likely be papers
   dealing with the topic from a variety of points of view, as
   unanimity on any issue is rare in any heterogeneous group of
   students. A variety of student perspectives is the best evidence
   that the teacher has not sought to inculcate a particular point of
   view on the issue and the teacher's best protection against parental
   criticism. This is also the case when a teacher encourages letters
   to a public official as a culminating activity for a particular
   research project (because there is a bill on the issue under
   consideration at the local, state, or national level). A public official
   who receives a set of classroom-sponsored letters conveying a
   monolithic point of view on a controversial issue is apt to wonder
   whether the students are being used by the teacher for the
   teacher's political ends.

4. *Students should locate some of their own sources of information.*
   Independent thinking begins with a student's own effort to locate
   relevant information about an event or issue under discussion.
   No matter how broad a range of materials teachers believe they
   have provided for class discussion, they may not be aware of all
   the relevant information or points of view on an issue or event.
   Principle 1 under *Commitment to the Student* in the Code of Ethics
   of the Education Profession mentioned above states that the
   educator "shall not unreasonably restrain the student from independent action in the pursuit of learning." This principle might
   well be stated positively with respect to discussions of social

issues in the classroom: the educator should encourage, if not require, independent action in the pursuit of learning. There are at least two good reasons for this: students should be actively involved in their own learning, and teachers should not be the sole source of the information students use for writing about a social issue or for sending a letter to a public official, both to avoid the possibility of excluding relevant material and to give students the opportunity to make independent judgments about what is relevant. For example, after the study of *Hiroshima* or *Sadako and the Thousand Paper Cranes* (two popular books in the secondary school), a Korean-American student might well raise the question of why the focus is only on what happened to the Japanese, when 20,000 Korean slave laborers were among the 150,000 people who died at Hiroshima and were there because it was a major military supply center—facts that few, if any, reference materials mention. As another example, after the study of *Dances With Wolves*, independent student research might call attention to *Pawnee Passage* by Martha Royce Blaine, wife of Pawnee head chief Garland J. Blaine, and contribute to class understanding of why all Indian tribes were not antagonistic to the white man.

5. *Students should locate a variety of sources of information.* Teachers have an obligation to discourage polarized and simplistic thinking. There is perhaps no greater myth about controversial issues than the notion that there are always just two sides. Most issues are much more complex than that, and students need to learn how to deal with complexity and moral ambiguity, not polar extremes, or an opposition between a so-called liberal position and a so-called conservative position. For example, students who wish to discuss the case being made by some black and Hispanic educators in New York City for separating urban black or Hispanic males in special schools of their own need to know that many respected black Americans, such as Kenneth B. Clark (see his letter to the editor in the *New York Times*, 1991, for example), do not favor such schools and that many people who consider themselves liberal, such as the representatives of the local chapter of the American Civil Liberties Union, are opposed to this proposed policy. Similarly, students who wish to explore the controversy about the negative psychological effects of affirmative action policies in this country and elsewhere need to know that prominent black Americans are on both sides of this controversy, with

some claiming that both blacks and whites have been damaged by the way in which these policies have been implemented in this country and elsewhere. (See, for example, the Winter 1991 issue of *Issues & Views*, which focuses on the way in which outspoken black Britons are trying to deal with this issue in Great Britain.)

Principle 2 under *Commitment to the Student* in the Code of Ethics of the Education Profession states that the educator "shall not unreasonably deny the student access to varying points of view." Again, this principle can be reworded positively: educators should encourage, if not require, students to locate varying points of view. Students who locate multiple points of view *and* multiple sources of information, and try to address them all in their writing, are apt to develop a greater understanding of the real world than those who limit themselves or are limited to a clear negative or affirmative point of view on a controversial question. What is at stake here is the basic academic purpose of such classroom activities. It should be an enhanced understanding of an issue, not simply the ability to stake out a position and defend it.

6. *Students should use a complete drafting process for participatory writing.* Writing to real audiences for real purposes should entail a student's best efforts because this writing conveys an image of the writer as well as a sense of a teacher's standards for public writing. Letters to the editor or to public officials should undergo response, revision, and editing in the same way that other experience-based writing may. What is the image of the writer that is coming through? Is it an image that the student or the teacher really wants the public official to have? Teachers should encourage students to consider whether the tone of their letters to a public official or editor would make readers listen to and respect the writer or simply turn them off.

The content and form of a piece of student writing tell a public official or editor something about not only a teacher's expectations for his or her students but also the teacher's view of the value of their time. Are the students spouting off opinions without evidence, advocating ill-informed or naive solutions to a problem, or simply demanding that more tax dollars be allocated to address the problem? Or do the letters show a grasp of the basic problem, provide supporting facts, and suggest how students might contribute to the solution of the problem with their own labor and time? And, while public officials tend to excuse deficiencies in protocol in a letter from an older person who may not have the advantage of formal schooling, they are disturbed by letters from students that do not demonstrate easily learned courtesies such as a proper greeting or inoffensive stationary. What students send from a classroom to an outside audience is as much the teacher's responsibility as the writing they do for each other or for the teacher.

Illustrations of Unethical Teaching Practices

To demonstrate concretely why teachers need to think about the dividing line between education and indoctrination when asking students to write about current events, problems, or issues, I offer an analysis of two sets of directions for writing activities in the secondary school. The first set was created by Patricia Taylor (1988, 18), a university-level teacher, for a suggested high school literature unit on the theme of the search for justice and dignity.

For this unit, Taylor has explicitly grouped *Death of a Salesman, I Know Why the Caged Bird Sings,* and *Farewell to Manzanar* in order to lead students to see this country as she apparently sees it—as materialistic, racially prejudiced, discriminating against women, and unjust—that is, with all vices and no virtues. The main teaching goal she offers for *Death of a Salesman* is to "study the struggle of the individual to find personal dignity in a materialistic society." The main teaching goal for *I Know Why the Caged Bird Sings* (Maya Angelou's autobiography describing her childhood and adolescence in a small town in Georgia) is to "see how the main character, through her struggle to mature as a black female, evolves into a person who has a strong feeling of self-worth." The main teaching goal for *Farewell to Manzanar* (a true story about the internment of Japanese-born immigrants and their American-born children in California while Japan and America were at war in the 1940s) is to "show how the members of the Wakatsuki family struggled to maintain dignity in an unjust society." The latter story, published in 1973, is narrated in the first person by its author, Jeanne Wakatsuki Houston, one of the daughters in the family, who was seven years old at the time the internment began.

Among her recommendations for discussion and writing topics, Taylor suggests that students prepare for reading *I Know Why the Caged Bird Sings* by writing in their journals about a time when they "felt discriminated against." To prepare for reading *Farewell to Manzanar,* she suggests that students "interview parents or grandparents to determine their ancestry and report on any injustices perpetrated upon their ancestors." After they have finished reading the book, Taylor suggests as a follow-up activity that they "conduct a mock trial of our government's policy of internment during WWII and write persuasive letters to the legislators regarding reparations for those who were interned." Why are these assignments unethical? There are several reasons. First, the students are not being asked to respond to these works of literature with their own fresh views or to bring their personal experiences in their own way to whatever meaning they create from reading these works. Instead, Taylor's assignments structure closed learning; they rigidly shape student responses in a particular direction by means of a process that is similar to religious indoctrination although the goals are very different. Second, Taylor's writing assignments seem designed to stimulate students' feelings of victimization by others, to foster inter-ethnic animosity, and to encourage negative feelings toward their own government and, by implication, their own society. Finally, she suggests using, without parental knowledge or permission, students in political activities on behalf of public policies she apparently desires.

One might argue that Taylor is trying to stimulate "social consciousness" and "cultural literacy" in students—not necessarily unethical goals if they are integrated with literary criteria. Yet, the ahistorical and negative thrust of her writing topics suggests that "cultural literacy" is not the aim of this unit. Why are there no questions, for example, about the current economic and educational status of Japanese-Americans, and their high rate of inter-marriage with other ethnic groups in America, despite the prejudice toward them? The present doesn't excuse the past, but places it in an historical context.

The design of the unit as a whole is also unethical. Clearly, all three works individually merit a place in the curriculum if a teacher so chooses. Students should become familiar with the dark view of American society that Arthur Miller and many other writers share. They should also learn about the long history of prejudice against black Americans and Japanese immigrants in this country. And they should understand that Japanese immigrants were long denied the opportunity to become citizens. These are morally reprehensible aspects of this country's history whose details the latter two works illuminate. What is unethical is a teacher's deliberate grouping of literary works primarily to allow her to foster negative feelings in students towards each other and towards their own society. Indeed, Taylor offers almost no topics for discussion or homework that focus on these three authors' skill in creating, for example, images, character, setting, or mood—

that is, that focus on literary elements in the three works. Her interest in these three works seems to lie almost exclusively in their social or political content, thus making the reading of a literary work an "efferent" rather than an "aesthetic" experience, to use Louise Rosenblatt's (1968) terms. Some readers may be tempted to excuse what Taylor has done on the grounds that she seeks to combat injustice and intolerance in this country. But a curriculum that seems motivated by animosity and that seems designed to foster animosity cannot be justified professionally. Nor is it likely to promote justice and tolerance. Nor is an attempt to use, not teach, literature apt to foster a love of literature.

The set of directions which follow was created and used in 1989, the culminating activity to an eight-week interdisciplinary unit in grade 7 on several American Indian tribes. During the eight weeks, the social studies teacher dealt with their history while the English teacher taught several literary works about American Indians. The directions were obviously designed to connect the study of literature and history to a current social issue. (Note: I have removed identifying information.)

Objective: To understand the political, economic and social problems facing Native Americans as a minority group.

To understand that Native Americans have used a variety of methods to address the need to gain equal rights and to maintain their cultural identity.

Directions: Complete one of the tasks below by using the packet of newspaper articles, the pictograph, cartoons and outside research. The product will be collected and graded.

1. Write an essay entitled "Native Americans Struggle to Survive as a Minority Group in the United States." Include each of the following topics:
   A. The variety of methods used by Native Americans to maintain their cultural identity and gain equal rights.
   B. Evidence that social and economic conditions have worsened on Indian reservations in the 1950s.
   C. The reasons why social and economic conditions for Native Americans are worse than the total American population.
   D. Proposals made by experts to improve the quality of life for Native Americans.

2. You have been hired on a trial basis by the editorial board of a newspaper whose policy has been to support the rights of minorities. Your assignment is to create a series of political cartoons that portray the economic, political and social problems of Native Americans.

3. You are attending a demonstration for Native American rights

being sponsored by the American Indian Movement. Each demonstrator has been asked to bring three signs for participants to carry. Create three signs that inform the audience about the problems of Native Americans or make suggestions to improve the conditions of this minority.

4. Write a letter to the editor of our local or metropolitan newspaper designed to inform the reader of the struggle of Native Americans to survive as a minority group and to influence the attitude of the reader regarding the plight of this group of Americans.

5. Write a persuasive letter to our state's senators or our Congressional representative informing them of the problems of Native Americans and proposing a suggestion to improve the conditions of this group.

6. Use the *Reader's Guide to Periodic Literature* to locate a magazine article published in 1987 or 1988 that updates the social and economic conditions of the Native Americans or reports on a method used by a particular group to achieve equal rights or to maintain their cultural identity. Write a summary of the article. Use the topics in Task 1 as a guideline.

What is unethical about these assignments? Let us begin with the writing tasks themselves. Not one requires critical or independent thinking. The students are not asked to make any judgments of their own or to come to any conclusions of their own. The assignments simply require twelve- or thirteen-year-olds to regurgitate content selected by the teachers. First, the teachers have precluded almost completely the students' own independent research by giving them, in a prepared packet, almost all the information they are to use. This material consists of a chart showing the "shrinking lands of American Indians" from 1500 to 1977, a cartoon suggesting the continuing mistreatment of American Indians by the U.S. government from 1820 to 1980, and four short newspaper articles dating from 1984 to 1986 on: the burning down of an illegal bar on a reservation by some Mohawk Indians; the status of lawsuits by the Oneida Indians asking for vast tracts of land and monetary compensation from the State of New York; a report by the Interior Department on unemployment rates and poverty levels on Indian reservations, on the decrease in the federal budget for Indian programs, and on its recommendations to stimulate economic development on the reservations; and the sentencing in South Dakota for riot and assault of an Indian activist who said he was working against racism and discrimination. Only Task 6 requires outside research, and here the students have been guided specifically to the year of publication and the thrust of the topic. They are also told exactly how to write it up—as a summary and with no critique at all.

For the writing of an essay in Task 1, the students have been given no choice of topic or of content. The teachers have supplied the "story-starter," and outlined, paragraph by paragraph, the exact content of the entire "essay." Nothing is left open for exploration and individual thinking.

In Tasks 2, 3, 4, and 5, the students have been given no choice in the point of view they role-play; they have been told exactly from what perspective they should write and for what purpose, whether they create a cartoon, sign, letter to the editor, or letter to a legislator. Specifically, they have been asked to write as advocates for the American Indians and told exactly how. But there is no real legislative context for this advocacy writing, and they have not been directed to demonstrate critical thinking about the difficult issues underlying the plight of American Indians. For example, they are not asked to compare alternative proposals for improving the conditions of American Indians, suggesting which methods or policies may have more merit than others and arguing the case. In sum, the whole series of assignments violates almost everything that is recommended by writing teachers and researchers about the way in which writing should be used for learning in the classroom.

Let us now consider the objectives driving this series of writing assignments. The first is clearly not an appropriate academic objective for seventh graders. Even adults without much knowledge of the history and status of American Indians would have difficulty understanding the intellectual and emotional complexity of their problems, particularly their deep ambivalence towards the Bureau of Indian Affairs. According to a lengthy article by Timothy Egan in the *New York Times* (1991), it seems that many American Indian tribes want not so much "equal rights" as the rights of citizens of sovereign, independent nations, but small nations that happen to be within one, much larger nation. A small number of tribes are now wrestling with the possibility of complete nation-status and self-government as a substitute for continued dependence on the Bureau of Indian Affairs. On the other hand, other tribes do not want the federal government to abandon its trust responsibility for Indians, which it has maintained through the Bureau of Indian Affairs for over 150 years. Apparently, Indian communities do not agree upon the course of action they should take because different tribes have different histories and face varying conditions today. Much of the debate within Indian communities also centers on how to handle corruption in their own tribal governments.

Clearly, neither the complexity of the problems nor the complexity of their possible solutions can be grasped by normal seventh graders. It is unlikely that they could understand even a few of the basic issues involved in these debates among the Indian tribes today. Nor was any of this basic political material discussed in the newspaper articles the students were given.

As for the second objective, it is simply not an academic one. Why should twelve-year-old students need to learn a list of "methods" used by Indian communities to achieve "equal rights"? Moreover, at their age, they can barely begin to understand, as one example, the legal basis for lawsuits to reclaim the millions of acres of land sold by Indian tribes to various state governments in the 1700s or 1800s. What seems likely is that the teachers really want them to learn that lawsuits against their government, riots, assaults, and bar-burnings are all morally equal methods for achieving equal rights. We all know that lawsuits are legitimate and acceptable methods for achieving legal rights. But there is a clear dividing line in a democratic society between violent and non-violent means to political ends. The fact that the directions for these writing assignments do not ask students to make a moral distinction among these methods suggests that the fudging of this critical moral distinction was the basic aim of this non-academic objective. Legal and/or peaceful means to redress grievances or to seek reforms exist in all functioning constitutional democracies, and all teachers are obligated to teach that as a general rule at all educational levels.

Some readers might be tempted to condone these assignments, despite the fact that they were academically inappropriate for seventh graders, on the grounds that they were designed to make students sympathetic to the problems of American Indians. This is an unacceptable excuse: when these students can study academic materials (not just advocacy journalism) on the complex problems of the American Indians in the context of their study of United States history (probably in grade 11), they will naturally become sympathetic toward a group of people who have had a tragic history and for whom all reasonable Americans have sympathy.

Why, then, was it unethical to require students to deal with a political problem or issue they cannot grasp in an intellectually adequate manner? There are two reasons. First, asking young students to spend time regurgitating information they cannot really understand deprives them of valuable time for learning something that is appropriate for their intellectual level of development. But, more important, students who are not developmentally ready to handle an intellectually complex or morally ambiguous political issue will deal with it simplistically and emotionally. The psychological result is the internalization of simplistic political stances. And this intended result, I suggest, is the main reason for the lack of substantive information in the packet of material the students were given and for the tightly structured and directed writing assignments. The materials were designed to ensure that the process of internalizing both an uncomplicated sympathetic stance towards the Indians *and* a negative stance towards the force depicted as most damaging to the Indians (the U.S. government), as well as a simple-minded view that racial discrimination is the root cause of the Indians' problems, was not inhibited by analytical thinking about complex and, possibly, morally ambiguous factors. In other words, what is taking place is political indoctrination, not liberal education. What are being developed are not the habits of mind necessary for understanding a complex topic, but specific political attitudes. As evidence for this argument, I offer in Appendixes A and B two student letters that illustrate the non-intellectual, simplistic thinking that results from these assignments. The teachers considered these letters "outstanding products."

In the letter to the editor in Appendix A, the author shows almost no ability to deal intellectually with the problem that she is writing about. She attributes suicide and alcoholism among Indians to their feeling that "we" don't care about them, and although, in her final paragraph, it looks at first as if she will offer a solution to the "suffering" of the Indians, her solution is simply a vague, emotional position—to put "ourselves in their position when making decisions." She offers no clue as to what decisions they might need to make. In fact, instead of any glimmer of understanding of what the American Indians themselves might want in order to improve their economic and political position, she apparently views them as incapable of helping themselves. A condescending paternalism runs through the whole letter, with a particularly patronizing touch in the last sentence: "We should treat them equally, but we should always keep in mind that they are accustomed to their own culture, and not so much to ours."

In Appendix B, a letter to one of the state's senators, the student has copied much of the information he gleaned from the newspaper articles provided by the teacher. (Interestingly, he apparently wrote in grade 6 to this same senator about nuclear power—another topic far too complex for elementary school students.) He, too, is incapable of addressing the causes of unemployment and poverty or how the Indians might preserve their culture within a larger nation. Modes of economic development and self-government are far beyond his intellectual grasp. And like the writer of the letter in Appendix A, he has concluded from the materials offered by the teacher (and perhaps from class discussions over the eight-week period of study on the Indian unit) that racial discrimination is a major cause of the Indians' plight. To address the problems of the American Indians, all he can do is to propose increased federal funding, but he does not indicate how this would relieve unemployment. A paternalistic tone also permeates this student's letter; the American Indians are portrayed as a group of people hapless and hopeless in coping with their complex problems. They need attention called to them and funds raised for them.

The paternalism in these letters is a direct result of the attempt to manipulate these young students politically with inappropriate materials and closed writing assignments. The American Indians are portrayed as a helpless group of people without rational leadership of their own. Even if one believes the teachers are not unethical in attempting to induce guilt in their students for the suffering of the American Indians and to make the students feel hostile to the force that has been depicted as most inimical to the Indians' interests—their own government—they are unethical in using the American Indians for this purpose, something some of them are aware of. One well-known Indian leader is reported in Egan's article as saying: "Self-government, if it works, is a historic opportunity to get rid of the people who thrive off the miseries of Indians."

Concluding Remarks

I hope the ethical issues raised in this essay will be discussed by English teachers who believe, as I do, that some of the serious events, problems, and issues of our time warrant some class discussion and student writing. All students need to become more aware of the events and issues that shape the world they live in, and they badly need to learn how to discuss those events and issues intelligently. One English teacher I know regularly discusses current events one day every two weeks; the issues are selected by the students, who are responsible for bringing in the information on these issues. This format is worthy of emulation not only because the issues are chosen by the students but also because it allows the teacher to keep literary discussion separate from discussion of current events, if the teacher so desires. There are many issues that students can discuss if they are relevant to course content. Students can talk meaningfully about such issues as drunken driving, teenage pregnancy, drug- related criminal activities, vandalism, smoking, or drug abuse. And their views in writing about how best to deal with these social problems may be welcomed by public officials because students may have the best insights into what is possible and what is not useful.

But teachers do have an obligation to make sure their students are intellectually and emotionally capable of understanding the issues they discuss. To encourage students to talk or write on topics that are beyond meaningful comprehension is a waste of their academic time, and, if they send letters to people outside the classroom, a waste of the time of others. Unless students have the ability and the background to deal with the sophisticated concepts and multitude of factors that surround many social and political issues, extemporaneous discussions and writing activities may be inimical to the development of rational thinking and healthy civic behavior.

References

Clark, K.B. 1991. Schools for Minority Men Violate '54 Segregation Decision. Letter to the editor. *New York Times*, National Edition. January 15: 18.

Egan, T. 1991. Sovereign Once Again, Indian Tribes Experiment with Self-Government. *New York Times*, National Edition, Wednesday, January 16: A16.

Issues & Views. A quarterly newsletter on issues affecting the black community. Winter, 1991, Volume 7, No. 1. Elizabeth Wright, Editor. Box 467, Cathedral Station, New York, NY 10025.

Scheffler, I. 1967. Philosophical Models of Teaching. In *The Concept of Education*, edited by R. S. Peters. London: Routledge and Kegan Paul, Ltd.: 120–34.

Sizer, T. 1984. *Horace's Compromise*. Boston: Houghton Mifflin Co.

Stotsky, S. 1987a. *Civic Writing in the Classroom*. Bloomington, Indiana: Social Studies Development Center, Indiana University.

———. 1987b. Writing in a Political Context: The Value of Letters to Legislators. *Written Communication 9*: 394–410.

———. 1989. How to Restore the Professional Status of English Teachers: Three Useful but Troubling Perspectives. *College English 51*: 750–758.

———. 1991. *Connecting Civic Education and Language Education: The Contemporary Challenge*. NY: Teachers College Press.

Strike, K., and J. Soltis. 1985. *The Ethics of Teaching*. NY: Teachers College Press.

Taylor, P. 1988. None of Us Is Smarter than All of Us: The Reform in California's Curriculum. *English Journal*. December (77): 14–19.

Appendix A:

The issue I want to tell you about is of the problems of the Native Americans that are living either on reservations or amongst the majority of people living in the cities of the United States. These people suffer greatly from economic and social problems. As you know, suicide and alcoholism are very common alternatives for Indians. This, I think, is because they feel that we don't care about them, that we wouldn't mind at all if they just suddenly died out. Why do they get this feeling? They get it because the many jobs that are suddenly "not available" to them, and because of the ever depressing fact that they live in poverty and always will. Of course, these feelings are not how all of us feel about them. Throughout the course of history, Americans have done what they thought would help the Indians, but it usually resulted in even more harm. For instance, in 1887, the individual Indians were given 40 acres to 60 acres of land to help them "stand on their own feet." This was called the Dawes Act. The Indians, not knowing how to use this land sold it to white developers. This resulted in even more suffering.

Even though we try to help them, we often discriminate against them and we don't take their feelings into consideration. Take what happened in Madrona Point, on the southwest edge of Orcas Island near the state of Washington's San Juan Islands. Developers have planned a 88-unit condominium development for this breathtaking area, but the local Lummi Indians can't bear the thought of that happening. They believe it is a sacred burial plot. Hearing this, the developers did some research and said that they found no evidence of the Lummi's claim. They will probably have their way.

How can there be "evidence" that at Madrona Point there is a plot of land that is a sacred burial point to the Lummis? This is just like saying that there is no "evidence" that there is a God. Our "evidence" (the Indians included) is our faith, and everyone should keep the things that in their faith are important.

I think the way to end the suffering of the Native Americans is by putting ourselves in their position when making decisions. We should treat them equally, but we should always keep in mind that they are accustomed to their own culture, and not so much to ours.

Appendix B: Student Letter to a Senator

My name is   . I am a student at Junior High School in   . Last year I wrote to you about nuclear power. I am now writing to you about the native Americans. They have many problems including unemployment, poverty, health, discrimination and preserving their culture.

There is an extremely high rate of unemployment on reservations. This is due to the fact that these reservations are isolated and the land is eroded, and the native Americans' lack of education. Unemployment causes many problems, such as poverty. Living in poverty is very upsetting and sad so native Americans turn to alcohol as a solution. They have a very high suicide rate. The native Americans' health problems are very severe. Not only are they alcoholics, but tuberculosis is an extremely common disease among native Americans. Their life expectancy is ten years less than the average American. Another major problem is racial discrimination. Almost anywhere they go in the world today they are discriminated against. Their hardest problem of all though, is probably trying to preserve their culture. With everything there is in the world today, like war, violence and drugs, it is extremely hard to keep your own heritage, not only for native Americans, but for all minorities.

Government help to the native Americans has decreased, not increased, lately. I received the following information from a newspaper article published in *The New York Times* on December 11, 1986, entitled "Plight of Indians on Reservations Is Worsening, Interior Dept. Says." The article, by Philip Shabecoff, says that 41% of native Americans living on reservations were below the poverty level compared to 12% for all Americans. It also says 58% of the male population 20-64 years old living on reservations are unemployed compared to 12% for all Americans. It shows that total federal spending on Indian programs went from $2.7B in 1981 to $3.1B in 1984 and then back down to $3.0B in 1985. Financing for employment and anti-poverty programs went from $264M in 1980 to $117M in 1984.

In order to improve the native Americans' problems we need to make this problem more nationally known. Funding to improve the lot of native Americans needs to be increased in coming years, not decreased as it has been in the past. A possible way of bringing attention to the native Americans' plight would be to have a national rally and raise funds for them there. Your support in continuing to draw national attention to this subject would be appreciated.

18 Textual Authority and the Role of Teachers as Public Intellectuals

Henry A. Giroux
Pennsylvania State University

Traditionally, the notion of literacy, defined in the larger sense of learning how to read and write, has been tied to pedagogical practices in which the student is often defined primarily as a passive consumer and the teacher is reduced to a dispenser of information, information which parades as timeless truth. Such pedagogical and ideological practices are evident in approaches to reading and writing which argue that the meaning of a text is manifested either in the intentions of the author or is revealed in codes that govern the text itself. For example, what unites advocates of the Great Books approach, such as Alan Bloom (1987) and remaining champions of the New Criticism, is the view that readers are relatively passive—their role is either to decipher the intentions of the author, or to search for the universal codes that inform the meaning of the text (Aronowitz and Giroux 1988). In both instances, the question of pedagogy is reduced less to a dialogue, much less a dialectic, between teachers and students, than to a form of pedagogical training in which teachers provide the learning conditions for students to discover the "truth" of the texts in question. What is missing is any notion of how teachers both produce and authorize particular forms of political, ethical, and social literacy. Also missing from this dominant position is any sense of how the ideologies that inform teacher authority, with its particular view of knowledge and curriculum on the one hand and pedagogy on the other, serves to legitimate and introduce students to particular ways of life, and their corresponding narratives and cultural values. In both cases, the emphasis on mastery, procedure, and certainty functions to exclude the voices, histories, and experience of subordinate groups from the ideologies, practices, and normative orderings that constitute the symbolic hierarchies of the dominant English curriculum.[1]

In what follows, I argue, first, that dominant approaches to curriculum and teaching English largely serve to legitimate and maintain current relations of inequality in society. Second, I analyze the importance of developing critical literacy through a particular approach to reading texts. Third, I make the case that the teaching of English has to be linked to the struggle for democracy. Fourth, I make a case for defining teachers of English as transformative intellectuals. Fifth, I attempt to lay out the basic elements of a critical pedagogy by analyzing the concept of student voice and its importance for teachers of English.

Rethinking Mainstream Curriculum Theory

Within dominant forms of curriculum theory, learning is generally perceived as either a body of content to be transmitted or a body of skills to be mastered. In the first instance, curriculum is usually made synonomous with acquiring the ideas and values associated with the "great books." Within this view, schools are seen as cultural sites, and English departments become cultural fronts responsible for advancing the knowledge and values necessary to reproduce the historical virtues of Western culture. In the second instance, the emphasis is on what Mary Louise Pratt (1986) calls knowledge as technique or method. This approach can be seen in the formalism reified in the New Criticism, in the methodology at work in cruder versions of deconstruction, and in those versions of cultural literacy in which the mastery of discrete pieces of information (i.e., Hirsch 1987) displaces learning as a form of critical engagement and understanding. Contrary to what is often claimed by academic critics, these approaches undermine the principles and practices of both critical literacy and critical pedagogy. More specifically, literacy as a form of social criticism within the dominant approaches to teaching English is often stripped of its value as a subversive force. For instance, reading critically is often reduced to understanding the true intentions of the author, discovering the codes that inform the text, or simply memorizing the basic assumptions that characterize an assigned work. At work here is a pedagogy that denies the voices and experiences of students; it is a pedagogy that treats knowledge as an inert object that simply has to be discovered and mastered, rather than as a social and historical construction that has to be remade and produced by students. As Jim Merod (1987) points out, this is a criticism without vision or hope, one particularly suited to the social function of the university (or the public school) in the age of big business. He writes:

> As it stands now, criticism is a grossly academic enterprise that has no real vision of its relationship to and responsibilities within

> the corporate structure of North American (for that matter, inter-
> national) life. It is simply a way of doing business with texts. It
> is in fact a series of ways, a multiplicity of methods that vie for
> attention and prestige within the semipublic, semiprivate profes-
> sional critical domain. (9)

It is important to acknowledge that dominant forms of curriculum
theory, as manifested in various English departments throughout the
United States, not only legitimate a particular version of Western
Civilization and an elitist notion of the canon but also serve to exclude
all those other discourses which attempt to establish different grounds
for the production and organization of knowledge. What is at stake
in the battle over curriculum is the struggle to control the very grounds
on which knowledge is produced and legitimated. This is both a
political and pedagogical issue. It is political in that the curriculum,
along with its representative courses, texts, and social relations, is
never value-free or objective. Curriculum, by its very nature, is a social
and historical construction which links knowledge and power in very
specific ways. For example, the curriculum used in English departments
always represents a particular ordering and rendering of knowledge
selected from the wider society. This becomes clear in the preference
for courses that legitimize the dominant notion of the "canon" at the
expense of courses organized around writers labeled as "others"
because of their marginality with respect to dominant representations
of power. The normative and political nature of the English curriculum
is also clear in its division between courses on literature and those
that focus on writing, with the teaching of writing being devalued
because it is falsely defined as a pedagogy of skill acquisition rather
than a "creative and genuine" form of cultural production.

Curriculum does not merely offer courses and skills, it functions to
name and privilege particular histories and experiences. In its dominant
form, it does so in such a way as to marginalize or silence the voices
of subordinate groups. For critical educators, then, the English curriculum has to be seen as a site of struggle. The issue here is how can
teachers of English educate students to be critical, rather than good,
citizens. The distinction is central for educating students either to adapt
to existing relations of power or to learn how to read society differently
so as to apply the principles of a critical democracy to the creation of
new and radical forms of community. In this case, the teaching of
English must be seen as a form of citizenship education that seeks to
expand, rather than restrict, the possibilities of democratic public life.

I want to argue in more concrete terms that the English curriculum
has to be viewed as someone's story, one that is never innocent, and,

consequently, has to be analyzed for its social and political functions. This not only suggests examining the curriculum and the institutional authority that legitimates it in terms of what it includes, but also examining it in terms of its "articulated silences"—those forms of knowledge, stories, and ideology that it has refused to acknowledge or represent. Not only does such a strategy allow us to understand that knowledge is not sacred, something to be simply received and revered, but it also allows teachers and students to use their own knowledge in the effort to read texts productively and critically, rather than passively. In this case, texts can be questioned and challenged through the experiences that students use to give meaning to the world, and the production of knowledge itself can become part of the process of reading and rereading a text.

Literacy and the Politics of Texts

Within dominant pedagogy, texts often become objects to be read independently of the contexts in which they are engaged by readers. That is, the meaning of a text is either already defined by the author, whose faithful representations have to be recovered by students, or the meaning of the text inheres in its fixed properties which can only be understood by analyzing how the text functions formally to mobilize a particular interpretation (Bleich 1988). In both cases, though the terms vary considerably, the meaning of the text appears to exist outside of the dominant and oppositional reading strategies in which the text could possibly be mobilized and engaged. Dominant approaches to reading limit the possibilities for students to mobilize their own voices in relation to particular texts. In its dominant form, literacy is constructed in monolithic rather than pluralistic terms. Literacy becomes a matter of mastering either technical skills, information, or an elite notion of the canon (Freire and Macedo 1987). Mainstream notions of literacy refuse to engage the varied contexts in which literacies develop and correspond within different social and cultural contexts. This is a form of literacy buttressed by a refusal to engage the voices and experiences that students might produce in order to give meaning to the relationship between their own lives and school knowledge. It is important to stress that this approach to reading and writing in the English classroom is eminently political—it has little to do with a pedagogy of empowerment and possibility, and a great deal to do with the production of students who learn quickly how to conform to, rather than challenge, the established culture of power and authority.

Linda Brodkey (1989) points out that dominant approaches to literacy are more concerned with initiating students into an existing culture than educating them to change it. She argues that these approaches, by denying students the opportunity to express their own voices and interests, obscure the wider social inequalities that, in part, construct who they are and how they live their lives. She writes:

> [Teachers] are energetic and inventive practitioners committed to universal education. In their writing, however, that commitment manifests itself in an approach to teaching and learning that many educators share in this country, a view that insists that the classroom is a separate world of its own, in which teachers and students relate to one another undistracted by the classism, racism, and sexism that rage outside the classroom. Discursive hegemony of teachers over students is usually posed and justified in developmental terms—as cognitive deficits, emotional or intellectual immaturity, ignorance, and most recently, cultural literacy—any one of which would legitimate asymmetrical relationships between its knowing subjects, teachers, and its unknowing subjects, students. (139)

Implicit in Brodkey's analysis is the notion that traditional forms of teaching literature and writing are connected to two forms of silencing. In the first instance, students are silenced in the interest of a dominant culture that wants to reproduce citizens who are passive rather than critical and actively engaged in the reconstruction of society. In the second instance, they are silenced by being denied the opportunity to engage texts within a context that affirms the histories, experiences, and meanings that constitute the conditions through which students exercise their own voices. Both of these insights are important for the ways in which they suggest that the dominant approaches to reading and writing function to police language, reproduce a dominant cultural capital, and deny the contradictory and often complex voices that inform how students produce and challenge the meanings that constitute their lives.

Extending these criticisms demands that we work toward developing a pedagogy organized around a language of both critique and possibility, one that offers teachers of English the opportunity not only to engage critically their own teaching practices, but also to create pedagogical practices that take up the radical responsibility of ethics in helping students to confront social injustices and imagine a more just society. In part, this means creating the opportunity for students to analyze the conditions which serve to legitimate particular forms of authority, texts, and social relations as immutable and to critically assess how the manifestations of such authority in various texts and cultural practices function to influence students in particular ways.

Teaching English and the Struggle for Democracy

One major challenge that these concerns will pose for teachers of English is the need to create a new language for engaging the debate over cultural literacy, student diversity, and educational reform by reclaiming schools in the interest of extending democratic possibilities, combating domestic tyranny, and preventing assaults on human freedom and dignity. Clearly, this must be an empowering language that defines teaching as part of an ongoing attempt to create opportunities to produce curricula, to dignify the voices of different students from dominant and subordinate groups, and to help to redefine higher education as central to the reconstruction of democratic public life (Giroux 1988a, Mouffe 1989). This suggests that educators rethink the meaning of both public and higher education, the role that teachers might play as transformative intellectuals, and the importance of developing a theory of critical pedagogy for teachers of English.

The problem with our educational system lies ultimately in the realms of values and politics, not in the realm of management or economics. Consequently, educational reformers, including those concerned with developing a critical pedagogy for the English classroom, need to address the most basic questions of purpose and meaning. What kind of society do we want? How do we educate students for a truly democratic society? What conditions do we need to provide for both teachers and students in order for such an education to be meaningful and workable? These are questions that link schooling to the issues of critical literacy, civic courage, democratic community, and social justice. Teachers of English need to put forth a clearer vision of what education is supposed to do outside the demands of industry and the inflated appeal to alleged rewards and benefits of social and economic mobility. By linking higher education to the imperatives of democracy, for instance, rather than to the narrow demands of the market place, it becomes possible to provide a rationale and purpose for higher education which aims at developing critical citizens and reconstructing community life by extending the principles of social justice to all spheres of economic, political, and cultural life. By viewing higher education, especially the liberal arts, as primary to the formation of a critical and engaged citizenry, the classrooms of English teachers can be reconstructed as important social sites in contributing to the knowledge, skills, and values students need as active critical citizens in a democratic society.

Reconceptualizing Teachers of English as Transformative Intellectuals

There is an important, but related, issue at work in defining universities as democratic public spheres. Such a perspective also serves to suggest the role that teachers of English might play as transformative intellectuals (Aronowitz and Giroux 1985, Giroux 1988b). Let me be more specific about what this means. The category of "intellectual" is useful for a number of reasons. First, it provides a theoretical basis for examining teachers' work as a form of intellectual labor linked to public life, as opposed to defining it in terms that celebrate its technical expertise or its alleged free-floating imperative to merely transmit knowledge and skills. The notion that teachers should be viewed as intellectuals is at odds with the idea of teachers of English as objective, non-partisan, dispensers of an unproblematic truth. The normative and political category of "intellectual," at the very least, provides a theoretical starting point for recognizing ideologies which conceal private interests under a universal rhetoric, for recognizing the values which structure and authorize teacher language, and for acknowledging the role that teachers of English might play in addressing important political and social concerns that characterize the larger society. Second, the concept of teacher-as-intellectual carries with it the imperative to critique and reject those approaches to teaching that reinforce a technical and social division of labor that disempowers teachers and students by subordinating the discourse of ethics and substantive vision to the language of disciplinary specialism, cultural uniformity, clever methodologies, and operationalized research. In this case, the concept of intellectual provides both a referent and a critique of those aspects of school life which undermine the broader vision and imagination necessary for sustaining the ethical and intellectual conditions necessary for the development of democratic public life.

The notion of teachers as transformative intellectuals is not one that reduces leadership and literacy to an issue of management and efficiency. Rather, it is a model of leadership and pedagogical practice which combines a language of possibility with forms of self-criticism and social criticism that require educators not to step back from society as a whole but only to distance themselves from being implicated in power relations that subjugate, corrupt, or infantilize. This is criticism from within, it is the telling of stories that speak with the voices of those who have been silenced, it is the willingness to develop pedagogical practices and experiences in the interest of a utopian vision that is synonomous with the spirit of a critical democracy. This is not a call for teachers of English to become wedded to some abstract ideal that removes them from everyday life, that turns them into prophets of perfection and certainty; on the contrary, it represents a call for teachers to undertake social criticism not as an outsider but as public and concerned educators who address the most pressing social and political issues of their neighborhood, community, and society. It suggests that teachers of English develop an intimate knowledge of the workings of everyday life, and make organic connections with the historical traditions that provide them and their students with a voice, history, and sense of belonging (Walzer 1987).

Teachers of English need to provide models of leadership that offer the promise of reforming universities as part of a wider revitalization of public life. Central to this notion of literacy would be an education that prepares students to govern. Primary to developing an empowering approach to critical literacy would be questions regarding the relationship between power and knowledge, learning and empowerment, and authority and human dignity. These questions need to be examined as part of a pedagogical discourse that organizes the energies of a moral vision and raises issues about how teachers and students can work for "the reconstruction of social imagination in the service of human freedom" (Simon 1987, 375). In short, this means providing the opportunity for teachers of English and their students to engage more critically what they know and how they come to know in a way that enables them to presuppose a pedagogy of democratic life that is worth struggling for. This means understanding the limits of our own language as well as the implications of the social practices we construct on the basis of the language we use to exercise authority and power. It means developing a language that can question public forms, address social injustices, and break the tyranny of the present. Finally, teachers of English need a language of imagination, one that both requires and enables them to consider the critical means for developing those aspects of public life that point to its best and, as yet, unrealized possibilities. This means struggling for a language of democratic possibilities not yet realized. This represents quite a challenge in the age of Reagan/Bush, but it is part of a struggle that has to take place if the teaching of English is to make a vital contribution to the reconstruction of a society in which liberty, equality, and social justice provide the political and pedagogical foundation for democratic public life.

Toward a Critical Pedagogy for Teachers of English

Thus far, I have argued that teachers of English need to take up the question of the purpose and meaning of schooling in order to provide an ethical and political referent for the forms of authority they enact in their classrooms; similarly, I have claimed that they need to reconstruct their roles as transformative intellectuals in order to create the conditions necessary for linking schooling to democratic public life. In what follows, I want to argue further that teachers of English need to address, as a pedagogical concern, how knowledge, learning, and teaching might be understood *in relation to,* rather than *in isolation from,* those practices of power and privilege at work in the wider society. Central to such a task is the need to develop a theory of critical pedagogy whose principles are consistent with the notion of schools as democratic public spheres and supportive of teachers as transformative intellectuals. I want to elaborate on this point by articulating a definition of critical pedagogy as a form of cultural politics, and in doing so I want to focus on some of the elements central to its language and practice. I will elaborate on three issues: pedagogy as a form of cultural production, pedagogy as a form of cultural practice, and pedagogy and the politics of student voice.

Pedagogy and the Production of Knowledge

Critical pedagogy, as a form of cultural politics, is not merely about the discourse of skills and techniques administrators and teachers use in order to meet predefined, given objectives. The teaching and learning of skills is insufficient for referencing what administrators and teachers actually do in terms of the underlying principles and values that structure their beliefs and work, and for providing the language necessary to critically analyze how pedagogical practices relate to future visions of community life. What critical pedagogy refers to is a deliberate attempt on the part of teachers to influence how and what knowledge and identities are produced within particular sets of classroom social relations. It draws attention to the ways in which knowledge, power, and experience are produced under specific conditions of learning. *It does not reduce educational practice to the question of what works. It stresses the realities of what happens in classrooms by raising concerns regarding what knowledge is of most worth, in what direction should one desire, and what it means to know something* (Giroux and Simon 1989). But the language of pedagogy does something more. Pedagogy is, simultaneously, about the knowledge and practices that administrators, teachers, and students might engage in together, and about the cultural politics such practices support. It is in this sense that to propose a pedagogy is at the same time to construct a political vision. In what follows, I want to pose the problem of pedagogy as a challenge to those knowledge/power relationships that treat the curriculum as a sacred artifact that has merely to be transmitted in order to be learned. I will then focus on the importance of student voice as a central aspect of critical pedagogy.

Pedagogy as a Cultural Practice

The notion of pedagogy being argued for rejects the notion of culture as an artifact immobilized in a storehouse. Instead, the pedagogical principles at work here analyze culture as a set of lived experiences and social practices developed within asymmetrical relations of power. Culture, in this sense, is not an object of unquestioning reverence, but a mobile field of knowledge, social relations, and values that are unfinished, multilayered, and always open to critical analysis. What must be rejected here is the dominant view: that culture, along with the authority it sanctions, is merely an artifact, a warehouse of goods, posited either as a canon of knowledge or as a canon of information that simply has to be transmitted as a means for promoting social order and control (Giroux 1988b). Instead, culture must be seen as a set of lived experiences and social practices developed with asymmetrical relations of power. That is, what counts as a legitimate expression of culture, what counts as important forms of history, knowledge, and values, is inextricably related to who has the power to select and legitimate particular stories and traditions as important and valued. Equally important, it is crucial to acknowledge that knowledge has to be made meaningful before it can be made critical in order to make it emancipatory. Knowledge never speaks for itself and must be related to the categories of meaning that students bring to the classroom. To situate learning merely in the school knowledge we teach is to assume that students don't come to school with histories, voices, sets of presuppositions about life—it is to forget that students read the world before they read the word.

Curriculum and the Pedagogy of Voice

The concept of voice refers to the ways in which students produce meaning through the various cultural resources, memories, and traditions that are available to them in the wider society. In effect, voice is organized through the cultural resources and codes that anchor and organize experience and subjectivity. It is important to stress that students do not have a singular voice. Such a concept suggests a static notion of identity and subjectivity. On the contrary, student voices are constituted in multiple, complex, and often contradictory discourses. The concept of voice points to the ways in which one identity as an elaboration of location, experience, and history constitutes forms of subjectivity that are multi-layered, mobile, complex, and shifting. A critical theory of voice points to the social and political practices which provide students with the experiences, language, histories, and stories that construct the categories and identities through which they give meaning to their lives (Giroux 1988c, Giroux and Simon 1989).

To speak of voice is to address the wider issue of how people become either agents in the process of making history or how they function as subjects under the weight of oppression and exploitation within the various linguistic and institutional boundaries that produce dominant and subordinate cultures in any given society. In this case, voice provides a critical referent for analyzing how people are made voiceless in particular settings by not being allowed to speak, or how people silence themselves out of either fear or ignorance regarding the strength and possibilities in their voices (Rockhill 1987). At the same time, voices forged in opposition and struggle provide the crucial conditions by which subordinate individuals and groups reclaim their own memories, stories, and histories as part of an ongoing attempt to challenge those power structures that attempt to silence them.

This means that the issue of student experience will have to be analyzed as part of a wider relationship between culture and power. Let me be more specific. Schools are not merely instructional sites designed to transmit knowledge, they are also cultural sites. As cultural sites, they generate and embody support for particular forms of culture as is evident in the school's support for specific ways of speaking, the legitimating of distinct forms of knowledge, the privileging of certain histories and patterns of authority, and the confirmation of particular ways of experiencing and seeing the world. Schools often give the appearance of transmitting a common culture, but, in fact, they more often than not legitimate what can be called a dominant culture. Moreover, schools are not uniform places simply catering democratically to the needs of different students; they are characterized by the presence of students from both dominant and subordinate cultures, with the dominant culture often sanctioning the voices of white, middle-class students, while simultaneously disconfirming or ignoring the voices of students from subordinate groups, whether they be black, working-class, Hispanic, or other minority groups.

Crucial to this argument is the recognition that it is not enough for teachers of English to merely dignify the grounds on which students learn to speak, imagine, and give meaning to their world. This is important, but it is also crucial for teachers to understand how schools, as part of the wider dominant culture, often function to marginalize, disconfirm, and delegitimate the experiences, histories, and categories that students use in mediating their lives. This means understanding how texts, classroom relations, teacher talk, and other aspects of the formal and hidden curricula of schooling often function to actively silence students.

At issue here is the notion that student experience has to be understood as part of an interlocking web of power relations in which some groups of students are often privileged over others. Voice in this case is a category for understanding how a politics of difference functions in classrooms to articulate particular readings and constructions of gender, race, ethnicity, class, history, and community. But if we are to view this insight in an important way we must understand that it is imperative for teachers to critically examine the cultural backgrounds and social formation experiences of such students in order for them to examine both their strengths and weaknesses. Student experience, like the culture and society of which it is a part, is not all of one piece, and it is important to sort through its contradictions and to give students the chance not only to confirm themselves but also to raise the question: *What is it this society has made of me that I no longer want to be?* This means that teachers of English have to be attentive to the categories of meaning that students use to produce knowledge in their classrooms. For example, English teachers can give students the opportunity to connect their own experiences to classroom knowledge by writing papers in which they explore particular readings by analyzing how they relate to issues that make up their own daily lives. English teachers can use reading and writing assignments that engage community and cultural traditions that students are familiar with. Moreover, English teachers can incorporate selective aspects of popular culture as an object of study, particularly as a basis for developing forms of literacy that enable students to read and write about the everyday in a critical and transformative fashion.

At the very least, there are two important pedagogical issues at work in dealing with students' experiences. *First,* it is important for students to both understand and self-critically address the prejudice and contempt that often constructs the identity of those labeled as the

Other. Pedagogically, this means teaching students to understand how difference is produced, legitimated, and sustained with regards to the categories of race, class, ethnicity, sexual preference, and gender as part of the discourse of deficit and domination; and that this discourse reproduces particular interests and identities which must be challenged and transformed as part of a movement into self-love, self-respect, and self- and collective determination. *Second,* it is important for students to affirm their histories and voices while simultaneously analyzing how the dominant powers and groups create experiences and policies that affect those who are powerless. *This suggests teaching students forms of literacy that not only engage the richness of their own communities, it also means teaching students how to critically appropriate the codes and vocabularies of different cultural experiences so as to provide them with the skills they will need in order to define and shape, rather than simply serve, in the modern world.* In other words, students need to understand the richness and strengths of other cultural traditions, other voices, particularly as these are constructed within a politics of difference in which the relationship between the self and other is mediated by the principles of equality, justice, compassion, and free-dom. Literacy, in this case, is grounded in the imperative to educate students to learn how to become ethical and political agents capable of practicing critical citizenship and civic courage. I want to amplify the pedagogical basis of a critical approach to literacy and voice by exploring in more concrete terms what such an approach might look like as part of a theory of critical pedagogy.

I want to set the present discussion around a hypothetical American literature class. I want to argue that it would seem appropriate in such a class to use texts that have not only played a major role in shaping the history of American literature, but also those that have been either ignored or suppressed because they have been written either from an oppositional stance or authored by writers whose work is not legiti-mated by the dominant Eurocentric tradition. What I am arguing for here is a deliberate attempt to decenter the American literature cur-riculum by allowing a number of voices to be read, heard, and used. This approach to reading and writing literature should be seen as part of a broader attempt to develop pedagogically a politics of difference that articulates with issues of race, class, gender, ethnicity, and sexual preference from a position of empowerment rather than from a position of deficit and subordination. Let me be more specific.

Let's assume that a large number of students in an English class are minority students. Central to affirming the voices of these students is the need to use texts that come out of an experience that they can both relate to and engage critically. Not only do such texts allow these particular students to connect with them in the contexts of their own histories and traditions, they also provide another language and voice by which other students can understand how differences are constructed, for better or worse, within the dominant curriculum. Similarly, different texts offer all students forms of counter-memory that make visible what is often unrepresentable in many dominant English classrooms. The benefit of such a pedagogical approach can be defended from a number of positions. First, using the literature of the "Other" provides an organic connection to the voices of students in the class who generally cannot locate their own histories in the traditional literature that constitutes the official canon. Minority literature captures the living experiences and struggles of groups whose repressed narratives provide the grounds for new ways of reading history—that is, knowledge of marginal histories represents a way of reclaiming power and identity. Second, literature of the "Other" provides *all* students the opportunity to identify, unravel, and critically debate the codes, vocabularies, and ideologies of different cultural traditions. What is crucial here is the opportunity for students to read texts as social and historical constructs bound up with specific discourses and forms of institutional power. Third, reading texts as part of a politics of difference that *makes a difference* must be highly discriminate in providing students with the opportunities to challenge authoritative bodies of curricula knowledge as well as transmission models of pedagogy. That is, reading texts in order to affirm and engage difference does not serve to merely validate the achievements of minority cultures, it offers the broader opportunity to provide a sustained critique of the historical and institutional practices that exclude them while simultaneously engaging such texts for the possibilities they may or may not have for democratic public life. This suggests that debates about including texts by minority authors is about more than a politics of representation; it is fundamentally about "addressing the ways in which our society is structured in dominance" (Carby 1989, 37). At the same time, the rewriting of authoritative texts and the reclaiming of excluded histories and narratives offers the possibility of reconstructing new communities that move outside of textuality into the world of material practices and concrete social relations (Agger 1989). Critically deconstructing texts is about more than analyzing ideology as discourse, it is also about the unrealized possibilities that exist in ideology as lived experience.

Of course, what actually happens in classrooms is that dominant and subordinate voices constantly interact to qualify and modify each other, though this occurs within relations of power which are, for the most part, asymmetrical. The language that teachers use never completely excludes the voices or interpretations of students. Students respond, they interfere, raise questions, and sometimes openly challenge or dialogue with teachers. In all of these instances, language, in varied degrees, gets negotiated and the discourse or voice of the teachers is modified. Though the process is more dialectical than I am suggesting, it is never simply pluralistic in the liberal sense described by Gerald Graff, Richard Rorty, and others.[2] That is, while different views may be expressed in class, classroom interaction always takes place within asymmetrical relations of power. The contexts, of course, differ, and in some cases some students are not allowed into the discourse, in others the voice of the teacher predominates, and in others there might be a genuine dialogue. What is at stake here is recognizing how language and authority combine with power to enable or disable human capacities to reason, think, assert one's voice, and challenge existing configurations of authority. To speak of voice in these terms is to raise questions about how teachers of English can validate student experiences in order to provide students with the opportunity to read and write culture differently within a variety of meanings and social relations that empower rather than disempower them.

Conclusion

I have argued that teachers of English can draw upon the cultural resources that students bring to the class in order to understand the categories such students use to construct meaning and to locate themselves in history. By analyzing texts in light of their diverse readings and by interrogating such readings so as to allow students to bring their own experiences to bear on such engagements, teachers of English can better understand the histories and communities of meaning that give their students a sense of voice and multi-layered identity. This suggests not only teaching students forms of literacy that engage their own communities and the discourse of the dominant culture but also means teaching students how to critically appropriate the codes and vocabularies of different cultural experiences so as to provide them with some of the skills they will need in order to define and shape, rather than simply serve in, the modern world. In other words, students need to understand the richness and strengths of other cultural traditions and other voices, particularly as these point to forms of self- and social empowerment. That is, teachers must take seriously what it means to educate students to learn how to govern critically and ethically in the broad political sense. In addition, students need to address as part of the pedagogy of the Other how representations and practices that name, marginalize, and define difference as deficit are actively learned, internalized, challenged, or transformed. At stake here is the need for teachers of English to address how an understanding of these differences can be used to change the prevailing relations of power that sustain them.[3]

Teachers of English must also take seriously the articulation of a morality that posits a language of public life, emancipatory community, and individual and social commitment. In other words, students need to be introduced to a language of morality that allows them to think about how community life should be constructed. A discourse of morality is important, both because it points to the need to educate students to fight and struggle in order to advance the discourse and principles of a critical democracy, and because it provides a referent against which students can decide what forms of life and conduct are most appropriate morally amidst the welter of knowledge claims and interests they confront in making choices in a world of competing and diverse ideologies.

Finally, I want to reiterate the point that schools need to become places that provide the opportunity for literate occasions. That is, teachers of English need to offer the conditions for students to share their experiences, work in social relations that emphasize care and concern for others, and be introduced to forms of knowledge that provide them with the opportunity to take risks and fight for a quality of life in which all human beings benefit. This suggests a pedagogical practice that recognizes that the principles of diversity, dialogue, compassion, and tolerance which are central to the teaching of English are at the heart of what it means to strengthen, rather than weaken, the relationship between learning and empowerment on the one hand, and democracy and schooling on the other.

Notes

1. This theme is taken up in a number of articles and books too numerous to mention; for a recent commentary, see: Hazel Carby, (1989); June Jordan, (1987); James Donald, (1985).

2. Gerald Graff (1987); Richard Rorty (1979); Mary Field Belenky (1986).

3. I develop these issues extensively in Giroux 1988c.

References

Agger, B. 1989. *Fast Capitalism: A Critical Theory of Significance.* Urbana: University of Illinois Press.

Aronowitz, S., and H.A. Giroux. 1988. Schooling, Culture, and Literacy in the Age of Broken Dreams: A Review of Bloom and Hirsch. *Harvard Educational Review,* 58(2): 172–194.

Bakhtin, M.M. 1986. *Speech Genres and Other Late Essays.* Austin: University of Texas Press.

Bakhtin, M.M. 1981. *The Dialogic Imagination,* translated by C. Emerson and M. Holquist. Austin: University of Texas Press.

Belenky, M.F., et al. 1986. *Women's Ways of Knowing: The Development of Self, Voice, and Mind.* New York: Basic Books.

Belsey, C. 1980. *Critical Practice.* New York: Methuen.

Bennett, T. 1987. Texts in History: The Determinations of Readings and Their Texts. In *Post-structuralism and the Question of History,* edited by D. Atridge, G. Bennington, and R. Young, 70–71. New York and London: Cambridge University Press.

Bleich, D. 1988. *The Double Perspective: Language, Literacy, and Social Relations.* New York: Oxford University Press.

Bloom, A. 1987. *The Closing of the American Mind.* New York: Simon and Schuster.

Brodkey, L. 1989. On the Subject of Class and Gender in "The Literacy Letter." *College English,* 51(2): 125–126.

Brodkey, L. 1987. *Academic Writing as Social Practice.* Philadelphia: Temple University Press.

Carby, H. 1989. The Canon: Civil War and Reconstruction. *Michigan Quarterly Review,* XXVIII(1): 35–43.

Donald, J. 1985. Beacons of the Future: Schooling, Subjection and Subjectification. In *Subjectivity and Social Relations,* edited by V. Donald and J. Donald, Milton Keynes: Open University Press.

Eagleton, T. 1982. *Literary Theory: An Introduction.* Minneapolis: University of Minnesota Press.

Foucault, M. 1980. *Power/Knowledge.* New York: Pantheon Press.

Freire, P., and D. Macedo. 1987. *Literacy: Reading the Word and the World.* South Hadley, Mass.: Bergin and Garvey Press.

Giroux, H.A. 1988a. *Schooling and the Struggle for Public Life.* Minneapolis: University of Minneapolis Press.

Giroux, H.A. 1988b. *Teachers as Intellectuals.* Granby, Mass.: Bergin and Garvey Press.

Giroux, H.A. 1988c. "Postmodernism and the Discourse of Educational Criticism: Border Pedagogy in the Age of Postmodernism." *Journal of Education,* 170(3): 5–30; 162–181.

Giroux, H.A., and R. Simon. (eds.) 1989. *Popular Culture, Schooling and Everyday Life.* Minneapolis: University of Minnesota Press.

Graff, G. 1987. *Professing Literature.* Chicago: University of Chicago Press.

Hirsch, Jr., E. D. 1987. *Cultural Literacy.* Boston: Houghton Mifflin.

Inglis, F. 1985. *The Management of Ignorance.* London: Blackwell.

Jordan, J. 1987. *On Call: Political Essays.* Boston: South End Press.

McLaren, P. 1989. *Life in Schools.* New York: Longman Publishers.

Merod, J. 1987. *The Political Responsibility of the Critic.* Ithaca: Cornell University Press.

Mouffe, C. 1989. "The Civics Lesson." *The New Statesman and Society,* 31.

Ohmann, R. 1987. *Politics of Letters.* Wesleyan: Wesleyan Press.

Pratt, M.L. 1986. "Interpretive Strategies/Strategic Interpretations: On Anglo-American Reader-Response Criticism." In *Postmodernism and Politics,* edited by J. Arac. Minneapolis: University of Minnesota Press.

Rocknill, K. 1987. "Gender, Language, and the Politics of Literacy." *British Journal of Sociology of Education,* 8(2): 153–167.

Rorty, R. 1979. *Philosophy and the Mirror of Nature.* Princeton: Princeton University Press.

Scholes, R. 1987. *Textual Power.* New Haven: Yale University Press.

Simon, R. 1987. "Empowerment as a Pedagogy of Possibility." *Language Arts,* 64(3): 370–382.

Simon, R. 1988. "For a Pedagogy of Possibility." *Critical Pedagogy Networker,* 1(1): 1–4.

Stimpson, C.R. 1988. *Where the Meanings Are: Feminism and Cultural Spaces.* New York: Methuen.

Walzer, M. 1987. *Interpretation and Social Criticism.* Cambridge: Harvard University Press.

19 Teaching, Feminism, and Social Change

Kathleen Weiler
Tufts University

I take as my central theme the concept of change: the changes in our lives and society that all too often leave us feeling helpless and unimportant; the desperate need to change inhumane social relationships; the complexity of creating change as we struggle with our historically constructed subjectivities, our given positions of power or oppression. I begin with a stanza from a recent poem by Adrienne Rich:

> What would it mean to live
> in a city whose people were changing
> each other's despair into hope?—
> You yourself must change it.—
> what would it feel like to know
> your country was changing?—
> You yourself must change it.—
> Though your life felt arduous
> new and unmapped and strange
> what would it mean to stand on the first
> page of the end of despair?* (1983)

Of course, cities and countries are changing, and changing very fast, but in ways that all too often injure and oppress people. These changes are the results of worldwide economic and political forces; they are driven by the desire for profit, the need to create desires for consumption, the search for a cheap work force anywhere and everywhere in the world, the exploitation of the environment, the logic of competitive and destructive social relationships. But these same forces of exploitation and oppression in turn give rise to resistance and struggle. The change Rich is talking about, a need to change despair into hope, is, in a sense, a call for the imagination, for Utopian dreams. It rests on the recognition that we change and grow in our own lives, and

* From: "Dreams Before Waking" by Adrienne Rich. In Adrienne Rich, *Your Native Land* (W. W. Norton & Company, 1986, pp. 44–46). Copyright © Adrienne Rich.

322

that we need to struggle collectively to create social change in vitally needed, more humane directions.

Political struggles for change occur in the context of people's lived worlds: for decent work and housing; against racist, sexist, and homophobic practices and attitudes; against violence toward women; for a meaningful education for students and decent conditions of work for teachers. The changes that have already taken place in women's lives in the United States in the last two decades reflect both the successes of an ongoing struggle for equality for women and equally powerful continuing and increasing exploitation of poor, working-class women and women of color. In the years since 1970, the number of women in the work force has increased markedly. While the number of women in professional jobs has increased in a variety of areas, in other areas not much has changed or the changes have been for the worse, reflecting the overall shift of resources from the poor to the rich, with women, and particularly single mothers and women of color, suffering the most. In 1986, the percentage of households in poverty headed by women increased to 48%, up from 20% in 1959. More than 50% of households headed by black and Hispanic women were below the poverty level in 1986.[1] Violence against women continues unabated, and women's bodies continue to be objectified and exploited in the media to sell anything.

It is realities like these that make it so important that those of us who hope for a more just and humane world think seriously about the ways we can work in our own lives to attain our goals. This hope is based on the knowledge of past struggles and a confidence that the actions of human beings matter. I am writing specifically here about teachers and feminists, women and men who hope to contribute to the building of a more just society for all students through their work as teachers. In this sense, the work of feminist teachers, concerned with equality and justice for girls and boys, cannot be divorced from wider social goals of equality and justice for all people. Anti-sexist teaching in this context must also be anti-racist, anti-homophobic teaching, sensitive to overlapping oppressions. But for women teachers, we must begin with our own experiences, and our own goals as feminists. To begin, I would like to take a question framed by Adrienne Rich: What do women need to know?[2] I want to expand that question to consider what we, as feminist teachers working for change, need to know. What does it mean for a teacher who is a woman and a feminist to teach for social change in a way that challenges sexist practices and attitudes? To what extent are we, as teachers, responsible for our own continuing self-education as we struggle to teach responsibly for change?

I have been thinking a great deal about my responsibility as a teacher and a white feminist for my own continuing self-education. I remember a conversation with a black South African student who had been imprisoned in South Africa and who was deeply involved in the liberation struggle there. When, in the context of our conversation, I referred to the genocide against the Armenians, he replied, "I haven't had a chance to educate myself about that yet." I was deeply struck by his comment: first, that he felt the importance of knowing about examples of historical oppression other than his own; and second, that he took the responsibility of that education on himself. This same student spoke of his experience of learning the official curriculum of a South African university in order to pass the exams, and then his unlearning and relearning that material in order to proceed with the education he needed. As teachers for social change, we are in the same relationship to knowledge as this South African student. We also have the ultimate responsibility of educating ourselves, and we need to unlearn and relearn the knowledge that we need to know. The question: what do women teaching for social change need to know? thus becomes our guide as well as the question we raise with our students. How can we best create a setting in which we can define and explore this question? I want to suggest that part of our own self-education includes an investigation of the way men and women, boys and girls, have been constructed within existing society, the way we approach learning, and the histories each of us brings to the classroom. This perspective rests on the belief that our sense of our own identity, our subjectivity, is the result of a complex process of social construction. Thus, one important starting point for thinking about issues of knowledge and teaching is an examination of who we are as men and women, students and teachers, within the society in which we live.

One goal of feminist pedagogy, as of other liberatory pedagogies, has been to provide a place where students can find their own voices and can take control of and responsibility for their own educations; that goal implies a need to understand the experiences, identities, and ways of knowing of those varied students. This points to the need to examine who we are now as men and women in terms of class, race, sexual orientation, age, and other socially defined identities, and the ways those identities shape our lives as students and teachers. The patterns of ways of knowing and learning of men and women have been the focus of the work of numerous feminist sociologists and psychologists in the past decade. These researchers have examined the nature of the moral and cognitive development of men and women.[3] Earlier studies of human development had been based on the study of male subjects, with the then common assumption that male experience was, in fact, human experience; if women's psychologies were different, that difference reflected their truncated or incomplete development. Gilligan, in her ground-breaking study of the moral development of men and women, challenged the well-established theories of human moral development of Kohlberg. Gilligan argued that Kohlberg's supposed universal stages of development in fact rested solely upon his study of young men, and represented male, and not necessarily human, development. In her work, Gilligan described different approaches to moral questions of men and women, with boys and men defining problems by an abstract morality of rights, while girls and women's views reflected a contextual morality of responsibility and care. Redefinitions of moral development to take account of the differences between men and women have in turn grounded the work of a number of subsequent feminist psychologists studying women's cognitive as well as moral development.

In their influential book *Women's Ways of Knowing* (1986), Belensky, Clinchy, Goldberger, and Tarule turned from the study of moral development to the study of cognition. Their extensive research on college women documents the ways in which the women they studied approached knowledge and responded to different forms of classroom instruction. They argue, echoing Gilligan, that women students approach knowledge through a connection with their own emotional and personal lives; these women are alienated by competitive and antagonistic classroom relationships and by a presentation of classroom knowledge as pure and abstract or of education as a process of individualized "mastery" of this knowledge. The authors of *Women's Ways of Knowing* argue that women students need to be encouraged to build on their own more connected approach to learning; that it is, in fact, positive to view education as an ongoing process of exploration of the world, not as a finished product to be consumed. They argue that it is only in this way that students will see that they also have valuable knowledge and can be theorists. As the authors comment, "So long as teachers hide the imperfect processes of their thinking, allowing their students to glimpse only the polished products, students will remain convinced that only Einstein—or a professor—could think up a theory" (215). Belensky, Clinchy, Goldberger, and Tarule thus propose a form of education that acknowledges the incomplete and ongoing nature of understanding based on what they call a "connected classroom," one in which teacher and students are both respected as knowledgeable and as creators of knowledge. They frame their proposal in the context of their research into women's emotional and cognitive development, arguing that "connected knowing comes more easily to many women than does separate knowledge" (229).

The work of researchers such as Gilligan and Belensky, Clinchy, Goldberger, and Tarule has been invaluable in calling into question existing forms of classroom pedagogy and our assumptions about the nature of academic knowledge. It has also highlighted the previously unexamined assumption that men's development, experiences, and psychologies were archetypical of true humanity. By studying and giving voice to the different lives and psychologies of women, feminist researchers have revealed the deeply gendered nature of human experience and raised significant questions for both pedagogy and knowledge itself. However, there are certain pitfalls and problems with these developmental studies. Some of these studies, particularly Gilligan's *In A Different Voice* (1982), imply that the experiences and attitudes of white middle-class girls and women are representative of all women. This assumption simply replicates the earlier male assumption that men's experience was representative of all human experience, and fails to explore the experiences and development of gays and lesbians, people of color, or the effect of different class positions; it does not address the homophobia and racism that so mark our society. Women of color, lesbians, and a number of white women theorists have challenged this valuing of white middle-class women's experiences as the basis for a feminist pedagogy or an analysis of women's psychologies, and argue instead the need to articulate differences among women and to recognize that we all speak from a particular history and standpoint.

A second criticism that has been raised to the work of feminist developmental psychologists lies in their failure to discuss the social and historical construction of subjectivities and the resulting implication that there is an unchanging women's "essence." These studies fail to explore the possibility that women may act in particular ways in response to specific experiences of oppression. While these writers mention the social construction of gender, they do not make the process of historical and social construction a major focus of their work. It is thus possible to read these studies not as descriptions of one group of women at one moment in history but as descriptions of an unchanging essential nature of men and women. While a recognition of the differences in men's and women's present life experiences and approaches to knowing is very useful in thinking about feminist teaching, the assumption that such differences are innate calls into question the possibility of change and suggests an inevitable division of men and women, with women seen as "naturally" nurturing and intuitive and men seen as equally naturally rational and abstract in their thinking. The consequence of this kind of view for the political and social organization of society is, to my mind, obvious and dangerous. It assumes the inevitable continuation of the present organization of society by gender. Although feminist developmental psychologists emphasize that women's nurturing work should be valued, they leave unaddressed questions of power. If the "naturally" rational and dispassionate people (men) continue to control economic resources and positions of political power, then even if the important work done by the nurturing and emotional people (women) is acknowledged, ultimate power relationships will remain unchanged. While there are many valuable insights in the work of the feminist developmental psychologists, I want to argue for an additional need to emphasize and examine the historical and social context within which we have learned who we are and which has shaped our "ways of knowing."

If we challenge the "naturalness" of existing gender arrangements and consider relations of power and oppression as they now exist, we raise the question of the ways in which a system based upon domination and oppression is distorting to both groups. As Virginia Woolf wrote, middle-class women

> are between the devil and the deep sea. Behind us lies the patriarchal system; the private house, with its nullity, its immorality, its hypocrisy, its servility. Before us lies the public world, the professional system, with its possessiveness, its jealousy, its pugnacity, its greed. The one shuts us up like slaves in a harem; the other forces us to circle, like caterpillars head to tail, round and round the mulberry tree, the sacred tree, of property. It is a choice of evils. (74)

Woolf's vision of the private sphere of women focuses not on the positive qualities of connectedness and nurturance, but on the hypocrisy and servility implied in a subordinate role; her vision of the public world of men points not to the power of rational analysis, but to the competition, aggressiveness, and greed of her society. Woolf argues that the way men and women now know and act in the world is not a "natural" way of being in the world. By examining the historical and social processes that brought existing gender relationships and definitions into being, we can celebrate what we see as positive, including the aspects of women's lives that have been condemned or slighted, but at the same time we can acknowledge the damage that has been done to us by a system of patriarchy, racism, or relationships of class privilege and oppression. This implies a more complex view of feminist teaching, not just celebrating "women's ways," but analyzing and trying to understand the complexities in the construction of our subjectivities and the differences among us—a more complex task, but one that addresses more directly our lived experiences and that of our students, male and female, black and white, straight and gay, and of such a wide range of class and ethnic positions.

The claim that identities are socially and historically constructed implies that we are all shaped by ideology and by the society in which we move. What does this mean for men and for women, for white people and people of color? The way we know the world is part of our experiences of dominance or oppression, of being taught that we meet what Audre Lorde has called "the mythical norm" or that we are "deviant" or "incomplete" if we are different from that norm. Cameron McCarthy (1988) has called these overlapping positions the "nonsynchrony of oppression." When we talk of our subjectivities, we refer both to the way society defines us and thus treats us, but also to the ways in which our sense of who we are is shaped by the very categories we use to make sense of our own experiences and the world around us. We live in a society that damages everybody—marked by racism, sexism, greed, violence, anger, the world reflected in our television screens. This is the world through which we know ourselves. How do we find ourselves if the very experiences and feelings that most intimately define us are reinterpreted to us through media images and methods themselves shaped by a culture of domination and objectification? We turn to television oracles like Oprah for clues about who we are, but we don't think about who else we might want to be. How often do we analyze and struggle against our own distorted images of who we are? As Audre Lorde (1984) comments, "America's measurement of me has lain like a barrier across the realization of my own powers. It was a barrier which I had to examine and dismantle, piece by painful piece, in order to use my energies fully and creatively. It is easier to deal with the external manifestations of racism and sexism than it is to deal with the results of those distortions internalized within our consciousness of ourselves and one another" (147). Instead of turning to an unconditional celebration of everything we are now, we should recognize the distortion and limitations of our full humanity as well as the very real strengths of our lives. I am suggesting an exploration of what might be, teaching against oppression but also in the hopes of contributing to the creation of a world, relationships, and ways of being which do not yet exist.

Teaching for a world that does not yet exist calls for a Utopian vision on which we can base a feminist pedagogy. In seeking a model for a feminist pedagogy, Belensky, Clinchy, Goldberger, and Tarule, in *Women's Ways of Knowing,* as well as a number of other feminist writers, have looked to the work of Paulo Freire, whose call for a liberatory pedagogy has influenced a wide range of educators throughout the world. Freire emphasizes that the world is not "a 'given' world, but . . . a world dynamically 'in the making'" (1985, 106).[4] Freirean pedagogy rests on the process of "conscientization," what Freire calls a reading of both the word and the world, a critical reflection that leads to the transformation of the world. This pedagogy assumes a dialogue between teacher and student in which both are respected as creators of knowledge about the world. The Freirean teacher, then, engages in a mutual exploration of social reality with students. But while Freire's work is based on a deep respect for students and teachers as readers of the world, the conscientization he describes takes place in a relatively unproblematic relationship between an unidentified liberatory teacher and the equally abstractly oppressed. The tensions of the lived subjectivities of teachers and students located in a particular society and defined by existing meanings of race, gender, sexual orientation, class, and other social identities are not addressed by Freire.

In a recent class, I passed out one of Freire's codifications, a drawing used by literacy teams to begin their work with illiterate peasants. In the center of this drawing is a peasant man holding a book and a hoe. In the distant background is the small figure of a woman holding a child. As we discussed this picture, two women students began to ask questions about this image and about the Freirean liberatory process in wider terms. Who was being educated in the Freirean culture circles? Who held the book? Who held the child? Who stayed at home taking care of the kids and making dinner while the peasant learned to read his book? Questions like these echo the writings of feminists in the last decade, and, in particular, women of color, who have emphasized that in order to attempt liberatory teaching, the conscientization of our students and ourselves, we need to ask the hard questions. What are the material conditions of existence lived by different people in this society? Who has the right to speak and who takes care of others? Who do we envision as actors in the public world? In Michele Russell's words:

> In every way possible, take a materialistic approach to the issue
> of black women's structural place in America. Focus attention on
> the building where we are learning our history. Notice who's still
> scrubbing the floors. . . . Do we ever get to do more than clean

up other people's messes, whether we are executive secretaries, social workers, police officers, or wives? (65)

Freire's deeply humane and impassioned pedagogy can provide an inspiration and a model for feminist teachers, both men and women. But women teachers in particular also need to think about our own specific issues that have emerged from our experiences as women. In thinking about how to move from an analysis of where we are to a vision of what we might become, we do have guides and models in the feminist writers of the past and present. I want to turn to the powerful writings of two women of radically different lives and circumstances: Virginia Woolf and Audre Lorde, writers I have referred to throughout this essay. The writings of Woolf, a privileged member of the English intellectual elite, and Lorde, the daughter of Caribbean immigrants to Harlem, from very different and complex positions of privilege and oppression, both contribute to the exploration of what feminist teaching for social change might look like.

Virginia Woolf's life has become well known as a drama of a creative woman. The story of her private education at home with her father, her bohemian life as a key figure in the Bloomsbury group, her marriage to Leonard Woolf, her bouts of depression and eventual suicide have gained an almost mythic status. Virginia Woolf's importance as a major modern novelist is well known. But equally important for feminists have been her two long essays, "A Room of One's Own" and "Three Guineas." In "A Room of One's Own," Woolf explored the impact of a patriarchal world on female creativity and women artists. In the less well known "Three Guineas," she considers the nature of women's education through an exploration of the relationship of patriarchy and war. Her central question asks what she, as a woman, can do to help to prevent war. In exploring this question, Woolf calls into question existing roles of men and women. She examines the symbiotic relationship of existing gender positions, challenging the subordinate role of women and the dominance of men as working together to justify and support a society organized around hierarchy and militarism. As she points out, "the public and the private worlds are inseparably connected . . . the tyrannies and servilities of the one are the tyrannies and servilities of the other" (142). She turns her attention to the question of what women should do in such a society. One obvious approach is to attempt to gain access to male-dominated institutions, and that means, at first, access to male-dominated education. This leads her to the larger question of what accepted education actually is and what function it serves. First of all, says Woolf, it is clear that while education is valuable, it is also clear that education "is not good in all circumstances, and good for all people; it is only good for some people and for some purposes" (26). Given the fact that the men who control and define a society organized around oppression and greed have been educated in the great universities, Woolf asks, shouldn't we look at what exactly they have learned in that expensive and celebrated education? As she argues:

> For do [the facts] not prove that education, the finest education in the world, does not teach people to hate force, but to use it? Do they not prove that education, far from teaching the educated generosity and magnanimity, makes them on the contrary so anxious to keep their possessions . . . that they will use not force but much subtler methods than force when they are asked to share them? (29)

For Woolf, then, a woman's education must imply more than simply gaining access to traditionally male-controlled universities or the appropriation of traditionally male modes of knowledge. She calls upon women who seek an education to look closely at the nature of traditional education and traditional knowledge. In a famous passage from "Three Guineas," Woolf asserts:

> Let us never cease from thinking—what is this "civilization" in which we find ourselves? What are these ceremonies and why should we take part in them? Where in short is it leading us, the procession of the sons of educated men? (63)

In many respects, Woolf's analysis of male-defined education anticipates the critique of the abstract and competitive male model of education described by Belensky, Clinchy, Goldberger, and Tarule in *Women's Ways of Knowing*. But Woolf does not simply juxtapose women's superior ways of knowing or being in the world to overly rationalistic and violent male ways of knowing. Instead, she also questions the nature of women's traditional experience and informal education. As she points out, the private world of women and the public world of men are symbiotically related. It is the nurturing and affective work of women that makes possible the rational public world of men. Woolf questions the effect of a life of subordination and subterfuge implied by this existing arrangement of public and private, gender-defined rationality and emotion. As she points out, women have received an "unpaid-for education" for centuries, an education that taught them to negotiate the world as it was given:

> Biography thus provides us with the fact that the daughters of educated men received an unpaid-for education at the hands of

poverty, chastity, derision, and freedom from unreal loyalties. It was this unpaid-for education, biography informs us, that fitted them, aptly enough, for the unpaid-for professions. (78)

For Woolf, then, what she calls the "unpaid-for education" of women is not in itself adequate as a model for women's education in the future. Women, in their traditionally defined emotional work of connection and nurturance, have in many ways made the public world possible, but for Woolf that work and women's unpaid-for education have demanded a high price. While women have been allowed a freer expression of emotion than men, they have also been forced to deny other aspects of their being and intelligence. And in their subordinate and relatively powerless role, they have been forced to subterfuge and manipulation. For Woolf, the nurturance and caring of women like Mrs. Ramsay in *To the Lighthouse* should be celebrated, but it is not adequate as a model for everything women might become.

Woolf argues for a vision of a new society in which new relationships and an education not based on privilege and oppression would make possible new ways of being in the world for both men and women. Writing in 1938, living in the shadow of fascism, Woolf saw educated women as members of what she called "the Outsiders Society." Women like Woolf had received the education of men (although Woolf herself, of course, was not allowed to attend University, but was tutored by her father, Leslie Stephen, at home). But while they were given the same traditional education as men, they were expected to live in the traditional roles of women. Thus, they were thrust into the position of outsiders, educated and articulate, and yet denied authority and voice. As Woolf scathingly shows in "Three Guineas," educated women in English society were denied adequate work or equal pay, and were excluded from positions of power and authority. Yet, as educated outsiders without loyalty to existing structures of power, they could speculate on a future for which there is as yet no blueprint, a future based on "the capacity of the human spirit to overflow boundaries and make unity out of multiplicity" (143).

Woolf provides a vision for a rethinking of what women's education should be. But while she wrote from her experience of oppression as a woman, she also benefitted from the privilege of being a white, upper-class European. She makes clear she is writing for educated middle-class women like herself, and in this respect her work is limited. A vision of education based on the multiplicity of oppressions can be found in the writings of Audre Lorde, a Black lesbian poet and essayist whose work emerges from the lived experience of racism and homophobia, as well as that of sexism. Lorde is one of the leading U.S.

poets and essayists of our time. Her work centers around the question of difference and the need to acknowledge and explore the depth of feeling that she sees as the ground of knowledge. Lorde's own life has been shaped by profound experiences of oppression, of being defined as on the margins or excluded from the dominant and somehow "correct" world. As Lorde has said, echoing Rich's question, she writes the things she needs to know. Central to her thought is an exploration of feelings as "hidden sources of our power from where true knowledge and, therefore, lasting action comes" (37). Lorde's ideas are complex, and for this discussion of teaching and social change I want to focus on two of her most important essays: "The Uses of the Erotic" and "The Master's Tools Will Not Dismantle The Master's House," from *Sister Outsider* (1984).

In "The Uses of the Erotic," Lorde extends Woolf's analysis of the split between male rationality and control and female nurturance and emotion to consider where women might look for a grounding for a feminist theory of change. She finds that source in our deepest feelings, not the constructed desires of advertising and mass media or the limitations of the domestic role, but the deep longings and capacity for pleasure that always exist in human beings. As she argues in her essay, "Poetry is not a Luxury," "within living structures defined by profit, by linear power, by institutional dehumanization, our feelings were not meant to survive" (39). Lorde argues that feeling, as a source of knowledge and power, has been denied by a male-dominated knowledge that values abstraction and control over feeling and creativity. But once in touch with that deep emotion, what she calls the erotic, Lorde argues that women will be able to draw upon that erotic power to begin to transform the world. She writes, "Once we begin to feel deeply all the aspects of our lives, we begin to demand from ourselves and from our life-pursuits that they feel in accordance with that joy which we know ourselves to be capable of" (57). Thus, a deep creative force becomes the source for an imaginative and visionary reordering of the world through working in the world. This view of the erotic, which Lorde calls "the measure between the beginnings of our sense of self and the chaos of our strongest feelings," challenges accepted definitions of gender. As Lorde puts it,

> For as we begin to recognize our deepest feelings, we begin to give up, of necessity, being satisfied with suffering and self-negation, and with the numbness which so often seems like their own alternative in our society. Our acts against oppression become integral with self, motivated and empowered from within. (58)

Central to Lorde's vision, then, is a rejection of the suffering and self-negation that is the condition of the oppressed, and a turning to the creative and emotional powers that we as human beings have within us. And in a society in which even the process of knowing has been gendered, it is women who have been allowed connection with that deep creative and emotional source.

In "The Master's Tools Will Never Dismantle the Master's House," Lorde argues that the oppressed, those who deviate from the norm, must consciously work to free themselves from dominant ways of knowing. That is the meaning of "the master's tools," the dominant forms of abstract rationality. As Lorde argues,

> [The master's tool's] may allow us temporarily to beat him at his own game, but they will never enable us to bring about genuine change. And this fact is only threatening to those women who still define the master's house as their only source of support. (112)

In seeking other tools with which to build a new world, Lorde looks to the erotic as a source of knowledge, but also to the history and experience of those who have been oppressed, what she terms the "dehumanized inferior." And as Lorde points out, "Within this society that group is made up of Black and Third World people, working-class people, older people, and women" (114). Lorde thus calls for the uncovering of subjugated knowledges of past struggles and an acknowledgment of the specific histories of different individuals and groups. And that process should not be an appropriation of the experiences or histories of oppressed or subordinated groups by dominant groups, but must be a dialogue. As Lorde argues, "Difference must be not merely tolerated, but seen as a fund of necessary polarities between which our creativity can spark like a dialectic" (111). This dialogue should be grounded in a recognition of the realities of material life, the actual experiences of privilege and oppression, work and authority, lived by different people in different relationships to power:

> Insight must illuminate the particulars of our lives: who labors to make the bread we waste, or the energy it takes to make nuclear poisons which will not biodegrade for one thousand years; or who goes blind assembling the microtransistors in our inexpensive calculators? (139)

Lorde, like Woolf, points to the injustices and exploitation of the existing society, and like Woolf, argues for the need for a vision of the future we cannot yet fully imagine. But she extends Woolf's analysis by grounding her vision more specifically in the powerful creative emotions, the erotic, and in a more self-conscious awareness of the power and possibility of the differences among us.

Feminist teaching for social change must take account of the valuable work that, traditionally, has been done by women teachers. Its basic starting place is grounded in women's varied lived experiences and ways of knowing and in this it provides a much more situated pedagogy than the more abstract theories of Freire. But the work of writers like Woolf and Lorde reminds us as well not to celebrate this women's work unproblematically. They point out that women need to expand our understanding of the effects of an oppressive gender, class, and race system on women as well as men, and to seek a vision of new relationships and definitions of ourselves and our students. Teaching for change from a feminist perspective calls into question accepted social reality and challenges students to begin the process of critique and self-critique, a process of conscientization. It entails taking risks and it can be frightening. Teaching of this kind is based on raising questions rather than providing answers. It invites students to engage in a dialogue, with the teacher, with other students, and with themselves about their own lives. This kind of feminist teaching asks developing adolescents to question the social world they have inherited. It touches upon sexuality, the privileges of boys, the oppression of girls, the accommodations mothers sometimes make, perhaps the ways boys, fathers, or brothers have used male privilege to counter the racism or classism they have suffered in their own lives. This kind of teaching is deeply personal and makes both teacher and students vulnerable. It must be engaged in with the greatest sensitivity to the culture and families of students. Such teaching is difficult and may be met with opposition from students, families, other teachers, or administrators.

Public schools are highly political institutions responsive to the political pressures of local constituencies and to the state; in their internal structure they express existing race, gender, and class inequalities. And students themselves are subjects in process whose lives reflect the racism and sexism of the wider society. To teach against the grain of dominant ideology and institutional structure of the school is a difficult task, particularly if undertaken in isolation, and it can make us vulnerable and afraid. As Freire comments:

> To the extent that I become more and more clear concerning my choices, my dreams, which are substantively political and ad-junctively pedagogical, to the extent to which I recognize that as an educator I am a politician, I also understand better the reasons for me to be afraid, because I begin to foresee the consequences of such teaching. Putting into practice a kind of education that

critically challenges the consciousness of the students necessarily
works against some myths which deform us. (1987, 55)

This fear of critically challenging the dominant myths of the society
which deform us should not turn us away from critical teaching. But
it does point to the need to build collective institutions and what
Henry Giroux speaks of as the struggle for a democratic public life. A
wider social movement such as the women's movement and a collective
movement is essential for teaching for social change. For our own
empowerment and in order to organize against the increasing bureau-
cratization of schools, progressive teachers must seek out ways of
working collectively and collaboratively. As Audre Lorde comments,
citing Malcolm X: "We are not responsible for our oppression, but we
must be responsible for our own liberation" (144).

Notes

1. R. Albelda, E. McCrate, E. Melendez, J. Lapidus, and The Center for
Popular Economics. 1988. *Mink Coats Don't Trickle Down.* Boston: South End
Press, 41–55.

2. Rich, A. 1986. "What Does a Woman Need to Know?" *Blood, Bread and
Poetry* (New York: W. W. Norton), 1–11.

3. See Carol Gilligan. 1982. *In A Different Voice.* Cambridge: Harvard
University Press; Nancy Chodorow. 1988. *The Reproduction of Mothering.*
Berkeley: University of California Press; Belensky, Clinchy, Goldberger and
Tarule. 1986. *Women's Way of Knowing.* New York: Basic Books; Sara Ruddick.
"Maternal Thinking." In *Feminist Studies* 6: 70–96; Nel Noddings. 1984. *Caring.*
Berkeley: University of California Press.

4. See, for example, bell hooks, *Talking Back.* Boston: South End Press,
1989.

References

Albelda, R., E. McCrate, E. Melendez, J. Lapidus, and The Center for Popular
    Economics. 1988. *Mink Coats Don't Trickle Down.* Boston: South End Press.
Belensky, M., et al. 1986. *Women's Ways of Knowing.* New York: Basic Books.
Freire, P. 1985. *The Politics of Literacy.* Massachusetts: Bergin and Garvey.
Freire, P. 1987. "What are the Fears and Risks of Transformation?" in P. Freire
    and I. Shor, (eds.). *A Pedagogy of Liberation.* Massachusetts: Bergin and
    Garvey.
Hooks, B. 1989. *Talking Back.* Boston: South End Press.
Lorde, A. 1984. *Sister Outsider: Essays and Speeches.* Trumansburg, N.Y.: The
    Crossing Press.
McCarthy, C. 1988. "Rethinking Liberal and Radical Perspectives on Racial

Inequality in Schooling: Making the Case for Nonsynchrony." *Harvard Educational Review,* 58, 3, 265–79.

Rich, A. 1986. "Dreams Before Waking" in *Your Native Land, Your Life.* New York: W. W. Norton.

Rich, A. 1986. "What Does a Woman Need to Know?" in *Blood, Bread and Poetry.* New York: W. W. Norton.

Russell, M. 1983. "Black-Eyed Blues Connection: From the Inside Out" in C. Bunch and S. Pollack (eds.). *Learning Our Way: Essays in Feminist Education.* Trumansburg, N.Y.: The Crossing Press.

Woolf, V. 1938. *Three Guineas.* New York: Harcourt Brace Jovanovich.

Index

Editors

C. Mark Hurlbert is an associate professor of English at Indiana University of Pennsylvania. He teaches in IUP's graduate programs in Rhetoric and Linguistics, and Literature and Criticism, and undergraduate courses in writing, literature, and English education. Mark has collaborated with Michael Blitz for several years. They have edited *Composition and Resistance* for Boynton/Cook Heinemann, and have written articles about cultural studies, the politics of literacy education, and the rhetoric of academic institutions for *PRE/TEXT*, for James A. Berlin and Michael Vivion's forthcoming *Cultural Studies in the English Classroom: Theory/Practice*, and for *Works and Days: Essays in the Socio-Historical Dimension of Literature and the Arts*. In addition, Mark has written about a collectivist approach to teaching literature for James Cahalan and David Downing's *Practicing Theory in Introductory Literature Courses*. He has also written with Ann Marie Bodnar about how the United States' then impending war with Iraq affected the undergraduate literature class that he was teaching and she was taking in the fall of 1990, for David Downing's *Changing Classroom Practices: Resources for Literary and Cultural Studies*. Mark has guest edited *Works and Days* and has written for *Progressive Composition, Studies in the Humanities, WCH WAY/New Wilderness Letter,* and *The Writing Instructor.*

Samuel Totten is currently an associate professor of curriculum and instruction at the University of Arkansas, Fayetteville. He is also a member of the Council of the Institute on the Holocaust and Genocide (Jerusalem, Israel). Prior to entering academia, he was an English teacher in Australia, California, Israel, and at the U.S. House of Representatives Page School in Washington, D.C. He also served as a principal of a K–8 school in northern California. A major focus of his current work is the areas of middle level education, international human rights education, the place of social issues across the curriculum, and the development of a genocide early-warning system. He is currently co-editing a volume entitled *The Place of Social Issues in the Middle School Curriculum.*

Contributors

Debbie Bell is a bilingual teacher at Ohlone Elementary School (formerly Pájaro Elementary School) in Watsonville, California. She is an active member of the Central California Writing Project (CCWP) and the California Association for Bilingual Education (CABE). She and colleague Sarah-Hope Parmeter have presented their Partnership work at various national conferences as well as at the 1990 International Council of Teachers of English (ICTE) conference in New Zealand.

Michael Blitz is an associate professor of English at John Jay College, CUNY. He collaborates regularly with C. Mark Hurlbert, with whom he has coedited *Composition and Resistance* and coauthored numerous articles for journals and books. He is also the author of *Partitions, The Specialist,* and *Five Days in the Electric Chair.*

doris davenport is a writer/educator. She was an assistant professor of English at the University of North Carolina, Charlotte, until December 1991. She has published in diverse African American and feminist publications, including *This Bridge Called My Back. Voodoo Chile/Slight Return* is her third book of poetry. Others are *It's Like This* and *Eat Thunder and Drink In.* In 1990 davenport received a grant from the Kentucky Foundation for Women to live and write poetry in Italy.

Henry A. Giroux is the Waterbury Chair in Secondary Education at Pennsylvania State University. He is coeditor with Roger Simon of the University of Minnesota Press series Pedagogy, Representations, and Cultural Practice. He is also coeditor with Paulo Freire of the Critical Studies in Education and Culture series, published by Bergin and Garvey Press. In addition to his journal articles, book chapters, and edited books, he has written a number of books, including *Schooling and the Struggle for Public Life; Teachers as Intellectuals; Postmodern Education; Politics, Culture and Social Criticism* (with Stanley Aronowitz); and, most recently, *Border Crossings: Cultural Workers and the Politics of Education.*

Ellen Louise Hart teaches in the writing program at the University of California, Santa Cruz. She has taught English as a Second Language at City College of San Francisco and has been a teacher and consultant at Project Bridge, an adult literacy program at Laney College in Oakland. With Sarah-Hope Parmeter, she makes presentations on teaching against homophobia and about the concerns of lesbian and gay student writers at community workshops, CCCC and NCTE conferences, and through the Central California Writing Project. She was a contributor to the first anthology of writings by lesbian teachers, *The Lesbian in Front of the Classroom*. She has published articles on Emily Dickinson's poetry and letters, and is currently writing a dissertation on Dickinson and the erotics of reading.

Edythe Johnson Holubec is an associate of the Cooperative Learning Center at the University of Minnesota. She has taught English and remedial reading at the middle school and high school levels in urban, suburban, and rural schools. She has also taught English and English Education courses at the college level. In addition to journal articles, she is a coauthor of *Circles of Learning: Cooperation in the Classroom* and *Advanced Cooperative Learning* with her brothers, David and Roger Johnson. She currently teaches courses in cooperative learning to educators world-wide.

David W. Johnson is a professor of Educational Psychology at the University of Minnesota. He has served as an organizational consultant to schools and businesses in such areas as management training, team building, ethnic relations, conflict resolution, interpersonal and group skills training, and evaluating attitudinal/affective outcomes of educational and training programs. He is a practicing psychotherapist and author or coauthor of over thirty books, including *The Social Psychology of Education; Reaching Out: Interpersonal Effectiveness and Self-Actualization; Joining Together: Group Therapy and Group Skills; Circles of Learning: Cooperation in the Classroom;* and *Cooperation and Competition: Theory and Research*.

Roger T. Johnson is a professor of Curriculum and Instruction with an emphasis on Science Education at the University of Minnesota. His public school teaching experience includes kindergarten through eighth grade instruction in self-contained classrooms, open schools, nongraded situations, cottage schools, and departmentalized (science) schools. At the college level, Roger has taught teacher-preparation courses for undergraduate through Ph.D. programs. The author of numerous articles and book chapters, he is the coauthor of *Learning Together and Alone* and *Circles of Learning: Cooperation in the Classroom*.

Daphne Kutzer is an associate professor of English at the State University of New York at Plattsburgh, where she has taught since 1979. She has published journal articles and book chapters on the subject of children's literature, has presented papers on writing at various conferences, and since 1988 has written, lectured, and taught extensively on the subject of AIDS. In 1991 she devised and taught a literature course, AIDS & Its Metaphors, and was a presenter at the third annual Northern New York HIV/AIDS Conference. She is currently working on a study of Paul Monette's writing.

Vincent A. Lankewish is a former high school English teacher and author of several teachers' guides and pedagogical articles. Mr. Lankewish is currently working on his Ph.D. in English at Rutgers University, New Brunswick, and is planning a book on Chaucer's place in Victorian culture.

Nancy Mack is an assistant professor of English at Wright State University in Dayton, Ohio. She teaches undergraduate courses in Composition and graduate courses in whole language for teachers in addition to working with teachers in whole language support groups, school district inservices, and state professional organizations. During the summer, she codirects an institute for teachers, Writing and Its Teaching. Prior to her work at Wright State, she taught in a middle school and at several Ohio prisons.

Jimmie Mason is a high school teacher of English at John Muir High School in Pasadena, California. She has worked on rewriting the core literature/ social science curriculum for junior high students in Pasadena. She is currently writing her Master's thesis, "Repression in the Works of Charlotte Bronte," at California State University, Los Angeles.

Cecelia Rodríguez Milanés is an assistant professor of English at Indiana University of Pennsylvania. In addition to teaching African American and multi-ethnic literature and composition at the university, she taught English as a Second Language to elementary school students, and English to high school students. She has made presentations at various conferences on subjects ranging from Latina writers, Toni Morrison's novels, and feminist criticism and pedagogy, to reading her own works of fiction and poetry.

Sarah-Hope Parmeter is a lecturer in writing at the University of California, Santa Cruz. She coedited the collection *The Lesbian in Front of the Classroom: Writings by Lesbian Teachers*, and has served for two years as the cochair of the Conference on College Composition and Communication's Lesbian and Gay Caucus. In addition to her advocacy work on behalf of lesbian and gay teachers and students, she serves as codirector of the Central California Writing Project and directs a writing-based early outreach partnership between USCS students and students in the local Spanish-speaking community.

Alan Shapiro taught secondary school English and social studies for many years in the New Rochelle, New York, public schools. He is the director of an international education project for Educators for Social Responsibility and coleads institutes on democracy and social responsibility themes in the United States, the former Soviet Union, and Poland. Among his publications are language, literature, and history textbooks. The latter include a series of six thematic paperbacks, *America, Land of Change*.

Sandra Stotsky is a research associate at the Harvard Graduate School of Education, and Director of the Summer Institute on Writing, Reading, and Civic Education. She also serves as the editor of *Research in the Teaching of English*, and is the editor of *Connecting Civic Education and Language*

Education: The Contemporary Challenge, an anthology of essays based on papers given at her institute.

Carol Stumbo teaches English and coordinates a writing program at Wheelwright High School in Floyd County, Kentucky. She and fellow teacher Delores Woody produce an oral history magazine, *Mantrip,* twice a year using the Foxfire teaching philosophy. Carol has taught on the college level and has published in the *Harvard Educational Review* as well as state publications. A chapter on her work will appear in *Students Teaching: Teachers Learning,* scheduled to be published soon by Boynton and Cook.

John Tassoni is an adjunct faculty member at Indiana University of Pennsylvania. He is currently completing his doctoral dissertation there.

Gail Tayko is an adjunct faculty member at Indiana University of Pennsylvania. She is currently completing her doctoral dissertation there.

Kathleen Weiler is an assistant professor of Education at Tufts University. She is the author of *Women Teaching for Change* and coeditor with Candace Mitchell of *Rewriting Literacy* and *What Schools Can Do: Critical Pedagogy and Practice.* She is currently at work on a history of women teachers in the country schools of Tulare County, California, in the period 1860–1960.

William W. Wright, Jr. set up and directs BreadNet, the network of the Bread Loaf School of English. His background includes work as an English teacher and as a project director for American Institutes for Research. In the latter role he helped computer companies design manuals and screens that are easy for people to use. He has helped develop online services for education groups and companies, and is currently involved with the effort to set up a network for NCTE.

James Thomas Zebroski is assistant professor of Writing and English at Syracuse University, where he teaches courses in composition theory and expository writing. He has spoken and published widely on the social foundations of literacy, on Lev Vygotsky's psychosocial theory of process, and on writing theory and practice. His work includes "The English Department and Social Class: Resisting Writing," "A Hero in the Classroom," "Rewriting Composition as a Post-Modern Discipline," and other essays, articles, and reviews in *The Writing Instructor, Composition Chronicle, Correspondences,* and *English Journal.* He is author of *Thinking Through Theory,* a forthcoming book that looks at ways theory can (and cannot) be of value to the writing teacher.

Daniel L. Zins is an associate professor in Liberal Arts at the Atlanta College of Art. He has taught a variety of peace-studies electives, and also teaches a course on the environmental crisis. His articles on peace, security, and the environment have appeared in *The Hollins Critic, College English, Papers on Language and Literature,* and elsewhere.